Greek Political Imagery from Homer to Aristotle

Greek Political Imagery from Homer to Aristotle

Roger Brock

BLOOMSBURY
LONDON • NEW DELHI • NEW YORK • SYDNEY

Bloomsbury Academic
An imprint of Bloomsbury Publishing Plc

50 Bedford Square	1385 Broadway
London	New York
WC1B 3DP	NY 10018
UK	USA

www.bloomsbury.com

Bloomsbury is a registered trade mark of Bloomsbury Publishing Plc

First published 2013
Paperback edition first published 2014

© Roger Brock, 2013

Roger Brock has asserted his right under the Copyright,
Designs and Patents Act, 1988, to be identified as Author of this work.

All rights reserved. No part of this publication may be reproduced or transmitted in any form or by any means, electronic or mechanical, including photocopying, recording, or any information storage or retrieval system, without prior permission in writing from the publishers.

No responsibility for loss caused to any individual or organization acting on or refraining from action as a result of the material in this publication can be accepted by Bloomsbury or the author.

British Library Cataloguing-in-Publication Data
A catalogue record for this book is available from the British Library.

ISBN: HB: 978-1-7809-3206-4
PB: 978-1-4725-9166-1
ePUB: 978-1-47250-217-9
ePDF: 978-1-47250-218-6

Library of Congress Cataloging-in-Publication Data
Brock, Roger.
Greek political imagery from Homer to Aristotle / Roger Brock.
pages cm
Includes bibliographical references and index.
ISBN 978-1-78093-206-4 (hardback) – ISBN 978-1-4725-0217-9 (epub) – ISBN 978-1-4725-0218-6 (epdf) 1. Greek literature–History and criticism. 2. Classical literature—History and criticism. 3. Politics in literature. 4. Politics and literature–Greece. 5. Imagery (Psychology)–Political aspects. 6. Greece–Politics and government–Early works to 1800. I. Title.
PA3015.P63B76 2013
880.9'358–dc23
2013000816

Typeset by Fakenham Prepress Solutions, Fakenham, Norfolk NR21 8NN
Printed and bound in Great Britain

Contents

Conventions	vii
Acknowledgements	ix
Introduction	xi

1	Gods as Kings, Kings as Gods	1
2	The State as a Household and Family	25
3	The Shepherd of the People	43
4	The Ship of State	53
5	The Body Politic	69
6	Leaders and Communities: The Archaic Period (*c*.750–480 BC)	83
7	Democracy and Autocracy: The Fifth Century (*c*.480–404 BC)	107
8	Orators and Philosophers: The Fourth Century to Alexander (*c*.400–322 BC)	147

Epilogue	197
Bibliography	199
Index of Authors and Images	221
Index locorum	227
General Index	249

Conventions

Abbreviations generally follow *LSJ* and *OLD* for authors, and *OCD*³ for epigraphy and papyrology; note additionally R&O = Rhodes & Osborne (2003) and P-W = Parke & Wormell (1956). Fragments of tragedy are cited from *TrGF*, of comedy from *PCG*: in the latter case 'KA' normally refers to the critical notes of Kassel & Austin. Fragments of lyric poetry follow the numeration of *PMG*, while for iambus and elegy I follow West; fragments of Pindar are cited from Maehler's edition.

Acknowledgements

This book has been a long time in the making, though I believe that it is all the better for it: in the long period of its gestation I have incurred many debts, and it is a great pleasure now to able to express my gratitude for the assistance I have received from the generous and collegial community of Classics. My only regret is that some of those to whom I am indebted are no longer alive to see the project completed.

It began life as an Oxford DPhil thesis, 'Political imagery in Greek literature before Plato': the topic was suggested to me by Oswyn Murray and the thesis was supervised by George Forrest and Kenneth Dover, and examined by Tom Stinton and John Gould. The award of the Derby Scholarship, for which I again thank the Derby Trustees and the Craven Committee at Oxford, also enabled me to spend a rewarding academic year in Toronto, where I benefited from the advice of Desmond Conacher, Leonard Woodbury, John Cole and Mac Wallace. In the following year I was a Postdoctoral Fellow at the Ohio State University, where I began the extension of the period covered to the rest of the fourth century and enjoyed the company and generous hospitality of the postgraduate community and academic staff, especially Charles Babcock, Carl Schlam, Joe Tebben and my adviser David Hahm.

Thereafter progress was slowed by the lack of uncluttered time in which to be able to reorganize all of the great mass of material into its final form: in the event, in the absence of any institutional sabbatical leave provision this was only made possible by the award of a Leverhulme Research Fellowship in 2002–3 and of a British Academy Senior Research Fellowship in 2008–9. I am profoundly grateful to both organisations, without whose support the book would not yet have seen the light of day even now.

I was able to try out earlier versions of the content and ideas on audiences in Cambridge, Columbus, Edinburgh, Exeter, Hull, Lampeter, Leeds, Liverpool, London, Manchester, Oxford, Rennes, Rethymnon, St. Andrews, Sheffield and Toronto, and I thank the organisers in each case for the opportunity and the audiences for comments, criticisms and suggestions which have improved my thinking. I have also benefited over the years from the assistance of a great many individuals who have helped me with encouragement and advocacy, provided advice and guidance, given me access to inaccessible, unpublished or forthcoming work, answered questions, and otherwise supported me. After all this time there will inevitably be some whose names are omitted here, but however fallible my memory, I am sincerely grateful to all those who have assisted me in any way. In particular I should like to thank Umberto Bultrighini, John Davies, Kyle Erickson, Elaine Fantham, Philip Ford, Mogens Hansen, Steve Heyworth, Richard Hunter, Gregory Hutchinson, David Konstan, Stratis Kyriakidis, Lynette Mitchell, Robin Osborne, Robert Parker, P.J. Rhodes, Fabio Roscalla, Richard Rutherford, Malcolm Schofield, Richard Seaford, Oliver Taplin, Christopher Tuplin, Matthijs Wijbier and Peter Wiseman. In addition, Pat Easterling, Melissa Lane,

Chris Pelling, Liz Pender, Emma Stafford and Hans van Wees read earlier versions of particular chapters, and Douglas Cairns, Malcolm Heath and Simon Hornblower read the whole text in draft, and all enhanced it by numerous acute criticisms and helpful suggestions. None of these is, of course, in any way responsible for any remaining shortcomings.

Deborah Blake at Duckworth displayed patience exemplary even by the standard of academic publishers and I am glad finally to have justified her encouraging optimism; I am also grateful to her successor at Bloomsbury, Charlotte Loveridge, for guiding the project through its final stages, and to Chloe Shuttlewood and Dhara Patel at Bloomsbury and to Kim Storry at Fakenham Prepress Solutions and the copy-editor Erika Cox for seeing the book efficiently through the press. An earlier version of chapter 5 appeared as Brock (2000): I thank Routledge for permission to re-use that material here.

My colleagues past and present in the Department of Classics at Leeds have been a tremendous source of warm friendship and collegiality which has been all the more valued in the difficult conditions in which we have been operating for the past few years. Finally, Elaine, Katherine and Sarah have supported me in my work, sometimes distracted me from it, and generally kept me sane: I owe them more than I can say.

The book is dedicated to my parents, and to those who have taught me, both at Oxford and earlier (especially Ned Campbell, Brooke Dowse, Peter Marriott and Roger Nichols): only I am to blame for whatever faults it may have, but insofar as it – and I – have turned out well, that is in great part due to them.

Introduction

Imagery can be revealing. In an interview in *Vanity Fair* a few months after her deposition, Margaret Thatcher observed that she had never been defeated by the people in an election.[1] The formulation is striking, implying that she viewed herself as engaged in a contest or conflict[2] not with the other political parties and their leaders, but with the electorate at large. Yet at the same time it is recognizably an extension of the long-established self-representation of politicians as fighting against each other, or enemies within or outside the state,[3] or, more laudably, against abstract foes such as poverty or injustice.

That model, or at least the image of politicians in combat, can be traced back to ancient Greece and the encounters of Aeschines and Demosthenes, the latter another politician who enlisted figurative warfare as part of his self-presentation.[4] While some at least of the underlying conceptual framework was doubtless culturally specific – one might surmise in this case that the image of politics as war was licensed by the Greek ideology of harming enemies as well as helping friends[5] – the origins of the western tradition of figurative representation of politics, as of political theory, lie in ancient Greece, and form the subject of this book. My objective is to study the emergence of political imagery as a historical and cultural phenomenon which runs in parallel with the Greek 'discovery of politics' and illuminates that process and the ideas behind it: in the earlier part of the period 'politics' has yet to emerge as a discrete field of experience and knowledge with its own terminology, so the capacity of imagery to illuminate thoughts which are not yet explicitly formulated is especially revealing. As overt discussion of politics emerges with its own terminology, political imagery continues to occupy a distinctive space between the crude propaganda of slogans and catchwords on the one hand and explicit theorizing on the other (which is not to say that theoretical writers eschew imagery, Plato above all). At the same time, many of these images have persisted in literature in other European languages down to the present day and have continued to be exploited in politics: political imagery is part of the Greek legacy to western culture.

Yet while the use of such imagery begins in the western tradition with the Greeks, we cannot be certain that they should be credited with the invention of all the images which they handed down to later eras. In fact, of the major complexes of imagery treated in the first half of this work, only the ship of state and the body politic are directly a legacy from Greek antiquity; since the others are attested as firmly established at a much earlier date in the Near East, it is an economical hypothesis that they were taken over from there at an early stage of Greek history.[6] Since they first appear to us in Homer at the end of the process of their development through the tradition of oral poetry, we cannot pin down the manner or date of their adoption; all we can say is that, as with other cultural borrowings from the Near East, the Greeks selected and adapted, and so, for example, the comparison of the king to a herdsman, widespread in the Near East, has in Homer been confined to a conventional formula with limited military reference (below 43) while the analogy between king and father appears only in a stock phrase focused specifically on parental gentleness (below 30, 83). That process of adaptation suggests that from the start the development of Greek political imagery involved a degree of reflection and an awareness that possible analogies might be more or less suited to their experience, and therefore draws attention to the question why certain fields of imagery were favoured: although this work is not directly concerned with the theory of metaphor (or indeed political science), it will be appropriate to say a little on a general level about the way in which these images seem to me to function.

First, Greek political imagery is largely drawn from experience; indeed, it must be due to the essential familiarity and communicative capacity of the source domains that models such as the state as household, the ship of state and the body politic have retained a perennial appeal as expressions of community and the working of power relations within them across the long span of time to the present and in a culturally diverse range of contexts. The presentations of the ruler as father or shepherd were taken over from Near Eastern tradition because the models were familiar and effective in making sense of the Greeks' experience of power relations, while the differences in their application show that they underwent adaptation to fit a somewhat different context in Iron Age Greece. The experiential basis of much of this imagery is at its clearest in the Archaic period: it is not simply that many of the new fields of imagery are drawn from other aspects of life, and particularly of elite experience, such as seafaring and the control of animals, but that there is a broader interaction between elements of the elite lifestyle, so that the symposium can be seen as a sea voyage, a woman can be a ship, and the pursuit of the beloved, or his or her demands, can be represented as the hunting or taming of animals, or sport, or warfare, or a game.[7] Indeed, the imagery of the ship of state is only a small part of the broader field of maritime imagery in which the course of life, or of a poem, can be figured as a voyage and all kinds of people, institutions and enterprises can be aided by a fair wind, or else storm-tossed and, in the worst case, shipwrecked – and the same of course applies to other fields of imagery.[8]

Secondly, the tendency is for political imagery, or at least the main fields from which it is drawn, to become conventional. In assembling the material for this study I was able to group most of it under a handful of broad headings – Animals, Elements and the Natural World, Farming, Household, Maritime, Medical, Military, Religion, Sport – and the imagery set out here tends to involve variations on established themes: even a poet as creative in his metaphors as Pindar operates almost entirely within established categories in his political imagery.[9] That is not particularly surprising, since the objective of much political imagery is to establish or consolidate consensus, and that is likely to be more effectively achieved if it proceeds on a basis which is either already accepted or sufficiently familiar and plausible that the target audience can be induced to endorse it. One would therefore not expect political imagery in general to work through the surprising suggestion of a connection to something unfamiliar or unexpected, as literary metaphor frequently does.[10]

It might be objected at this point that all Greek political imagery is literary metaphor; however, while it is true that the sources are almost exclusively literary, in most cases the works from which my material is drawn were intended for mass audiences. That is obviously true of oratory at Athens and elsewhere, of Attic drama both comic and tragic and, in a different way, of early Greek hexameter poetry; much of the sympotic poetry of the archaic period also circulated widely and must have been intended to be accessible to an elite public beyond the particular polis. The main exceptions are the other prose genres, particularly historiography (where use of imagery is relatively sparse, and much of that in embedded speeches) and philosophy (to which should be added Presocratic works in verse): it is probably not coincidental that philosophers, above all Plato, are among the most creative authors in their use of political imagery, though he is something of a special case because of the substantive functions that his images can perform in his philosophy.[11] Even here, however, a good deal of Plato's imagery is founded on existing usage, while in the use of craft analogies he is plainly operating within a broader Socratic tradition; there are indications, too, of a degree of dialogue between philosophy and Athenian public discourse in the fourth century.[12] The inventiveness of comic poets, on the other hand, is probably due to the way in which the unexpected can create humour. At all events, I suggest that we are rarely dealing with the kind of individual and personal creativity normally implied by describing imagery as 'literary': most political imagery works within, and trades on, established frameworks.

At the same time, the degree of conventionality should not be overstated. Certainly it would be relatively easy to define a set of underlying structuring concepts which serve to organize ancient Greek perceptions of their experience of community and power relations, and these could be expressed as conceptual metaphors such as 'The community is a family' or 'The community is a body', but each individual image in our sources represents an expression of the concept which develops it in a particular context for a particular purpose. The fact that an image has become conventional will tend to reflect the continuing validity of the conceptual metaphor(s) underlying it; hence images often dismissed as 'dead metaphors' can continue to have communicative power, even though the conceptual metaphor may no longer be consciously acknowledged.[13]

Although each image will therefore normally involve an element of creativity, however modest, this study is nevertheless only incidentally concerned with individuals, whether authors or political actors. It is only rarely that we can attribute the creation of an image to a specific person, as in the cases of Solon or Cleon,[14] and equally I have usually avoided discussing the imagery of particular authors (or indeed works), not least because there is already plenty of good scholarship on such topics.[15] Furthermore, a major difference between this work and studies of modern political imagery is that although Greek political imagery often has persuasive aims, it is relatively rare to be able to observe it directly being deployed to persuade in specific situations:[16] much more frequently what we can detect are the broader terms of debate, the underlying ideological landscape which dictates, and is further constituted by, the imagery actually employed. The ideological context is, of course, equally revealed by what is not said, and the images which are absent or appear only to a limited extent:

for example, although Greek politicians do make use of images of conflict, as we have seen, what is striking is the limited development of the equation of politics with war. That makes sense when we reflect that it was largely self-serving, since it lent the status and respectability of warfare to internecine quarrels, and insofar as those quarrels *did* come to resemble warfare, the risk of collateral damage posed potentially negative implications for the community involved. In fact, both political competition and argument in general were more frequently assimilated to the combat sports, and particularly wrestling with its combination of violence and trickery.[17] Politicians were thus largely denied self-identification with the more straightforward prowess of the runner, which involved no chicanery, though it may also be the case that the relatively minor role of election, as opposed to sortition, in the Athenian constitution left little place for the model of 'first past the post'. At any rate, other appealing models of self-representation such as the helmsman or doctor were apparently completely off limits to Athenian politicians in the fifth century: the fact that they only become available in the less radically democratic environment of the succeeding century strongly implies some form of ideological control over political imagery before then.[18] Similar factors may be at work in the limited and late emergence of imagery drawn from craftsmanship, the earliest of which would seem to be the weaving metaphor in the *Lysistrata*, i.e. that while political or constitutional order might be perceived as an artefact, it was not appropriate to assign the role of creator to an individual.[19] However, it is also possible that the sense of the polis as a 'citizen-state', and so a community of living beings, made it inappropriate to conceive of its population as material to be worked on, in the same way that we find no imagery which treats the polis or *politeia* as a structure or mechanism. When imagery from the plastic arts finally does appear, it is significant that it is in works of political theory.[20]

Ideological investment in well-established imagery, whether expressed through continuing service paid to the trope of the politician as servant (115, 154) or through policing of the limits of self-presentation, demonstrates that while such images may be essentially conventional, they retain real force and are not just 'dead metaphors'. That can also hold good of fields of imagery which through changing historical circumstances have lost their currency. Thus the father and the shepherd, images of individual leadership and particularly of monarchy, are revived and developed in the fourth century when political developments create a propitious climate (Chapter 8): the potential was presumably always there, albeit dormant. Equally, it was always possible to elaborate the core imagery for a specific purpose, as Plato does with the ship of state, enriching it with intertextual allusion to make a particular point about the relationship between philosophy and politics (below 58).[21]

Since the terminology of metaphor itself was not developed until the time of Aristotle, doubt has sometimes been expressed as to whether it can be appropriately applied to ancient Greece before then, and indeed whether the Greeks previously had a conception of metaphor, especially in the archaic period: in particular, it has been suggested that what appear to us to be metaphors in medical or scientific language are literal, or else involve an extension of meaning of normal terms.[22] However, the way in which, as we have noted, the king as shepherd and the king as father were restricted to a specific focus – military organization in the one case, parental affection in the other

– is a clear indication of reflection on the appropriateness of these models to Greek circumstances and therefore of figurative thinking rather than a simple extension of meaning; that is natural enough, since on any close scrutiny Homeric *basileis* were not really the fathers of their subjects, nor herdsmen leading sheep out to fight.[23] The same goes for the reciprocal interrelation of seafaring and other aspects of archaic life described above, where the source domain shifts from one to another with the context. Even with the body politic, the concept of 'semantic stretch' only really applies satisfactorily to the basic antithesis of health and disease: that will suffice to describe a malfunction of the polis as a body-like system, but as soon as the question of how to redress it arises, it raises the question of what constitutes 'health' in this body, how it is to be restored, and who is to be responsible for treatment, all of which again reveals the figurative nature of the analogy.[24] However, this does not so clearly hold good for the representation of the cosmic order in political terms, where it could be argued that what we are observing is an analogy between seen and unseen, in which the structures and principles regulating the invisible order of the cosmos are assumed to be of the same kind as those governing human society. That is a natural interpretation, especially if one accepts Durkheim's argument that gods represent the apotheosis of the society which creates them.[25] Given that there were powers in the universe superior to men and that these were conceived of as personalities, it was natural to imagine that hierarchy between gods and men in terms of the relation between human kings and their subjects (and since all the gods were 'kings' in that sense, the position of Zeus was that of an Agamemnon among the other *basileis* rather than a supreme cosmic ruler, despite his superior power),[26] and likewise to think of kings as gods or godlike. However, if that was so natural a step as to have been more or less instinctive, when one moves beyond the basic structures of Greek religion it seems likely that thinking about the cosmos entailed more conscious deliberation, since in considering its operation it was not inevitable that it should be conceived as a political order, and other models were available (e.g. that the universe was a body); furthermore, as Greek political institutions developed, it became possible to imagine different versions of a political cosmic order. Even if we should restrict ourselves in such cases to speaking in terms of analogies or models, we ought not to assume that they have necessarily been adopted without reflection.[27]

Whatever their status, cosmological analogies seem to me illuminating for early Greek ideas about social order and the exercise of power. Indeed, as far as formal status is concerned I have been deliberately inclusive: to borrow the helpful formulation of Rutherford (2012, 119), '"imagery" … is used to include words and expressions which communicate a non-literal sense, and particularly comparisons, of which the main categories are metaphors and similes'; hence he also discusses personifications, and I would add such looser forms of comparison as allegory and fable.[28] I have also given some attention to the 'flip sides' of images such as the body politic, where the way in which from an early stage medical writers were thinking about the body in political terms is, I think, helpfully suggestive about the way in which the analogy between body and community functioned. That is more conspicuously the case for Plato, for whom body, city and cosmos are parallel systems, and hence imagery of direction such as steering a ship can be applied across all three.[29] I have also included cases where reference is made figuratively (mainly at Athens) to political institutions and terminology, since these too are expressive of ideology. On the other hand, I have tended to conservatism about whether an image is a political image, particularly in tragedy, where leading characters tend to exercise authority within a (royal) household as well as the wider community.[30] I have also adopted a fairly restrictive sense of 'political' as relating to the exercise of power and to relations within communities; although it is not unreasonable to maintain that *ta politika* in the sense of 'the affairs of the polis' could include a considerably wider range of matters with which the community was concerned (e.g. education, marriage), to include those would vastly increase the scale of this already substantial volume and diminish its focus. Because of its very broad scope and the wide range of topics on which it touches, I have also had to be selective in the citations of the bibliography to keep that within bounds. For the most part I cite items which have contributed to the argument, or which point to a different line of interpretation, and I have tended to favour recent publications on the principle that they will direct the reader to earlier scholarship on a given topic.

By the same token, the majority of examples are simply cited or alluded to, and quotation is of necessity sparing, but I have tried to be thorough in including all the material which I have collected, as also in covering all archaic and classical Greek literature: frequency of usage, both absolutely and across time, is in itself a measure of the currency and significance of an image – or, contrariwise, its distinctiveness. More specifically, the more comprehensive our knowledge of an image is, the more confident we can be of the way(s) in which it was used and the meaning(s) it carried. That in turn can helpfully guide our interpretation in doubtful cases: because political images tend to the conventional, as we have seen, one would expect them, all other things being equal, to fit into the existing pattern. It is not that an image cannot be applied against the grain, but one would expect to see clear signals in the context to that effect. So, for example, 'ironic' interpretations of Xenophon's *Cyropaideia* which read the father images in that work as negative face the difficulty that this image is otherwise (including elsewhere in Xenophon) entirely positive, and that Xenophon offers no hint that his intentions are any different in this case.[31]

I anticipate that the material collected and analysed here will be of interest both to ancient historians and to those working on literature (and to a lesser extent philosophy) from ancient Greece and Rome and from later periods, and the volume is structured accordingly. The first five chapters deal thematically with fields of imagery which have proved particularly influential in later periods, and these are followed by three diachronic chapters which deal with the development of these and other images in their historical context. Because of this bipartite structure, points made at length at one point are on occasion reprised more briefly elsewhere for ease of comprehension (since by the nature of the subject not all readers will want to read from cover to cover), supported by extensive cross-referencing which, together with the indexes, will, I hope, enable readers with diverse agendas to find the particular topic of interest to them; Greek is very largely transliterated and translated for the convenience of non-specialists. In order to maintain the flow and momentum of the argument, it has also been necessary at many points, especially in Chapters 6–8, to divert to footnotes arguments on particular points such as fifth-century military imagery (139n.127), and I have sometimes treated synchronically images of which there are only a few instances so as to reduce fragmentation of material.

The scattered nature of the material, together with its sheer volume, is probably a principal reason why Greek political imagery has hitherto been unjustly neglected: I trust that what is, as far as I am aware, the first book-length study of the subject will demonstrate its capacity to throw fresh light on major themes such as the evolution of the idea of community in the archaic period and the perennial ideological struggles between democrats and anti-democrats, and so stimulate interest in the topic, and I shall be pleased if it prompts other scholars to give political imagery the attention it merits in the study of ancient Greek literature, history and society.

Notes

1 ' "I have never been defeated" by the people, she said no fewer than five times during our interview. "I've never been defeated in an election"': *Vanity Fair*, June 2001 (accessible at www.vanityfair.com/magazine/archive/1991/06/thatcher199106).

2 I suspect that the implicit model was warfare: I can recall that when she was tantalizing the media over the timing of the 1983 General Election, she said that it would be a poor general who gave away his plan of campaign, and it is an obvious suggestion that 'the Falklands Factor' influenced her outlook; cf. also her post-deposition remark that 'no general can fight without a really good army behind them' (*Guardian* 29 May 1991). Charteris-Black (2005) 89–98, 112–14 similarly concludes that the conceptual metaphor POLITICS IS CONFLICT was central to her rhetoric and leadership style.

3 'We had to fight the enemy without in the Falklands. We always have to be aware of the enemy within, which is much more difficult to fight and more dangerous to liberty.' (quoted e.g. at news.bbc.co.uk/1/hi/3067563.stm); again, Charteris-Black (2005) 92–4 identifies INDUSTRIAL RELATIONS IS A BATTLE as an important conceptual metaphor for her.

4 Below 162–3.

5 The statement in Pl. *Men.* 71e that a man's virtue consists in doing good to friends and harm to enemies while managing public affairs is a classic expression of the principle; for a detailed study see Blundell (1989).

6 The alternative possibility of convergent evolution cannot be excluded, since the image of the ruler as father occurs in other societies (e.g. China; and NB below 77n.2 for parallel development of culturally specific versions of the body politic in Greece and China), but the restricted and stylized form of the image of the leader as shepherd (below) seems to point to modification of an earlier model and so is suggestive of at least some Near Eastern influence within the process studied by West (1997), and that assumption is followed here.

7 Symposium as ship: below, 97n.28; woman a ship: Thgn.457–60; love a voyage: Thgn. 1273–4, 1361–2, 1375–6, Anacr. fr.403; love as hunting or being hunted: below 101n.64; as animal taming: below 99n.41; as warfare: below 102n.77; as boxing: Anacr. frr.346 (2), 396; as knucklebones/dice: Anacr. fr.398. The use of images with multiple reference is nicely illustrated by the debate as to whether the ships in Alc.

frr.73 and 306 (i) col. II are to interpreted in a political or erotic sense: Rösler (1980) 121, Gentili (1988) 206–12 and below 97n.26.

8   For discussions of the wider field of maritime imagery see e.g. Luccioni (1959), van Nes (1963), Peron (1974), Steiner (1986) 66–75; Rutherford (2012) 129–30.

9   Steiner (1986) is an excellent study of the fertility of Pindaric imagery; the recent study of Hutchinson (2012), which focuses on the target domains to which imagery is directed, implicitly treats politics as a subordinate aspect of the topic of the victor or city.

10 And for all his eloquence, the metaphors deprecated by Orwell in 1946 as 'dying' and 'flyblown' (1961, 340, 349) were effective for the same reason. On the other hand, the example of Solon shows that ancient Greece was capable of persuasive political metaphor of a genuinely creative kind, though in that case facilitated by literary allusion to earlier poetry (below, 90–1).

11 Pender (2000), (2003).

12 See below 148 for the Socratic tradition of craft analogy, and NB Merkelbach (1949) for an anonymous example of the same technique, whose author argues against distinguishing constitutions on numerical grounds on the analogy of lyre- or pipe-playing, which are the same skill whether practised by few or many. The interplay between Plato and contemporary Athenian politicians is discussed below 156–8, 161–2.

13 The classic study of conceptual metaphor is Lakoff and Johnson (1980); for the continuity between conceptual metaphor and literary metaphor see Lakoff and Turner (1989) esp. 50–6 ('conventionalization' is discussed at 55–6), 67–72, also 136–9, and for an application of the principle to Pindar see Hutchinson (2012) 277–81. Not all the conceptual metaphors behind political images are peculiar to those images: one of the underlying images Hutchinson treats, 'fame is light', surely rests on a more general 'light is good, darkness is bad', which also underlies the image of the 'light of salvation', and both the more specific versions of the concept feature in political imagery (below 89). In the same way, the ship of state image is to some extent informed by the broader conception of processes as journeys, of which the voyage is one form (above x). We can also point to a very basic conceptual metaphor of orientation in which 'up' has a positive value (Lakoff and Johnson 1980, 14–21) underlying some spatially conceived political language: political leaders are described as *koruphaios* ('head-man') and kingship as 'the head of things' (Hdt. 3.82.3; Pi. *O.* 1.113–14), and leaders as 'top man (*akros*)' e.g. E. *Supp.* 118, *Pho.* 430, 1245, fr.703.1; *LSJ* s.v. III. For the conceptual metaphor of politics and debate as conflict see above nn.2–3 and below. The view taken of 'dead metaphor' here is of course very different from that of Silk (1974) 27–56, whose approach is literary, and specifically lexical (and whose concern is with *poetic* imagery); see further below.

14 Solon: 90–1; Cleon: 118–19. In fact, it is usually impossible to attribute the creation of any aspect of ideology to a particular individual, though there is a tendency to assign any initiative to the leading figure in the period (e.g. Pericles for the third quarter of the fifth century BC) which should be firmly resisted.

15 For example (most of them cited below on particular points): Homer: Moulton (1977); Lonsdale (1990); Aeschylus: Lebeck (1971); Sophocles: Goheen (1951), Knox (1957); Euripides: Barlow (1971); Aristophanes: Taillardat (1962); Plato: Louis (1945), Pender (2000). Rutherford (2012) 119–62 is a valuable study of a whole genre. However, I am hopeful that the indexes to this work will enable those who wish to pursue such lines of investigation to do so.

16 E.g. Charteris-Black (2005) or many of the contributions in Carver and Pikalo (2008).
17 Hence we can see in Greek thought a conceptual metaphor related to that proposed by Lakoff and Johnson (1980) 4–6 and *passim*, ARGUMENT IS WAR: for argument as wrestling, see e.g. E. *Ba.* 200, 800 with Dodds (1960), Ar. *Ach.* 385, 565, 704 with Olson (2002), Pl. *Euthd.* 277d, and below 138n.111; Protagoras wrote a work entitled *Kataballontes* ('Knock-down arguments'; B1 DK).
18 Ch. 7, esp. 117–18, 121.
19 Contrast the frequent use of craftsman imagery for poetic creation (Steiner 1986, 52–6), and the recurrent imagery of construction in the speeches of Bill Clinton and Tony Blair: Charteris-Black (2005) 121–5, 156–7.
20 On the use of such imagery by Plato and Aristotle see 160.
21 Rutherford (2012) 125–7 makes some good observations on this question; NB also Ortony (1975) 49–50.
22 E.g. Lloyd (1966) 225–9, (1987) 172–214, (2003) 8–13 – the latter two passages make use of the concept of 'semantic stretch'; Padel (1992) 9–11, 33–5 and *passim*.
23 More generally, it is clear that Homer has a conception of metaphor: Pelliccia (1995) 37–8n.58, Leidl (2003) 38, the latter with reference to *Od.* 20.13–15, where the extension of the 'barking' or 'growling' of Odysseus' heart in the simile of the bitch and her pups indicates recognition of the preceding metaphorical usage of the verb *hulaktein*.
24 Which is not to dispute the more specific arguments of Lloyd (n.22) regarding the development of technical language in science and medicine.
25 More recently, the phenomenon has been explained in terms of cognitive psychology: Boyer (2001) 155–91, who notes that Greek gods were unusually anthropomorphic (162); Atran (2002) 51–79.
26 Below 1, 4, though the picture is complicated by the fact that Zeus is also imagined as the head of a family: see also 84.
27 The recent study of 'metaphor and cosmology', with particular reference to Aeschylus and Heraclitus, in Seaford (2012) 240–57 is rich and suggestive, though a little constrained by an implicit opposition between 'metaphor' and 'reality'. The way he writes about the former ('merely metaphorical' 244; 'more than mere metaphor' 247) implies that he views it as (simply) a literary feature, and so following Lloyd (above n.22) he treats cosmological accounts as non-metaphorical. Yet when he says that 'Herakleitos directly describes the cosmos' (251), that does not seem quite right, since the philosopher has presumably not (for example) observed a cosmic child playing *pessoi* (B52; below 20n.69); he must at least be making an analogical surmise. Elsewhere, however, the distinction between abstract and concrete is less clear-cut, and when Seaford writes that 'presocratic cosmology derives ... in large part from preconceptions rooted in the changing life of the polis', that '[c]osmological ideas reflect social formation' (241) and that the universality of his key paradigms, ritual and monetary exchange, 'is, like that of monarchy or the polis, unconsciously projected onto the cosmos' (250), we seem to be much closer to structures of thought analogous to conceptual metaphors (so also Cairns 2012, lii). Indeed, the working of ritual, dreams, omens and abstractions as he presents it suggests to me that they would fit comfortably into a loose definition of 'imagery', alongside features such as personification and myth, as indirect expressions of ideas or beliefs (below).
28 Hutchinson (2012) 278 suggests that myths, too, are 'a kind of imagery'. Given this broad formulation of 'imagery', I make no formal distinction between metaphor and simile: for a theoretical justification see Ortony (1975) 52–3.

29 Below 174n.50.
30 See, for example, 36n.4 on E. *Pho.* 486 for a characteristic blurring between *oikos* and polis; again, Clytemnestra's hyperbolic praise of Agamemnon in A. *Ag.* 966–72 seems more likely to refer to him as head of the *oikos* than as king.
31 E.g. the claim of Tatum (1989) 82–3 that the effect of Cyrus as father is 'infantilization'; against such readings see now Gray (2011) 5–69, esp. 44, and NB 31 and 169n.23 below.

1

Gods as Kings, Kings as Gods

Political imagery is a feature of Greek literature from its very beginning, in the poetry of Homer and Hesiod, and the most prominent complex of such imagery is the parallelism between the authority of kings and that of the gods. This parallelism is expressed in two forms: on the one hand, the anthropomorphic gods are depicted in terms of an organized society corresponding to human society, and the power exerted by Zeus and other divinities is presented as corresponding to that of human rulers; on the other, mortal rulers are assimilated to gods, by the attribution to them of a divine or at any rate more than human nature, in a way that serves to enhance their status. Strictly speaking, these are of course different types of political imagery: in the former case, the world of human power relations supplies the term of comparison[1] (i.e. this is imagery drawn from politics) while in the latter the comparison is used to describe politics – that is, it is 'political imagery' in the more commonly used sense.[2] Nevertheless, there is a strong sense in which the two fields of imagery can be viewed as reciprocal and founded on a steady conception of the two levels of authority as parallel and hence mutually illuminating.[3] The political image of 'kings as gods' clearly has parallels with the (self-) representation of earlier and contemporary Near Eastern rulers; however, in Homer and Hesiod it is found only in a relatively attenuated form which persists in later usage until the concept undergoes a significant change in the later fourth century. By contrast, the parallel conception of 'gods as kings' undergoes a steady development which reflects changing political conditions as well as the evolution of cosmological thinking, and so I shall consider the latter first.

Gods as kings

The conception of the gods as living together on Olympus seems to be a creation of the epic tradition, perhaps influenced by the expression of similar ideas in the Near East.[4] There is more to this than a divine household, however, though the genealogical aspects of the tradition obviously contribute to the picture: Homer and Hesiod conceive of the gods as forming an organized society like their own,[5] and since the gods are self-evidently powerful, their relations reflect those between powerful humans, and have a political aspect. The divine society is a form of monarchy: both Homer and Hesiod represent Zeus as a king, using the same terms (*anax*, *basileus* and cognates) as for mortal rulers.[6] Thus he is styled *anax* ('lord') and his rule described as *anassein* ('reign') and he is given the titles *basileus* ('king'), 'king in heaven' and 'highest of rulers', 'king (or 'lord' or 'commander') of the gods' and 'king of all gods and men' (or simply 'of all').[7]

In Homer, the authority of Zeus appears firmly established. It is now generally agreed that the *Iliad* displays an awareness of an earlier stage in the cosmic order, revealed in allusions to the division of the three zones of the world between the three sons of Kronos (below) and the insurrections of the Titans and Typhoeus which feature prominently in the *Theogony*.[8] All that, however, is in the past, and while the Homeric poems certainly refer to conflicts between Zeus and the other Olympians (as also between other gods), in many cases the basis of these is familial (especially the friction between Zeus and Hera over Heracles); the only case in which Zeus' authority is represented as having been violently threatened is the conspiracy of Hera, Poseidon and Athena which Thetis is supposed to have thwarted with the aid of the 'hundred-hander' Briareos (*Il*. 1.396–406). It is possible that the episode is simply Homer's own invention, and that the three gods named are chosen because, as supporters of the Greeks in the *Iliad*, they would be most opposed to Zeus' acceding to the request of Thetis, in which case the implications for the poet's view of the cosmic order would be limited.[9] However, it has also been argued that there are oblique allusions in this context and elsewhere in the poem both to the divine succession which established the supremacy of Zeus and to a version of the myth of Thetis in which she was destined to bear a son greater than his father and so, to obviate the threat to the cosmic order, had to be married to the mortal Peleus.[10]

That aspect of the divine order is to the fore in the *Theogony*, where the emphasis is on the origins of Zeus' power through the overthrowing of his father Kronos, who had overthrown his own father Ouranos. On the one hand, such a model tends to imply that the origins of power lie in force,[11] yet the succession of generations also implies a sort of regular system in which each father is overthrown by a more powerful son; Zeus himself would have been subject to the same process, had he not found a way to negate the threat. The two aspects of the monarchic position are suggested by Hesiod's use of the language of kingship: on the one hand, in applying it to Kronos, he implies that his position was a legitimate one,[12] while on the other, when, in describing the consequences had Typhoeus defeated Zeus, he says that he 'would have ruled' (*ken ... anaxen Th.* 837), he seems to suggest that legitimacy rests on strength. The possibility of a threat to Zeus' position is also demonstrated in the Homeric *Hymn to Apollo*, both in the Prologue, in which the advent on Olympus of Zeus' son by Leto causes initial turmoil, and later in the poem where it is Hera who begets Typhaon to challenge Zeus.[13] As Clay notes, it is an innovation to locate the threat to Zeus within the Olympian family, though one which harks back to Hera's own descent from Gaia, and the usurper is not a son of Zeus, but engendered parthenogenetically by Hera; in a sense, therefore, the challenge is also to the very patrilineal succession process through which Zeus has become established (and so even more threatening to cosmic order), and the issue is resolved only by the incorporation of Apollo into the Olympian regime as upholder of his father's order.[14] We should also make a distinction between the struggle against the Titans, who oppose the establishment of Zeus's regime, and the various uprisings of the giants and monstrous figures such as Typhon/Typhoeus, which constitute a revolt against that order once established.[15] In Homer, although the power of Zeus is mainly sanctioned by his greater strength and the threat of his violent anger,[16] there is also an explicit reference to primogeniture as the basis of his greater wisdom and hence, by implication, the authority which Poseidon avoids challenging directly.[17] This is in contrast to the Hesiodic model, in which the new ruler is in each case the last-born son.[18]

Interestingly, although Hera is evidently the consort of Zeus in the Homeric poems, Homer never actually describes her as such, unlike later hexameter poetry: in a fragment of the Hesiodic *Catalogue of Women* she is called 'queen of gods and men', and she is 'Olympian queen Argive Hera' in the *Phoronis*.[19] However, the stable order of the Homeric cosmos is reflected in the recognition of the kingship in their own right of the gods who control the other two spheres of creation, Poseidon and Hades (*Il.* 15.187–92). Poseidon is depicted as lord of the sea at the beginning of *Iliad* 13, and named as such (*anakta*) in line 28, while in the *Odyssey* Proteus is described as *Poseidaônos hypodmôs* ('servant of Poseidon': 4.386), and represented as tending the god's livestock, a picture which underlines Poseidon's authority in his own sphere. The concept of Hades as 'lord of the dead' is widely distributed in epic,[20] and his authority in his own realm is nicely pointed up by two passages in the *Hymns*: in the *Hymn to Demeter* he promises Persephone power over all living creatures, with elegant irony, since she will derive that power from being his consort, and in a similar passage the ambitious infant Hermes is threatened with having his authority restricted to children if he is sent down to Hades as one himself.[21] No other god is regularly assigned such a position: when Athena is described as ruling all other gods and men with Zeus (*Od.* 16.260–5), it seems to be due to a combination of the important position which she occupies in the poem, and in Odysseus' mind, as his patroness, while on a lower level, Apollo can be described as ruling all mortals (*hAp.* 29) in recognition of his exalted power and wisdom. There does seem to be a distinction of status between the gods who are siblings of Zeus and those who belong to the next generation, hence Poseidon's dismissive retort to Iris that Zeus would do better to threaten his own children than his brother (*Il.* 15.196–9).

Yet if the gods are clearly subordinate to Zeus, within the Olympian order each has his or her *timê* or privileged sphere of influence. In Homer, the term is used of the established cosmic division between Zeus, Poseidon and Hades (*Il.* 15.189); Hesiod alludes several times to Zeus assigning the *timai* of the gods, and the proper attribution of powers and spheres of influence to each divinity is a major concern of the Homeric hymns.[22] By extension, gods can be described as ruling the places of which they are patrons: the word *medôn/medeousa* is already used in the *Iliad* and the *Hymns* to associate the 'rule' of a god with a particular place, and later the idea is particularly prominent in Pindar, who applies the concept to Apollo (*P.* 1.39 cf. 3.27) and the nymphs Cyrene (*P.* 9.7, 54, 69–70) and Thebe (*I.* 8.21–2).[23] So, too, in *O.* 7.64f. Helios exacts a sworn legal title to Rhodes as his *geras* ('portion, privilege'), and in *P.* 9.56–7 Cyrene is assured of a similar legal right (*ennomon* 57) to her portion of Libya.

The stable political organisation of Olympus is also reflected in its institutions. Like humans, the gods meet in assembly;[24] sometimes this is simply so that Zeus can make his will public, as when he warns the other gods off the battlefield (*Il.* 8.5–27) and dares them to challenge his strength, but at other times it can act as a genuine forum, within which Athena can raise the case of Odysseus (*Od.* 5.7–20) and get her way. Likewise, the gods are envisaged as having a system of justice: in the *Odyssey* this is simply a matter of financial compensation for an evident wrong (*Od.* 8.332, 347–56), but the *Hymn to Hermes* presents a more sophisticated picture of search and testimony followed by a hearing before an arbitrator.[25] The Cyclopes of the *Odyssey* represent the other pole, a totally uncivilized society without either political or judicial structures (9.106, 112–15 cf. 189, 215), each being an independent king in his own household; such a situation is described by Plato in the *Laws* (680b-d) as *dynasteia* (autocracy) and as the most primitive system of government, though Aristotle assimilates it to the democratic freedom to choose one's private life (*EN* 1180a26–9).[26] Polyphemus boasts that the Cyclopes do not even fear the gods, a position based entirely on strength (9.273–80, esp. 276). He duly comes to grief, and as a whole the picture of stable justice among the Homeric gods is of a piece with the stable cosmic government of Zeus, counterpointing the mutability of human affairs and the fallibility of mortals.

While the other gods are ultimately subject to Zeus, as Ares avows (*Il.* 5.878), he is nowhere in Homer autocratic; he shows respect for other powers such as Night (*Il.* 14.261) and expresses concern that he may antagonise other gods such as Poseidon and Hera when his actions are in conflict with their wishes (*Il.* 1.518–23; *Od.* 1.64–79). There is an additional complexity in the relations of the gods, in that they also constitute a family and household;[27] inasmuch as there are tensions between them, these seem to owe as much to family as to political dynamics, while at the same time the social interplay between the gods serves to prevent serious escalation in tension: by day Zeus and Hera may quarrel over the fate of Troy, but they sleep together by night. There is the same kind of ambiguity in Zeus's position at the head of two patriarchal systems, house and kingdom, simultaneously; in both cases the term used is the same, *anax*. One may suggest, however, that insofar as Zeus appears influenced by the disapproval of other gods, this is due more to his familial position.

At bottom, the state of affairs described by Homer and Hesiod is the same, but seen from different perspectives. Hesiod is concerned with the aetiology of the cosmic order, and this tends to lend prominence to questions of the origin and basis of power. Homer on the other hand is more concerned with the exercise of power. Indeed, the balance which Zeus strikes between asserting his superior position and exercising tact and respect for the *timai* and opinion of other gods can be seen as in counterpoint to Agamemnon's negotiation of a similar position of relative superiority among the Greek leaders: Zeus represents an ideal of kingship both for earthly kings, in his secure and potent authority, and for the ruled, in his tactful reluctance to use it.

We can trace an evolution of both the 'steady state' and the dynamic models of the divine political order in later Greek literature. Hesiod's succession of divine rulers is echoed in the Orphic theogony[28] and in later cosmogonies: Epimenides gives a couple of picturesque aetiological stories concerning Zeus's struggle with Kronos and his rise to power, and Pherecydes of Syros tells of a battle between Kronos and Ophioneus (an analogue of Typhon).[29] Herodotus (2.144.2) records a tradition reminiscent of Hesiod from Egypt, in which Horus overthrows Typhon/Seth and rules in his place.[30] In the late fifth century we also find more circumstantial stories in a Hesiodic vein: in fr.10 (Fowler) Epimenides seems to give an account of Typhon's attempt to overthrow Zeus which (apart from the decisive thunderbolt) is strikingly reminiscent of the coups that brought many tyrants to power: 'In Epimenides it is said that Typhon climbed up to the palace while Zeus was asleep, gained control of the gates and made his way inside; when Zeus came to the rescue and saw the palace taken he killed him with a thunderbolt.'[31] There is also a tantalizing fragment of Stesimbrotus preserved in Philodemus (*FGrH* 107 F17): 'he says that Zeus received his authority from his mother Rhea and was again deprived of it by her, and she then gave dominion to Artemis and Athena'; the picture of 'king-making' by a female may owe something to Greek perceptions of Persian practice.[32] The mythical background here is obscure, but given the reference in Empedocles to Aphrodite as queen (below) a model of alternation between male and female rule in the cosmos is conceivable.

We find a development of the same realism in the *Prometheus Bound*, in which relations between the gods are treated in terms of fifth-century politics. Zeus' seizure of power was a datum of the myth,[33] but the political detail is striking. Zeus is a tyrant,[34] new, hard and autocratic, with complete power; no-one is free but he, he keeps justice to himself, mistrusts his friends, receives the other gods in his *aulê* (court) like a Homeric king and allots their privileges and powers. He possesses the emblems of royalty, sceptre and throne, too, but can expect a deposition as violent as his accession.[35] Most interesting is the treatment of Zeus' rise to power as an exercise in power politics (198f.): initially the gods are split by *stasis* into pro- and anti-Zeus factions; at first Prometheus sides with the Titans, who in this version seem to be allies of Kronos rather than later rebels (221), but when they are unwilling to follow his advice he changes sides and puts his wiles at the disposal of Zeus, who duly wins. This is followed by the picture of the new king putting affairs in order (228f.). There is a general atmosphere of fear, particularly in the Oceanus episode; it is also in keeping with the tone of the play that Hermes, messenger of the gods, is here portrayed as the tyrant's lackey, adding his own bluster to his master's threats, like Euripides' heralds in *Heracleidae* and *Supplices*. It is a reflection of the fifth-century experience of political strife that its aftermath is seen as bitter and uncertain, rather than the stability previously associated with the rule of Zeus.[36]

The established political organisation of the gods is naturally carried over from epic to lyric poetry and becomes more or less commonplace, particularly the position of Zeus as king of the gods and heaven.[37] More loosely, he is styled 'master of all', 'chief of the Olympian gods' and 'commander of Olympus', while Hipponax uses a Lydian word, *palmus*, which is analogous to *turannos*. His rule is spoken of as *anassein*, and he receives the Homeric epithet *euruanax* ('wide-ruling'); reminiscent of Homer also is *ouranou … kreonti* ('ruler of heaven').[38] As with a Homeric king, Zeus' power is symbolized by his sceptre – Bacchylides calls him 'golden-sceptred'; Pindar speaks of a 'rule of Zeus', and Simonides calls him *aristarchon* ('best-ruling': 614). Occasionally his rule is set out at greater length, as by Theognis: 'for you rule over all, holding honour (*timên*) and great power … your power is greatest of all, O king.'[39] In the same way, Hera is called queen of the gods, holds a sceptre and shares the throne of Zeus. Other deities accorded royal status in lyric are Hades 'the all-receiving king (*basilêa*) of the dead', Hermes '*palmus* of Kyllene' and 'queen' Athena;[40] Hestia is also accorded a sceptre in Pi. *N*.11.4, and the generality of the usage is implied by Pindar's description of the Olympians in *Pythian* 3.94 as *Kronou paidas basilêas* ('the kings, the sons of Kronos'). Empedocles too says that the men of the Golden Age were subject not to Zeus *basileus*, but to *Kupris basileia*.[41]

The case is similar in tragedy: in Aeschylus' *Supplices* Zeus is said not to defer to any higher authority, or owe respect to any superior power, but to plan and act at will,[42] and in *Ag.* 509 he is described as 'Zeus, highest of the land'. Likewise in Sophocles, Odysseus calls Zeus 'the lord of this land' (*Phil.* 989), in *Ant.* 608 he is called *dunastas* ('potentate'), and he is 'the king who governs everything' at *Trach.* 127–8, while in *O.T.* 903–5 the chorus appeal to Zeus as 'O governing (*kratunôn*) Zeus, ruling (*anassôn*) all things' and speak of 'your everlasting immortal rule'. Near the end of the fifth century, even the sophist Gorgias calls Zeus '*turannos* of all' (B11.3); it is hard to know whether the title is poetically neutral, or a provocative example of sophistic plain speaking, like the acknowledgement that Athens' empire is a tyranny (below 124). However, by the early fourth century, Isocrates can appeal to the kingship of Zeus as an argument in favour of earthly monarchy (3.26): if the tale is true, he says, the gods clearly favour monarchy, and if it is a matter of human conjecture, obviously the human inventors of the tale would have attributed the best of constitutions to the gods.

As in Homer and lyric, the tragic gods of the underworld have their own domain: in *Choephoroi* Aeschylus speaks of 'rulers of those below' (*nerterôn turannides* 405);[43] Agamemnon once dead is only an attendant on these powers (*Cho.* 357–9). A speaker in a tantalizing fragment of Euripides attempts to unite the two powers in a somewhat confused piece of theology: he or she apparently regards Zeus and Hades as alternative titles for one god ('whether you are pleased to be called Zeus or Hades' 2–3), yet says that this divinity wields the sceptre of Zeus and shares (*metecheis*, 8) the power of Hades. The context appears to involve necromancy, so perhaps the speaker's aim is to invoke the power of the god by any means possible.[44] At all events, this interesting rationalizing throws into relief the traditional independence of Hades, usually shunned by the other gods: for his independent rule one may compare the addressing of Persephone as *Chthoniôn basileia* ('queen of those beneath the earth') in the fourth-century Orphic tablets. Herodotus reports the Egyptian belief that Demeter and Dionysus were lords of the underworld; he also attributes this kind of expression to other non-Greek peoples, relating that Thracian and Paeonian women sacrifice to 'queen Artemis', and referring to Hestia as 'queen of the Scythians'.[45]

Later poetry also takes over and develops the idea that the society of the gods has political institutions analogous to those of the human world. By the fifth century, we encounter references to decrees (*psêphismata*) in Empedocles ('There is an oracle of necessity, an ancient decree of the gods, eternal, sealed with broad oaths') and his pupil Gorgias ('through the counsels of Tyche and … the decrees of Necessity').[46] Pindar also gives us a council of the gods (*I.* 8.29f.): he speaks of an 'assembly of the blessed ones (*makarôn agorai*)' which has apparently been called to decide whether Zeus or Poseidon should marry Thetis (33), but which ends, after the speech of Themis, by agreeing that she should marry Peleus;[47] the final vote is by the nod of divine assent (49–50), since the choice between Zeus and Poseidon has been superseded by the proposal of Themis, which can be settled simply by indicating approval or disapproval. Similar ideas are expressed in tragedy: there is an atmosphere of 'the chancelleries of

Olympus'[48] in the opening scene of Euripides' *Alcestis*, in which Thanatos lays stress on his *timê* (30, 53) and appointed task (49), while Apollo appeals to *charis* (60, 70) as if in a Homeric relationship of mutual benefaction. An incidental aspect of the developed view of the political organization of Olympus is the description of lesser powers as *xunedros* or *paredros* (assessor; lit. 'sitting with/beside'): in Pindar, Rhadamanthus (*O.* 2.76) and Themis (*O.* 8.21-2) are *paredroi* of Zeus, and Eileithyia has the same relation to the Moirai (*N.* 7.1); in Sophocles (*O.C.* 1382) we find the idea of Justice sitting as assessor beside Zeus, while in Euripides' *Helen* 878-9 *paredros* is used of the full council of gods attending Zeus. In all these cases the implication is of advice given to the higher power.[49]

Both the establishment of the divine order and its political operation can of course be parodied in comedy. Thus in an anonymous comic fragment (*Com. Adesp.* fr.1062), apparently part of a prologue, the speaker, Rhea, describes Kronos' precautions against being overthrown because he has received an oracle (with typical comic disregard for logic, from Apollo) 'that he will be expelled from the kingship by his child'. Similarly Aristophon fr.11 (*Puthagoristes*) describes the disenfranchisement of Eros by the Twelve Gods for causing *stasis* among them: he is banished to earth, and his wings are given to Nike to prevent his flying back.[50]

Both lyric and tragedy suggest a gradual broadening in the range of divinities who can be characterized as regal: Bacchylides styles Asopus 'lord of rivers' (9.45) and Pindar makes Boreas lord of the winds (*P.* 4.181), while the stars are *dunastai* in Aeschylus (*Ag.* 6). Even in Homer we can already see the beginnings of a related phenomenon, the tendency to extend the concept through the personification of abstract powers which are conceived of as dynasts in their own right: hence Hypnos (*Il.* 14.233) and Night (*Il.* 14.259) are described as having dominion over all gods and men, by virtue of the power which they exert (all must sleep, and Night brings sleep).[51] In Aeschylus' *Eumenides* (127-8) Sleep and *Ponos* (Toil) conspire to overcome the Furies, and Ajax acknowledges Sleep among the great cosmic powers in his 'deception speech' (*S. Aj.* 675-6). Pindar extends the range to Time (Chronos) and Nomos (Law or Custom): the former is described as 'surpassing all the blessed gods' (fr.33) and the latter as 'king of all mortals and immortals' (fr.169a.1-2).[52] Critias likewise speaks of Dike (Justice) as a *turannos* enslaving *hybris* (*TrGF* 43 F19.6-7), and by the end of the period, the thought is applied to Tyche (i.e. Fortune), the '*turannos* of all the gods'.[53] As with Night and Sleep and, perhaps, with Hades (who to some extent comes to stand for death[54] and, with Zeus, is the god most fully characterized as a monarch), the implication is of powers which compel ultimate submission rather than immediate obedience. Gorgias' description of Logos in the *Helen* as *dunastês megas* ('a great potentate', B11.8) is clearly in the same tradition (Isocrates characterizes it as leader or guide (*hêgemôn*) of every thought and act [3.9 = 15.257]), and the paean to Air in the Hippocratic treatise *On Breaths* (3) also seems to owe more to this mode of thought than to the ideas of the Presocratic philosophers: 'he is the greatest of all potentates (*dunastês*) in all respects, and his power is worthy of contemplation ... for what could happen without him, or from what is he absent, or on what does he not attend?'[55]

Another extension of this conception is the move towards characterizing in political terms any influence on the human mind or feelings. Thus political power is extended to the paraphernalia of the symposium: Ion invokes wine as a king and as 'ruler of men'[56] and an unknown character in tragedy claims that 'wine persuaded me, highest of the gods' (*TrGF Adesp.* fr.570), while in the comic poet Antiphanes he is represented as a general (fr.19.4). Likewise the flute is a *turannos* in Sophocles, and credited with ambitions to be a general (*stratêlatas*) of drunken comasts by Pratinas.[57] A doubtful fragment of Anacreon (505d) attributes power over gods and men to Eros, who is also called *turannos* of men in E. *Hipp.* 538 and of gods and men in fr.136.[58] The same term is also used of Persuasion, a power strongly associated with Eros (E. *Hec.* 816), and another form of persuasion is invoked in an anonymous tragic fragment (*TrGF Adesp.* fr.129) in which gold is addressed as 'most powerful of [or over] all, *turannos* of all'.[59] The latter image is developed by Plato, who speaks of the oligarchic man establishing the desire for wealth in himself as a Persian monarch with the royal insignia of tiara, collar and sword at *Republic* 553c4–7 (below 153).

There is a striking adaptation of Homer's picture of Zeus in Heraclitus B53: 'War is the father of all and king of all, and some he shows as gods, others as men; some he makes slaves, others free.' [tr. Kirk, Raven and Schofield]. Heraclitus has taken the traditional titles of Zeus, but bestowed them on War, an inanimate power which is his 'favourite metaphor for the dominance of change in the world'.[60] The elaborate parallelism suggests that he is saying that War as an engine of change performs the functions of father and king, inasmuch as whether one is a man or a god is a question of one's parentage,[61] whether one is a slave or a free man is at the whim of a king (i.e. the capricious fortunes of war). Such unhampered power might seem more typical of tyranny, but Heraclitus clearly chooses to exploit the twin roles of Zeus as cosmic ruler.

This passage is also a helpful bridge to the way in which the analogical view of the gods as cosmic rulers formed the starting-point for the political cosmologies of the Presocratics. The earliest such instances are concerned with cosmic justice and equality,[62] beginning with Anaximander B1, which speaks of cosmic justice and reparation for wrongs done: 'for they [the cosmic 'opposites'] pay penalty and reparation (*dikên kai tisin*) to each other for their injustice according to the assessment of Time'. With this one may compare Heraclitus' statement that the sun is deterred from overstepping his limits by the Erinyes 'helpers of Dike' (B94) and his belief in a cosmic justice which 'nourishes' all earthly law (B114).[63] While these passages assert a systematic arrangement in the cosmos, they have no detailed political context; there is, however, a definite political framework implied by certain passages of Empedocles. In B17 DK [=8 Wright] 27–9 he describes the circular course of creation in terms of the successive authority of powers otherwise entirely equal in standing and privilege; in B30 [=23 Wright, with commentary] he describes Strife rising to a power which has been agreed by compact, while in B35 [=47 Wright] 9–11 there are overtones of the opposite process, with Strife submitting rather reluctantly to cosmic relegation from the seat of power.

Resemblances to these ideas can be seen in certain passages of tragedy. In Aeschylus' *Agamemnon* the messenger describes a conspiracy to destroy the Atreidae between the elements fire and water. Ajax in his 'deception speech' speaks of the cycle of the seasons and days in terms analogous to the succession of magistrates at

Athens, giving way to due authority (*timais*) and resigning (*existatai*) in favour of their successors.[64] Likewise in Euripides' *Phoenissae* (535–50), though she gives it no explicit political colour, Jocasta uses the cosmic manifestations of *Isotês* ('Equality') to argue for equality and justice in Eteocles' political behaviour.

Conceptions of elemental balance comparable to those to be seen in cosmology are being applied around the same date to the internal order of the bodily microcosm: Alcmaeon (B4) represents the health of the body as dependent on a balance of power (*isonomia*) between the various elements (as opposed to fair succession), while the dominance (*monarchia*) of any one brings sickness,[65] and a similar doctrine lies behind the statement in the Hippocratic treatise *Airs, Waters, Places* (12) that growth and gentleness are most favoured in an environment 'when nothing prevails (*epikrateon*)[66] by force, but equal shares of everything hold sway (*pantos isomoiriê dunasteuêi*).[67] In the Hippocratics, the main rationale seems to be that widespread health implies a stable order, though since illness arises frequently, the balance of power is conceived of as less firmly established than in Presocratic cosmology. However, while internal balance is the leading concept in Hippocratic conceptions of bodily order, this did not prevent a minority of writers, like contemporary cosmologists, from founding their ideas on the predominance of a single element, as we have seen.[68]

From ideas of balance and equality we move to a single directing force in the cosmos. This idea is already present in Xenophanes (B23, 25), though without any overt political colour, and in two obscure fragments of Heraclitus (B52, 53).[69] In Anaxagoras and Diogenes we find the more straightforward identification of a single element in the cosmos as its ruler. In the case of the former it is Mind, while for his part Diogenes believed that Air was the intelligent element.[70] The Pythagoreans seem similarly to have conceived of the cosmos as in a general sense monarchic, to judge from the observation attributed to Pythagoras[71] that just as under a monarchy one would be foolish to seek favours by courting an underling while neglecting the supreme ruler and king, so one should seek all good things from the god; however, this authority does not appear to have been strongly characterized, since their description of the central fire as the 'tower', 'guard-house' or 'throne' of Zeus (B37) was clearly figurative. Plato makes some use of the idea of a sole intelligent ruler in the cosmos,[72] and the concept resurfaces in striking form at the end of *Metaphysics* Λ (1076a3–4), where Aristotle backs up his firm assertion that there can only be one first principle by quoting Odysseus in the *Iliad* (2.204): 'the rule of many is not a good thing: let there be one ruler'.

As Lloyd has pointed out,[73] the transfer of the political model to cosmology brings a significant change, in that while the power relations described involve entities which are in some sense personalities, these are not anthropomorphic; hence in the absence of human emotion and caprice, it is easier to conceive of their interaction as regular and orderly, as a model of the cosmos requires. Order, equality and balance are the keynotes of much Presocratic cosmology, as they are of the conception of the body in early Hippocratic writings; even a figure like Heraclitus who wishes to emphasize the dynamic character of the universe is still aiming to give a rational and structured account of it. No doubt the Greek desire for order, implicit in the word *kosmos* itself, also played a part; it certainly lies behind the Hippocratic doctrine of *krasis* ('mixture').

When these ideas first appear, they can be viewed as reflecting the emergent order of the polis, and are often seen as very much in line with contemporary political ideals of abstract justice and social order of the kind expressed by Hesiod and Solon and exemplified by the slogans *nomos* and *isonomia*; however, it is worth noting that these trends persist even into the fifth century, when more radical ideas of democracy have taken root and examples of democratic constitutions have become widespread, perhaps precisely because of their capacity to accommodate a diversity of conceptions of order and balance.[74]

The other characteristic feature of these cosmologies, more evident in the monarchic models of the cosmos, is the emphasis on the intelligence of the directing power, which we have already noted in Anaxagoras and Diogenes. Indeed, it is this aspect that persists even when at the end of the Presocratic period we encounter attempts to dispense with the personal and political elements of the picture. Already in Xenophanes (B23, 25) we find God divorced from the cosmos at large; Anaxagoras goes a step further with incorporeal Mind, though he still finds himself justifying its position in physical terms, while his pupil Archelaus develops the idea by reducing the role of Mind, bringing it back into the cosmos and, probably, reducing its role in creation.[75] The atomists, however, dispensed entirely with a directing intelligence, and instead resorted to 'necessity', a mechanistic process which is neither purposeful nor random, though while departing from the traditional picture of the rule of the gods, Democritus was content to leave a place for gods in the cosmos.[76]

By the later fifth century, the removal of the traditional government of the cosmos, combined with the personification of abstracts which can be conceived of as intelligent, paves the way for the idea of the rule of law. The sophistic treatise known as the Anonymus Iamblichi argues that 'the kingship of law and justice among men' was invented owing to the need for human society, and order within it. Lysias describes the Athenians as ruled (*basileuomenous*) by law, and Alcidamas speaks of 'laws that are kings of cities'. The characterization of Nomos as a personalized agent was further developed in the fourth century, particularly by Plato, who also describes the ideal constitution as divine; hence, submission to the laws may be represented as submission to the gods.[77]

Kings as gods

I turn now to the other side of the coin, kings as gods. In the Near East, there was quite a strong perception that kings were literally divine, or at least more than mortal. In Egypt the pharaoh was a god or gods, and he is often described as established by Re, the father of Horus.[78] Description of kings as divine is rare in Mesopotamia, but as holders of a kingship bestowed by the gods, and mediators between god and man, kings were felt to be of supreme importance, and for this reason were often referred to as 'sons of the gods', a description which also suggested the king's dependence on the gods, and the gods' interest in the ruler.[79] The same ideas presumably underlie addresses to the Israelite king as the Lord's son (e.g. *Ps.* 2.7; Dvornik 1966, 297), though in one exceptional case the king is apostrophized as 'divine' (*Ps.* 45.7). One link between Near Eastern and Egyptian ideas is the metaphorical styling of Near Eastern kings as 'the sun'; in Persia this assimilates them to Ahura-Mazda, and there is perhaps a connection with the radiant *Hvarena*, the kingly glory.[80]

In Homer, the linkage is significantly weaker: with the exception of Priam's epitaph on Hector 'who was a god among men' (*Il.* 24.258) – which implies the rejoinder 'and yet all too mortal' – it is confined to simile. Thus we hear that Homeric leaders are honoured like a god by their people, or will be so honoured, or are looked on as gods.[81] More strongly, they may be greeted as gods or even prayed to as gods: 'all prayed among gods to Zeus and to Nestor among men'; compare Hector 'to whom the Trojans in the city prayed like a god'; in the only example of the image in Hesiod the wise king receives the same adulation. Similarly, Nestor's flattering remark to Agamemnon 'with you I shall end, from you I shall begin' recalls the addresses to gods in the Homeric hymns.[82]

In the *Iliad* (and *Od.* 11.484, where the context is Iliadic) the reference is principally to the prowess and stature of the leader concerned, as in the simple assessment of Idomeneus' glory that 'he stood like a god' (*Il.* 3.230–1); the Trojan adoration of Hector has the same basis. In the *Odyssey* and Hesiod, on the other hand, the honour seems more due to the civic arts, especially the administration of justice. So Arete is noted for her wisdom in settling disputes (*Od.* 7.74), just as Alcinoos and the putative orator of 8.169f. are for their eloquence, and the same applies to the kings in Hesiod *Th.* 81f.

The attenuated character of the image is reflected in its sometimes perfunctory application to heroes. In two of the passages cited above, those honoured with quasi-divinity are only introduced to be none too gloriously killed by Greeks (Hypsenor *Il.* 5.78, Laogonos 16.604). The same is true of its extension well beyond royalty: thus in *Od.* 14.205–6 Castor is admired by the people as a god simply for his prosperity and his children, and in *Il.* 14.72–3 Zeus is said to exalt the whole Trojan army. In the *Odyssey* it is almost a commonplace of courtesy to enquire of well-favoured strangers whether they are gods;[83] both Odysseus and Telemachus promise prayers to their female benefactors as to a god (8.467, 15.181) and the author of the hymn to Apollo goes so far as to liken all the Ionians at their festival to immortals (*hAp.* 151).

While there is still a residue of admiration for kings as more than human, combined with the usual nostalgia for a heroic age when men were like gods and kings looked like kings,[84] the basis of the image is already the use of the gods as a general standard of excellence and blessedness: beauty in strangers suggests divinity, the wise counsellor is *theophin mêstôr atalantos* ('an adviser equal to a god') and the brave man *atalantos Arêi* ('equal to Ares'), while *dios* ('godlike') is used to denote excellence not only in heroes, but in women, swineherds, whole nations, horses, land, and so on. This trend leads in the classical period to a handsome man being called *seios* (i.e. *theios*, 'divine') at Sparta, and to Eupolis' saying that the Athenians prayed to their statesmen of the past 'like gods – because that's what they were'.[85] So too in Theognis (338–40) a man perfectly successful at requiting friends and enemies would seem like a god.

References in later Greek literature to men as divine or godlike in a political context occur in passages with Homeric colouring. The Delphic oracle is said to have hesitated whether to call Lycurgus a god or a man, and inclined to the former, no doubt in admiration of his status as a creator and upholder of law (nr.29 P-W), and one of the Harmodius skolia (*PMG* 894) is sure that the tyrannicide is not dead, but has been translated to the Isles of the Blest.[86] In the same way, Plato in a number of passages attributes to his ideal rulers and lawgivers a more than human quality: the reverential attitude towards Lycurgus is traditional (*Lg.* 691e, *Phdr*.258c),[87] but Plato extends this to his ideal rulers, referring to the Nocturnal Council in the *Laws* as *theios* (966d, 969b cp.945c), and attributing to the Guardians in the *Republic* the epithets *sôtêras te kai epikourous* ('saviours and protectors') which would be appropriate to gods.[88] After death the Guardians, like founders of colonies, will be honoured with sacrifices as *daimones*, subject to Pythian approval, or failing that as *eudaimones kai theioi* ('blessed and holy': 540bc); similarly, Xenophon suggests that the funeral honours for Spartan kings were devised by Lycurgus to reflect their heroic character (*Resp.Lac.* 15.9).

In a couple of instances in tragedy the effect of the image seems to be one of misdirection. While the priest states that Oedipus is not a god, but rather the first of men (*S. O.T.* 31–3), he is certainly god-like in receiving suppliants and being hailed as saviour (48 cf. the reference to 'your altars' at 16); he is taking the place of the god for the Thebans (14; contr. 904–5), and replies appropriately (216f.), creating a feeling of an enviable but dangerous eminence. In A. *Supp.* 373 the phrase *monopsêphoisi neumasi* ('with nods that vote alone') recalls the nod of Zeus; here the usage, like the whole stanza, is designed to create a picture of a king like a Persian monarch, with absolute, uncontrolled power, which Pelasgus can then refute by his constitutionality.

It is thus rare for Greek rulers to be straightforwardly characterized as divine. What we find instead are two more oblique uses of the concept. On the one hand, and unsurprisingly, the stronger Near Eastern use of the image is reflected in Greek literature concerned with Persians. Thus in Aeschylus' *Persae* Xerxes and Darius are described as gods (157, 642–3, 651) or as equal to gods (80, 634, 655, 711, 856; cf. Hecuba's reference to the throne of Troy as *tês isotheou turannidos* ('tyranny like that of a god': E. *Tro*.1169)). Herodotus gives us more detail: from the idea of the king as the best and fairest of men (4.91.2, 7.187.2, 8.68γ; cf. 3.20.2 – the king of the Ethiopians is chosen as being the biggest and strongest) and perception of his splendour comes the idea that the invading Xerxes is actually Zeus in disguise (7.56.2; compare Gorgias' phrase 'Xerxes, the Zeus of the Persians (B5a), criticized as bombast by Longinus 3.2); the Greek protestations in 7.203.2 that the invader is not a god, but a man, suggest that the Persians may have played on the idea for propaganda purposes. Certainly Alexander of Macedon speaks of Xerxes in terms of more than human power and reach (8.140β2), which perhaps reflects Greek accounts of the institutions of the King's eyes and ears, which extended his perception throughout his realm; so too Deioces had 'watchers and listeners' throughout his kingdom in Media (Hdt. 1.100.2).[89] Likewise Cyrus saw himself as more than human (Hdt. 1.204; NB Deioces' desire to appear *heteroios* ['of a different kind': 1.99.2]), and the kings of India seemed to Scylax to be of a different type from their subjects.[90] Kings of Persia were perceived not merely as rulers of their land, but as its possessors[91] and Xerxes' megalomaniac ambition is to make his realm co-extensive with what the sun can see (7.8γ). A further symbol of the distinct character of Persian monarchs, at least in Greek eyes, was the custom of *proskynesis* (ritual obeisance): Lloyd remarks, in reference to Herodotus' statement that Egyptians greet one another in this way, that 'to a Greek such prostration before another was not only regarded as degrading and ridiculous, but also as blasphemy; for προσκύνησις was a cult act in Greece.' One may compare the remark of the Spartans whom the Persians tried to force to fall before Xerxes, as reported by Herodotus, that 'it was not their custom to prostrate themselves before human beings (*anthrôpon proskuneein*)'.[92]

The other oblique approach is the satirical burlesque. Attic comedy contains a series of attacks on Pericles the Olympian.[93] Cratinus, who seems to have enjoyed a similar relationship with Pericles to that of Aristophanes with Cleon, refers to him on three occasions as Zeus, profiting each time by the opportunity to refer to the peculiar shape of his head, particularly by perverting traditional epithets of the god: in his *Nemesis* he calls him 'Zeus patron of foreigners and head of state (*Zeu xenie kai karaie*)' and in the *Cheirones* we find the marvellous *kephalêgeretan* ('head-gatherer').[94] In this fragment, Cratinus, in a comic cosmogony, calls him the son of Chronos (Time)[95] and Stasis; the reference to the overthrow of a divine tyranny in fr.171.22–3 (*Ploutoi*) might indicate that Pericles played this role there, though the details are not entirely clear.[96] Telecleides fr.18 (*Hesiodoi*) calls him 'the Olympian', Hermippus fr.47 (*Moirai*) refers to him as 'king of the Satyrs' and Plato Comicus fr. 207, in identifying Damon as his Cheiron, may have referred to him as one of the heroes.[97] In Aristophanes' *Acharnians* 530–1 the reference would seem to be chiefly to his Olympian anger, but in 531 there may also be a reference to the thunder of his oratory (cf. *Com. Adesp.* frr.288, 701), given that from Homer onwards the thunderbolt is a symbol of Zeus' power.

Aspasia is similarly a divine consort: Cratinus made her Hera to Pericles' Zeus in the comic cosmogony in *Cheirones*: 'and as his Hera, Buggery (*Katapugosunê*) bears Aspasia the shameless concubine (*pallakên kunôpida*)', and it would appear that this was also her title in Eupolis' *Philoi* (fr.294).[98] Elsewhere in Eupolis she was referred to as Helen; she was also called the new Omphale (presumably because she kept Pericles in bondage), perhaps by Cratinus, and further identified with Deianeira: presumably Pericles was therefore Heracles, the implication being in both cases that she was bad for him, and, perhaps, dominated him.[99]

By contrast, Cleon is depicted as a Typhon (Ar. *Eq.* 511) and a multi-formed monster (*Vesp.* 1030–6 = *Pax* 752, 754–9). Just as Aristophanes is the Heracles who takes on Cleon's monster (*Vesp.* 1030 = *Pax* 752), so Plato Comicus complains that politicians grow like the Hydra's heads, and need an Iolaus to cauterize them (fr.202); the philosophic Plato uses the image of the Hydra's heads to illustrate the futility of trying to cure social ills by ad hoc legislation (*R*. 426e).

By the end of the fifth century, however, we can detect a change in the fortunes of the image which reflects the rising stock of monarchy. The political context was beginning to shift, as the conferral of divine honours on living individuals began to creep into Greece, the earliest case being that of Lysander, to whom the Samians dedicated a festival (Plut. *Lys.* 18.4) and who had a paean written in his honour (*PMG* 867).[100] This calculated political use of divine honours seems to be of a different type from honours paid to an *oikistês* (founder of a colony) even in the fifth century, though the Amphipolitan treatment of Brasidas in 422, an overtly political gesture, perhaps marks the beginning of secularization. Plato's willingness to heroize his guardians needs to be viewed in this light. Even more striking is the case of Isocrates who, though hostile to *proskynesis* and Persian despotism when writing for a broad Greek public, intriguingly reflects it in his advice to Nicocles. Starting from the fairly trite observation that monarchs are considered godlike because of their advantages, he goes on to observe that kingship is not in fact like a priesthood, which anyone can fill; the king must be special. This is elaborated in terms reminiscent of Persian ideology: the king should want to be superior, and indeed the honour paid to him is because he is best (*beltistos*), so he should look worthy of his rule and be solemn and remote (*semnos*); in a related passage Isocrates attributes to Nicocles a claim to omnipresent omniscience of the sort achieved by the King's Eyes and Ears. That Isocrates should write to Philip suggesting that once he has subdued Asia there will be nothing left but to become a god is, in the context of these ideas, not surprising.[101]

Towards the end of the period, we can detect a convergence between the two fields of imagery addressed in this chapter in the emergence of the idea of the ruler as embodying law (*nomos empsuchos*), a concept which gained currency in the Hellenistic era, and which first appears in Xenophon's *Cyropaideia*. He attributes to Cyrus the belief that, while men are improved by written laws, the good ruler is 'a law with eyes (*bleponta nomon*) for men', able to instruct or chastise as appropriate. The king's capacity for close supervision, which seems to be the main issue here, is also attributed by Xenophon to the authority of the ephors at Sparta: like tyrants and overseers of the gymnastic contests, they can punish immediately anyone whom they detect in wrongdoing.[102] The thought of this passage is, however, not as close to the later development of the idea as Plato's concept of the ideal king as more flexible than, and hence superior to, law (*Plt.* 300c). For Plato, and for Aristotle, the concept clearly rests on the idea that such a man will be morally outstanding to such a degree as to be quite different from ordinary men, hence Aristotle's assimilation of such an ideal ruler to the divine (*Pol.* 1284a3–15, b25–34). Elsewhere, Aristotle seems to allow that a judge might ideally embody justice (*EN* 1132a21–2), but essentially the concept seems to envisage a single outstanding individual, and hence in constitutional terms a monarchy. Problems naturally arise when Hellenistic political philosophy takes the concept of the rule of a divine personified law and links it to the person of real kings, who are also conceived of as raised above ordinary mortals. Plutarch and Arrian relate that Anaxarchus consoled Alexander in his despair after the murder of Cleitus the Black by comparing him to Zeus, at whose side Justice sits as *paredros*, so that all his acts should be accounted just. Put so baldly, this sounds like a justification of unaccountable absolute power, and Hellenistic political philosophers devoted much effort to justifying and qualifying the position.[103]

Notes

1 The 'vehicle' in the terminology of I. A. Richards, while the 'underlying idea', the object of comparison, is the 'tenor': Silk (1974) 8–10. On the question to what extent such usage was originally conceived of as figurative, see above xiv–xv.

2 Again, it might be questioned whether this constitutes imagery as such, at least in

early hexameter poetry (see above xiv–xv), but it clearly reflects analogical thinking; what is noteworthy is the difference between Greek application of the concept and that found in the Near East (below, 10–12).
3 See above (xv) for this principle.
4 Aristotle observes that 'men imagine not only the forms of the gods, but their ways of life, to be like their own.' (*Pol.* 1252b26–7). The society of the gods itself seems to be an invention of the epic, being at odds with the general tenor of Greek religion, in which gods tend to operate independently: Griffin (1980) 186 with nn.19, 20. Finley (1978) 132–4 highlights one key difference between the two societies, the 'overwhelming' power of Zeus, 'beyond the dreams of even the greatest king', but notes that he nevertheless remains 'a special sort of first among equals'. There is a good overview of Homer's divine social order in Lloyd (1966) 193–200; see also Clay (1989) 8–16. For Near Eastern and Indo-European parallels see West (1997) 107–9, (2007) 131, and for Jahweh as king NB Dvornik (1966) 319, 324, 332–4.
5 In what follows I treat the two authors (and the composers of the Hymns) together where there is no difference in their practice, and cite major works without author name.
6 There does not seem to be any reflection on Olympus of the superiority of the Mycenean *wanax* over those styled pa_2-*si-re-u* i.e. *basileus*: both titles are used interchangeably (and juxtaposed in *Th.* 883), along with terms such as *koiranos* ('ruler') and *sêmantôr* ('commander, ruler'); nor is *anax* reserved for Zeus (below). The distinction is a little clearer, if still 'somewhat blurred', among mortals: West (1997) 15.
7 *anax*: *Il.* 1.502, *Th.* 493; *anassein*: *Th.* 403, 491, 883; *basileus*: *Th.* 897, Hes. fr.308, *hDem.* 358 cf. *basileuemen* in *Th.* 883; 'king in heaven': *Th.* 71; 'highest of rulers': *Od.* 24.473; king/lord/commander of the gods: *Il.* 4.61, 18.366, *Th.* 886, *Op.* 668, Hes. frr.5, 308, *Sc.* 56, 328, *hMerc.* 367; king of all: *Il.* 2.669, 12.242, *Od.* 9.552, 13.25, 20.112, *Th.* 506.
8 For Kronos and the Titans in Tartarus see *Il.* 8.479–81, 14.203–4, 273–4, 278–9, 15.224–5 – if it is they who are referred to in *Il.* 5.898 he also knew their parentage; for Typhoeus: *Il.* 2.782–3. Cf. the uprising of Otus and Ephialtes, of which different versions appear in *Iliad* (5.385–91) and *Odyssey* (11.305–20), though they do not feature in Hesiod.
9 Willcock (2001) 439.
10 Slatkin (2001), referring to Pindar *Isthmian* 8 and [Aeschylus] *P.V.* 907–27; Willcock (2001) 439–40 also sees a reminiscence of this myth in the description of Briareos as 'more powerful than his father'. See further Cairns (2001) 45–8 for judicious discussion.
11 Explicitly stated at *Th.* 49; cf. 403 and fr.308 for the language of *kratos* ('might'). NB also Schibli (1990) 98–9 for the idea that 'ordering-processes involve conflict' and ibid. 89–93 for a distinction between gradual cosmic development, which does not require a concept of authority (he cites Arist. *Metaph.* 1091b6–9) and change in stages or by succession, which is likely to do so. Vernant (1982) 108–16 likewise argues that the establishment of divine sovereignty is simultaneously the establishment of cosmic order.
12 *anax Th.*486; *basileida timên* ('kingly honour') *Th.* 462; *basilêi Th.* 476, 486; *ouranôi embasileuen* ('was king in heaven') *Op.* 111; cf. the spurious *Op.* 173a, where Kronos is said to govern (*embasileuei*) the Isles of the Blest.
13 Clay (1989) 19–29, 63–74; Typhaon is a variant of the monster's name, as is Typhon.

14 Clay (1989) 68; 74, 91–4.
15 It is intriguing that there are no securely identified artistic representations of (generic) Titans nor of the Titanomachy (one lost example is attested), in contrast to the abundant Gigantomachies and a couple of dozen Typhons, both of which apparently serve to emphasize the durability of the divine order by depicting the defeat of challenges to it: 'La prééminence de Zeus n'est pas réellement menacée. Et c'est peut-être ce qu'il fallait montrer.' (*LIMC* s.v. Typhon [Odette Touchefeu-Meynier]); *LIMC* s.vv. Gigantes, Titanes, Typhon. On the epic *Titanomachy* of the late seventh or sixth century see West (2002) 111–18. Hardie (1986) 85–156, 384–5 discusses the later figurative use of the Gigantomachy to symbolize threats to order.
16 Strength: *Il.* 4.56, 15.165, *Od.* 5.4; anger: e.g. *Il.* 8.10–27, 402–6, 450–1, 463, *Od.* 5.146–7, 13.148.
17 Precedence of Zeus: *Il.* 13.345–56, 15.162–6; his especial wisdom (*mêtis*) is recognized in two formulas linked exclusively to him, *Zeus mêtieta* ('Zeus the counsellor') and 'equal to Zeus in *mêtis*'. The Homeric gods also display a more general deference to age: *Il.* 4.58–61, *Od.* 6.329–30, 13.341–2. In point of fact, though, Zeus was only the first-born because regurgitation by Kronos reversed the order of birth of his children: West (1997) 293–4.
18 In either case there is a contrast with the lack of any clear rule of succession for earthly monarchs noted by Qviller (1981) 115–17.
19 Hesiod fr.10(d).9 M-W, *Phoronis* fr.4.1–2; cp *anassês* in line 4, *hHom.* 12 and Panyassis fr.6c Davies/25 Bernabé, if the citation *reginam ... Iunonem* reflects the poet's words. 'Queen' was also a common cult title, particularly of Hera (e.g. R&O no.62 B5, from Cos), though also of Artemis, Aphrodite and Persephone: *RE* s.v. Basileia (5), Basilis (2); NB below, n.41.
20 *Anax* and cognates in *Il.* 20.61, *hDem.* 347, 357, *Th.* 850; *koiranos*: *hDem.* 87; *polusêmantôr* ('ruler of many'): *hDem.* 31, 84, 376; *sêmantôr* is applied to divine rulers in *hMerc.* 367, *Sc.* 56, Hes. fr.5 as well as to human commanders (LSJ s.v. 1); hence *polusêmantôr* is loosely equivalent to *eurukreiôn* ('wide-ruling'), applied to Poseidon at *Il.* 11.751.
21 *hDem.* 365, and NB Richardson (1974) on 363ff. for 'the ambiguity and subtlety of the speech'; *hMerc.* 259 with Allen, Halliday and Sikes (1936) *ad loc.*
22 For the meaning of *timê* applied to gods and their distribution by Zeus, see West (1966) on *Th.* 74 and Richardson (1974) on *hDem.* 85f.; on their centrality in the *Hymns*, Clay (1989) 15 and index s.v. *timai*. The allotment seems to have featured in Pherecydes' cosmology as well: Schibili (1990) 52–3, 100. The epic *Titanomachy* appears, like Homer, to have represented the division of the cosmic spheres as done by lot: West (2002) 114–16; again, there are Near Eastern parallels: West (1997) 109–11.
23 *medôn/medeousa*: *Il.* 3.276, 320, 7.202, 16.234, 24.308; *hMerc.* 2, *hVen.* 292, and this language persisted: a cult of Athena 'who rules Athens (*Athênôn medeousa*)' is attested by boundary markers found in states subject to Athens' fifth-century empire: Parker (1996) 144–5. In Pi. *O.* 10.13 the personification Atrekeia (Strict Truth or Justice) is said to rule over Epizephyrian Locri; Anacreon (fr.348) similarly applies the imagery of shepherding to Artemis of Magnesia (NB 44 below). There is an intriguing oddity of usage, apparently related to this image, in Aeschylus' application of *polissouchos* ('city-protecting'), otherwise the epithet of guardian deities (more often in the form *poliochos*: LSJ s.v.), to the Athenian people (*Eum.* 775, 883, 1010). Two less forceful bridging examples in the Euripidean *Rhesus* (*poliochou turannidos* 'city-protecting tyranny' 166; *poliochon kratos* 'city-protecting might' 821), applied to

Hector and his kingship in a manner reminiscent of Near Eastern ideas, show that it will not do to pension off the Aeschylean passages under a separate heading, as do *LSJ*, and that there is a continuity, with the same keynote of protection. Such high praise of the demos is appropriate in *Eumenides*, where the resolution of the crisis rests with the demos, and we can perhaps detect a certain role reversal, with Athena taking on some of the government of the city (NB the references to her *thesmoi* ('ordinances') in 571 and 681), while the people assume some of the responsibility for its protection.

24 *Il.* 4.1, 8.2, 20.4, *Od.* 5.3–4, *hDem.* 92, *Th.* 802; both divine and human assemblies are convened by Themis (*Il.* 20.4–6, *Od.* 2.68–9). The normal term for this gathering in Homer is *agora*, while Hesiod calls it *boulê*. There are similar assemblies of Near Eastern gods: West (1997) 177–81, and NB (2007) 150–1 for wider Indo-European parallels; cf. (1997) 190–3 for divine messengers.

25 *hMerc.* 264=364, 312, 324; in 370–3 Hermes protests at an abuse of procedure: Allen, Halliday & Sikes *ad loc.* observe that 'the writer models heaven on his own *polis*'; NB also Richardson (2010) 21 for the legal colour of the hymn.

26 In the *Politics* (1259a37-b17) Aristotle distinguishes different aspects of the authority of a householder, which is kingly only over his children; see further below 34.

27 Rutherford (1996) 47 puts it the other way round: 'The gods are presented as an extended family, mostly resident together on Olympus; like any family, they have their disagreements and their changing moods ... In other scenes, the appropriate human parallel may be rather the court of a king and his fellow-nobles.' More frivolously, Collins (1996) 144 remarks that the gods 'often suggest characters from *The Marriage of Figaro* obliged to manage a Wagnerian Valhalla'.

28 Lines 5–7, 11, 17–9, 25 and 29 of the Derveni theogony reconstructed in West (1983) 114–5 with 84–8; the poem abridges an earlier cosmogony of *c.* 500 BC. By the late fifth century, the succession myth could be adduced by Timotheus (fr.796) as an argument for progress in art: 'the young Zeus is king, and Kronos ruled in ancient times'; the latter had become proverbial for the old and out-of-date: Ar. *Nub.* 398 with Dover (1968) *ad loc.*

29 Epimenides B23–4 (24=2 Fowler; on 23 see ibid. 101); Pherecydes F78 Schibli = B4DK; see Schibli (1990) 78–103 for full discussion, arguing that Kronos and Zeus act here in full accord (Zeus may have been the champion of the gods in the field) and that the peaceful succession of Kronos by Zeus follows their victory.

30 The word used, *katapauô*, is almost a technical term for carrying out a coup d'état: *LSJ* s.v. II.3.

31 = *FGrH* 457 F8. My translation of Diels' text; the supplements are unreliable, but the outlines are clear, since [*ba*]*sileion* ('palace') seems secure (West 1983, 48 n.42); for a conservative text and alternative supplements, see Fowler's *apparatus*. For the date of the poem attributed to Epimenides, see West (1983) 49–51 (*c.* 430 BC?), though Fowler (2000) 79 suggests early fourth century.

32 For example Herodotus' account of the struggle over the succession to Darius I (7.2–3); Sancisi-Weerdenburg (1993) discusses the perceived influence of women at the Persian court.

33 Reflected, for example, in E. *HF* 1317–8, Pl. *Euthphr.* 6b7–9, R. 377e6–8b5. See, however, A. fr.281a for a different version in which, though he evidently still used violence, Zeus was retaliating and justified: he had the personal support of Dike, who is one of the speakers.

34 The play contains two thirds of the instances of *turannis* in the Aeschylean corpus

(10, 224, 305, 357, 756, 909, 996) and three quarters of those of *turannos* (222, 310, 736, 761, 942, 957, and NB *monarchos* 324); even if the play is not Aeschylean, the frequency is striking.

35 Zeus autocratic: 310, 324; power: 389; freedom: 50 cf. E. *Hel.* 276 with 108 below; monopoly of justice: 186f.; cf. E. *Supp.* 429–32 with Collard (1975) and Stinton's addendum (ibid. 440–2); mistrust: 224–5; court: 122; allotment of privileges: 229–31; sceptre: 171, 761; throne: 228, 767, 910, 912 cf. 389; deposition anticipated: 756–7, 908f.

36 On *P.V.* see Podlecki (1966) ch. 4, pointing out the similarity between Zeus and Aristotle's stock tyrant. Conacher (1980) 38–40 emphasizes Prometheus' own political pragmatism, but his defection seems already to have featured in the epic *Titanomachy*: West (2002) 114.

37 king: Thgn. 285, 376, Sol. fr.31.1, Alc. frr.296.3, 387, Pi. *I.* 8.20; of the immortals: Thgn. 743, Pi. *N.* 5.35, 10.16; of heaven: Pi. *N.* 4.67; of the gods: Pi. *O.* 7.34, *N.* 7.82; supreme king (*pambasileus*): Alc. fr.308b.3–4; Stesich. S14.1–2 (suppl. Lobel).

38 Master: Pi. *I.* 5.53 (Ammon, the Egyptian divinity syncretized with Zeus, is likewise 'master of Olympus' in a hymn addressed to him: fr.36); chief: Bacch. 5.179; commander: Pi. *O.* 9.57 cf. fr.52r (a).3 [?]; *palmus*: Hippon. fr.38, and also applied to Hermes (below); compare the suggestive sequence (from choral lyric) *antessinôturanniazeusk* in *P.Oxy.* 2736 2b14. *Anassein*: Thgn. 373, 803; *euruanax*: Bacch. 5.19–20, Pi. *O.* 13.24; *ouranou ... kreonti*: Pi. *N.* 3.10.

39 Sceptre: Pi. *P.* 1.6, fr.70b.7, Bacch. 9.100; 'rule of Zeus': Pi. *O.* 2.58–9, Simon. fr.614, Thgn. 373–6. For the ubiquity of the sceptre as symbol of power in the Near East see West (1997) 17, 134–5; often it is associated with the throne: ibid., 563. The commonplace persists in the fourth century: 'the son of Kronos who reigns (*anassei*) mightily over all' (Antim. fr.3); 'by Zeus the king (*ton anakta*)' (D. 35.40). Similarly, the historians Aristodicus (*FGrH* 36 F1) and Aglaosthenes (*FGrH* 499 F2) allude to Zeus' accession to the kingship of the gods.

40 Hera as queen: Pi. *N.* 1.39, fr.52v.3,11,19; cf. *megistoanassa* ('greatest queen') in Bacch.19.21; sceptre: *PMG Adesp.* 960; throne: Pi. *N.* 11.2. Hades: *PMG Adesp.* 925 (e).11; Hermes: Hippon. fr.3; Athena *basilêid*[: *Lyr.Adesp.* S415.4. However, *Arês turannos* (Tim. fr.790) is different: 'war is our lord' amounts to 'we will fight come what may', according to Hordern (2002) *ad loc.*

41 B128.2–3; compare the cult of Aphrodite *basilis* at Tarentum and Persephone *basilis* at Katane: *RE* s.v. Basilis (2).

42 A. *Supp.* 595f. (the text is partially corrupt) cf. *anax anaktôn* 524; the tone is what West (1997, 557–8) calls 'Zeus orientalized'.

43 As Garvie (1986) notes *ad loc.*, the term *turannos* is not inherently derogatory in such contexts (cf. below 110–11 and n.27 on Turannis in E. *Pho.* 506). Compare *Supp.* 791 and fr.612, where Hades is called *hagêsilaos* ('leader of the host').

44 E. fr.912; cf. references to Hades as a Zeus of the dead in A. *Supp.* 158 and 230–1, and for the ambiguities of Zeus Chthonios see West (1978a) on Hes. *Op.* 465. Hecuba invokes Zeus in similarly unconventional terms before her crucial debate with Helen (*Tro.* 884–9 with Lee 1976 *ad loc.*).

45 Persephone: A1–2 in Zuntz (1971), with p.308. Egypt: Hdt. 2.123.1 (*archêgêteuein de tôn katô*) cf. 4.33.5, 127.4.

46 Emp. B115 DK [=107 Wright] 1–2 (tr. Inwood); Gorg. B11.6, though Empedocles' gods are not immortal (Wright 1981 *ad loc.*, who notes the reminiscence of the oath between Love and Strife (B30)). Gorgias adds a little sophistic colouring concerning

the inevitable rule of the stronger. *Psêphisma* is an unusual expression for a divine decree (MacDowell 1982 *ad loc.* compares Ar. *Vesp.* 378), but note the more striking conceit in Gorgias' *Palamedes* (B11a1, echoed in Xenophon's *Apology* 27; the verb in both cases is *katapsêphizô*) that we are condemned to death at birth by nature.

47 He uses the formal language of political decision making: *edox' ara kai athanatois* ('so it was resolved by the immortals', 65).

48 Dodds (1929) 102.

49 Cf. also *O.C.* 1267: *esti gar kai Zêni synthakos thronôn Aidôs* ('for Zeus too shares his throne with Compassion'). *TrGF Adesp.* fr.655.19-20 *he toi par[e]dron theôn dromon kektêmenê | Dikê*, ('Justice who runs the course that sits alongside the gods') though mixing its metaphors, must have a similar sense. NB below, 14 for exploitation of this idea in support of the concept of the king as embodying law. For such attendants in Hades cf. E. *Alc.* 743 with Dale (1954), Isoc. 9.15. In Ar. *Av.* 1753, Basileia ('Princess') is the attendant of Peisetairos as he supplants Zeus (see Dunbar 1995 *ad loc.*).

50 The same kind of rationalization can be seen in another fourth-century source when Xenophon makes the Athenian politician Callias style the Dioscouroi 'citizens of Sparta' (*HG* 6.3.6).

51 Note the slide from 'sweet sleep' to 'all-subduing Sleep' in *Il.* 24.3-5. Lloyd (1966) 200-2 notes that in Homer such natural phenomena can be both personified and thought of in material terms; for the phenomenon see Stafford (2000), esp. 1-44, with references to earlier studies; she also discusses the evidence for Sleep as a god receiving cult in Stafford (2003). NB also below 125 for personification of political concepts.

52 For the influence of this passage and the later personification of Nomos, see below 166. Nomos here is taken by Lloyd-Jones (1972, 55-6) to mean cosmic law or order, as generally administered by Zeus. However, while it is clear that Callicles (or Plato) is perverting the sense of the passage in the *Gorgias* for polemical ends, it is equally clear that Herodotus (3.38) took it in the sense 'custom', for that is the point of the story which precedes it, and this also makes more sense of Pindar's sympathetic tone towards Diomedes and Geryon (fr.81); his point is, in modern terms, that justice can be a matter of perspective (cf. fr.215 (a) 2-3). For this line of interpretation see Ostwald (1965). There is an ambiguity over the sense in E. *Hec.* 799-800, the first instance ('*nomos* which rules the gods') being closer to 'law' and the second to 'convention'.

53 *TrGF Adesp.* fr.506 = *Com. Adesp.* fr.883, cf. fr.881, also of Tyche.

54 *LSJ* s.v. Ἅιδης II ('after Hom.'), alongside the straightforward personification of Thanatos.

55 For a power (*dunamis*) or powers at work in the body, see below 152.

56 fr.26.12W, *PMG* 744.5; the reference of 27.1 is probably the same or similar: see West 1974 *ad loc.* and below 39n.31).

57 S. *Tr.* 217, Pratin. fr.708.9; NB the *sêmata* of the lyre in Pi. *P.*1.3, and compare Telestes fr.806 'Phrygian king of the fair-breathing holy pipes', referring to Olympus.

58 Cf. S. fr.941.15, where it is said that Kypris *Dios turannei pleumonon* ('rules the guts of Zeus').

59 For the power of speech NB above. Peithô as divinity is one of the case-studies discussed by Stafford (2000), 111-45; for Peithô and love, see Buxton (1982) 29-48, and for πείθω in the sense 'bribe', *LSJ* s.v. A II.2.

60 Kirk, Raven and Schofield (1983) 194.

61 Though the concept of parentage is itself being used figuratively here if the reference is to Heraclitus' doctrine that some could become gods through death in battle (Kirk, Raven & Schofield 1983, *loc. cit.*). Robinson (1987) 117–18 suggests the possibility of separating this off from any view of War as an agent of cosmic change.
62 On this see Vlastos (1947); more generally, Lloyd (1966) 210–32, Pender (2000) 94–6, 106–7; Grossmann (1950) 48–70 argues for a concept of proportional *isonomia* in thinkers influenced by Pythagoreanism.
63 NB Empedocles B135 DK [=121Wright] for Law extending throughout the cosmos, and the identification of *nous* ('mind') with *to dikaion* ('the just') in Anaxagoras A55 for the rational basis of law; also Kirk, Raven & Schofield (1983) 210–12 for this theme in Heraclitus.
64 A. *Ag.* 650–1; for cosmic conspiracy cf. *Eum.*127, above 7; S. *Aj.* 669f. with Knox (1961) 23–4. The idea could be reversed: in his peroration, a fourth-century Athenian speaker appeals to the administration of the cosmos and the seasons by *nomos kai taxis* ('law and order') as evidence of the universality of law: [D.] 26.27.
65 Strictly speaking, the balance is between pairs of opposites (Ostwald 1969, 99–106), but what is in question is not necessarily absolute equality, but appropriate balance, as the diversity of physical constitutions and temperaments, as well as the changing seasons, would imply: Cambiano (1982) 235; Caserta (2007) traces affinities with Pythagorean mathematics and rules of proportion in sculpture. See also below 75, 114.
66 In the sense 'prevail, be prevalent' (so *LSJ*, who compare *Aph.* 3.5, of a prevailing wind).
67 My rather literal translation attempts to capture the paradoxical quality of the expression.
68 *Flat.* 3 (above, 7), 15; cf. *Vict.* 10. For fuller discussion see cross-references at n.65 above.
69 For the cosmic supremacy of War in B53, see above. Even more perplexing is B52: 'Lifetime (*aiôn*) is a child playing, moving pieces in a board-game; kingly power is in the hands of a child.' Robinson (1987) reads this in a cosmic sense, while arguing that the child is only apparently senseless to those without true perception; Marcovitch (1967; his fr.93) interprets it as meaning that men, even kings, have no more sense than a child. For images based on the board-game *pessoi*, see below 104n.91; Plato *Lg.* 903d has a divine draughts-player (*petteutês*) moving human souls up and down according to their actions (Pender 2000, 108 n.188).
70 Anaxagoras: A48, B12; Kirk, Raven and Schofield (1983) 362–5; Diogenes: B5; ibid. 441–5.
71 DK58 D2; NB Kirk, Raven & Schofield (1983) 349 for its authenticity; cf. D3.174.
72 Lloyd (1966) 220, Pender (2000)106–7; below 152.
73 Lloyd (1966) 210–13, 224–5.
74 Lloyd (1966) 222–5 offers a cautious assessment of the implications of these cosmologies, noting that individual political convictions need to be allowed for, though they are not always influential. For equality in Solon see especially frr.34.9 (*isomoiriê*) and 36.18–20 (equal laws for all). It should also be remembered that rotation of office is a hallmark of constitutionality, but not necessarily of democracy, as shown by the constitutions of the cities of Boeotia *c.* 400 BC (*Hell.Oxy.* 16.2, cf. [Arist.] *Ath.Pol.* 30.3). For the flexibility of *isonomia* as a principle see above n.65 and below 114; for the fourth-century doctrine of 'proportional equality' see Harvey (1965) and NB below 160.

75 Anaxagoras B12; as Kirk, Raven and Schofield (1983) 364 point out, he has not quite succeeded in defining an incorporeal abstract; Archelaus: Kirk, Raven and Schofield (1983) 386-8.
76 Taylor (1999) 188-95; for Democritus' theology see ibid. 211-16.
77 Anon. Iambl. 6.1 (NB below 145n.158), Lys. 2.19; Alcidamas ap. Arist. *Rh*.1406a22-3 = fr.17 B-S. Kingship of law in Plato: below 166; ideal constitution: ibid.; for Nomos = 'custom' as king, see above, 7 and below 166.
78 Pharaoh as divine: e.g. Pritchard (1969) 227; 245, 247-8 (Amenhotep II); 329; 378-9 (Ramses IV); 431; 446-7 (Thutmose III); established by Re: ibid. 231 (Hatshepsut); 232 (Kamose); 257 (Ramses II); 329; 373-5 (Thutmose III); 375-6 (Amenhotep III); imitated in the subordinate kingdom of Ethiopia *c.* 600: ibid. 447-8. The object lesson given to the Egyptians by Amasis in turning an ordinary polluted foot-bowl into a sacred statue (Hdt. 2.172), evidently designed to show that kingship transforms human material as sanctity does ordinary artefacts, comes closer to Persian ideas of the 'magic of kingship' (below, n.90) than to regular Egyptian belief, the special pleading being necessitated by Amasis' usurpation.
79 Rarity: Frankfort (1948) 224-6; Dvornik (1966) 71-2, 81-7, 95-6 and n.59; see Frankfort (1948) 295-9 for kings as consort of a goddess, with 301-12, 324, 327 and Dvornik (1966) 25-9 for other quasi-divine aspects of Mesopotamian kingship; mediation: Dvornik (1966) 127-9. 'Sons of the gods': ibid. 26, 49-50, noting the closeness implied by a filial relationship; Frankfort (1948) 299-301; for a recent general account see West (1997) 132-4.
80 'The sun': Pritchard (1969) 318, 529 of the Hittite Suppiluliumas (cf. Frankfort 1948, 338 for Hittite practice); Pritchard (1969) 389 n.10 (Sumero-Akkadian) and cf. the address to the king as 'the Star' in one of the Akkadian Mari letters (ibid. 632). Assimilation to Ahura-Mazda in Persian ceremonial: Dvornik (1966) 113-4; *Hvarena*: ibid. 84-96, 119 and below 100n.49. In general see Frankfort (1948) 307-9 for comparison of the king to the sun in Mesopotamia and New Kingdom Egypt; there is a similar idea in David's final speech (*2Sam*. 23.3-4): 'he who rules men in justice ... is like the light of morning at sunrise, a morning that is cloudless after rain' (NEB).
81 On the unbridgeable divide between the godlike hero and true gods, see Griffin (1980), esp. 81-94, 187-90. Leaders honoured like god: *Il*. 5.78, 10.33, 11.58, 16.605, *Od*. 11.484; *Il*. 9.155 = 297, 302 = 603; looked on as gods: *Il*. 12.312, *Od*. 7.71, 8.173, 15.520.
82 Greeting: *Il*. 22.434-5 cf. *Od*. 7.72; prayer: *Il*.11.761, where the chiasmus reinforces the point, 22.394; in *Th*. 91 the different verb *ilaskontai* ('propitiate') refers more specifically to seeking divine favour; Nestor to Agamemnon: *Il*. 9.97. The suggestion that kings might be invoked in prayer is perhaps the strongest residual indication of an earlier belief in their more than human nature; for others, see Mondi (1980). It is still felt that kings are established by Zeus (*Il*. 1.279, 2.197, 205, 9.37-8, 98-9, *Od*. 1.386-90, *Th*. 96 cf. Tyrt. fr.4.3) and epithets such as *diogenês* and *diotrephês* ('sprung from/fostered by Zeus', applied, with the exception of *Il*. 4.280, only to royalty) and the formulas *hieron menos* and *hierê is* (holy might/force), used, with one exception (*Od*. 18.34, of Antinoos), of Telemachus and Alcinoos (cf. *hypermenês* ('surpassingly powerful'), normally an epithet of Zeus, at *Od*. 13.205, 20.222) are suggestive of a lingering sense of their divine descent and consequent distinctiveness; compare the observation that 'it is a terrible thing to kill one of royal blood (*genos basilêion*)' (*Od*. 16.401-2).

83   6.149f., 243, 280–1, 7.199f., 16.181f. Such greetings might originally have been motivated in part by a cautious sense that the gods could move among men (*Od.* 17.483–7 with Steiner 2010; West 1997, 122–4), but they have clearly become conventional when the topos is exploited for irony in real divine epiphanies: *hAp.* 464–5, *hVen.* 91–106 with Richardson (2010) *ad locc.*; in *Od.* 13.231 Odysseus similarly supplicates the disguised Athena as a god. Odysseus' reception 'like a god' by the Phaeacians does not seem to have anything to do with his royal status (5.36,19.280 = 23.339), since it is a long time before he reveals his identity; and when Phemius talks of singing before him 'as to a god' (*Od.* 22.348–9) this is surely the desperate flattery of a man pleading for his life.
84   Men like gods: *Th.* 968 = 1020; kings like kings: *Il.* 3.169–70, 211; *Od.* 2.13, 4.63, 17.416, 20.194, 24.253; *hDem.* 213f.; *Vita Hom.* 427–8; imitated *Batr.* 21–2.
85   *theios/seios*: Pl. *Men.* 99d, Arist. *EN* 1145a28–9; Athenian statesmen: Eupolis fr.384.6, and cf. the address *ônax* ('o Lord') *Miltiadê kai Periklees* (fr.104.1); the passage combines Homeric reminiscence (a touch hyperbolic) with nostalgia for a lost golden age of leadership. For alternative exploitation of golden age motifs see below, n.95.
86   i.e. is enjoying the blessed afterlife granted to the race of heroes (*Op.* 166–73 with West 1978), or at least to certain figures such as Menelaus and Achilles (*Od.* 4.561–9, Pi. *O.* 2.70–80, Pl. *Smp.* 179e–80a) as a hero himself; by the end of the classical period Athenian orators can apply the conceit to rank and file war casualties: D. 60.34, cf. Hyp. 6.35, 39.
87   Note also Hdt. 1.65.2–66.1, the context of the earliest citation of the oracle to Lycurgus, for fifth-century Spartan attitudes and the establishment of posthumous heroic cult of Lycurgus.
88   463b with Adam (1902); on heroization NB n.100 below. The title *Sôtêr*, hitherto normally an epithet of divinities, comes to be applied to kings from the early Hellenistic period (Dornseiff 1927, 1211–14); it is occasionally attested earlier (e.g. D.S. 11.26.6; but Ion fr.27.1W is most likely to refer to a god: below 39n.31), but in such cases may simply reflect an appreciation of salvation in reality (Nock 1972, 720–2 takes a minimalist view even of Hellenistic usage, while acknowledging the difference made by using the word as a title or epithet), though the Syracusans' salutation of Dion as 'saviour and god' (Plut. *Dion* 46.1) is suggestive and could go back to contemporary sources (whereas e.g. *Pelop.* 12.4 may well be influenced by the common usage of Plutarch's own time).
89   For the hand as a symbol of royal power, see How and Wells (1928) *ad loc.*, and for Persian admiration of long arms, Cook (1983) 75 and 248 n.4. Briant (1996) discusses the stature and beauty of the Great King (237–9) and his prowess in battle and the hunt (239–44) as aspects of Achaemenid royal ideology, and that ideology is reflected in Herodotus (below 110); one might compare Saul: 'there was no better man among the Israelites than he. He was a head taller than any of his fellows' (*1 Sam.* 9.2 [NEB]). For the King's eyes and ears, NB Ar. *Ach.* 91–125, Hdt. 1.114.2, X. *Cyr.* 8.1.10–12; the fullest recent treatment, by Hirsch (1985) 101–39 is highly sceptical, but NB Cassio (1985) 41–2. For a king's ministers as additional hands and feet, eyes and ears, NB Arist. *Pol.* 1287a29–31, and for Greek tyrants making use of eavesdroppers, 1313b11–16.
90   Scylax *FGrH* 709 F5 ap. Arist. *Pol.*1332b23–5; see *Pol.* 1288a6–29 for the relevance of this to Aristotle's ideas. For the idea that the ruler is, or should be, superior to his subjects NB X. *Cyr.* 5.5.34, 7.2.24, 5.78, 83, 8.1.37, 40–2. In Egypt the pharaoh's *ka* (vital force) was different from that of a commoner (Frankfort 1948, 62–78). For the

Gods as Kings, Kings as Gods 23

magic inherent in kingship, compare the idea that only sons born to a king after his accession can succeed to the throne (Hdt. 7.3.2–4; Plut. *Artax.* 2.3), and the Scythian belief that if the king fell sick, it was due to someone's foreswearing themselves by his hearth (Hdt. 4.68.1–2). Hdt. 7.15.3 likewise hints at a special power conferred by sitting on the throne. For ideas of the dual nature of kingship in later antiquity see Kantorowitz (1957) 497–505, and for the special quality of royal blood in the Middle Ages, ibid. 331–3 and n.63.

91 Hdt. 1.87.3, 7.5.2, 9.116.3; cf. 2.115.6 of Proteus and contrast the Greek attitude: when Creon asks 'Is the city not held to belong to the ruler?' (S. *Ant.* 738) he is skating on very thin ice. For the concept of the Persian empire as 'the King's house', see below 110.

92 Hdt. 7.136.1; Lloyd (1975–89) on Hdt. 2.80.2 cites Isoc. 12.151, X. *An.* 3.2.13; cf. E. *Tro.* 1021, *Or.* 1507, *TrGF Adesp.* frr.118a, 664.9, Ar. *Vesp.* 516, X. *Ages.* 1.34. Compare the inference of Deinon (*FGrH* 690 F27) that the Persian queen is worshipped by the concubines from their doing obeisance to her; for the purported obeisance of the Pamphylian sea to Alexander in Callisthenes' history, see below, 167.

93 Comic attacks on Pericles are comprehensively if somewhat speculatively discussed by Schwarze (1971). The origin of the concept of Pericles the Olympian is a puzzle: Delcourt (1939) 371–6 argues that it arose first from the thunderous quality of his oratory, and came later to be applied to his distant, philosophic demeanour. It seems possible, however, given that some of the mythological burlesques must go back to the context of the ostracism of Thucydides son of Melesias, that the initial seed was comic satire of his pre-eminence (one thinks of French satire in the 1990s of François Mitterand as 'Dieu').

94 Cratinus frr.118 (tr. Bakola), 258: *kephalêgeretan* is only two letters different from the Homeric *nephelêgeretan* ('cloud-gatherer'); cf. 'the squill-headed (*schinokephalos*) Zeus': fr.73 (*Thrattai*) – we would say 'onion-headed'. All this material comes to us from Plutarch's *Pericles* 3.3–7: NB Stadter (1989) *ad loc.*, Bakola (2010) 172–3, 184, 222–3.

95 The manuscript reading, though some scholars prefer to read 'Kronos' with the Hesiodic succession in mind: see KA *ad loc.* and Olson (2007) 207–8; for a Hesiodic succession of demagogues and climactic Gigantomachy in Aristophanes *Knights* see Bowie (1993) 58–66, and for the clear Hesiodic colour in Cratinus' *Ploutoi*, Bakola (2010) 52, 135–6, 209.

96 Schwarze (1971) 44–5, 54, 59–60; NB also Telecl. fr.47 'alone he raises up much tumult (*thorubon*) from a head big enough for eleven couches' (for *thorubos* in politics cf. E. *Supp.*166, *Or.* 905). For recent discussion of the implication of tyranny NB Morawetz (2000) 86–93; on the play and its political background see Bakola (2010) 49–53, 122–41 (esp. 122–5), 208–20: the scenario was evidently that of the tragic Prometheus, so the tyranny would again have been that of Zeus.

97 On Pericles' probable appearance as Theseus in Pheidias' Amazonomachy, see Boardman (1982) 18–19.

98 Cratin. fr.259 (*Cheirones*) tr. Olson; NB Olson (2007) 208 for commentary: *Katapugosunê* stands for depravity in general and *kunôpida* (literally 'dog-eyed'), the Homeric Helen's self-description, is substituted for *boôpis* ('ox-eyed'), Hera's normal epithet, which Eupolis also used, presumably with reference to Aspasia (fr.438 with KA *ad loc.*).

99 Helen: Eup. fr.267 (*Prospaltioi*); Omphale and Deinaneira: Cratin. fr.259 with KA, *Com.Adesp.* fr.704; on the attacks on Aspasia in all these passages see Storey (2003)

137, 243, 265; also Schwarze (1971) 165, 170; Powell (1995) 258–60. Given that critics referred to Pericles and his associates as 'the new Peisistratids' (*Com.Adesp.* fr.703), the suggestion that the Athenian tyrant Peisistratus deliberately exploited the image of Heracles may be relevant here: see now Stafford (2012) 163–7 for discussion of the continuing debate.

100 Lysander was the earliest person to be honoured in his lifetime as a god, but this was anticipated by the heroization of Euthymos of Locri around the middle of the fifth century (Currie 2002, esp. 37–8, 43) and Hagnon at Amphipolis a couple of decades later (Hornblower 1991–2008, II.452–5, on Thuc. 5.11.1). On the antecedents of Alexander's divinity, see also Bosworth (1988) 278–90.

101 Advantages: 2.5; kingship not a priesthood: 2.6 cf. 15.71 with Mathieu 1960 *ad loc.*; office-holding is compared in the Demosthenic corpus to initiation into the Mysteries, but ironically ([D.] 13.19, D. *Pro.* 55.3); in the latter case the word *ateleston* ('uninitiated') puns on the sense 'exempt from tax' to get in a further blow at rival leaders. Persian ideology: Isoc. 2.14, 15.72; *beltistos*: 3.15; appearance: 2.32 (cf. X. *Cyr.* 8.3.1f. on the style of the Persian king); remoteness: Isoc. 2.34, 9.44. Nicocles' omniscience: 3.51 cf. 2.23. Philip: *Epistle* 3.5.

102 *Cyr.* 8.1.22, quoted more fully below, 166; *Resp. Lac.* 8.4, on which see below 173n.47.

103 Plut. *Alex.* 52.2–4 with Hamilton (1969) *ad loc.*, cf. *Artax.* 23.5; Arrian *An.* 4.9.7 with Bosworth (1995); note Isoc 3.26 (above 6) for the appeal to Zeus to justify the monarch. Justice already sits beside Zeus in Hes. *Op.* 256–60: see West (1978a) on 259 for later developments of the idea, and NB 7 above. Bosworth (1996) 104–8 discusses the contemporary context of this episode; on the development of the concepts see the overview in Hahm (2000) 457–64; fuller discussion in Goodenough (1928) esp. 59–73, 84–6, 91–101 and Dvornik (1966) 245–9, 269–77 and (for later periods) Index s.v. *nomos empsychos*.

2

The State as a Household and Family

At their *dokimasia* (scrutiny), candidates for the Athenian archonship were asked not only who their parents were, but whether they treated them properly ([Arist.] *Ath. Pol.* 55.3). The questions, which suggest that the *dokimasia* was an ancient institution (Rhodes 1981, 617), indicate how natural it was to make associations between *oikos* and polis and assume that there were affinities between a man's behaviour in the two spheres; Creon takes a continuity between moral behaviour in domestic and public arenas for granted (S. *Ant.* 661–2).[1] In the same way, the use in Homer of *anax* ('lord') to denote the head and master of a household implies a perception of a correspondence between the two levels of authority.[2] However, the conception of the state as a household is slow to emerge as a fully-fledged political image: only in the late sixth century, the context of the story in Herodotus (5.29) that the Parians chosen to act as arbitrators in the civil strife at Miletus placed the administration of the city in the hands of those whose lands they saw to be well managed, do we encounter a clear if still only implicit analogy between domestic and political administration.[3] The development of the image in the succeeding period is hard to trace and attested only by a scatter of images of the ruler as steward in Pindar (see below); it is not until the second half of the fifth century that we see evidence that the image was firmly established and indeed commonplace in the use of the verb *oikein* in place of *dioikein*, the standard term, to denote administration, particularly when applied zeugmatically to both cities and households in Euripides, Xenophon, Plato and the orators, and in the figurative use of *oikonomia* and its cognates.[4]

In the early fourth century this theory becomes explicit: Plato claims that there is a universal art of rule which embraces the householder as well as the king and slave-master (*Plt.* 258e–259c) and makes Protagoras say that his teaching covers both domestic and political administration (*Prot.* 318e–9a).[5] In the same way, Xenophon in the *Oeconomicus* draws the comparison between order in the household and organization in the state, suggesting that both require not simply to be set on a proper basis initially (in a city, by the establishment of good laws) but also, subsequently, call for proper administration. Thus Ischomachus' wife must uphold the laws of the household, inspect and scrutinize, and impose appropriate rewards and punishments 'like a queen' (9.14–5). Later in the work, Socrates argues that there is one consistent art of rule, so that a man who can train a bailiff to command can make him a master or a king (13.5); indeed, since the skill of command (*to archikon*) is a constant in every business, including politics and household management (*oikonomikê*; 21.2), the authoritative householder will possess an element of kingly nature (*ti êthous basilikou*; 21.10). This principle is expressed again in inverted form in the *Memorabilia* when Socrates, told that Euthydemus is studying to enter politics, exclaims 'surely, Euthydemus, you are aiming at that virtue by which men become statesmanlike and good managers (*politikoi ... kai oikonomikoi*) and capable of ruling', a virtue which he identifies as 'part of the fairest virtue and the greatest art: for it belongs to kings and is called kingly' (4.2.11). In 3.4.7–12 he demonstrates to a surprised Nicomachides that the good *oikonomos* will have the qualities necessary to be a good general. It was therefore a deliberate and quite substantial theoretical divergence on Aristotle's part to draw firm distinctions between the various sorts of rule and authority in the first book of the *Politics* (1252 a7–16; below, 170n.24).

Once the polis is linked to the household by the common theme of administration, attention naturally falls on the individual responsible. Pindar applies the term *tamias* ('steward') to Greek monarchs in Sicily and Libya: he calls Battus 'steward of Cyrene' (*P.* 5.62), says to Hieron *pollôn tamias essi* ('you are a steward of many people/things', *P.* 1.88) and describes Aegina as 'in the stewardship of a Dorian people (*Dôriei laôi tamieumenan*) since Aiakos' (*O.* 8.30). However, it is not clear to what extent Pindar's use of the image is based on the idea of the city as household, or even whether it carries any strong notion of authority held in trust (the address to Hieron would come closest), since from an earlier period *tamias* and *tamieuô* are used to denote control and administration, often with overtones of dispensation, in several spheres.[6] Nevertheless, at the very least the words would seem to imply a responsible and rational oversight, as well perhaps as some consideration for the interests or needs of other parties.

In Athens, however, this aspect of the image came very much to the fore in a distinctively democratic development that shifted its focus from administration as such to the relationship between politicians and the *demos*, which came to be expressed in terms of various forms of service. The most conspicuous example is Aristophanes' *Knights*, in which Athens is represented as the household of a personified Demos, a ploy which might be viewed as a way of giving new energy to a commonplace, even if the allegorization is not consistently sustained. Within this household, the various politicians are presented as his slaves, a point made all the more sharply at the outset of the play if we accept that the two characters labelled *oiketai* were identifiable as the contemporary politicians Nicias and Demosthenes.[7] By the fourth century, the idealized picture of the politician as the servant of the people, whose duty it is to serve the people (*diakonein / therapuein / hupêretein*) is a familiar trope in the orators.[8] Likewise Isocrates claims that in Golden Age Athens it was held that the demos should have the power to appoint and chastise magistrates and to decide disputes, while men of wealth and leisure should care for the common good like servants.[9] Within this framework, there is plainly a sharper ethical focus to any reference to a politician as a steward (*tamias*) which, in an Athenian context, must have evoked overtones of trust and careful management, given the use of the term *Tamias* for officials such as the Treasurers of Athena, of the Other Gods, of the Boule and, in the fourth century, others besides, all of whom were accountable to the demos and subject to close scrutiny. In his prosecution of Demosthenes over the Harpalus affair (5.12), Hyperides uses the terms *tetamieusai* ('you administered') and *epistatên* ('overseer') ironically to point up his opponent's dishonesty and abuse of his leading position. More generally, Isocrates in the *Panegyricus* (4.76) declares that the statesmen of old did not profit from public resources as if they were private (*idia*) while neglecting them as if they belonged to others (*allotria*), but cared for them as household property (*oikeia*) while keeping their hands off them 'as one should with things to which one has no claim'; the passage implies a contrast not only between profit and service, but also between what is one's private property (*idia, prosêkonta*) and that which concerns one (*oikeia*) but which one is nevertheless not free to appropriate. These ideas are already evident in a less fully articulated form in Aristophanes: when in *Knights* 947–8 Demos uses the verb *tamieuein* in demanding the return of his ring[10] and handing it over to the sausage-seller, the term implies that the Paphlagonian has betrayed his trust.

The same vocabulary is used in both the plays of female reform, associated with notions of careful management, when the women's proven domestic ability is cited as an argument for putting the affairs of the city in their hands (*Lys.* 493–5; *Eccl.* 210–2 cf. 600), and the same argument from domestic experience underlies the protracted image from wool-working in the *Lysistrata* (567f.; below 122). A related term, *epitropos* ('household supervisor'), is linked with *tamias* at *Eccl.* 212 and fr.305, from the other *Peace*, and applied to political leadership at *Peace* 686, while the Paphlagonian uses the cognate verb *epitropeuein* to refer to his primacy in the house of Demos at *Knights* 949; given that elsewhere in that play (212, 426) the phrase *epitropeuein ton dêmon* ('oversee the demos') is used simply to mean 'be a/the leading politician', it may be that Aristophanes is taking advantage of the allegorical domestic context to give new energy to a faded metaphor.[11] However, when in two passages at the end of the play Demos puts himself in the charge of the Sausage-Seller with the words *emeauton epitrepô* ('I entrust myself': 1098, 1259), the reference must surely be to a different sense of *epitropos*, 'guardian', and his specific duties are defined as *gerontagôgein*, 'guide an old man', which is obviously modelled on *paidagôgein* 'guide a child, tutor'.[12] In the context this is a positive development, if unrealistically optimistic, since this guardianship restores Demos to his old capable self; the same is true of the Athenian decision to 'entrust (*epitrepein*) the city' to the women in the *Ecclesiazusae* (455–6), though the latter term is more or less literal.[13]

Outside comedy, there is a striking figurative passage in the sophistic treatise known as the Anonymus Iamblichi (7.14) in which the author suggests that tyranny is the result of a breakdown in normal law and order which itself supplies the need for law and order: 'when therefore these two things, law and justice, cease to be present in the mass, at that juncture the guardianship (*epitropeian*) and preservation (*phulakên*) of these things devolves on a single individual.' This view of the tyrant as holding the rule of law in trust is in sharp contrast to the normal view of the tyrant as a law unto himself, and reflects the late fifth-century conception of the importance of law in itself (for the monarchy of law in *Anon. Iambl.* 6.1 see above 10). Whereas in the Aristophanic images it is the Demos which is given a guardian, here it is law which has to be taken from them (or taken up when they have abandoned it) and looked after for itself, because the need for law and justice is the highest imperative (7.13). A related democratic version of the concept which represents the justice, laws and legal procedure of Athens as deposited on trust with the jurors (using the technical term *parakatathêkê*) appears in the fourth-century orators.[14] A more orthodox perception of the tyrant is implied in Aristotle's advice to such rulers in the *Politics* (1314b6–7, 14–18, 37–8, 1315a40–b2) that their financial exactions should appear to be made to meet the needs of administration (*tês te oikonomias heneka*), that they should in general present themselves as guards and stewards of what by implication is common property and that they must appear to their subjects 'a good manager and kingly and not self-interested but a guardian (*epitropon*)'. Here guardianship remains a positive model, like stewardship and household management, despite the cynical use made of it.[15]

As a developed political image, the concept of guardianship seems thus to be entirely positive, though in reality not all guardians in Athens seem to have met their obligations.[16] Unreliability is also a problem with servants – indeed, this is taken for granted in the exposition of *Knights*, where it is made clear that Demos' servants are engaged in a competition to become the master's favourite by gratifying his desires (46f.). This situation obviously reflects badly on Demos as well as on his servants: if it was a stock charge against politicians that they pandered to the people, it was equally true that the people lapped up such attentions, and recent scholarship has tended to argue that the issue remains unresolved at the end of the play.[17] In oratory, however, the finger of blame points squarely at the servant, as in Demosthenes' regular charge that the demos has been reduced to slavery by contemporary politicians (2.14, 3.30–1, 22.54f., 23.209–10, 24.143, [D.] 13.31, cf. Aeschin. 3.3)[18] or that other *rhetors* display the ingratitude of liberated slaves, rather than thanking the demos for their advancement (24.124); lack of *charis* is compounded by the implication that such men have become rapidly, and dubiously, wealthy (Ober 1989, 225–6; the same slur is made explicitly in 18.131). When the servant is given a specific identity, this is usually negative: hence the Paphlagonian in *Knights* becomes a nurse, shooing away flies, spoon-feeding the old man meagrely and tidying him up. Here the normal position is reversed, with the slave in control, as it is when the fourth-century orator Democrates compares politicians to nurses who chew up food for babies, but swallow the lion's share themselves.[19] Corruption is assimilated to starving the demos on the visual plane in the 'meal scene' of *Knights* (1151–1226) and, in a slightly different context, when Aeschines (3.251) says that ordinary citizens leave an assembly monopolised by professional politicians 'having not debated, but shared out the left-overs, as from a pot-luck meal (*hôsper ek tôn eranôn*)'. The same idea of control of the demos by politicians who hold the purse-strings is conveyed by a fragment of Aristophanes (fr.699) which likens them to wine-stewards: 'you stir up our city and dole out cupfuls (*kotulizete*) to the poor'. The consequence of this financial control is that the jurors in *Wasps* (and presumably the demos at large), like itinerant olive-pickers, will go wherever the money is (*Vesp.* 712).[20]

Plato also portrays democratic politicians (*prostatai*) as bad wine-stewards (*R.* 562cd), though his point is about irresponsibility rather than dishonesty. This is in line with his consistently negative use of the image of service: in the *Republic* he speaks of the politicians who pamper the chronically ill state (426c), and this portrait of politicians as pandering servants is more fully developed in the *Gorgias*: the speakers 'treat the citizens like children, simply trying to please them (*charizesthai*)' (502e). Plato calls this sort of unreflecting gratification of the people's desires, which undermines the city's health, 'pandering' (*kolakeia*: 463b–6a, 503a, 513d) and refers to it by the term *diakonein* (517b–8a, 521a), a word he applies to the form of service which has been provided by the politicians of the past (517b); the two expressions appear side by side when the dialogue considers what kind of politician Callicles will be (521ab).[21]

Servants, then, may be dutiful or dishonest, principled or cynical. There is also a clear difference between the sort of service normally posited of politicians as servants and the imagery of wage labour which is applied by fourth-century orators to accusations of corruption. This latter can be described from the perspective of both employer and employee: the briber, for his part – typically Philip II – is said to hire or buy the services of a politician. To sell oneself outright clearly carries overtones of slavery, but one does little better if, in another favoured image, one hires oneself out, whether to a foreign power or to domestic interests. In so doing, one loses one's independence of action and speech, and so much of one's status as citizen and politician, and there can be an implication of prostitution – one notes Aeschines' use of *misth*-words (i.e. 'hire' or 'pay') in the case of Timarchus.[22] Evidently, the implication that the speaker's opponent is a servile tool and a traitor rather than a citizen is the primary objective of such imagery, though it would seem from Demosthenes' repeated dismissal of the relationship between Aeschines and Philip and Alexander not as friendship and *xenia* (ritualized guest-friendship) but as that of master and hireling, as if Aeschines were an agricultural labourer (18.51–2, 284), that he felt the need to disperse the reflected glamour and prestige which Aeschines derived from it, by stressing that they did not meet on equal terms or without an ulterior motive. Such images are only applicable to relations between politicians and outside powers or among themselves: one cannot hire oneself, still less prostitute oneself, to the demos.[23]

The precise nature of the relationship between the demos as master and its servants was equivocal: while it would have been demeaning to describe oneself as a slave, not all stewards, treasurers or other holders of delegated authority necessarily had this status. Furthermore, there is a suggestive link to the allusions to politicians as 'lovers of Demos' which appeared in the fifth century and remained current in the fourth (below 115–17, 154–5), since the mot juste for a lover's attentions is *therapeuein* or *therapeia*, which can also refer to domestic service, as well as to courting political favour.[24] This overlap in terminology thus left open to politicians the possibility of an alternative self-conception which, though still a little ambiguous (in that it entailed a degree of subordination), was nonetheless more positive both in reflecting an elite lifestyle and in being essentially voluntary.

The Athenian image of the politician as servant thus expresses central tenets of democratic ideology, the subordination of politicians to the demos and their accountability before it,[25] but it seems to be intended primarily for internal consumption, inasmuch as it is focused on power relations within the democracy rather than expressing a virtue of democracy in comparison to other constitutions. The consistent manner in which it is deployed both by individual politicians to promote themselves and disparage their rivals and by Aristophanes, the comic poet as internal critic, likewise implies that this imagery, while retaining a persuasive force, is intended to regulate the operation of Athenian democracy.

Even the opponents of democracy found it difficult to evade, as we can see from the way that speakers in Xenophon's Socratic works express their hostility to the concept but offer no riposte, and can only respond by opting out of political activity. In the *Symposium* Callias expresses admiration of Antisthenes' spiritual wealth (and physical poverty) 'because the city does not give you orders and treat you (*chrêtai*) like a slave' (4.45). Equally, Aristippus in the *Memorabilia* (2.1.9) is unwilling to enter politics and make himself the people's servant, a concept which he expresses in the most unfavourable terms possible: 'cities expect to use (*chrêsthai*) office-holders as I use my servants (*oiketais*).' As he explains, he expects his servants to provide him with the necessities of life in abundance but not to lay hands on them themselves, and similarly cities expect their leaders to provide them with all possible benefits while themselves abstaining entirely from those benefits (the contrast in tone with Isocrates 4.76 [above, 27] is very marked). From this perspective, submission to the authority of the demos seems to be considered slavish; we are close to the idea of the tyranny of the demos which is explored overtly in the amusing dialogue between Pericles and Alcibiades in *Memorabilia* 1.2.40–6.[26] As we have seen, Plato was able to turn the concept into a stick with which to beat democratic politicians in the *Gorgias*, though his treatment shades into a different devotion, that of the lover of the *demos*, and his agenda is in any case principally philosophical. Ultimately the escape for anti-democrats seems to have lain in accepting the idea of service, but assigning that service to the laws rather than the *demos*: Xenophon describes a Spartan king as 'doing service to the laws' and Aristotle in commending the rule of law recommends the appointment of individual rulers as guardians and servants of the laws; only when monarchy made clear the subordinate position of the demos in reality would kings embrace the paradox of styling their position 'distinguished slavery'.[27]

If Athenian democracy was able to exert its authority over the figure of the servant, it had more difficulties with the other possible conception of the *oikos*, as the locus of the family. In part this may have been because images derived from the family had deeper roots which can be traced back to Homer. In the *Odyssey*, Odysseus is three times described as 'gentle like a father' (*patêr d'hôs êpios êen*: 2.47 = 234 = 5.12), just as Helen in *Iliad* 24.770 credits her father-in-law Priam with the gentleness of a true father.[28] These resonances are also typical of the regular use of the image of the king as father in the early Near East: Azitawadda of Adana says 'Baal made me a father and a mother to the Danunites' and goes on to boast that other kings look on him as a father because of his righteousness, wisdom and kindness of heart. Similar is the claim of Kilamurra of Y'dy Sam'al: 'To some I was a father, to some I was a mother. To some I was a brother ... They were disposed to me as an orphan is to his mother', in which the variation in the relationship suggests that the king supplies the appropriate care and comfort to each.[29] Given the currency of the image in Near Eastern contexts, it is surprising that it is not more frequently used of Homeric kings; it is much more often applied to Zeus, the 'father of gods and men', or simply *patêr*, the father par excellence.[30] Instances of the image are equally sparse through the archaic period and into the fifth century: Pindar addresses Hieron as *patêr*, but since this is in the context of the foundation of Aitna he may have the biological implications more in mind.[31] More obviously in the Homeric mould is the opening of Sophocles'

Oedipus Tyrannus, where Oedipus enters with the words 'Oh children' (*ô tekna* cf.6, 58, 142): the implication that Oedipus is thinking like a father was picked up by the ancient commentator, who viewed this in a positive light. However, we might be more hesitant, and might wonder whether Sophocles is not allowing the audience the chance to see the image as more equivocal, when we note that all other contemporary references to the king as father are in Near Eastern contexts.[32] Thus the chorus in Aeschylus' *Persae* refer to Darius as 'father' (664 = 671) and Atossa as 'mother' (215), and in Herodotus we find the same image used of Croesus – 'you who were more than a father to the Lydians' (1.155.1–2), and of Cyrus, whom the Persians called 'father' 'because he was gentle (*êpios*) and contrived every good thing for them' (3.89.3).[33] The latter case is noteworthy as the image is unusually not a piece of royal propaganda, but a tribute from his people, and inverts the advertisement by kings in Near Eastern inscriptions of their own past munificence and kindness.

In the early fourth century, the heyday of monarchic imagery, the image of the ruler as father takes on a new life. Perhaps the most enthusiastic exponent is Xenophon: in the *Cyropaideia*, Chrysantas is made to say of Cyrus 'I have often noticed that a good ruler is no different from a good father: for fathers take thought for their children, that they may never want for good things, and Cyrus now seems to be advising us of the ways in which we can best continue to prosper' (8.1.1). The same image is said to have been applied to Cyrus by his newly conquered subjects, the principal point being that of benefaction (8.1.44, 2.9, 8.1).[34] In applying the image not only to Cyrus' Persian subjects, but also to those whom he has conquered, Xenophon is going one better than Herodotus (3.89.3), for whom Cyrus is a father only to the Persians (and in contrast to his successors, whom they hold in less high regard). The image is equally applicable to Greek leaders. Xenophon says of Agesilaus that the Greeks in Asia mourned his departure 'as not only of a commander, but of a father and a comrade' (*Ages*. 1.38), and later describes his behaviour to his political opponents as father-like, chiding their errors, honouring their successes and supporting them in adversity (7.3). Finally, Xenophon as commander of the Ten Thousand is twice equated with a father in speeches made in his own defence: in *An*. 5.8.18 he claims that any application of corporal punishment to maintain discipline should be judged in the same light as a father's chastisement of his sons or a teacher's of his pupils, while in 7.6.38, criticizing the troops for their ingratitude, he reminds them that they used to call him 'father' in recognition of his benefactions. Xenophon's application of the image to himself is suggestive of its attractions for him as a paradigm for the exercise of authority. For him, the chief implications of the image seem to be paternal care and guidance, reciprocated by respect and affection on the part of the children. At the same time, Xenophon also brings into the open another and potentially more problematic aspect of the father-figure, his right to chastise: Aristotle remarks on the need for a tyrant to administer punishment in a fatherly spirit (*Pol.* 1315a21), and Plato's description in the *Laws* of a father's rule over his household as 'the most just kingship (*basileia dikaiotatê*)' and his evaluation of the right of parents to rule over their children as self-evident (680e, 690a) similarly imply a more authoritarian view of the father's role than that taken by Xenophon.

A further, potentially controversial issue which has hitherto lurked in the background also emerges clearly in the fourth century: if the concept of the state as a household is combined with monarchy, it follows that the state may be seen as the estate of the ruler, a possession to be disposed of as he sees fit.[35] This idea is most prominent in Isocrates' *To Nicocles*, where the young ruler is encouraged to administer the state in the same way as his royal estate, and advised that all the property of those who reside in the city belongs to the kings who rule them well (2.19, 21 – there is a sharp contrast to the idea of Athenian politicians handling the state's property as stewards in the *Panegyricus* [above, 27]), but the same outlook underlies a couple of Xenophontic passages which imply a possessive attitude to the subject: Hiero compares the spirited citizen to a good horse which its master fears may cause him fatal harm, yet which he is reluctant to slaughter (*Hiero* 6.15–6), while Cyaxares compares Cyrus' winning over of his subjects to subverting the loyalty of watchdogs, servants or a wife (*Cyr.* 5.5.28–30). The concept is given a more characteristically positive slant in *Hiero* 11.14, where Simonides urges the tyrant to 'think of your fatherland (*patrida*) as your house, the citizens as comrades, your friends as your children, your children as your soul' and encourages him to outdo them in benefactions; the implication is that as paterfamilias he will not only show kindness, but will devote himself to the preservation and growth of his estate rather than simply exploiting it. The unspoken implication is that in so doing, he will change from a tyrant into a true king.

Both these elaborations point to the continuing utility of the image of the father as an expression of the position of the monarch,[36] but they also highlight the distinctly problematic character for democracy, which closely policed any handling of public assets by officeholders, and in which the application of physical sanctions to one citizen by another came close to being taboo.[37] When the *Athenaion Politeia* (28.5) describes the leadership of Thucydides son of Milesias and Nicias as 'treating the whole city in a fatherly manner (*têi polei pasêi patrikôs chrômenous*)', it is clearly analogous to the judgment of Thucydides (the historian) on Pericles in 2.65.8–9, and equally difficult to align with democratic ideology.[38] However, there are indications that Athenians adopted an alternative approach to family which avoided many of these difficulties by marginalizing or distributing parental authority, and which seems to be linked to the myth of autochthonous origins.[39] Since all Athenians shared a common descent from the land of Attica, they were all siblings, as Plato says in the *Menexenus* (238e–9a), and all legitimate children too (D. 60.4 cf. Lycurg. 1.48). This shared ancestry is sometimes expressed by referring to them as 'sons' of one of the mythical kings, of Erechtheus or Theseus,[40] but attention more often focuses on the land itself. Recent scholarship has tended to focus attention on the masculine aspect of the title *patris* ('fatherland') but it might be argued that this is to over-emphasize the gendered aspect of a tendency, not unique to Greece, to conceive of descent and inheritance in terms of the male line (which was after all the commonest form of inheritance),[41] and to neglect the way in which the earth is also conceived of as nurturing and hence as maternal, or at least specifically female where the reference is to Attica as nurse. This is the aspect highlighted by Isocrates (4.25): 'alone among the Greeks, we have the right to call the same land nurse and fatherland and mother',[42] and he goes on to associate this with the origins of agriculture in Attica, acknowledged by the other Greeks in first-fruit offerings to Eleusis (4.26–31). He returns to the theme in his last speech, the *Panathenaikos* (12.124–5), where there is an explicit reference to autochthony: 'having as nurse this land from which they sprang, and loving her as the best of men love their own fathers and mothers'. Lycurgus likewise refers to Attica as nurse of Athenians (in two quite different epochs) in *Against Leocrates*, a speech with some marked resemblances to the funeral orations.[43] The emotional bond reinforces the obligation on children to defend their parents: Lycurgus (*Leoc.* 48) notes that this is naturally stronger for legitimate than for adopted children, while Demosthenes (18.205) spells out the point, claiming that the Athenians of old felt that they had been born not simply for their biological parents, but also for their fatherland, and were consequently ready to face premature death to defend Athens from slavery and dishonour. Such sentiments were not unique to Athens – Isocrates puts in the mouth of Archidamus (6.108) an appeal to the Spartans to repay their upbringing to the fatherland – but the ideology gives a particularly sharp edge to Lycurgus' denunciation of Leocrates for failing to meet this obligation by defending Athens in her hour of need (1.53).[44] The parental role is thus displaced onto the polis at large, or onto the whole community of citizens of which it is constituted, while the individual citizen, or any group of citizens considered in relation to the polis, is figured as a child. It was presumably on this basis that the newly enfranchised Agoratus could describe the Athenian demos as his father, a ploy to which Lysias ripostes by appealing to the Athenian law against mistreatment of parents. More fanciful variants could be fashioned to suit particular rhetorical contexts: Demosthenes, arguing in the *Fourth Philippic* in favour of harmony between rich and poor and against the unwillingness of the former to contribute to the support of the latter, states that all citizens should be viewed as parents of the city as a whole, and hence entitled to the support which is guaranteed for individual parents by law and custom.[45]

It is noteworthy that Plato's familial imagery proceeds on the same assumptions. The common ancestry of citizens means that the citizens whom a tyrant murders are all his kin (*R.* 565e with Adam 1902), a fact which emphasizes his impiety and explains his lycanthropic transformation, and likewise it is the kinship of citizens which Socrates regards as obliging him to devote his philosophic efforts to Athens (*Apol.* 30a). Plato also locates parental authority in the permanent social structure, the city or its laws. Thus in the *Euthyphro* Socrates talks of Meletus' denouncing him to the city as if 'telling on him' to his mother (2c), and the image of the laws as standing in a similar though superior relation to the citizen as his parents is a major part of the argument of the *Crito*: the laws claim that, being ultimately responsible for the birth and upbringing of Socrates and every other citizen, they are entitled to the same respect and obedience in all reasonable demands from their 'offspring' as adults, and in a greater degree inasmuch as the city is higher than individuals. In particular they are entitled to immunity from any violence at the hands of citizens, which would be as impious as violence against parents.[46] Likewise in the *Laws*, the proper model for the lawgiver is that of loving, wise parents, not arbitrary tyrants (859a).[47] In the same way, unjust behaviour suggests familial disobedience: timarchic individuals will indulge their pleasures in secret 'running away from the law like children from their father' (*R.* 548b),[48] while the tyrant is described as the prodigal son of the demos, not respecting and supporting his father but doing violence to him and consuming his property (568e–9c).[49]

It is perhaps not surprising that Plato makes use of Athenian conceptions when dealing with Socrates as a citizen of Athens, but the way in which they seep into his more idealizing works is more striking, and perhaps suggests that he could not entirely escape his own ideological conditioning as an Athenian. His avoidance of the king as father, on the other hand, is probably due rather to the fact that, in an era before Dr Spock, parenthood was not a *technê*, and the implications of sympathetic concern which were useful when he applied the image to gods[50] were not part of his ideal of earthly authority, in which orthodox monarchy plays little part.

Aristotle's disagreement with Plato and Xenophon on the uniformity of the art of rule has already been noted. It may be that he is concerned at the outset of the *Politics* to establish terms of reference, which in this case leads him to distinguish between different forms of authority in order to isolate the one with which he is properly concerned. It may also be relevant that he is much less interested at a practical level in monarchy than he is in oligarchy and democracy, and so rejects a model which has little practical application for him. At the same time, the father's relation to his children remains a useful analogue of kingly power, which is itself to be distinguished from his 'statesmanlike' authority over his wife. Yet this is not the whole story, for there is another set of comparisons of the domestic and political in the *Nicomachean Ethics*, in the discussion of friendship: here Aristotle is primarily concerned with relationships between individuals, which he illuminates by reference to politics, and the parallels are grounded in the affective relation between ruler and ruled, not only between parent and child and husband and wife, but also between brothers; this last, however, Aristotle compares to timocracy, not democracy, which for him is the anarchy of a household with no master, or a weak one. It looks as though Aristotle the metic is rebuffing in one brief passage both the versions of the household espoused by his Athenian hosts.[51]

Whatever his theoretical preoccupations, Aristotle acknowledges the long-standing appeal of the analogy between monarch and father, which had returned to prominence with the resurgence of monarchy as an effective form of government at the beginning of the fourth century. It is less straightforward to account for the development of the Athenian models of the *oikos* which, as we have seen, may not emerge until the fifth century. *Prima facie*, the alternative family is the later of the two, since it is not attested in literary sources until the tail-end of the century, but other considerations suggest that this is misleading. As we have seen, the conception of all Athenians as siblings sprung from Attic soil is associated with the discourse of autochthony and its expression in speeches at Athenian public funerals, both of which are probably to be assigned to the period shortly after the Persian Wars.[52] In undertaking the burial of war-dead, the state appropriated to itself what had previously been an obligation of individual *oikoi*, and it went further in maintaining war orphans to adulthood at public expense, an initiative also dating from this period.[53] The role of the polis as surrogate parent was underlined by the suppression of patronymics on the lists of war casualties erected as part of this process.[54] Finally, Pericles' citizenship law in the middle of the fifth century effectively enacted what the concept of autochthony symbolized.[55] It is often suggested that the growth of Athens problematized the relation between polis and *oikos*.[56] At the most basic level, it is possible that the growth of the city, in increasing a general consciousness of a separation between the two, simply made individuals more aware of the household, which had previously been so universal and obvious as to escape notice as an entity. However, the development of the city as a democracy and a power in Greece placed increasing demands on its citizens, not least in military service: increasingly citizens were expected to risk their lives on behalf of the city, but not directly in defence of its territory or of their own homes and families, although many of the casualties in the period when this ideology seems to be taking shape fell in fighting with the Persians and hence still in the cause of the security of the polis in a wider sense.[57] Insofar as there were tensions between household and state, however, the model of the alternative family avoided them by figuring the state as a super-*oikos* which by virtue of its size and inclusiveness transcended the individual *oikos*, and at the same time by representing all members of that household as siblings the Athenians succeeded in side-stepping the problems of hierarchy and paternalism which are sometimes seen as inherent in such imagery.[58] To some extent the potential for this development had always been present: there seems to have been no recognition of the *oikos* as such in Athenian law,[59] while the institution of the civic hearth suggests that an unarticulated sense of the city as a single community resembling a household had always been present.[60] The analogy between house and city is already implied by the imagery of the ruler as father, which we can see from Pindar was current in this period, and if Herodotus is to be believed, other Greeks had already started to assimilate political administration to household management. The particular form which that concept took in Athens is easier to understand if the alternative family was already in place: in the absence of a father to head the household, the householder could only be (the) [D]emos, and anyone aspiring to an individual role could only achieve it by subordinating himself.[61] Given the prevailing character of political systems from the Hellenistic period on, it is hardly surprising that household imagery has become almost uniformly paternalistic (above n.58); today, however, when almost all countries proclaim themselves democratic, their citizens might find it salutary to revive the model of a household without a head.

Notes

1. cf. Aeschin. 1.28–30, and NB Strauss (1993) 45–7 on both passages.
2. Naturally prominent in the *Odyssey*: e.g. 1.397, 14.8, 18.303, cf. *Il.* 24.734; also applied to ownership of animals, e.g. *Iliad* 10.559, 23.417, *Odyssey* 17.303; NB Calhoun (1935) 4–8. West (1997) 545–7 cites Semitic parallels for the broad semantics of *anax* and *anassein*.
3. The sixth-century date is of course the historical context, the image being well-established by the time of composition, and some commentators have expressed scepticism about its historicity, though without explaining their grounds: How & Wells (1928) II.11 ask 'is not the story a political parable inserted here for some unknown reason?', and Legrand (1946) remarks on 30.1 'il est douteux que les Pariens aient opéré comme le dit Hérodote.' Van Wees (2008) 29 puts forward a literal interpretation of the passage in which the estates in good order are those least damaged in *stasis*, but this does seem to me rather to stretch Herodotus' language.

4 *oikein*: E. *El.* 386–7, fr.200 (*Antiope*), X. *Mem.* 1.1.7, 4.1.2, Pl. *Men.* 73a, 91a, *Grg.* 520e, *R.* 600d, *Lg.* 714a, 790b, Isoc. 2.19, Aeschin. 1.153, Thphr. *Char.* 26.3. *oikonomia*: *LSJ* s.v. 2 and (e.g.) X. *An.* 1.9.19, *Mem.* 4.3.14, *Cyr.* 5.3.25, Theopompus *FGrH* 115 F224, Dinarch. 1.97, Demad. fr.131, Arist. *Pol.* 1288a34, 1308b32, *Poet.* 1453a29; note also *dioikêsis* 'maintenance' in [Arist.] *Ath.Pol.* 24.3 with Rhodes (1981). In Euripides' *Phoenissae oikein* is used with *oikon* (486, 1231) and *domon* (602) of ruling Thebes. To some extent this is a literal statement, given the confusion caused by the multiple statuses of Polyneices and Eteocles; Pearson (1909) remarks on 486 ' "to administer my own estate" was in Polyneices' case to be sovereign of Thebes', but *oikein oikon* seems also to have been a proverbial phrase (Stevens 1971 on E. *Andr.* 581; NB the alliteration, characteristic of proverbs and popular expressions (Silk 1974, App.IV)), familiar enough to be parodied by Aristophanes (*Ran.* 105). So perhaps Euripides is bringing the proverb to life by making it literal, suggesting that absolute identification of the two spheres can lead to an excessively proprietorial attitude, and expansion of family quarrels to embrace the city at large. Cf. the similar *oikein oikian* of the financial mismanagement of Philip II and his Companions in Theopompus F224.

5 Universal art of rule: cf. *Alc. I* 133e, *Laws* 690a. Plato's view of the evolution of the state from the household as the basic administrative unit suggests belief in a historical basis to this argument, but though Aristotle gives a similar account of the growth of the state in the *Politics* (1252a24–53a1), he regards the state as logically prior (1253a19–29).

6 Thgn. 504–5, 1186, 1242, Pi. *I.* 6.57–8, Hdt. 2.121.α2, Thuc. 6.78.2; in.6.18.3 *tamieuesthai* means 'regulate', cf. 6.79.2. We should remember that *tamiai* often operated outside the domestic sphere (see next para.), just as at Athens there were public slaves and slaves living independently as well as domestic slaves, though the imagery seems very much to focus on the household.

7 For other personifications of Demos produced on stage NB Pl. Com. fr.201 (below 181n.97) and perhaps Eup. fr.346. On the allegory in *Knights* and its inconsistency see Dover (1972), 93–5, who is guarded on the identification of the two slaves in the prologue, and on this play NB also below 115.

8 e.g. D. 18.206, 311, 51.7, *Ep.*2.11, [D.] 50.2, Aeschin. 3.13, 15, Hyper. 5 col.30. For Isocrates, the characteristic of the successful constitutional politician is effective *tou plêthous therapeia* ('service to the masses': 2.16), and attention to the people is praised in *Evagoras* (9.46) and commended to Nicocles as one of the paths to success (2.15–6). For *epimeleisthai* and *epimeleia* used of political service, NB Isoc. 1.37, 3.22, 7.25–6, 8.127, 12.56, 15.103, 116, 131, 133; Aeschines (3.13, 16) points it out as slippery political terminology, linking it in the former passage with the more overt *diakonia*, and *diakonein* can also be applied pejoratively to non-Athenians doing the bidding of a foreign despot: D. 9.43, 19.69. Demosthenes also tends to use *hypêretein* negatively, of service to a foreign power: 9.53, 56, 19.85, 299, *Ep.*6.1, [D.] 17.17; the word is used favourably (of service to the city and the laws) only at 47.42, 48 which is not Demosthenic and perhaps to be attributed to Apollodorus (Trevett 1992 50–76); NB also Whitehead (2000) on Hyper. 5 col.30. In the newly discovered speech of Hypereides *Against Diondas*, *hypêretôn* is used to denote Diondas' legal services to others, so branding him as a sycophant with a mercenary attitude and implicitly contrasting him with Hypereides and Demosthenes as true servants of Athens (175v line 6 – 174r line 4).

9 *epimeleisthai tôn koinôn hôsper oiketas*, 7.26 cf. 12.146, though Isocrates' commitment to the ideal is questionable: below 177n.68.

10 There may be a reference to the *dêmosia sphrêgis*, the public seal: Neil (1901) on 948–9.
11 Note how in *Pax* 686 and *Eccl*. 212 the noun is governed by *chrêsthai* ('make use of'), which also appears in Xen. *Mem*. 2.1.9 in a context of political service (below 30).
12 Landfester (1967) 24–5, 57 n.165 treats all uses of this terminology as meaning 'guardian', 'be a guardian', 'entrust oneself to a guardian', since it is part of his thesis that Demos is himself incapable until the last scene; Olson (1998) on *Pax* 685–7 on the other hand regards them all as referring to supervision. Landfester (67–8) also links *gerontagôgein* to the idea of the sausage-seller as guardian; the line is adapted from a passage of Sophocles (fr.487, from the *Peleus*), where there were clearly overtones of benign care (NB the expression *kêdeuein tên polin* ['care for the city': S. fr.683, E. *I.T.* 1212]), though Aristophanes may also have felt a reminiscence of *dêmagôgein*: see further below, 134n.82.
13 Compare Thuc. 6.15.4 where *epitrepsantes* is apparently used absolutely to mean 'hand over' (Gomme, Andrewes and Dover 1945–81 *ad loc*.) and, for the concept, X. *Mem*. 2.6.38.
14 D. 21.177, [D.] 25.11, Aeschin. 1.7, 187. Dinarchus (1.81) describes the entrusting of Athens to Demosthenes as both *parakatathesthai* and *epitrepsai*; cf. the looser *egcheirizein* ('put in the hands of') at D. 19.99. For the sophist Lycophron, law itself was a 'guarantor (*egguêtês*) of reciprocal rights' (Arist. *Pol*. 1280 b10–11, tr. Robinson).
15 Aristotle applies this image to subordinate authority (below 175n.55), whereas Plato is prepared to employ it of cosmic rule (below 174n.51) as well as in the general sense 'govern' (e.g. *R*. 519c), which we can see from Thrasym. B1, a model preface (Yunis 1997), had become conventional by the end of the century. In Herodotus, however, besides two references to guardianship and six to 'rule in another's name' (Powell 1938 s.v. 1 and 2), *epitropeuein* is three times applied to unlimited monarchy (3.36.3, 82.2, 5.92ζ.2, all in speeches); in each case the implication seems to be competent management (though the first passage, part of Cambyses' attack on Croesus, is ironic).
16 Plato's passing reference to corrupt guardians at *Tht*. 144d is suggestive. There was a specific procedure against such dereliction, the *dike epitropês* (Harrison 1968–71 I.119–21), and protection of wards was part of the workload of the eponymous archon (Rhodes (1981) 629–36).
17 e.g. Hesk (2000b) 255–8, drawing on the fuller treatment in Hesk (2000a), esp. 248–61.
18 Compare D. 2.30 for the idea that the demos must become its own master rather than leaving politicians and generals in the position of tyrants; so too [D.] 58.61: jurors and laws must be in control of speakers, not vice versa.
19 Paphlagonian as nurse: *Eq*. 60; for the motif of brushing away insects, which recalls Athena in *Iliad* 4.130–1, cf. 1038 and *Vesp*. 596–7; spoon-feeding: 716–8; tidying up: 908; NB fr.416 for rejuvenation by removal of grey hairs, a stock flatterer's trick (Thphr. *Char*. 2.3) which contrasts with the real rejuvenation in the finale. Democrates fr.1 Baiter-Sauppe = Arist. *Rh*. 1407a8–10.
20 *kirnantes* is punningly combined with the idea of 'stirring up trouble' which also occurs frequently in *Knights* (below 132n.68; NB *Eq*. 859 for giving short measure). For the status of wage labour in ancient Greece see below 132n.69; compare its employment as an image of corruption (below 29), and NB Morawetz (2000) 15–47 for the antidemocratic concept of the *banausos* (lit. one who practises a craft or trade).

21 Note that in *R*. 562cd Plato distinguishes between irresponsible politicians and the authorities (*archontes*) who come under pressure from the city they have corrupted. The audience of children in *Grg*. 502e recalls the contest before an audience of children between a confectioner and a doctor which Socrates imagines in his account of 'pandering' (464de, 521e–2a). There is a clear association between these ideas and Plato's broader concern with health: the doctor is a favourite model of expertise for Plato (below 150n.1), with which Socrates implicitly associates his own true statesmanship here. For the concept of *kolakeia* in democratic politics, note *Alc. I* 120b and Arist. *Pol*. 1292a15–38.

22 Briber hires or buys: D. 10.9, 15.32, 18.33, 51, 149, 284, 19.316; Aeschin. 3.218 cf. [D.] 7.7; politician sells self: D. 8.61, 10.63, 18.46, 19.13, 16, 102, 109, 116, 118, 156, 167, 236, 301, 331, fr.11.2, [D.] 17.13; cf. *ônios* ('for sale') = 'bribable': Din. 1.20; hires self out: D. 9.54, 10.19, 59, 18.21, 38, 42, 49, 51–2, 131, 138, 149, 236, 307, 320, 19.29, 68, 110, 118, 125, 286, 289; Aeschin. 3.86, 220; Din. 1.15, 28, 3.12 cf. fr.I.2 Conomis; within Athens: D. 24.14–5, 67, 200, 25.37, 51.22. Timarchus and *misth*-words: e.g. Aeschin. 1.51–2, 72, 154, 163–4. Harvey (1985) discusses Athenian attitudes to bribery (NB also Ober 1989, 277–9); on political prostitution see Scholtz (1996). The negative implications of commerce are perhaps prefigured in Theramenes' contemptuous reference to 'those who out of poverty would sell the city for a drachma' (X. *HG* 2.3.48).

23 There is a unique instance of the language of pimping (*mastropeuein*) in Xenophon's *Symposium* (8.42), where it is suggested that Socrates might act as a go-between for Callias to establish him in the affections of the polis: this plainly provocative idea (contrast the language of matchmaking [*promnômai*] at Pl. *Tht*. 151b) picks up Socrates' earlier claim to expertise in this field (3.10), that is, in relationships, with a philosophic slant (4.56–64), for which cf. *Mem*. 2.4–6, 3.11 and Scholz (2007) 135–44.

24 On *therapeuein* see Landfester (1967) 58 and below 115 and NB Isoc. 2.16, 9.46 (cited above, n.8). Plato seems always to use *diakonein* pejoratively in the *Gorgias*, though not necessarily elsewhere (e.g. *R*. 467a, *Lg*. 782b), but his handling of *therapeuein* is more equivocal: while in *R*. 426cd it is applied to political gratification in association with the verb *charizesthai* ('give pleasure'; NB *Grg*. 502e, above n.21) it can also be used of informed care, for example, by doctors: *Grg*. 521a makes explicit the existence of two types of *therapeia*; cf. 464c, 513de, 517e. See further below 155.

25 Full discussion in Roberts (1982). It is striking that while the imagery of service continues in the present to be applied to administrators ('civil servants'), it seems more or less to have disappeared from the discourse of politicians themselves.

26 Compare the assertion of Callias in the *Symposium* (4.32) that whereas formerly he was treated like a subject ally and made to pay tribute (*phoros*), now as a poor man he is like a tyrant, since the city supports him. From another viewpoint, it is acceptance of the status of subject which is servile, hence Socrates' assimilation of being ruled in Greece to the condition of the Syrians, Phrygians and Lydians as Persian vassals or the subjection of the Libyans to the Carthaginians in his assault on Aristippus' proposed withdrawal from public life (*Mem*. 2.1.10–12) and the assertion that politicians (*hoi ... en tais polesi prostateuontes kai tôn demosiôn epimeloumenoi*) are considered freer, not more slavish, on that account (2.8.4; cf. *Lac.Pol*. 8.2 – non-Spartan elites regard submission to officials as *aneleutheron* – and the anecdote in *Cyr*. 8.3.21–3).

27 X. *Ages*. 7.2; Arist. *Pol*. 1287a20–2; Ael. *VH* 2.20; below 196n.188. Früchtel (1952) insists that *douleia* means 'servitude', not 'service'; so also Adcock (1953) 173.

28 The formula is also used at *Od.* 15.151–3 (Nestor and Menelaus); cf. 16.17, 17.111 for paternal affection as the essential aspect of the relationship.
29 Pritchard (1969) 653, 654–5; other examples cited by Graziosi & Haubold (2010) on *Il.* 6.429–30; West (2007) 421 notes wider Indo-European parallels.
30 'father of gods and men' (e.g. *Il.* 1.544, 22.167, *Od.* 17.137, *hDem.* 6, Hes. *Th.* 47, 524), or simply *patêr* (*Il.* 8.69, 245, 14.352, 16.250, *hCer.* 325 [restored]; cf. Pi. *P.* 4.24); Calhoun (1935) emphasises the patriarchal character of Zeus. Pindar also uses *patêr* of Kronos in *O.* 2.76 and refers to the gods as *hupatôn paterôn* ('highest fathers') in fr.75.11. Stanford (1959) comments on *Od.* 13.125–8: 'πάτερ is often a term of respect, not relationship, and the combination is Indo-European, cf. *Iu-piter, Dies-piter'*; on 'father' as a respectful form of address from younger to older, see Dickey (1996) 76–81, 89, 269; the usage appears on the human plane already in the *Odyssey* (e.g. 7.28, 48, 18.122, 20.199).
31 Pi. fr.105. For founders as fathers, see Weinstock (1971) 201 n.1: Ennius had Romulus called *O pater, o genitor* (*Ann.* 108 Skutsch); for 'fathers of liberty', note Pl. *Mx.* 240de on the heroes of Marathon, and compare Cic. *Rab. Perd.* 27, of Marius. In Pi. *P.* 3.71 *xeinois de thaumastos patêr* ('and to strangers a father to be admired'), the reference is presumably to Hieron's hospitality. There is one other instance of the image before the fourth century, Ion of Chios 27.1 W *chairetô hêmeteros basileus sôtêr te patêr te* ('Hail to our king, our saviour and father'); unfortunately, it is impossible to tell whether the reference is to a Spartan king or, as Campbell (Loeb) suggests, to Dionysus or wine.
32 Scholars disagree as to how far Oedipus' words are to be seen as figurative: Dawe (1982) *ad loc.* insists that the only adults present are Oedipus and the priest, but Jebb (1887) notes that other groups are implied; Kamerbeek (1967) comments that while children are in the majority, the group is representative of the whole city and hence *tekna* is also 'expressive of the father-son relation between the good ruler and his subjects'; in this vein see also Budelmann (2000) 206–10. The comments of the scholiast – 'Oedipus' character shows affection for the people (*philodêmon*) and forethought for the public interest, and the masses are well-disposed to him because of his benefactions to them, so that his use of "children" like a father is natural' – are bound to be influenced by the elaboration of kingship theory in the Hellenistic and Roman periods and the place of the father image within it (on which NB Stevenson 1992). Family relationships are a problematic category for Oedipus from the start of the play, as Peter Burian has reminded me.
33 In the former passage, however, the image is intriguingly tangled with the idea of killing the father but sparing the sons (for which see *Cypria* fr.25 Davies = 33 Bernabé), which may throw light on Cyrus' character, if the remark is authentic. Note the Homeric reminiscence in *êpios*, on the tone of which see de Romilly (1974) 95–6. In Timotheus 791.154 'father' is a respectful term of address (above n.30), but *pace* Hordern (2002), we should not take the same view of other vocatives in oriental contexts in tragedy, given Dickey's emphasis on age-differential as the norm.
34 The last clause in 8.1.44 'so that they would continue to be slaves for ever without dispute (*anamphilogôs*)', implies a cynicism of which there is no hint in Xenophon's other uses of this image, and in my view should be bracketed, given that there is no hint that the image is to be read against the grain; in favour of retention see however Due (1989) 213 n.21, who attributes objections to anachronistic moralizing, and Gera (1993) 295–300, esp. 295 with n.66, who argues that Cyrus slips from the earlier ideal. Gray (2011) 282–3 retains the phrase while softening it by making the slavery

a philosophical one to pleasure, but still has to treat it as an exception to the positive reading of the leader as father which she wants to adopt overall (325–8, 370). In 8.8.1 *etima* ('he honoured') seems to express an expectation of certain behaviour on the king's part not found elsewhere in connection with this image; this could be taken as an argument against the authenticity of the controversial final chapter, or as an element introduced to point up the decline from past to present. Due (1989) 211–12, 221 has a good appraisal of the blend of affection and authority underlying the father image in the work as a whole.

35 In the fifth century, the idea of the king as owner of his realm was associated with Persia and hence carried implications of autocracy: above 12.
36 In Rome, the title *parens patriae* is applied first to Cicero as saviour of Rome from Catiline, and then to Julius Caesar, Augustus and his successors, whose authority it reinforces through the concept of *patria potestas* (Weinstock (1971) 200–5), though Dio 53.18.3 stresses the affective aspects of love reciprocated with respect in the title's origin. The image continued to develop: note for example Cic. *Cat.* 1.17 (Catiline as would-be parricide) and Plut. *Dion* 39.4 (fatherly restraint), and see Alföldi (1952–4) for an exhaustive study. Kingship theory in the Middle Ages evolved the concept of the ruler as husband of the realm, drawing both on classical sources, notably Aristotle, and on Christian theology: Kantorowicz (1957) 214–23, while modern times have shown both that the image is still alive and that ripostes to it have evolved: '[Mobutu] says he is father of the nation. If he was a good father, he would visit his children' (quoted in *The Guardian* 4 January 1993).
37 Financial accountability: *Ath.Pol.* 54.2 with Rhodes (1981) *ad loc.*; physical sanctions and ideology: Hunter (1994) 154–84.
38 Strauss (1993) registers (e.g. 214–15) but does not properly address the difficulty of extrapolating the father-son relationship onto the polis level caused by paternal authority; Griffith (1998) faces the issue directly (esp. 24–6, 30–3, 68, 75) in a stimulating psychologizing treatment, though he seems to me to concentrate rather too much on elite concerns (but NB 76 for the suggestion that the wide spread of office-holding might have made father-figures good to think with for the demos at large).
39 For the autochthony topos, see in general Loraux (1993) 35–70, and on its development, Rosivach (1987), suggesting (305) that this may essentially belong to the period *c.* 480–450; for its significance in funeral speeches, Loraux (1986) 148–53, 193–4, Nouhaud (1982) 60–1. As Rosivach notes (297–8, 305–6), other groups also claimed to be autochthonous; I suggest that we should include among these the Thebans, through the myth of the Spartoi, the original inhabitants sown by Cadmus as dragons' teeth; Rosivach 296 seems to me unduly restrictive on this point.
40 Children of Erechtheus: e.g. E. *Med.* 824, *Supp.* 702; of Cecrops, *Ion* 296, *Pho.* 855, Ar. *Eq.* 1055. 'Children of Theseus' in S. *O. C.* 1066 seems to be unique, and all the more notable in a play in which Theseus is a character, though no commentator remarks on it.
41 Loraux (1993) 10, 15, 65–6, 121–2, Strauss (1993) 44–5, 57–9. The noun *patris* itself is feminine, like *gê* and *chôra*, the other regular words for land or territory.
42 Cf. the very similar 'the same land as mother and fatherland (*mêtera kai patrida*)' in L. 2.17, and 'our earth and mother' in Pl. *Mx.* 237e. By the time of Menander, this has become a commonplace of universal reference: *Mon.* 145, 511 (and cf. fr.247); cf. the proposition in Arist. *Oec.* 1343a30-b1 that agriculture is natural because 'all are nourished by their mother'.

43 Lyc. *Leoc* 47 (Chaeronea), 85 (time of Codrus); the verb *trephô* ('rear') could apply either to a mother or a nurse. Creon's appeal to Oedipus to return to his 'old nurse' Thebes (S. *O. C.* 759–60) shows that the concept was not conceived of as unique to Athens. The formula 'nurse and mother' makes a perplexing appearance elsewhere in Sophocles, applied at *O. T.* 1091 to the mountain Cithairon by the chorus during their speculations about Oedipus' true birth, just after it has been revealed that he is not the son of Polybus and Merope: perhaps they mean to suggest that he is an autochthonous Theban (above, n.39) whose mother is the earth rather than any mortal.

44 Nielsen (2004) 50–1 documents the widespread association of *patris* with familial terminology.

45 L. 13.91, D. 10.40–1; the former image is a kind of inversion of Tecmessa's identification with Ajax as the only homeland (*patris*) she has (S. *Aj.* 514–8; cf. also Andromache's appeal to Hector as her whole family at *Il.* 6.429–30). Compare the appeal of Demetrius to the Roman Senate, in which he claimed to regard all the senators as his fathers (Plb. 31.2.5; the title *patres conscripti* might be a factor here). Filial obedience is put to a different use in another Demosthenic passage (*Ep.* 3.45), where he argues that the relationship between a politician and the demos should be that of a son who hopes that his parents will be reasonable, but puts up with them as they are, submission being the honourable course.

46 50d–1c, 51e with Kraut (1984) especially 48–52, 91–114, 143–8. The analogy is reinforced by the use of *patris*: Kraut 54 n.1. This image reappears in the *Seventh Letter* as an argument against using violence to change even a constitution which one regards as bad (331cd).

47 The similarity in expression to the two types of doctor-legislator (720; below 72) suggests that such lawgivers will explain and persuade.

48 Aristotle picks up the underlying link between the timarchic state and Sparta when he echoes the phrase at *Pol.* 1270b34–5 (below, 191n.155).

49 The corresponding tyrannical individual literally behaves in the same way (574ac), though the link to the polis is made at 575d (NB *mêtrida te...kai patrida*, 'motherland and fatherland').

50 Discussed by Pender (2000) 104–6, who also notes Plato's use of the generative aspect, which is almost entirely absent from political imagery (only perhaps hinted at with reference to the founding of cities: above, 30 and n.31); this is applied to the artistic creation of immortal offspring, of which laws are treated as one form, in the *Symposium* (209de).

51 *Oikonomia* is stated to be a domestic kingship, and kingship the domestic administration of a city or one or more nations, at *Pol.* 1285b31–3, i.e. the relationship between the two is reciprocal. Father and husband as analogues: *Pol.* 1259a37–b17. Types of friendship in house and state: *EN* 1160b22–61b10, esp. 1161a6–9; cf. the briefer discussion in *EE* 1242a1–13. At *EE* 1241b27–31 he remarks that all the constitutional forms, good and bad, are present in the household at once.

52 Autochthony: above, n.39; public funeral: Hornblower (1991–2008) on Thuc. 2.34.1 usefully summarizes the debate; the *epitaphios logos* may have been added later, but NB Rosivach (1987) 303–5 for the ideology of autochthony as a stimulus to the patriotism and defence of freedom which the speeches eulogize.

53 Both points made by Kallet-Marx (1993) 140; date of support for war orphans: Hornblower (1991–2008) on Thuc. 2.46.1. Pl. *Mx.* 249a-c makes considerable play with the language of familial relationships in describing these provisions: particularly

striking is his allusion to orphans who have just reached adulthood returning 'to their ancestral hearth' (b1–2), presumably from the civic hearth.
54 Noted by Osborne (1997) 29.
55 Osborne (1997) 3–11.
56 Finley (1981) 77–94, Humphreys (1983) 1–32, Roy (1999); NB also, more generally, Strauss (1993) 33–53.
57 Three of the six theatres of operation named at the head of *IG* I³ 1147 (460 or 459 BC) saw action against the Persians, for example; the extent to which all these developments are motivated simply by aggressive imperialism can easily be overstated.
58 e.g. Sennett (1980) 50–83; Ringmar (2008) 60–1; Honohan (2008) 73–4.
59 Hansen (1998) 135–7.
60 Glotz (1929) 19–20; Gernet (1981) 322–39; Jameson (1990) 105–6; Parker (1996) 26–7.
61 Not that any distinction between public and private was thereby effaced: just as the Athenians regarded an individual's conduct in regard to his domestic obligations as indicative of his character in public life, and good personal behaviour as a kind of service (Liddel [2007] 211–27), so living well could be represented as a kind of liturgy (Is. fr.30 Thalheim, L. 21.19; below, 164), and bad living as a form of treason: Isoc. 15.305.

3

The Shepherd of the People

One rarely encounters the 'shepherd of the people' these days, at least in the western world: the image is hardly at home in an era in which almost all regimes profess to be democracies, and the shepherd as such has more or less disappeared from public perceptions, which think instead in terms of 'farmers' in general. Yet if the image has withered in the last century,[1] it is an ancient and deep-rooted one: its origins are elusive, but it is found earliest and most widely in Mesopotamia, and is commonly used in the ancient Near East.[2] Its implications seem to be particularly of care and responsibility: we hear of Adadnirari III 'whose shepherding [the gods] made as agreeable to the people of Assyria as is the smell of the Plant of Life', and the establishment of the king as shepherd by the gods is often stressed, while a text of Hammurabi lays stress on the abundance provided by the king.[3] The idea of care is likewise central to the prophets' criticism of the shepherds of Israel and their promises of intervention by the Lord, the true shepherd.[4]

In Greek literature the image is present from the beginning, in Homer and other early hexameter poetry, but in the particular shape of a formulaic metaphor, the expression 'shepherd of the people', which occurs some 65 times as a formula at the end of a line.[5] The formulaic quality of the image (Silk 1974, 30 calls it 'epic cliché') makes its implications hard to assess, but I would suggest that its particular significance lies not in ideas of pastoral care, but in the idea of directing and marshalling an unruly crowd; one may compare the simile of the Greek commanders sorting out their men like goatherds separating flocks (*Il.* 2.474f.),[6] the comparison of Odysseus to a bellwether (3.196–8) and the description of Aeneas followed by his men like a ram (13.491–5).[7] This might also explain why the formula is found much less frequently in the *Odyssey* and in other early hexameter poetry than in the *Iliad*. The military aspect is to the fore in certain Near Eastern texts: the leaderless Ethiopian army as 'like a herd which has no herdsman', and in Mesopotamia leaderless soldiers could be compared to sheep without a shepherd, though it is clear in the Ethiopian example that the king's functions extend well beyond the military. It is also worth noting that Xenophon in the *Memorabilia* attributes to Socrates an exposition of the epithet as applied to Agamemnon with specific reference to generalship (though for the revaluation of the image in the fourth century see below).[8]

The most recent extended treatment of the Homeric image is that of Haubold (2000, esp. 17–32) who emphasizes two aspects: the marginal and subordinate status of the shepherd, and his failure to protect the flock. The former point is true enough and has been noted by others, but was presumably equally true of the contemporary

Near East, where it is clear that human shepherds are entrusted with the flocks of the gods.[9] Indeed, in Mesopotamia, gods are also called shepherds, and the idea of Jehovah as 'the Shepherd of Israel' is familiar to every reader of the Bible.[10] Occasionally, such ideas are echoed in Greek literature, as when Anacreon (fr.348) says of Artemis of Magnesia 'the citizens you herd (*poimaineis*) are not uncivilised (*anêmerous*, lit. 'untamed').[11] Clearly, then, there is nothing inherently demeaning in the concept; it is certainly hierarchical, but since it assigns a humble status to both parties, it neither widens the gap between them, nor does it necessarily simply reduce the herd to mute beasts,[12] for all that it makes plain their need for care and protection. Haubold's claim that the Homeric shepherd fails to provide this protection, which is important for his wider argument, relies on supplementing the unforthcoming formula with the frequent similes in which a lion or other predator raids a flock or steading; this, however, fails to allow for the context in which such similes tend to occur, namely the battlefield dominance of an individual hero which is emphasized when the poet identifies it with the prowess of a beast of prey. In such contexts the focus is obviously on the successful onslaught of a hero who at other times may function as a shepherd; only at those times when the predator is fended off (for example, in a struggle over the corpse of a hero) do the similes reflect successful defence. Thus the corpus of similes is rather skewed, and will tend to produce a skewed view of shepherds and herding.[13] Contrariwise, the fact that in Hesiod the epithet seems to be simply ornamental (most contexts in which it appears are concerned with parentage, in fact) implies a positive view of the pastoral analogy at an early date.

After Homer and Hesiod, the image is strikingly uncommon down to the end of the fifth century: the majority of instances are found in tragedy and usually reflect both Homeric influence and a military context.[14] In a fragment of Aeschylus, Achilles refers to Agamemnon as a 'bad shepherd', and in another the Greek leaders who awarded the arms of Achilles to Odysseus are called shepherds (*p[oi]mandridai*), while in a fragment of Euripides' *Temenos* a wise adviser applies the verb *poimainein* ('tend') to a general (*stratêlatên*).[15] Similarly, when in Euripides' *Supplices* Adrastus describes Theseus as a 'good shepherd', the reference may be narrowly military, since he continues 'for want of which many cities have perished, lacking a general' (191–2). In the *Persae*, Aeschylus alludes to the widespread use of the image when he refers to the Persian expeditionary force as *poimanorion* ('flock' 74–5) and has Atossa ask the chorus concerning Athens 'what shepherd (*poimanôr*) is set over them as master?' (241); at the same time, however, the identification of the shepherd's role with mastery underlines the contrast between an absolute monarchy and Athenian democracy and hints at related imagery of the control and taming of animals, setting up the reply that the Athenians are no man's slaves.[16]

In other passages, we can detect some articulation in a broader context of the functions of a shepherd as, for example, the source of nourishment: hence, Pindar speaks of Iamus praying for 'the honour of nourishing a people (*laotrophon timan*)', and the same concept may lie behind the name of the Spartan king Leobotes ('Feeder of the people').[17] The principle that the herdsman cares for his charges is by now taken for granted, as one can see from the generalised use of *poimainein* and the related *boukolein* ('herd cattle') and their cognates in the sense 'take care of'.[18] Likewise when the chorus of Aeschylus' *Agamemnon* state that their king is (or should be) 'a good knower/judge of the flock (*agathos probatognômôn*)' (795) and so able to identify the genuinely loyal, the implication that a good king will know his flock is starting to develop the potential of the image,[19] and the identification of ruler and shepherd might also lie behind the story that the lawgiver Zaleukos of Locri was a shepherd who was inspired by a vision (Arist. fr.548R = 555 Gigon).[20]

Nevertheless, even if we can infer that imagery from animal husbandry was popular in other contexts, the shepherd appears only sparsely as a political image up to this point, and almost entirely in high poetry and contexts set in the mythical past, which makes the resurgence of the image from the turn of the fourth century on all the more striking. Though it is still limited in distribution, this time to philosophic and quasi-philosophic literature, it is clear that its significance and validity had become a topic of lively debate. In his defence of Socrates, Xenophon quotes him as having criticized the Thirty for being like a cowherd who makes his cattle fewer and worse, yet will not acknowledge his incompetence, an analogy which apparently annoyed Charicles and Critias. Given the apologetic context, this anecdote ought to be reliable: if so, then it is a reasonable inference that the image of the shepherd was, like other political imagery derived from practical activities, in common circulation in Socratic circles, and indeed, as we have seen, Xenophon also represents Socrates as exploring the implications of the Homeric formula.[21] The tendentious use of the image by Thrasymachus also gives the impression of being well-developed, as if by the time of the first book of the *Republic* we are tuning in to a debate which has been going on for some time.

It is Thrasymachus who introduces the figure of the shepherd there, accusing Socrates of childish naivety because he cannot distinguish between sheep and shepherd and supposes 'that shepherds or herdsmen look to the good of the sheep or cattle, and fatten them up and care for them with some other object in view than the good of their masters and themselves' (343ab). This is clearly an attempt to mobilize the shepherd in support of his contention that 'justice is the interest of the stronger' and to side-step the conclusion of the previous discussion of *technai* such as medicine and seafaring that any art, including the art of rule, is exercised in the interest of the subject. In so doing he is implicitly substituting a different authority relation, between a ruler and subjects unlike him, rather than between one human and others like him.[22] Socrates, however, ripostes by insisting on extending the principles of the previous discussion to animal husbandry: the true shepherd will look to the benefit of his charges, since that is the objective of the art of shepherding (*poimênikê* [sc. *technê*]) in the true sense (345cd). In thus assimilating animal husbandry to other arts, he also legitimizes it as a model of the exercise of authority of wider scope than medicine or seafaring. Of course, in reality rulers may well fall short of this ideal, hence the suggestion in the *Theaetetus* (174de) that in the philosopher's eyes the king or tyrant will resemble a herdsman whose success lies in the scale of his exploitation ('milking', *bdallein*), his mind cramped by the difficulty of imposing on subjects more bad-tempered and treacherous than domesticated animals.[23]

After this initial prominence, the image of the shepherd largely disappears from the ensuing discussion in the *Republic*: the Guardians are only characterized as shepherds in regard to their relationship with the Auxiliaries, who are characterized as watchdogs. Initially, indeed, the image is applied to the whole group of Guardians in the broader sense (375a–6c) who share the same initial education, hence the suggestion that the proper watchdog, who can distinguish friend and foe and act appropriately, is in a sense *philosophos* (376ab), but when the Auxiliaries are separated out from the Guardians proper, what is important is that they be properly trained and obedient, as dogs obey their shepherds.[24] It is the job of the Auxiliaries, both male and female, to guard the flock, but the higher authority of the Guardians as shepherds over the flock remains only latent, and their superiority to their subjects is likewise left implicit, though the 'tough and wiry watchdogs' are contrasted with the 'fat and tender sheep' who inhabit other states.[25] Plato seems to want to downplay, or at least not to emphasize, the disparity between ruler and ruled which is to the fore when he next makes use of the image, in the *Statesman*.

Certainly the shepherd plays a more prominent part in that dialogue, but the use which Plato makes of the figure is idiosyncratic and ultimately abortive. The attempt to define the expertise of the statesman is initiated by a process of a series of divisions intended to isolate it with ever-increasing precision: at an early stage in this process, the art of the statesman is said to be akin to the rearing of living creatures in herds (as opposed to being concerned with individual animals or inanimate things: 261b-e), and by implication tame animals (263e–4a). His charges are then successively distinguished as land-dwelling, non-flying, hornless, non-interbreeding and without cloven hooves, which leaves them in the same class as pigs (265b–6c); an alternative process identifies them immediately as bipeds and lacking feathers (266de); clearly this is as much an exercise in method as in political thought.[26] The combined results are summarized (267a-c), but then immediately critiqued, first (267d–8c) on the grounds that whereas the herdsman deals with all aspects of the care of his flock, including nutrition and medicine, there is a whole range of professions dealing with the care of humans – 'merchants, farmers, millers and bakers … and gymnastic trainers too, and doctors' (267e [tr. Rowe]) – who could dispute the statesman's claim and so must be excluded in order to isolate him; and then in the myth of the age of Kronos, which highlights the problem that the image of the shepherd suits the relationship of a god to humans much better than human statesmen who are 'far more like their subjects in nature' (275c) while at the same time leaving the precise nature of the statesman's activity ill-defined, given that it does not consist in 'rearing' (*trephein*).[27] Although a token effort is made to address these problems by substituting a more neutral terminology of 'herd-keeping' (*agelaiokomikê*) or 'care' (*epimeleia*), explicitly distinguishing human kings and adding the further criterion of voluntary rule to separate the king from the tyrant, the image is evidently still unsatisfactory, since at that point it is essentially discarded in favour of the paradigm of weaving: insofar as herding is still relevant as providing the raw material for that process, it functions in a distinctly subordinate role, though a couple of passing mentions hint that it has not quite been abandoned altogether.[28]

If the image of the shepherd is not entirely discredited in the *Statesman*, it is certainly distinctly problematized; however, the difficulties which he raises do not appear to trouble Xenophon. One probable reason for this is that Xenophon is very largely concerned with contexts in which the exercise of power is in any case rather authoritarian, and his shepherds tend to be generals, or else the Great King of Persia. In the latter case, the image was also culturally appropriate, since the shepherd and kingship were associated in Persian ideology, a link exemplified in the ritualized return in the investiture of each Persian king to the purported pastoral origins of the Achaemenid monarchy in the time of Cyrus, and the issue of difference presented no problem, since Persian kings were in fact believed to be of a superior nature to their subjects.[29] It was therefore natural for Xenophon to introduce the image programmatically at the very beginning of the *Cyropaideia* (1.1): reflecting on the nature of human authority, he contrasts the difficulty which men have in ruling men, even at the level of the household, with the ease with which they control herds of animals. Animals are more willing to obey their herdsmen in everything and to allow them to profit from them as they wish and, so far from rebelling, are more compliant towards their herdsmen than to outsiders. He concludes that man's natural condition makes it easier for him to rule other creatures than others of his own species.

However, the case of Cyrus shows that such rule is not impossible, although Xenophon acknowledges that he was very different from other kings (1.1.4). The singling out of Cyrus, and the course of the succeeding narrative, imply that Xenophon has in mind a role considerably more substantial than basic care and provision of necessities: Cyrus gathers together the Persians as a flock and actively leads them militarily and politically to a new imperial destiny. At the same time, his expert man-management, founded on his knowledge and understanding of individual character, mimics the shepherd's knowledge of his flock.[30] The benefits conferred on the Persians also do much to address the charge that the shepherd simply exploits his flock: towards the end of the work Cyrus is made to expound the argument that the duties of the good shepherd and the good king are very similar: both must make their subjects happy (*eudaimonas*) as they make use of them (*chrêsthai*; 8.2.14). That perception of a relationship which is to some degree reciprocal, and hence implies that the shepherd's power brings with it duties, underlies Socrates' interpretation of the formula *poimên laôn* (*Mem.* 3.2.1), namely that both general and shepherd must keep their charges safe and supplied with life's necessities and ensure that the object for which they exist is attained.[31]

The stress laid on pastoral care suggests that Xenophon feels, or wishes to imply, an affective aspect to the idea: the shepherd's concern for his flock is more than simply mercenary, and so the flock can put their trust in his leadership and protection.[32] Xenophon's position is the easier to maintain as he has no latent moral or didactic agenda:[33] provided the relationship is mutually beneficial, then as long as the needs of the sheep are provided for, there is no need to deny the element of exploitation, particularly since it is surely conceived of as operating at a limited and sustainable level, and in terms of milk, cheese and wool rather more than meat. Since livestock were both a measure and a major component of wealth, particularly in the pre-monetary economy of Homeric times, one would expect their preservation to be a high priority, and indeed the herdsman is frequently expected or enjoined to increase the flocks.[34] What subverts the relationship is dereliction of duty on the part of the shepherd: in Jehovah's denunciation of the shepherds of Israel in *Ezekiel*, their crime is not exploitation, but failure to deliver their part of the bargain by caring for their charges: 'How I hate the shepherds of Israel who care only for themselves! Should not the shepherd care for the sheep? You consume the milk, wear the wool and slaughter the fat beasts, but you do not feed the sheep. You have not encouraged the weary, tended the sick, bandaged the hurt, recovered the straggler or searched for the lost; and even the strong you have driven with ruthless severity' (Ezek. 34.2–4, NEB).

Having not quite rejected the image of the shepherd, Plato returns to it once more in the *Laws*. It would seem that he did so in response to Xenophon, since in his account of the Persian monarchy as constitutional model, he criticizes Cyrus for having failed to educate his children in the art of herding, even though he left them great herds, including human herds, and despite the fact that the Persians were by tradition 'shepherds and offspring of a rugged land' (695a): while that tradition made them tough, ascetic and warlike, the royal princes were brought up in the lap of luxury by women and so corrupted. The implication is that while the analogy of the shepherd is not completely inappropriate for a king as leader (and the Athenian concedes that Cyrus was a good general: 694c), the morally corrosive environment of monarchy makes it extremely difficult to hand on or teach the qualities on which it depends for its validity.[35] Yet as in the *Statesman*, the image does not quite disappear: when the discussion comes to the selection of the citizen body for the new ideal state, the Athenian invokes the model of animal husbandry to validate the principle that, as the herd must be cleared of unhealthy and inferior animals before the herdsman can apply himself to its care, so the population of the state must be purged of unsuitable individuals. It is noteworthy that here too, it is the legislator who is authorized to apply this process: even if it is conceded that he is unlikely to have tyrannical power, he is clearly envisaged as operating from a position of superior expertise which authorizes his acting thus.[36]

Nor is Plato's quite the last word: notwithstanding his criticisms, Aristotle aligns himself closely with Xenophon when he observes (*EN* 1161a12–15) that a king, if he is a good king, treats his subjects well so that they benefit, just like a shepherd, and he cites the Homeric formula in evidence.

That last example brings us full circle, and it also illuminates the development of the image from an invariant formula of mainly military significance to a carefully articulated paradigm of benign authority. Hardly any of that process of articulation takes place before the fourth century: the essential point about pastoral care is made explicit, moving the image away from its military origins, but the controversial nature of one-man rule, especially in Athens, makes it easy to understand why shepherding is not part of contemporary political discourse in the fifth century. Such attitudes clearly persisted into the fourth century: hence discussion of the shepherd remains for the most part theoretical and exploratory, critiquing or justifying the concept rather than deploying it as an image whose implications can be taken for granted. More than any other complex of imagery, the imagery of animal husbandry illuminates for us the process of the reconstitution of the conception, ideology and presentation of monarchy prompted by the changing political landscape of the fourth century: if Greek images of the shepherd are sparser than in earlier or later periods, they are more thoughtful than many.

Notes

1. For the later history of the image see Murray (1990), Dvornik (1966), Index s.v. 'shepherd, good, ruler's title', and more generally Foucault (2002), though he rather understates the extent of Greek usage, not least because he takes no account of Xenophon. Even today, the crozier of a bishop or abbot is a symbolic crook, harking back to Jesus' injunction to St Peter to 'feed my sheep' (*John* 21.15–17).
2. Murray (1990) 3–5, West (1997) 226–7; and beyond: West (2007) 421; Watkins (2001) 45 considers the shepherd of the people formula 'probably of Indo-European antiquity'.
3. Adadnirari: Pritchard (1969) 281; divine establishment: Pritchard (1969) 298 (Ashurbanipal), Frankfort (1948) 238 (Gudea of Lagash, Hammurabi; for Gudea cf. 256). Among a wealth of material, see also Pritchard (1969) 289 (Esarhaddon), 558 (Ashurbanipal III); 604 (Uruk) – Gilgamesh too is shepherd of Uruk, 'the sheepfold of Eanna' (*Gilgamesh* I i-ii); 481, 574, 583–5, 641, 648 (Sumeria); Frankfort (1948) 252 (Nabonidas). Hammurabi: Dvornik (1966) 34, and see 266–8 for an excellent brief survey of the pre-Hellenistic use of the image in the Near East.
4. e.g. *Ezek.* 34 (vv.2–4 quoted below, 48), 37.24; *Jer.* 23.1–4; further examples in Murray (1990) 5. Persian propaganda trades on this tradition when Cyrus is called the Lord's shepherd in *Isaiah* 44.28: Dvornik (1966) 327.
5. The phrase appears in the accusative and dative, *poimena/poimeni laôn*. There is a useful tabulation of instances in Haubold (2000) 197; for *poimena laôn* add Hesiod frr. 10a47, 40.1, *Scut.* 41, and for *poimeni laôn*, Hes. *Th.* 1000. Besides Homer and Hesiod, the formula is attested in the *Iliupersis* (fr.4.2 Davies = 6.2 Bernabé) and Asius (fr.1.3).
6. Compare the prayer addressed to the Good Shepherd in the *Dies Irae*: *inter oves locum praesta et ab haedis me sequestra*. The *laos* is frequently assembled (*ageirô* e.g. 2.438, 4.28, 377) or dispersed (*skedannumi* e.g. 19.171, 23.162), just as the shepherd constitutes the flock by his actions (Foucault 2002, 301–2); note also that *sêmantôr* can mean both 'commander' and 'herdsman': Collins (1996) 28–9.
7. Collins (1996), who grounds on the same basic approach a more elaborate interpretation then I offer, remarks that 'warfare in the *Iliad* is a matter of pastoral management' (24); see also Gutzwiller (1991) 24.
8. Pritchard (1969) 447, cf. 443, from Egypt; Frankfort et al. (1946) 202; X. *Mem.* 3.2.1, and cf. Arist. *EN* 1161a12–15 (below 48). Lonsdale (1990) 20–1 notes the intrusion of military language into the description of lions attacking a herd of cattle on the Shield of Achilles (*Il.* 18.573–86) which implies some reciprocity between the two fields.
9. Noted also by Collins (1996), 20–1 and Blondell (2005) 27–8, who also discusses the association of pastoralism with primitivism in Greek thought (28–31).
10. Mesopotamian gods: Pritchard (1969) 337, 574–6, 613 (Enlil), 387–8,556 (Shamash), 398 (the Hittite sun-god); the idea is also basic in the lamentation for the destruction of Ur, sheepfold of the gods (ibid. 455–6, 460–1). In Egypt men can be called 'the cattle of the god' (ibid. 417); for Israel NB Murray (1990) 4–5; West (2007) 131 notes wider Indo-European parallels.
11. The Homeric formula 'shepherd of the people' is applied to a god, probably Zeus, in a Samian inscription of the fourth or third century: *CEG* II 852.2.
12. *pace* Collins (1996) 20, 25–35, for whom the expression of power through speech

relations is a central concern. He (20–1) and Murray (1990) 3–4 also suggest an element of nostalgia for a simpler era.

13 Lonsdale (1990) 39–110 provides an excellent discussion of the subtleties and complexities of Homeric lion imagery: he counts seven instances out of 27 in which lions attack livestock and are actually or potentially defeated. Haubold does not comment on the episode on the shield of Achilles (*Il.* 18.520–9) in which shepherds (*nomees* rather than *poimenes*, but NB his 19 n.28 for the lack of distinction in the terms) are killed by another *laos*, highlighting the risks that they too run.

14 There is a striking contrast with the prominence of herdsmen themselves in drama: Gutzwiller (1991) 45–65.

15 A. frr.132c8, 451q8 [dub.]; E. fr.744. A. fr.451 p12 [dub.] might also identify shepherd and king, though the text is fragmentary and the attribution uncertain, but in *Agam.* 657 the 'evil shepherd' is best understood as the storm which wrecks the fleet (so Fraenkel [1950] *ad loc.*).

16 Below, 107–8; there are similar overtones in the use of *elaunei* ('drives' 75) of Xerxes' command.

17 *O.* 6.60 (below, 112; Hdt. 1.65.4, 7.204. These ideas are sarcastically perverted in Aristophanes *Knights*, where the Paphlagonian calls on the jurors 'whom I feed' (256), since as Neil (1901) remarks *ad loc.*, the verb in question, *boskô*, is properly used of animals, so that the jurors are in a sense the Paphlagonian's flock. Here comedy is clearly evoking negative implications of democracy; cf. Murray (1990) 7 for the dangers of ovine docility in a democracy.

18 E.g. *h.Merc.*167, Pi. *O.* 11.9, A. *Supp.* 767, *Eum.* 91; Lloyd-Jones and Wilson (1990) 17–8 (on S. *Aj.* 360) cite extensive parallels.

19 As Fraenkel (1950) *ad loc.* remarks, noting that *probatognômôn* may have been coined by the poet for this context.

20 So Dunbabin (1948) 69, though the motif of the lonely shepherd who has visions or meets divinities is probably also involved: Hes. *Op.* 23 with West (1966) 159–60; Gutzwiller (1991) 29–35.

21 X. *Mem.* 1.2.32, 37; for the argument that *technê* analogies can be traced back to Socrates and the late fifth century, see below, 148. The particular point is echoed in the comparison of Athenian politicians to incompetent keepers of animals or charioteers in Pl. *Grg.* 516a-e (below 150).

22 For the egalitarian Herodotus, by contrast, the creation of Median court ceremony and protocol is motivated by Deioces' desire to conceal the fact that he is *not* superior to his subjects (1.99), and the tyrant Polycrates is criticized for 'mastery over men like himself' (3.142.3); contrast Xenophon's approving account of Cyrus' use of ceremony in *Cyr.* 8.1.40–2, 3.1–18. Skemp (1952) 52–66 discusses the implications of inequality in fourth-century herding imagery with particular reference to Pl. *Plt.*

23 Cf. Solon fr.37.8 (below 91) and the analogous language of olive-harvesting applied to exploitation by politicians in Ar. *Eq.* 326, Cratin. fr.214. By the same token, *basileis* who ought to be shepherds can be denounced for devouring their flocks (Hom. *Il.* 1.231 cf. Hes. *Op.* 38–9, 263–4; below 90) without invalidating the image in principle.

24 415e–16e, 440d, 451cd, Halliwell (1993) 17, 140; at 440cd canine imagery is applied to the idea of reason calling passion to heel, suggesting a correspondence between the tripartite relationship between shepherd, dogs and sheep and Plato's individual psychology.

25 422d (tr. Lee); cf. the association of canine toughness and vigour with the training of the Guardians at 404ab. Plato also makes play with the ascetic character of the herdsman's life in the *Laws* (694e–5a; below 48).
26 Rowe (1995) 3–4, Lane (1998) 13–97; note in particular the discussion of principles at 262a–3e (cf. 285b–6c). Rowe also observes (1–2) that the word translated as 'statesman', *politikos*, is almost unique to Plato, and hence that what is being sought, both the expertise and its practitioner, are more theoretical than actual.
27 274e–5c; cf. the allusion to divine shepherding in the age of Kronos at *Lg.* 713d. On mistakes in this process of division see Rowe (1995) 197–8, Lane (1998) 117–19, Blondell (2005) 38–43. For divine shepherds in Plato see Pender (2000) 108–10, 119–23, 139–44.
28 275c–6e; weaving is introduced at 279b (below 161): for the subordinate role of the shepherd see Blondell (2005) 54–5, who also notes the residual use of the image of the legislator's subjects as 'herds' at 294e, 295e. Despite the attempt to separate off king and tyrant, Miller (1980) 43–54 suggests a problematic association between the shepherd image and contemporary enthusiasm for strong one-man rule.
29 Murray (1990) 4–5; the ritual is described in Plut. *Art.* 3. On belief in the superior nature of Persian monarchs, see above 12, below 160; however, if the re-emergence of the image in Greece goes back to the later fifth century, it is less likely that Plato and Xenophon were more generally influenced by Persian practice, as Dvornik (1966) 267–8 suggested.
30 Foucault's comments on the resonances of the image are instructive here: (2002) 301–3.
31 That herdsmen profit from their charges is already acknowledged in 1.1.2, though Xenophon uses the neutral word *karpos/-oi* ('fruit[s], profit[s]').
32 NB Brock (2004b) 249–51 for this aspect of Xenophon's political imagery, which is also implicit in his fondness for father imagery.
33 Indeed, although imagery of animal husbandry can slide into that of the taming or control of animals, as we have seen, strictly speaking the notion of taming or training is alien to the image of the shepherd: even if the herdsman may seek to improve his flock, he does so by acting on his understanding of their needs and interests, and by guiding natural processes in breeding, as the charming portrait at Pl. *Plt.* 268ab indicates. Gray (2011) 48–51 sets out a positive evaluation of Xenophon's animal imagery in general as a model of leadership; for a more cynical reading, see Tatum (1989) 63–6.
34 Animals as measure of wealth: Hom *Il.* 6.234–6; as constituent: (e.g.) *Od.* 14.96–104. Increasing the flock: 'May he multiply the sheepfolds like a trustworthy shepherd': Pritchard (1969) 641 ('Inanna and the King'); for the pharaoh's duty to his flock see Frankfort *et al.* (1946) 78–9, and cf. nn.3–4 above for examples from Babylon and the Old Testament. The same outlook is reflected in the analogical claim in Hp. *Vict.* 25.2 that the strong *dunastês* is one who can 'nourish (*trephein*)' most men: one may compare *Proverbs* 14.28: 'In the multitude of people is the king's honour; but in the want of people is the destruction of the prince.' The importance of moderation is reflected in the dictum attributed to Tiberius, that the good shepherd should shear the sheep, not shave them (Suet. *Tib.* 32.2, Dio 57.10.5).
35 *Lg.* 694a–5b; the pattern recurs with Darius (an outsider not brought up as a prince) and Xerxes: 695c–6a. For the passage as anti-Xenophontic polemic see Tatum (1989) 225–34, who notes the criticism of Cyrus as (actual) father and householder at 694c; the passage echoes other contexts where Plato remarks on the inability of real-world

political leaders to pass on skills to their offspring (cf. *Men.* 93a–4e, *Prt.* 319d–20b; below 179n.86).

36 *Lg.* 735b–6c: the concept is supported by quasi-religious language of purification (*katharmos, katharsis*: England 1921 on 735b3), by medical imagery of disease and purgation (below 170n.29) and by an analogy from the selection of sources of pure water (below 79n.23).

4

The Ship of State

Maritime imagery comes naturally to those who live by the sea and get their living from it.[1] For example, Holland in the sixteenth and seventeenth centuries abounded in images of the ship of state, and in other communal images of seafaring, particularly the related image of the Ship of the Church and its antithesis, the Ship of the Heresy,[2] a reminder that ship imagery does not have to be positive and that some of those who put to sea are, like Edward Lear's Jumblies, neither well-advised nor competent. Indeed, probably the most influential ship image of the Early Modern period was a negative one: Sebastian Brant's *Das Narrenschiff*, inspiration for a host of translations and imitations produced all over Europe.[3] *Das Narrenschiff* also goes to show that the appeal of maritime imagery is by no means confined to seafaring peoples, having been originally published in land-locked Basel in 1494. Another product of land-locked central Europe was the mechanical galleon in the British Museum, made in Augsburg around 1585: here the central figure is the Holy Roman Emperor, surrounded by the empire's seven Electors, and the ship is evidently to be read in part as symbolic of the hierarchical order of the empire, as well as of its wealth and sophistication.[4] It is the immediate comprehensibility and perennial adaptability of the image of the ship of state which has kept it alive through the ages and maintains its status as a popular trope in political discourse even today.[5]

As far as the somewhat scanty surviving evidence allows us to judge, the ship of state comes into view only gradually. The first instance of maritime imagery used in a communal context is in Archilochus, who describes the sudden and alarming onset of an impending storm, and calls on his comrade Glaukos to aid him in shortening sail and other precautions.[6] At first glance, the passage is a realistic description of a storm at sea; for its allegorical nature we have to accept the testimony of the ancient scholar Heraclitus, writing in the first or second century AD (*Alleg. Hom.* 5.2), who unlike us knew the context of the passage and before citing it states that the poet 'compares the war to a surging sea'. That statement, and the fact that he distinguishes the military context of this image from the political one of Alcaeus fr.208, which he cites immediately afterwards, shows that we have not yet quite arrived at the concept of the ship of state:[7] on one level, Archilochus' use of the metaphor of storm may be seen as an early instance of the general use of maritime imagery in Greek literature to indicate trouble or distress, while the specific reference to a military threat echoes the comparison of the surge of Trojan warriors attacking the Achaean camp (and its ships) to a vast wave.[8] However, the references to the crew in the first person plural and to the sails of the ship in fr.106 show that the concept of the ship as some kind of community already underlies the image, though that is more likely to be the poet's *hetaireia* or war-band than any more extensive grouping.[9]

The next stage of development is the appearance of overtly political examples in Alcaeus (frr.6 and 208). Although both passages, like the Archilochus fragments, read superficially like naturalistic storm descriptions without an obvious political reference, as Heraclitus remarks, he again assures us that the passage cited is a political allegory, and this is confirmed by references to the Mytilenean tyrant Myrsilus in ancient commentators on both fragments. More importantly, each passage contains terms which hint at its true significance: Silk points out that in fr.6.2 *steichei* ('advances') is intrusive in the maritime context, being normally used of soldiers on the march, while in fr.208.1 the pun on *stasin* serves to explain the allegory 'without violation of its own terms'.[10] All of this makes it clear that we are dealing with considered and artful imagery. This is not to say that we can necessarily identify the significance of each detail in the nautical descriptions,[11] but the implication of the images as a whole is clear: whereas Archilochus is reacting to a clear external threat, here there is a shift to focus on internal dissent, or to the need for internal solidarity in the face of external dangers on all sides: Alcaeus cannot tell from where the wind is blowing.

The simple conception of the ship of state menaced from without and, perhaps, within finds an echo in the early fifth century when Herodotus attributes to Miltiades before the battle of Marathon the fear that failure to engage will cause a great *stasis* to fall upon (*empesousan*) Athenian will to resist and shake it apart (*diaseisein*), though here if there is any specific implication, it is of the treachery of a fifth column siding with the Persians, and that association with an invader implicitly locates the threat to the community predominantly outside it, as the squall surrounds the ship.[12]

Internal disorder is also a feature of an extended and again highly self-conscious passage at an earlier date in the Theognid corpus (667–82):[13] this ship is also storm-tossed by night, but in this case the danger posed by the elements is exacerbated by the behaviour of the passengers, on which the emphasis falls. The poet complains that they will not bail out the water washing over both sides of the vessel and indeed have deposed the expert (*epistamenôs*: 676) helmsman; discipline has collapsed, the cargo is being plundered and mere porters[14] are in control. This is a fairly transparent allegory of the collapse of political and social order, the reading made easy by the use of language which can be read in two senses, with reference to seafaring and to life in the polis.[15] Although the poet concludes the passage by saying that he fears that the ship will be swamped (680), his attention is clearly focused on what is happening on board, and for the first time we start to see some articulation of the ship's internal organization.

Hitherto, the helmsman has not played any significant role: in Archilochus and Alcaeus, insofar as he is implied, he is as bewildered as the other passengers, and even in the passage just discussed he has lost control (675–6).[16] Another couplet in the Theognid corpus (855–6) similarly likens the poet's city to a ship which, through the negligence or cowardice[17] of its commanders, has often listed and run close to shore: here the focus is shifting from the ship to the helmsman, though as yet only as someone to blame.[18] From now on, however, the helmsman rises to a position of increasing prominence in the ship of state.

The earliest reference to the statesman as helmsman of the ship of state which can be reliably dated is the Delphic oracle said to have been given to Solon: 'Sit in the middle of the ship, straightly guiding the helmsman's task (*kubernêtêrion ergon euthunôn*): many Athenians are your allies.'[19] Since the image of the helmsman is almost entirely confined to individuals in a position of sole direction, the oracle looks suspiciously like an exhortation to tyranny, which is how Plutarch interprets it; however, the reference to sitting in the middle of the vessel, rather than at the stern, where the rudders are, suggests that the encouragement to take power, if such it is, is being masked or muted by an implication of moderation.[20] After this, however, although the frequency with which helmsman imagery is used of divine and cosmic guidance from the beginnings of Presocratic philosophy implies that it is firmly established as a model of leadership, it is strikingly uncommon in actual political contexts: only when Pindar speaks of 'pilotings of cities' with reference to the Aleuadae of Thessaly and exhorts Hieron to 'guide the host with a just rudder' does the image refer to men exercising power in reality.[21]

By contrast, the helmsman features widely in tragedy. In Aeschylus the earliest example concerns Darius, who 'captained the host well';[22] the image suits a good king even if he is a Persian. Next come three in *Septem*, a play rich in maritime imagery: Eteocles characterizes himself at the very beginning of the play as the man who 'keeps watch over affairs, plying the rudder in the stern of the city' (2–3), and the messenger calls on him 'to screen the city like a ship's careful steersman before the storm-blasts of Ares strike' and to 'judge how to command (*nauklêrein*) the city', while Eteocles criticizes the chorus for fleeing through the city like a sailor – by implication the helmsman – rushing from his post in the stern to the prow and jeopardizing the ship.[23] The helmsman image is used to criticize dereliction of duty again in Theramenes' trial at the end of the fifth century, when Critias, denouncing Theramenes' change of sides, says that a man who deserves to live should not lead his friends into trouble and then change sides at the first reverse, but persevere until the wind turns fair: sailors who put about at any obstacle will never reach their destination.[24] The use of the helmsman image by both Eteocles and the messenger promotes a uniformly favourable view of the king in the first two-thirds of the play: the people of Thebes look to him as an experienced commander and sole possible saviour, while he in turn is duly aware of his duty and responsibilities. However, the helmsman is not automatically a positive figure: the recognition of the chorus in the *Prometheus* that 'new rudder-guiders (*oiakonomoi*) control Olympus' makes it plain that the fundamental significance of the motif is of autocratic control.[25]

Similar usages are found in Sophocles: in the opening scene of the O.T., as Campbell shows, a complex of images establishes a perception of Thebes as a storm-tossed ship with Oedipus as her helmsman, but later in the play Oedipus' anxiety comes to alarm the passengers who depend on him. Likewise in *Antigone* Creon presents himself as a model helmsman who understands the priority of the safety of the ship of state over individual interests, but when Teiresias replies to his claim that he has never previously disagreed with the seer 'and so you steered this city rightly', he is warning him that there are limits within which the helmsman's authority should operate: Creon may steer the ship, but Teiresias has a better eye for the lie of the wind.[26] Euripides likewise has the Herald warn Theseus in *Supplices* that he must follow his advice if he is to keep his city in calm water, and points to the risk of wrecking the ship of state which is also implicit in a later allusion to the adverse impact of a bad helmsman on his city's reputation.[27]

An analogous expression, *prôratês stratou* ('bow-watcher of the army') appears in a fragment of Sophocles: although strictly speaking the *prôratês* is the lookout in the bows, and the reference is to a general, the notion of the watcher in the forefront is appropriate to the proper position of the general at the head of his troops (like the shepherd leading his flock); the speaker complaining of his inability to please all of the people all of the time is presumably Agamemnon, and his reference to himself as commander is natural in a Trojan War context; no doubt Eteocles is also seen in part, perhaps primarily, as a military leader.[28]

The spatial articulation of the ship is also elaborated in a related group of passages in which the ruler's position is spoken of in terms of the helmsman's bench (*zugon*). Aegisthus (another unappealing helmsman) chides the chorus 'do you talk like that, sitting at the lowest oar, when those on the bench are masters of the vessel?', and a position of political power is described in Euripides as 'the first bench of the polis' and 'the benches of office (*zugois ... archês*)'. Similarly, the description of the gods as 'sitting on the dread bench of the helmsman (*selma*)' gives a specifically nautical slant to the epithet *hupsizugos* ('seated on a high bench') which is applied to Zeus as ruler in the *Iliad*.[29] Since helmsman imagery is, naturally, used of individuals exercising power or authority – in the real world, monarchs or leading statesmen, and in lyric and tragedy, almost always of kings or tyrants[30] – it finds ready parallels in passages concerned with divine guidance or control, some of which we have already encountered, and in cosmological passages concerned with the direction of the universe which probably derive from the use of the image in connection with the gods; by the fourth century the language of 'steering (*kubernan*)' is freely applied to the bodily microcosm as well.[31] Body and ship can also be treated as parallel cases, as when Plato assimilates the integrity of the body and of a ship in treating both the cables which undergird a ship (*hypozômata* and *entonoi*) and the sinews of a body as analogies for the vital preservation of the unity and integrity of the polis, and the anchor, too, though strictly speaking external to the ship, is also perceived as crucial to its survival when he describes the Nocturnal Council as the 'anchor of the whole city'.[32]

Although the basic notion of the helmsman image would seem to be one of control, hence the occasional appearance of helmsmen who are simply autocratic, this is usually linked to notions of superior skill or wisdom, and the generally favourable tone of the earlier, lyric examples implies that this is an image which arose in aristocratic circles, as a comfortable view of themselves which grounded their claim to authority on a basis of ability and expertise, and framed it with the appealing implication that its ultimate object was the preservation of the community. We can see this clearly if we compare the ship of state with a related image, the chariot of state: the two images are structurally similar in the way that they depict an expert individual directing a larger, complex system, to the degree that at times they came to be reciprocal, with charioteers being described as helmsmen, and vice versa, and the language of 'steering' (*euthunein*) applied to both functions alike. The charioteer, however, is directly linked through the reins to animals which he must control and direct through his superior intelligence and skill, and the image of the chariot therefore carries associations with mastery over and taming of animals which, even if they are more muted in this context, imply a more openly authoritarian attitude to those who are ruled: the frequently used motif of the 'handing over' of the reins or goad of the state implies that while the holder of the reins may change, it is natural and desirable that the demos should remain in harness, under control. The position of the helmsman is much less ambiguous, which makes the ship of state an image capable of appealing to the wider community while remaining attractive as a model of rule: the statesman knows where to go and how to get there, and a sensible demos will entrust itself to him, hence the fact that in Plato's imagery the helmsman is aligned with the doctor, as another representative of the knowledgeable expert whose authority is justified by skill.[33] Yet there were limits to that appeal: although ship of state imagery is widespread in tragedy, it is strikingly uncommon in other fifth-century genres. The passage in Herodotus cited above is the only instance in prose, and there is little in comedy either – a mention of the ship of state in *Wasps* which marks it as a cliché and a couple of allusions to that ship as storm-tossed at the end of the Peloponnesian War is a pretty thin haul.[34]

Nevertheless, it is notable that even if poets may have seen the basic image as hackneyed, it had not lost its usefulness or potency, witness the fact that the ship of state and its crew continue to furnish imagery in fourth-century oratory. However, there are some significant changes in presentation: the ship itself is mentioned relatively sparsely, and – with the important exception of Plato (below) there is almost no interest in its internal organization,[35] while in contrast the helmsman, who as we have seen played no part in fifth-century political discourse, is now widely appropriated by politicians to enhance their status,[36] or to call into question the competence of their rivals. A speaker in the Demosthenic corpus draws a contrast between the minor consequences of error on the part of the individual sailor and the universal impact of blunders by the helmsman to emphasize the need for stringent supervision of politicians like Aristogeiton (26.3). Furthermore, in an atmosphere of political failure and decline, there is naturally an increased element of mutual recrimination and self-exculpation, bringing into renewed prominence the motif of shipwreck not simply as a danger, but as actually experienced. Thus Demosthenes accuses Aeschines of having failed in his duties as a statesman, and having overturned and sunk the ship of state and, as far as he could, put it in the power of the enemy. Aeschines returns the compliment in their later encounter, remarking that whereas the Athenians punish any ferryman guilty even inadvertently of capsize by banning him from the occupation, they are proposing to allow Demosthenes to continue to be their helmsman (*apeuthunein ta koina*) although he has turned turtle both Greece and Athens. In his reply, Demosthenes evades responsibility: like the good ship-owner or captain, he has taken every reasonable precaution against foreseeable dangers, but he cannot be blamed for the typhoon of Chaeronea, an act of *tuchê* (Fortune), and anyway, he was not at the helm, since he was not in command.[37]

Thus far, we have been entirely concerned with images of the ship of state in which the authors or speakers have a personal involvement, usually an anxious one – that is, they are on board. However, there is another possible point of view, namely, that of the detached external observer. This is a position which first emerges clearly in the works of Plato. Maritime imagery is a Platonic favourite, and in political contexts, occurs almost uniquely in variations of the picture of the helmsman: though Plato acknowledges it as a commonplace, it has, as already noted, a strong appeal for him as one type of the expert practitioner whose authority should be accepted.[38] The most celebrated of Plato's maritime images, however, is a burlesque one, that in *Republic* 488a–9a. Prima facie this concerns the relationship of philosophers to politics, but it shares with Plato's other maritime images a stress on skill and knowledge, and is also self-consciously literary and rich in echoes of earlier authors. Demos is the ship-owner (*nauklêros*), the biggest and strongest individual – this a perfunctory bow to democratic theory – but he is also somewhat deaf, like Aristophanes' Demos, short-sighted and with similarly vague notions of seafaring;[39] as the 'owner' he delegates his power to the helmsman and thus though, as Adam says, not positively vicious, he must bear a share of responsibility for failure to approach the true helmsman for help. The sailors (that is, the demagogues) are squabbling for the helm in a way that recalls Thucydides' account of the situation after Pericles' death, though they have no knowledge of or education in the skill (*technê*) and indeed they claim that it is not teachable and are ready to kill anyone who says it is.[40] Instead they spend all their time doing anything to get the captain to give them the helm: persuasion, killing or throwing overboard their rivals, or overpowering him with drugs or drink. Once they get control they plunder the stores, like the crew in the version of the image in the Theognid corpus which I discussed earlier, and go on a voyage of self-indulgence which may be expected to end in disaster, though that implication is not emphasized.[41] Their definition of nautical skill is the ability to seize control, and anyone who does not possess it is 'useless' – again, there are echoes of Thucydides here, this time analysing factional conflict (*stasis*), while as to true helmsmanship, with its requirement of detailed practical knowledge, they believe it impossible to acquire, and look down on those who practise it as mere daydreamers.[42] Plato's insistence here on the helmsman's need for a knowledge of matters such as the seasons, stars and winds (488d) is picked up in the *Statesman*, where he adds to the remark that the helmsman 'preserves his fellow-sailors … by offering his expertise as law' the observation that this expertise is not set down in writing, and he drives home the point with a satirical picture of an attempt to regulate seafaring and medicine by democratic procedure, enacting rules of procedure on the basis of an open debate, and even selecting practitioners by lot and subjecting them to popular review, while absolutely forbidding scientific study of these arts.

Here again there is a contrast between genuine experts and ignorant politicians, though in this case the latter are nevertheless credited with pretensions to knowledge when the Elean Stranger remarks that many cities have gone under through the mistaken belief of their helmsmen that they knew all about the art of politics.[43] As in the image in the *Republic*, the external danger from which the helmsman protects the crew and passengers is acknowledged, but remains more in the background than is usual in maritime imagery, though it implicitly underlies the justification of his position and the need for obedience to him,[44] and by the same token, although there is a destination implicitly in view, the focus is far more on the continuing process of steering a safe course than on the ultimate arrival. In this respect there is a significant divergence between the figure of the helmsman and that of the doctor, who is more strongly associated with the ultimate objective of health (in other words, with the concept of moral improvement), but whose position is less easy to justify: people will recognize an impending storm more readily than they will acknowledge that they are sick, and the two fields of imagery thus complement one another.[45]

If we return to the origins of the image of the ship of state and survey its historical evolution, we can sketch a coherent picture of the early stages. As we have seen, our evidence suggests that it emerges in the archaic period, being absent from Homer. There is, of course, no shortage of ships in Homer, but one may suspect that the very different character of power relations, and the absence of even a vestigial sense of the polis as a citizen-state, prevented any perception of the ship as a model of the community, which indeed emerges only gradually. Perhaps, too, there was insufficient distinction between the vehicle and the tenor for the image to be effective – and Odysseus' loss of all his ships on his homeward voyage hardly made him a good role model in this respect. By contrast, in the period of colonization a ship, or a small group of them, will have been more or less literally synonymous with a community-to-be, even though the earliest examples of the analogy, in Archilochus and Alcaeus, are sectional, and apply only to a faction or *hetaireia*;[46] there again, such a grouping might well form the crew of a ship, particularly a *pentekonter*, the early fifty-oared type which could be used for both military and commercial activity. The possibility that there might be more than one ship, and the scope for interaction with the surrounding elements of wind and water, left open a convenient indeterminacy as to just what community was being represented: hence the image perfectly suited a context in which issues of community definition and membership were still in flux, while the dangers created by struggles for power were mirrored in a perception of the hazards of seafaring and the horrors of shipwreck which is already attested by the Pithekoussai krater.[47]

Given the political climate of the archaic period, it is not surprising that the element of the helmsman should have achieved prominence; what might seem to us rather more odd is that democratic Athens seems to have evolved no maritime imagery to illustrate its ideals, the more so given the abundance and variety of maritime imagery in general in this period; at first sight the trireme would seem a paradigm of communal effort and mutual reliance – Barry Strauss has presented it as an engine of thetic political consciousness[48] – and yet it never appears as such in literature. Two possible explanations from internal factors spring to mind: first, despite broad citizen participation which in times of crisis could include hoplites and, exceptionally, knights, as in the crisis mobilization for the battle of Arginusai in 406, the Athenian navy in the Peloponnesian war was not in practice crewed exclusively by citizens: metics also rowed as did *xenoi* (foreigners), both as mercenaries and conscripts and so, in emergency, did slaves, notably again at Arginusae. Furthermore, within the ship, rowers were not all the same, but divided into three types, *thalamioi*, *zugitai* and *thranitai*, with the upper tier, the *thranitai*, being paid most and the *thalamioi* at the bottom least; above them were the professionals of the *hupêresia*, the specialist deck-crew, and there is evidence that it was possible for those with talent to work their way up the trireme from bottom rower to helmsman.[49] All this will have made it hard to regard the crew of a trireme as equal in any but the most superficial sense. Against this it could be argued that for the idea which the trireme would most naturally suggest, that of 'all pulling together', complete equality was unnecessary, and indeed the image could have been used to suggest that it was irrelevant. In fact, Aristotle does remark on the basic identity of sailors, as of citizens, despite their differing capacities and specialized roles, 'since the safety of the voyage is the task of all, and each of the sailors aims at that' (*Pol.* 1276b20–7).

The other possible social and political factor is prejudice against the navy, despite Athens' public naval pride; though the *nautikos ochlos* ('naval mob') is primarily a fourth-century phenomenon, there are already shades of it in the 'Old Oligarch' and in Euripides. How widespread such views were is hard to tell, given the restriction imposed by a popular audience; no doubt they enjoyed greater popularity among the trierarchic class, who had to foot the bill, and the feelings of their peers might have influenced Athenian authors. Nevertheless, it remains hard to explain the absence of positive maritime images in drama, especially comedy, which one would expect to be aimed at a popular audience, as indeed Dicaiopolis' allusion to 'the host of *thranitai* who save the city' implies.[50]

However, there is a further possible explanation, rooted not in the circumstances of fifth-century Athens, but in the character of the image of the ship of state. If we ask ourselves what kind of ship the ship of state is, it rapidly becomes clear that it is not a trireme, a warship, but a merchantman. When triremes make a journey, it is to fulfil some further military purpose; in the ship of state, it is the voyage from A to B in itself which matters, and the safe arrival of crew and cargo. Unlike the trireme, which notoriously had to put to shore every day in all but the most exceptional circumstances,[51] the ship of state is, like a merchantman, frequently portrayed on the high seas at the mercy of the elements, since she will tend to travel directly, and whereas triremes typically operated in substantial flotillas – the only regular exceptions would be those used to carry messages or for diplomatic missions, particularly the 'state triremes' *Paralos* and *Salaminia* – the ship of state is imagined sailing alone. The roles of those on board differ sharply, too: on a trireme, skilled rowers make up the bulk of the crew and provide the essential motive power, and command rests with the trierarch rather than the helmsman. On the ship of state, the *nauklêros* may be the owner, but he must defer to the expertise of the helmsman; under the command of the helmsman in turn come the sailors, and below them are the passengers, lacking all skill and completely passive as far as the journey is concerned, while it is the wind(s) which move the vessel. If this distinction is correct, it helps to explain why the image evolved as it did, with an emphasis on hierarchical command and differing levels of expertise. It would still, presumably, have been possible to create an image of the trireme of state, but all the weight of previous usage militated against it. It must, incidentally, be due to the aristocratic origins of the image that figurative seafaring is nowhere associated with fishing, in contrast for example to the biblical tradition: for the Greeks – and indeed Romans – fishermen were conceived of as poverty-stricken and socially marginal, even though the fish trade itself could be highly lucrative.[52]

Finally, we should consider briefly the relationship of the demos to the ship of state. As we have seen, the early ship of state was not necessarily imagined as carrying the entire population of the polis, and even after the concept of the polis as community becomes firmly established, it remains possible for the demos to be located outside it and implicitly perceived as a threat to it through the use of another field of imagery, the elements. Water and weather were equally natural sources of imagery for the Greeks. In a famous fragment of his poetry Solon states that the sea's nature is *dikaiotatê*, 'most just', and that any disturbance is due to external causes, a passage often seen as indicating that the demos is naturally just unless disturbed by agitators; that reading is encouraged by parallels in Herodotus, Polybius and Livy, but other comparisons of the demos to water are less favourable: in the constitutional debate which Herodotus sets in Persia, Megabyzus, the proponent of oligarchy, argues that the *hybris* of the demos is worse than that of tyranny because it is irrational, and compares its impetuous, irrational decision-making to a river in spate, an image echoed by the Spartan Lampito in Aristophanes' *Lysistrata* and by Isocrates in the fourth century. There is also in all these cases an overtone of powerful forward impetus (like our 'surge'), perhaps more emotional than physical, which is difficult to resist.[53] Euripides uses the related image of a storm-wind to describe the demos: 'but if one slackens sail and gives way to it when it exerts itself, watching for the right moment, perhaps it may become calm; and if it abates, you may easily get from it all you want.' The implication is that the demos is wild and primitive, unmanageable by normal methods of control, but it is also implied that there are ways of handling it (as indeed the speaker succeeds in doing later in the play) and this perhaps diminishes the extent to which it can be regarded as responsible for its own actions. A similar though less positive passage by an anonymous iambic poet observes that 'the demos is a restless menace, stirred by the wind like the sea, and if there should perchance be a calm, a slight breeze rears its head and, if there is any accusation, it swallows up the citizen.' In the images both of sea and of wind the demos is seen less as uncontrollable than as unpredictable, needing intelligent and judicious management. The recurrence of the 'torrent' image in Isocrates, and passages in which Demosthenes imputes the use of comparisons between the demos and the sea to his pro-Macedonian opponents, show that this strand of anti-democratic rhetoric persisted into the fourth century.[54] Thus anti-democratic perceptions of the demos found expression through a field of imagery which implicitly located it outside the ship of state, though since the two fields were never actually combined, the exclusion was never directly presented. The existence of this option also helps to explain why the Greeks never developed a negative version of the ship of state to set beside Brant's *Narrenschiff* or the Ship of the Heresy.

Maritime imagery is hugely adaptable, lending itself to a range of essential conceptions: a community or enterprise, threats from outside or from disorder within, trouble or destruction, process and progress, arrival and safety.[55] Much of this is specifically true of the ship of state (although as we have seen, the ship of state never reaches a final destination): the image of the helmsman enjoys its successful development because it is founded on an attractive, or at any rate acceptable, conception of the community at large. Given the political climate of the archaic period, it is not surprising that the element of the helmsman should have achieved prominence, but though this development reflects the dominant ideology, it also seems to attest to some awareness of the persuasive potential of the image, while concepts of control in more direct form over animals, though clearly available and even briefly aired, enjoy a much more limited development even in their most guarded form. At the same time, the image of the ship of state lends itself to ideas of process that is ongoing or open-ended,[56] and which can be seen as menaced by a present crisis or a future threat, calling in turn for an obedient response to the helmsman's commands. It seems to establish itself only slowly in Latin literature, but the frequency in Cicero of the image of the *gubernator*, the Latin helmsman, and of the shipwreck (*naufragium*) of the Roman republic, attests to its continuing appeal,[57] and it is doubtless through Cicero's influence that it continues into post-classical literature and so comes down to us. Thus one might say that we owe it to Archilochus and Cicero between them that what regulates our country's affairs is a 'government'.

Notes

1 Though strangely, the Vikings would seem to be an exception: runic inscriptions and skaldic verse seem to have no imagery for community or leadership drawn from ships, to judge from Jesch (2001), though seafaring is frequently described figuratively (see her Index svv. kennings, metaphor), including comparisons of sailing to horsemanship (176–7), like the Greeks (below, 56–7). Perhaps there was insufficient distance between tenor and vehicle to make maritime imagery effective.
2 See the survey in Knipping (1974) 355–60, who notes that the image goes back to early Christian authors (well discussed by Rahner 1963, 55–6, 85–6, 345–53, 371–86); Noah's Ark supplied an obvious model, while masts naturally suggested the Cross, and the main part of a church building is of course still called the 'nave', from Latin *navis*. On the other hand, it does not seem to be an important element of Old Testament imagery, though West (1997) 531–2 cites a couple of examples in the Hebrew prophets of the shipwreck of the city; however, there are parallels elsewhere in Indo-European poetry: West (2007) 420–1.
3 It was reprinted three times in the year of publication, and six editions appeared in Brant's lifetime, making it the most successful work in German before Goethe's *Werther* (Killy 1988–93, s.v. Brant), and was translated into Latin, French, English and Dutch, not to mention versions in Low German: Manger (1983) 66–94 gives full details.
4 MacGregor (2010) 490–6 gives a good brief account of the artefact and its symbolism.
5 One thinks of Canning's description of Pitt the Younger as 'the pilot that weather'd the storm' in a poem written for a banquet in honour of his birthday (28 May 1802), Whitman's 'O Captain! My Captain!', or Tenniel's depiction of Kaiser Wilhelm II 'dropping the pilot' Bismarck (*Punch*, 29 March 1890). Meichsner (1983) in her study of the 'Steuermannstopos' cites examples from German politics in the era of Helmut Schmidt and Franz-Joseph Strauss; more recently, *Private Eye* used the grounding of the submarine HMS Astute in October 2010 to paint a satirical portrait of the ship of state on the rocks (no. 1274, 29 October–11 November 2010, front cover), and the centenary during a global financial crisis of the sinking of the *Titanic* was a gift to political cartoonists.

6 Fr.105, with which fr.106 is probably to be associated on the basis of correspondences between its content and the reaction of the helmsman described by Plutarch (*Mor.* 169b) after his citation of fr.105: West (1974) 128–9.
7 'he ... compares the upheavals caused by the tyrants with stormy conditions at sea' (loc. cit, tr. Campbell); commentators nevertheless have a tendency to see a political context here: even West (1974) 129 speaks of 'the impending political situation'.
8. Maritime imagery for trouble in general: LSJ s.v. χειμάζω III.2, Collard (1975) on E. *Supp.* 269; Pearson (1917) on S. *Ichn.* 267 for the medical sense; a later military example: Musaeus fr.22 DK. In Pindar, for personal political downfall: *I.* 1.36; *eudia* ('calm') for political peace: *P.* 5.10, frr.52b.52, 109.1; NB also *P.* 8.98. Trojan wave: Hom. *Il.* 15.381–9.
9 See the discussion of Gentili (1988) 213–5, who notes the mention of 'ships' in the plural in fr.106.1, which must preclude identification of the singular 'ship' of l.3 with the community as a whole.
10 Heraclitus states that 'it is Myrsilus who is indicated' (loc. cit.): cf. frr.305b 8, 306C (c). Interactive terminology: Silk (1974) 144, 123: *stasis* can mean both 'direction' of wind and 'civil strife'.
11 That is, I read these passages as extended metaphor rather than as allegories, as Gentili (1988) 197–215 does, though his full discussion is valuable nevertheless.
12 Hdt. 6.109.5; How and Wells (1928) *ad loc.* comment 'the metaphor appears to be taken from a squall ... splitting a ship and causing a leak'; for an alternative medical significance to the verb *empiptô* and on *sathron* ('rotten') in the following sentence see Scott (2005) 384 and below 71 and n.16, 80n.37. Fear of treachery must have been acute after the betrayal of Eretria to the Persians (Hdt. 6.100–1).
13 West (1971) inclines to attributing these lines to Euenus of Paros (see critical note on Euenus frr.8a-c) but their authenticity is defended by Van Groningen (1966) 267–9 and Nagy (1985) 22–3.
14 Gentili (1988) 201 translates *phortêgoi* (679) as 'stevedores' and Campbell (1967) 369 suggests 'porters', though both note that the word elsewhere means 'merchant' (Nagy 1985 adopts the neutral 'carriers of merchandise'); however, given Theognis' attitude to *nouveaux riches*, either could be denoted as base men ruling over noble (679 cf. 53–68, 183–92), and either would suit the nautical context (though NB the argument of Coffee 2006 that merchants link it more appropriately to the social situation): the point is that the inexperienced passengers are in charge, not the expert crew.
15 Silk (1974) 125 n.10: *phulakê* (676) can refer to a 'watch' at sea or to military and political 'safety', *chrêmata* (677) can denote 'cargo' and 'property' more generally, *kosmos* can mean both 'discipline' and political and social 'order'. Hence the poet presents his vignette as a riddle (681), if to us a pretty transparent one.
16 If, that is, he is specifically identified: van Groningen (1966) 266 argues that the generality of *hotis* suggests the traditional governing class rather than any individual, but Dover in Gomme, Andrewes and Dover (1945–81) IV 199 draws attention to the Ionic use of *hostis* as a relative pronoun.
17 *Kakotêta* implies both incompetence and fear, presumably of going too far from land.
18 Though his skill is already acknowledged when he is called 'wise' in Archil. fr.211 and his ability to avoid reefs is made a point of comparison at Thgn. 576.
19 No. 15 P-W, *c.* 595 BC; on the dispute over its authenticity see below 98n.29. My translation attempts to capture the flavour of the artful periphrasis: *euthunô* can mean 'make straight' literally and figuratively, as well as simply 'direct' or 'steer'.
20 Silk (1974) 122 emphasizes what he sees as the message of moderation, but NB

below 98n.29 for the reading of Plutarch (*Sol.* 14). The language of the oracle looks deliberately ambiguous, too: *euthunô* could imply the righting of injustice, like *dikaiôsei* in the oracle for Cypselus (Hdt. 5.92β2), and *epikouroi* can denote the mercenary supporters of a tyrant.

21 *P.* 10.72, 1.86, and maritime imagery applied to politics is relatively rare even in Pindar (below 113).

22 *eu podouchei* (*Pers.* 656) is Dindorf's emendation of the transmitted text, but generally accepted (see Garvie 2009 *ad loc.*): since the verb means 'guide a ship by means of the sheet', Darius was technically speaking not a helmsman, but the idea is plainly the same, and *pace* Garvie, we do not need to look for a specifically nautical historical context; Hall (1996) appositely compares 767 for the metaphor. Van Nes (1963) treats all these Aeschylean passages in fuller detail.

23 A. *Th.* 2–3, 62–4, 652; 208–10; NB Hutchinson (1985) on 62–4 and 208–10. 'Stern' now denotes the helmsman's post: *prumnêtês* ('stern-man'), an Aeschylean coinage, appears twice in *Eum.*, once of Delphos, mythical eponymous ruler of Delphi (16), and once of a putative future aggressor against Athens (765), in both passages governing a word for 'land' in the genitive; the ancient commentators gloss the word with 'Delphos, who is the lord and helmsman of the land' and 'stern-man: ruler, helmsman'.

24 X. *HG* 2.3.31 (below 180n.89); cf. Ar. *Ran.* 534–41 for Theramenes as the experienced seafarer who knows how to roll to the comfortable side of the ship: was some such expression in general circulation?

25 [A.] *P.V.* 149; for divine helmsmen cf. *Ag.* 182–3 and below, n.31.

26 Campbell (1986): see esp. *O.T.* 22–4, 103–4 and contrast 922–3: 'Look at us, passengers in the grip of fear, watching the pilot of the ship go to pieces.' (tr. Fagles); *Ant.* 189–90, part of the passage quoted with approval by Demosthenes (19.247); contrast 994, and NB Goheen (1951) 44–51, locating these images in the wider context of divine action and power.

27 E. *Supp.* 473–4, 507–9 (with Radt [1970] 345), 879–80; there is also a more neutral allusion to the storm-tossed polis at *Rh.* 245–50.

28 Fr.524 (*Polyxena*); NB Murray (1990) 13 for the ancient shepherd leading his flock.

29 A. *Ag.* 1617–8, E. *Ion* 595, *Pho.* 74–5; A. *Ag.* 182 with Fraenkel (1950) *ad loc.* The symbolic importance of the stern as the helmsman's station is also reflected in a passage in Aeschylus' *Suppliants* in which the suppliant Danaids call on the king to 'respect the stern of the city thus garlanded' (345), on which Tucker (1889) comments (his line 316) 'i.e. that part of the ship of state in which the places of honour are situated'.

30 In Thgn. 855–6 and A. *Ag.* 1617–18 we find helmsmen in the plural, in the former case with reference, unusually, to oligarchy; in the latter passage the reference is to the joint tyranny of Aegisthus and Clytemnestra.

31 Divine helmsmen: A. *Ag.* 182–3, [A.] *P.V.* 515, S. *Aj.* 35, *TrGF Adesp.* fr.348g; Pi. *O.* 12.3, *P.* 4.274 (below 113), 5.122–3, frr.40, 214; B. 13.185; Pseudepicharmeia fr.240.3KA; Antiphon 1.13; Pl. *Smp.* 187a1, 197e 1 (Eros), 197b3 (Zeus); *R.* 573d4–5 (tyrant Eros), *Ti.* 42e3 and cf. *Criti.* 109c2–4, *Lg.* 709b8; cf. Anaxandr. 4 *oiaka strephôn* 'turning the rudder' of Tyche (Fortune), and Men. fr.372; steering the universe: Anaximander A15 (with Guthrie 1962–81, I 88), Heraclitus B41, 64, Parmenides B12 with Lloyd (1966) 272–4; *kubernan* linked with *kratein* of the directing element in cosmos: Diogenes B5; Guthrie (1962–81) II 369 notes the religious colour of Diogenes' language here. For the extension in Plato of *kubernan*

32 P. *Lg.* 945c (and for the concept cf. *R.* 616c); 961c. The proverbial principle that two anchors were better than one (Pi. *O.* 6.100–1; [D.] 56.44 with Carey and Reid 1985; van Nes 1963, 112–13) could be cited in Euripides as an argument for the superiority of joint rule over monarchy (fr.774 [*Phaethon*]), though the image of the two councils as twin anchors in Plut. *Sol.* 19.2 seems more likely to derive from Plutarch than Solon (see the cautious remarks of van Nes 1963, 74–5). It was presumably the implications of solidity and stability which led the Seleucid monarchs, though essentially rulers of a land power, to adopt the anchor as part of their symbolism (App. *Syr.* 56, Just. *Epit.* 15.4.3–9).

and its compounds to direction and rule on all planes of existence see below 174n.50; the verb is already applied to control of the body in fifth-century medical writing (Hp. *Vict.* 10; below 131n.60).

33 See below 96n.22 for helmsman and charioteer as interchangeable, and 86–7 for a fuller treatment of the underlying divergences between the two; for the subtler differences between helmsman and doctor in Plato, NB 150–1. It is rare for the crew or passengers to be depicted as disorderly, as in Theognis (above) or Plato's satirical ship of state in *R.* 488–9 (which alludes to that passage: below): insofar as the demos is unruly and a threat to the ship, it is more likely to be characterized as a force of nature, wind or wave (below 61).

34 Ar. *Vesp.* 29, *Ran.* 361, 704, the latter in fact derived from Archilochus: Dover (1993) *ad loc.* Taillardat (1962) 381 describes the ship of state in comedy as 'tout à fait banale', in contrast to the chariot of state. *Eccl.* 109 seems to refer to the ship of state lying dead in the water, but the expression verges on the proverbial (Ussher 1973 *ad loc.*) and may in any case be a sexual double entendre: Henderson (1991) 162.

35 Demades alludes to the ship of state positively at fr.29 (Athens is the greatest vessel [*skaphos*] in Greece), but more frequently describes it as in danger of sinking (frr.13 and perhaps 42–3; cf. fr.17 [below]). D. 9.69, calling on the Athenians to exert themselves for the ship's safety while they can, draws a rare distinction between helmsman and sailors. Other more developed Demosthenic images imply the ship's existence: in *Ep.* 1.8 he refers to different policies for salvation in terms of a choice between rowing and sailing (for which choice cf. Men. fr. 183); in 18.281 he compares the loyalty of a politician to 'riding at the same [sc. anchor] as the masses' and in fr.13.16 he refers to the demos as feeling seasick, either at its situation in general (so the ancient commentator) or because of the incompetence of some other helmsman.

36 Cf. Demades' retort to the criticism of having only one son that it was better to leave behind one trierarch than ten rowers (fr.56); also below 156.

37 D. 19.250; Aeschin. 3.158; D. 18.194: for the argumentation here NB Yunis (2001) *ad loc.*; cf. Demades' defence of his policies in terms of shipwreck in fr.17 (below 156). Aeschines' allusion to ferrying is apposite, since because of its importance it tended to be heavily regulated: Constantakopoulou (2007) 222–6.

38 External observer: Anderson (1966) 87–8. Commonplace in Plato: *Plt.* 297e, *Lg.* 905e cf. 906e and below 148; for full discussion of the helmsman as expert, see below 150–1. The view of the ship of state from an external viewpoint was to prove popular in later political analysis: one may compare Polybius' image of Athens as a ship with no-one at the helm (6.44.3–7; NB military examples at 3.81.11, 10.33.5, 11.19.3) and numerous passages in Cicero (e.g. *Sest.* 99, *Prov. Cons.* 38, *Att.* 2.7.4, *Fam.* 1.9.21, 16.27.1, *Q.F.* 1.1.5); see also below, n.57.

39 For the nod to democracy cf. the 'large and powerful beast' of 493a, but *gennaion*

40 ('honest' or 'worthy') in 488c4 is ironic (though perhaps also an echo of *kubernêtên ... esthlon* at Thgn. 675–6, and that passage or this one is presumably unconsciously echoed when *gennaion kubernêtên* is used positively at *Plt.* 297e11); Aristophanes uses the same word for partial deafness (*hypokôphon* 488b1) of his own Demos at *Eq.* 43. Socrates' mention of 'a ship or ships' at 488a7–8 presumably implies that what is true of Athens may apply to other poleis too.

40 Demos as 'placid and not deliberately vicious': Adam (1902) on 488a7; post-Periclean power-struggle: Thuc. 2.65.11. Socrates credits the Athenians with the belief that political expertise cannot be taught in the *Protagoras* (319a-d, esp. d6–7; cf. 319d–20b for the failure of politicians to educate their sons, and below 179n.86).

41 Plundering the cargo: Thgn. 667 (above 54); unlike the poet, Plato does not spell out the consequences of anarchy aboard ship, presumably because he wants to focus attention on the continuing situation of misrule. Equally, the evocation of luxury and self-indulgence attaches here to the crew/demagogues rather than referring to the negative consequences of indulging the demos as in the *Gorgias* or the sketch of the democratic constitution and individual in book 8. For Plato's knowledge of Theognis, NB *Men.* 95d–6a, *Lg.* 630a; Levine (1985) 195–6 and cf. X. *Smp.* 2.4, and see also Lane Fox (2000) 45–51 for the currency of the Theognid corpus in the symposiastic culture of late fifth-century Athens.

42 The assessment of nautical ability in terms of the ability to seize power (488d) has much in common with the pragmatic revaluation of ethical terminology described in Thuc. 3.82.4–5; daydreamers: *meteôroskopon te kai adoleschên* ('a stargazer and idle chatterer') 488e4–9a1, echoed almost verbatim at *Plt.* 299 b7–8 (below). Hunter (2012) 68–79 has an illuminating discussion of this passage from a Platonic perspective and reaches similar conclusions on the literary influences at work here.

43 *Plt.* 296e4–7a2 (tr. Rowe); democratic seafaring: 297e–9d and below 171n.33; cities go under: 302ab; Schofield (2006) 122–5 explores the philosophical implications.

44 The idea of constant peril at sea is most explicitly evoked at *Laws* 758ab; for the argument, cf. X. *Anab.* 5.8.20, Arist. *Pol.* 1320b33–21a1 (below 171n.35).

45 Hence the kinds of misdeed which the imaginary democrats of the *Statesman* seek to repress also differ: the doctor's treatments are inherently painful, whereas the charges against the helmsman – marooning passengers, throwing them overboard, causing shipwrecks – arise from malice or incompetence (298ab).

46 Cucchiarelli (2004) 195–200 rightly insists on the specificity of the situation and of Alcaeus' personal point of view, in contrast to the stock 'ship of state' of later periods; for the focus on the *hetaireia* see further below 97n.26.

47 See further below, 85–6; the evolving definition of the archaic polis and its members are discussed by the contributors to Duplouy & Brock (forthcoming). Pithekoussai Krater: Ischia Sp.1/1 (*c.* 725–700 BC); see e.g. Boardman (1998) pl.161 for an image.

48 Strauss (1996), though we should remember that oligarchic states such as Corinth and Aegina were also major naval powers. It is curious, too, how few warships in the fourth-century naval catalogues (*IG* I^2 1604–32) were named after democratic ideals: we do find *Dêmokratia* (two vessels of that name in *IG* I^2 1607), *Parrhêsia* ('Free Speech') and other less exclusively democratic values (*Eleutheria* ['Freedom'] *Homonoia* ['Unity'], *Dikaiosunê* ['Justice'], *Philotimia* ['Competition']), but these represent only a small fraction of the names attested.

49 Citizens as rowers: [X.] *Ath.Pol.* 1.2, Plut. *Cim.* 11.2–3, *Per.* 11.4; hoplites: Thuc. 3.16.1; knights: X. *HG* 1.6.24; metics: Thuc. 1.143.1, 3.16.1, 7.63.3; foreign mercenaries: Thuc. 1.121.3, and conscripts: Thuc. 7.13.2; slaves: Thuc. 7.13.2, X.

HG 1.6.24; Graham (1992), (1998). Tiers of rowers: Ar. *Ach.* 162 with Olson (2002), *Ran.* 1074 with the scholia, Morrison and Coates (1986) 132–51, esp. 136–8; pay for *thranitai*: Thuc. 6.31.3; for *thalamioi*: ΣAr. *Ran.* 1074; *hypêresia*: Morrison (1984); career structure: Ar. *Eq.* 541–4 (with Gilula [1989]), and cf. Pollux *Onom.* 1.95.

50 *nautikos ochlos*: Pl. *Lg.* 707a-d, Arist. *Pol.* 1304a17–24, 1327a40-b15; in the fifth century: [X.] *Ath.Pol.* 1.2 (and cf. Gigante 1957, esp. 70–1, for similar views in another apparently contemporary pamphlet); E. *Hec.* 606–8, *I.A.* 914; the same phrase is put in the mouths of Athenian oligarchs in Thuc. 8.72.2. NB also below 139n.125 for the rarity of visual representations of the navy in fifth-century art. Navy in comedy: Ar. *Ach.* 162–3; likewise Demos in *Knights* is imagined to have the calloused backside of a Salamis veteran (781–5), and paying the rowers in full is part of the 'happy ending' of that play (1366–8).

51 Highlighted by Gomme (1933).

52 The paradox is suggestively discussed by Purcell (1995). Xenophon briefly mentions the trireme as a model of orderly disposition at *Oec.* 8.8, but follows this with a much more elaborate account of a Phoenician merchantman as a model of organisation in a complex system (8.11–17 with Pomeroy 1994 *ad loc.*; for the theme cf. below 188n.147).

53 This negative characterization of water as a force is very persistent: as Polly Toynbee remarks, 'reason is irrelevant: the water metaphors always win. Images of human tidal waves of asylum seekers also swamp the facts' (*Guardian* 7 April 2004); cf. Charteris-Black (2005) 23–4 on the use of similar language by Norman Tebbit with reference to immigration.

54 Solon fr.12; cf. Hdt. 7.16α1; Plb. 11.29.9–10, 21.31.9–11; Livy 28.27.11, 38.10.5 (*vulgata similitudo*); demos a stormy sea: E. *Or.* 698–701, Iamb. Adesp. 29D; for parallels see below 88, 120 and 159, and cf. Cic. *Rep.* 1.65.4, Sen. *Her. F* 170 for Roman disparagement of the *mobile vulgus* by analogy with the sea.

55 e.g. Steiner (1986) 73–5 on the voyage of the poem in Pindar, and cf. West (2007) 40–5 for Indo-European images of poetry as a ship or other modes of travel.

56 Contrast the journey metaphors of contemporary politicians such as Tony Blair and Bill Clinton analysed by Charteris-Black (2005) 130–5, 152–4, which generally do envisage arrival, presumably because they are applied to particular policy goals within the constraints of a finite electoral term.

57 Fantham (1972) surveys early Latin maritime imagery (19–26) and looks in more detail at political examples in Ciceronian rhetoric (117–9, 126–8). Even allowing for the extent of the Ciceronian corpus, the number of figurative and, in particular, specifically political examples cited by the lexica (*TLL* s.vv. *gubernaculum, gubernatio, gubernator, guberno, portus* (B); *OLD* s.v. *naufragium*) is striking, and these entries suggest a process by which, under his influence, political examples slowly percolate into historiography (e.g. Liv. 4.3.17, 24.8.12–13, V. Max. 9.15.5) and imperial rhetoric, particularly panegyric, and thence into the language of the Christian church (though the latter must also be influenced by wider use of such imagery with reference to divinities).

5

The Body Politic

Beset by sickness and death in reality, the cities of ancient Greece were also subject to a range of symbolic and metaphorical diseases, among them disorder in the state (*stasis*) perceived as a sickness of the body politic. This image is not part of the Homeric repertoire and appears first in Greek literature in the early sixth century with Solon and Theognis;[1] it is thus the latest of the major complexes of political imagery to emerge and, like the ship of state, appears to be a distinctively Greek conception.[2] It is also significant, I think, that it emerges at a time when the sense of the polis as a community is becoming stronger and more inclusive than was the case at the time when the ship of state makes its appearance.[3] Solon and Theognis already strike the notes which will be characteristic of the image to the end of the classical period: first, there is very little anatomical detail in the picture of the body politic; and secondly, the overriding concern is with a disorder in that body which is increasingly identified with civil strife (*stasis*). As we shall see, it is also typical of the archaic period that the idea of treatment is less prominent than that of disease.

Indeed, when Theognis speaks of Megara as 'pregnant', he evokes a situation in which no treatment may be required, yet one in which the outcome is uncertain and potentially hazardous.[4] Elsewhere, he and Solon speak of a *helkos*, a wound or a sore: in Theognis the identity of the body afflicted by it is not spelt out, but Solon says explicitly that it 'is coming on the whole city' because of the behaviour of leading citizens, and the sense that this is a wound which they are inflicting is more in evidence.[5] Theognis also suggests the possibility of treatment, since he uses the word *pharmakon* ('remedy', whence our 'pharmacy'), though what that might be is far from clear; conversely, there are hints that Solon might have claimed to have avoided any medical intervention for fear of harming the patient, i.e. Athens.[6]

Thereafter, the tendency is for medical imagery to become more general, and by the fifth century the malady affecting the polis is normally simply *stasis*, dissension, civic strife, or in extreme cases civil war, to the point that the identification becomes almost conventional.[7]

It is of a piece with the generality of this identification that the disease (*nosos*) of *stasis* is not any disease in particular, in contrast to the modern usage of allusions to specific maladies such as tuberculosis, cancer and AIDS described by Sontag (1991). In one sense, this is not surprising at all, since classical Greek doctors apparently did not identify and name as such any infectious disease. What is more striking is that the disease of civil strife has no aetiology and few, if any symptoms: other than the term *helkos* which we have already encountered, the 'wound' or 'ulcer' which appears as an alternative term, or perhaps a precursor, to *nosos* ('disease') in the earliest instances of the image in Solon and Theognis, and Theognis' allusion to pregnancy, the only specific symptom associated with the political disease is swelling (*oidein*), applied to political upheaval in Herodotus; in the fourth century, Plato and Demosthenes add to the register of symptoms inflammation, swelling, fracture and sprain, but this is still hardly a great haul.[8]

Equally striking is the absence from the medical metaphor of any anatomical detail: the body politic is articulated only to the extent of distinguishing the head, as seat of authority, from the rest of the body. Thus, an oracle allegedly given to the Argives shortly before Xerxes' invasion (Hdt. 7.148.3) distinguishes between the body and the head: 'hated by your neighbours, dear to the immortal gods, sit on your guard, holding your spear drawn in and guard the head, for the head will save the body.' The oracle's instruction to guard the head is interpreted by commentators as a reference to the remnants of the Argive ruling class laid waste by the Spartans after the battle of Sepeia, the body being the mass of the population, including the so-called slaves.[9] A near-contemporary oracle given by Delphi to the Athenians (Hdt. 7.140.2) enumerates the parts of the body more fully: 'The head is unstable, the trunk totters; nothing – not the feet below, nor the hands, nor anything in between – endures; all is doomed'; here, however, the detail is elaborated for rhetorical emphasis, to underline the imminent danger of defeat at the hands of the Persians, and not to make a political point. In the same way, the nocturnal council of Plato's *Laws* is the intellect of the state, which the junior guardians serve as sense-organs[10] and, by inversion, the head governs the microcosm of the body in the *Timaeus*.[11] It might be held that the reference in an oracle given to the Spartans to a 'lame kingship' (*tên chôlên basileian*; X. *HG* 3.3.3) should furnish the body politic with legs, but Lysander's interpretation, that the lameness of which the Spartans were warned referred to a general dysfunction of the monarchy, is supported by other examples of the broad semantic field of the language of lameness; if there is a more specific point, it lies in an association between bastardy and a lack of the physical integrity particularly expected of kings.[12] The phrase *to tês poleôs sôma* ('the body of the state') itself does not actually appear until the later fourth century, in Deinarchus and Hypereides, by which time other orators have already attributed a soul to the city, either its constitution or its laws.[13] The detailed description of wounds in the *Iliad* attests to at least a basic knowledge of internal anatomy early in the archaic period, and so while we should acknowledge the very limited impact made by dissection before the Hellenistic period, and the persistence of unscientific conceptions of the internal economy of the body,[14] the failure to exploit what would seem to us the full potential of the image cannot simply be ascribed to ignorance, and must be explained in terms of other factors.

In fact, we do find parallels drawn between parts of the body and other human associations: Xenophon compares the dysfunction of strife between brothers to dysfunction in co-ordinate bodily systems such as the hands or feet. The image is also applied to military contexts: Polyaenus reports that Iphicrates compared the parts of an army to the parts of the body, the head being the general, without which the army would not simply be lame or maimed (as it would be by the loss of hands [i.e. light-armed troops] or feet [i.e. cavalry]) but helpless, and Aesop makes a similar comparison in a fable about the stomach and the feet, the stomach in this case somewhat surprisingly being the general. We might rather expect the lesson drawn from the same sort of analogy by Menenius Agrippa in Livy, that despite its apparent passivity, the stomach has a vital part to play, but in fact it is hard to find a parallel in the Greek world for his commendation of the Senate/stomach as 'sleeping partner'.[15]

Vagueness about anatomical and clinical particulars is paralleled by the very general language in which the disease of civil strife is described. To the symptomatic terms that I have already mentioned, we can add *arrôstia* of illness in general, the language of 'attacks' of disease, and *sathros* ('unsound'), *hupoulos* ('festering') and – perhaps – *eklelusthai* ('be faint, fail') of conditions of sickness.[16] None of these words can really be considered technical; even the language of Thucydides' description of the Plague of Athens, though it is now generally conceded that, in Adam Parry's words, it 'is not entirely, is not even largely, technical', is a great deal more varied and circumstantial, and the language of the Hippocratic writers, for example in the roughly contemporary *Epidemics* 1 and 3, is substantially more densely technical than that.[17] As with anatomical knowledge, the expressive resources were available, had they been wanted.

Indeed, a wider comparison between accounts of the sickness of *stasis* and the literary genre of the plague description is instructive. In examples of the latter, such as those in Thucydides, Lucretius and Virgil, the enumeration of the many forms and symptoms of the disease serves to reinforce the impression of its intractability, both rhetorically, by an overwhelming enumeration of details, and in a more explicit manner, by creating an impression of an enemy too versatile and cunning for its human opponents to master; one might compare modern presentations of viral mutation or the development of 'super-bacteria' resistant to all antibiotics. In contrast, the bare assertion in the imagery that the city is sick simply establishes the existence of the disease, leaving scope for the possibility of a more hopeful prognosis. Furthermore, literary plagues are epidemics which strike a whole community, passing by contagion or infection from one individual to another – and indeed sometimes from species to species – but this dynamic is absent from the imagery, which is only concerned with the presence of the disease within the single organism of the body politic.

I now turn from examining the descriptive qualities of medical imagery to consider its implications, which are more closely linked to the other side of the medical coin: the issue of treatment. Here I shall begin with Plato and work backwards, partly because his attitudes are fairly obvious and uncontroversial, and partly because they are much more in line with later usage of this sort of imagery.[18] Plato's medical imagery is based on two basic concepts: the idea of health or dysfunction within an organic unity, and the equation of those in political authority with doctors, an example of Plato's fondness for craft analogies to describe the practice of philosophical statecraft. That it is particularly dear to his heart is suggested by the close correspondence between passages in the *Republic* and the *Seventh Letter* which compare the Athenian democracy to a patient whom it is pointless to treat until he changes his way of life; in the *Seventh Letter*, the image is used to justify Plato's own refusal to intervene in Athenian politics.[19]

This field of imagery offers Plato a number of advantages in presenting his programme. Health is a universally recognized good, and therefore rhetorically persuasive; however, it is not universally understood, and the layman would therefore be well advised to submit to the judgment of the expert, not only as to what constitutes health, but also as to the most appropriate therapy for any given malady. Finally, since the good of the organism as a whole is what matters, it is reasonable to submit parts of the body to painful processes, or even to remove them altogether, if that is what is required to restore health. Medical imagery thus adds to the general claim of the craft analogies to superior wisdom and expertise a charter for intervention which the persuasive force of the concept of health makes it hard to resist (always provided that the diagnosis is accepted), and against which the idea of a living organism (with unspoken overtones of a finite lifespan) makes it difficult to temporize. This is true whether it is the maintenance or the restoration of health which is at issue: at times, as in the *Gorgias*, Plato distinguishes the former as the province of the trainer, but in the real world of flawed constitutions it is the doctor who is much more likely to be needed.[20] However, as we have just seen, Plato knew from personal experience that he would not necessarily be called on, and similarly in the *Gorgias* (521e–2a) he makes Socrates the true legislator identify himself with a doctor victimized by a pandering confectioner.

While the patient is expected to seek out the doctor and submit himself to him, he must not necessarily expect to have his treatment explained: in the *Laws*, Plato outlines two forms of treatment, corresponding to two modes of legislation, the authoritarian and the persuasive, and in the *Republic* rulers are the doctors of expert judgment who will know how to use the remedy (*pharmakon*) of lying.[21] There is also the expectation that medical treatment will be painful: Plato does not refer specifically in a political context to surgery and cautery ('the twin horrors of pre-anaesthetic surgery', as Dodds calls them) but references to them elsewhere in his works are common, particularly with the implication of necessary submission to a painful but beneficial process, and when the Athenian Stranger remarks in the *Laws* that the patients of doctors and trainers are content if they achieve their results without great pain, he is implicitly providing an apologia for the use of force or coercion.[22] The image of purging also occurs several times in Plato in a strikingly modern sense. In the *Statesman* the Eleatic Stranger suggests that true rulers may on their own authority carry out violent purges 'killing or else expelling individuals'. In the *Laws* the description of purges is superficially more moderate, distinguishing the gentler from the harsher, but even the milder option is admitted to be essentially exile under a euphemistic screen. As noted earlier, whatever is good for the body politic as a whole can be justified, and the philosopher-statesman is the only individual in a position to make that judgment.[23]

Contemporary political discourse in the fourth century seems to reflect the Platonic model, though inevitably in a debased form.[24] We have already seen how the orators mimic Plato in offering a slightly richer medical language than that of the earlier period; they also want to be seen as doctors of the state. The model of expertise not only enables them to claim the thanks of the demos for their medical services, but also to disparage their rivals: Demosthenes, in an ironic variant of the image, compares Aeschines' political wisdom after the event to the case of a doctor who fails to advise a sick man of the proper treatment while he is alive, but goes to the funeral and there specifies the régime which would have saved him. Medical imagery can also reflect competition between self-professed experts: Demosthenes likens the theoric distributions of his rivals to invalid food, which neither gives the patient strength nor permits him to expire, while Aeschines, accusing Demosthenes of divisiveness, contrasts his policy of opening new wounds (*helkopoiein*) with the amnesty of 403.[25] Like Plato, the orators seek authority for violent intervention by cautery or surgery to dispose of opponents whom they represent as cancers or ulcers, and resort in increasingly violent language to images of the demos being 'hamstrung' and Athens 'mutilated'.[26]

The medical imagery of the fourth century is, of course, shaped by personal interest, and usually wielded by men with an axe to grind.[27] Plato, with his sense of intellectual and moral superiority, regards the whole of practical politics as in need of his expert treatment, while Demosthenes and his contemporaries wrangle in a squabble for access to the patient which Galen would have had no trouble in recognizing. However, if one goes back to an earlier and less self-interested discourse, the picture is, I believe, rather different.[28]

One important difference is that earlier medical imagery displays little moral aspect. In this regard it is very different from the discourse which Sontag presents as associated with cancer in modern times. For Plato, of course, the practice of the statesman-doctor is tied up with the health of the soul and the moral good of the community, as emerges clearly from the discussion of punishment in the *Gorgias* (477e–79e), where it is the judge who is identified with the doctor, but such a clear-cut moral agenda is much less in evidence before his time. It is certainly true that Solon perceives the sickness about to befall Athens as divinely inflicted in response to the misdeeds of Athens' leading citizens, and Theognis' fears of the 'birth' of a man – by implication, a tyrant – 'to make straight our evil *hubris*' likewise suggests some form of requital for immorality which affects the wider community.[29] Such a perception is in line with the belief expressed in the earliest Greek poetry that the health and well-being of the whole community are dependent on the character of its rulers, so that it will flourish if they are virtuous but will suffer if they are wicked, and with the analogous perception of disease as frequently of supernatural origin.[30] However, such a perception is not apparent in later cases of the sickness of civil strife, partly no doubt because the figure of the charismatic leader has more or less disappeared. Certainly by the fifth century the sickness of civil strife is not presented as sent by the gods or as a judgment on the body suffering it or as a reflection of general corruption. Whereas the plagues visited by angry gods on the Achaeans at Troy in the first book of the *Iliad* or on Oedipus' Thebes reflect fundamental problems in the health of the community on a religious or ethical level, and so naturally have a moral dimension, the plagues and blights first threatened and then abjured by the Furies in Aeschylus' *Eumenides* embrace civil strife, but only within the wider framework of their relationship with the city of Athens and its moral values.[31] It should also be noted that the sickness of *stasis* is always denoted by the neutral word *nosos* ('disease') rather than *loimos* ('plague'); the latter term embraces a complex of disasters which include failures of crops and of human and animal reproduction, just as the benefits of a good ruler extend to healthy reproduction and bountiful crops.[32]

It would not be surprising if there remained in Greek minds in later periods a residual concern that the moral character of their leaders might carry risks for the city at large, as Parker argues, but it is far from clear that this carries implications of pollution or contagion, as Connor has argued, suggesting that there is an association between the demolition of the houses of those guilty of tyranny or treachery and the treatment of offences which clearly did attract pollution or divine vengeance, such as murder and temple robbery.[33] While the process may well represent the same objective in both cases, namely the complete removal of the criminal and his *oikos* (household) from the city, the motives may well be different. Where pollution is at issue, it is obviously important to eject or destroy any trace of the perpetrator from the polis lest the polis come to harm through contagion: in the case of a traitor, however, it makes equally good sense to regard the razing of the house and ejection of the offender's body without burial as a retaliation against one who has betrayed the community by expunging that person and his *oikos* from that community.[34] Insofar as traitors and other political malefactors have made themselves subject to *agos* (divine retribution), this is the product of curses which the community itself has pronounced as a pre-emptive sanction to prevent such behaviour and which they can hardly have believed would rebound on them.[35] Furthermore, almost all the evidence suggestive of a belief that bad leaders could bring disaster on their cities through a form of pollution derives from the heated and self-serving context of later fourth-century Attic oratory, at a nadir in Athens' fortunes which fostered recrimination and personal attacks.[36] As we have seen, for the politicians of the fourth century, medical imagery is associated with mutual charges of disloyalty, perceived as a disease in the body politic, or perhaps rather portrayed as such by speakers in order to seek a pretext for action by the demos against their rivals; this aspect is largely absent from the earlier imagery, and where it appears, is almost always applied to loyalty to the Greek cause in the Persian wars rather than to a polis.[37] Where a city's leaders are – or turn – bad, there are purely pragmatic reasons for civic surgery, above all in the case of tyrants, who are unquestionably morally repugnant; yet even in this case, while it is true that tyrants are regularly presented as the worst disease which can befall a city,[38] a city suffering from a tyrant does not seem to attract blame expressed in medical terms, and the same should apply *a fortiori* to references to other individual figures identified with disease.

One obvious objection to this view of sickness imagery would arise from the often perceived affinity between Thucydides' account of the Plague at Athens and his account of the *stasis* in Corcyra. Given that both seem to be presented as quasi-case histories, it has been suggested that he regarded the events in Corcyra as a kind of epidemic, and in both cases there are clear allusions to the collapse of moral standards.[39] However, these allusions are concrete, part of the actual experience brought about by an epidemic in one instance and chronic civil strife in the other. The two instances are parallel and co-ordinate, witness the very similar treatment they receive, with a symptomatic description, indications that both accounts are intended to have a prognostic function, and a recurrence of medical language in the introduction of his analysis of *stasis* in the Peloponnesian War; accordingly, the two are at most to be regarded as both symptoms of some sort of meta-disease, the wholesale collapse of civil society.[40] Moreover, Thucydides' reaction in both cases is direct (and disapproving): he regrets the abandonment of moral norms resulting from the disruption of society in both cases, but that reaction stands on its own, and is not extrapolated into any kind of global judgment.

This conclusion, if correct, may be aligned with another apparent difference, namely a much vaguer attitude to treatment, and a much gentler one. Agamemnon threatens to remedy any political malady which has developed in Argos during his absence by surgery: 'where anything is in need of healing remedies (*pharmaka*), we shall endeavour to turn to flight the harm of the disease by sage use either of knife or of cautery' (A. *Ag.* 848–50 tr. Fraenkel), but this threat is unique in the fifth century (and placed in the mouth of a not entirely sympathetic character).[41] Much more representative is Pindar's appeal to Arkesilas in his fourth *Pythian*: 'You are a most seasonable healer, and healing Apollo (*Paian*) honours your glory. You must tend the ulcer's wound with the application of a gentle hand.' Reconciliation is the keynote of the poem, and it is natural to expect Apollo's support for a Pythian victor.[42] If the inference from Plutarch that Solon spoke of refraining from giving medical treatment to Athens in the city's delicate state is sound (above, 69), that implies an appreciation that treatment is itself traumatic which engenders a cautious attitude rather than a radical one. In general, indeed, references to treatment are confined to vague mentions of *pharmakon* ('remedy') or *iasthai* ('to heal'), even when a specific measure is in view, as in Nicias' appeal to the *epistates* (presiding officer) in the Sicilian debate to re-open a debate already settled by vote and so 'act as physician (*iatros*) to the city when she has made a bad decision'.[43] Indeed, in the majority of references to the sickness of *stasis* in the sixth and fifth centuries, the figure of the doctor does not appear, and there is no specific allusion to treatment. Nevertheless, I suggest that there *is* a specific medical significance to the image, and that it resides in the concept of the internal economy of the body as a balance between humours, and of the need to maintain or re-establish a proper balance between them to promote or restore health.

This concept surfaces in political imagery in the late fifth century in the pages of Thucydides, when Alcibiades, perhaps as a riposte to the foray of Nicias into medical imagery just mentioned, speaks of 'the inferior, the ordinary and the really acute blended together (*xygkrathen*)' as being the strongest combination in the city; later in the work the historian himself observes of the government of the 5000 that it was 'a moderate blending (*xygkrasis*) of the interests of the few and the many'. Euripides, too, speaks of a blending (*sygkrasis*) of rich and poor, which shows that the concept was in general circulation by this time.[44] The inverse image, Alcmaeon's account of the internal economy of the body as an *isonomia* (equality of political rights) between the humours, permits us to trace the link between the two fields back to about the middle of the fifth century.[45] The later use of the image has been very well discussed by de Romilly, who analyses the close link between ideas of balance and blending on the one hand, and of organic unity on the other in early Hippocratic treatises such as *On the Nature of Man* and *On Ancient Medicine* and their application to political thought. These concepts of mixture and balance are not alien to Plato either, although they are not often expressed in a specifically medical form and seem to float between medicine, the symposium and even music.[46] However, if the scientific articulation of ideas of mixture is a product of the fifth century, I suggest that the basic principles behind such ideas can be applied to the image of sickness in the polis from its beginnings.

Of course, the application of the detailed concepts to political thought cannot antedate their articulation by the medical writers, but that does not necessarily preclude an intuitive appreciation of the organic unity of the body politic or of the need for balance and harmonious unity within it, and indeed such an appreciation of the value of blending and combination seems to be reflected in the use of words such as *mignumi* ('mix') and *amiktos* ('unmixed', hence 'unsociable, savage').[47]

Such an interpretation would help to explain why the figure of the doctor plays a minor role in the early development of the image and – in contrast to the common later use of disease imagery as an interventionist's charter – the approach to treatment is much more cautious. Furthermore, the perspective from which disease in the polis is usually viewed is that of the community itself, or else of a non-expert observer looking at the community as a whole. From such a perspective, and considering the body politic holistically (and we have already noted the late and limited development of the hierarchical anatomical model of the body politic), the important task is to remedy the dysfunction in it with minimal harm to the body. How exactly this is to be done is not spelt out, but the implication is that radical measures are not likely to be favoured; better to leave the body to heal, encouraged by a suitable regimen. In fact this is in line with the sort of treatment often implied by early Hippocratic writings for infectious diseases, in which interventions are cautious and relatively infrequent;[48] the only difference is that it seems to be implicit in the imagery that as often as not it will be the patient who knows what is best. A further attraction of the concept of mixture is that the optimal composition will vary from case to case or patient to patient and so is a matter of informed judgment, and indeed there is a degree of flexibility in the concept itself, which may be imagined sometimes as a tempering of a powerful element by a milder one (as in the dilution of wine with water in the symposium) and sometimes as the concoction of a recipe from a range of ingredients.[49]

If this approach is correct, the fundamental concept behind the image of the sickness of the body politic is of dysfunction within an organic unity and of the need for this to be remedied; in its origins, however, it is the patient who occupies the central position, and the patient's interests, *as perceived by the patient*, which are paramount. Detailed diagnosis is also much less important than prognosis, and this, as Sontag remarks 'is always, in principle, optimistic'.[50] That does not make the image as a whole positive, of course – the possibility of a cure does not guarantee a cure in any particular case, and the patient may die, or remain a chronic invalid – but it is free from the authoritarian tone of much medical imagery.[51] In these terms, the sickness of civil strife is a problem and a misfortune, but not a sign of pollution or corruption, and to draw attention to the disease is to issue a rallying-cry for the highest form of community medicine.

Notes

1 The language of suffering as illness appears in Archil. fr.13, but without any clear political reference. Lloyd (2003) 8–13 (cf. 147 for Plato) speaks in terms of 'semantic stretch' rather than metaphor; however, where such language is applied

2 Distinctive within the Western tradition, that is: early imperial China has its own very different conception of the body politic, founded, according to the tenets of Chinese medicine, on an ideal of '"free flow", interaction, intercommunication between parts, with each fulfilling its due and proper function', so that sickness and disorder are the product of stagnation, and deployed by advisers to the emperor rather than (actual or aspiring) rulers or legislators: Lloyd (1996) 190–4, 206–8 (quotation from p. 206).
3 Though the examples in Theognis do not certainly concern the polis as a whole: below 92–3.
4 Thgn. 39–40; the veiled suggestion that the situation will engender a tyrant (made more explicitly in the variant passage 1081–2; below 103n.83) focuses on the outcome of the birth, but we should bear in mind the considerable hazards of childbirth for the mother until relatively recently which caused pregnancy to be described as a medical 'condition' (*OED* s.v. II 9e).
5 Thgn. 1133–4, Sol. fr.4.17; for the ambiguity of *helkos* see below 103n.79. In Solon there are clear moral implications which hint at divine punishment (Lloyd 2003 stresses the persistence of the concept of disease as divinely inflicted), but there is also the suggestion that the harm has been knowingly inflicted: cf. Fantham (1972) 16–17 on Cicero's use of *vulnus* to denote injury at the hands of political enemies.
6 For the semantic range of *pharmakos/on*, which covers drugs, poisons, charms and scapegoats, see Lloyd (2003) 10–11; on the possibility that Solon alluded to treatment, see below 75, 92.
7 Hdt. 5.28, E. *HF* 34, 272–3, 542–3; D. 2.14, 9.12, 50, Isoc. 12.99, 165; Pl. *Mx.* 243e, *Plt.* 307d, *Soph.* 228a, *Lg.* 744d, [Arist.] *Ath.Pol.* 6.4, 13.3; cf. Pl. *Lg.* 628cd, Arist. *Pol.* 1273b18–24, 1284b17–22, where the word *nosos* does not appear. For the increasingly commonplace character of the image, note the evidence of the lexicographers: Hesychius has the gloss '"sick": in a state of civil war', and Pollux 8.152 gives '"to be sick": used of states of disorder and disturbance'. Likewise the commonplace used in D. 9.12 *nosousi kai stasiazousi* ('sick and split by strife'), has clearly been inserted in full in 2.14 by unthinking scribes, though two manuscripts have *stasiazousi* only: McQueen (1986) 140. Aristophanes parodies such language at *Vesp.* 650–1, though with specific reference to the behaviour of some dikasts (below 135n.88).
8 *helkos* appears also at Pi. *P.* 4.271, where Braswell (1988) sees it as an appositive genitive in place of an adjective ('an ulcerous wound'); swelling: Hdt. 3.76.2 and 127.1. Inflammation (*phlegmainô/phlegma*): Pl. *R.* 372e cf. 564b, *Lg.* 691e (imitated by Plut. *Lyc.* 5.2, *Numa* 8.1); swelling (*spargaô*): *Lg.* 692a; fracture (*rhêgma*) and sprain (*stremma*): D. 2.21 cf. [D.] 11.14).
9 e.g. How and Wells (1928) *ad loc.*
10 One might compare the conception of the associates of monarchs (particularly oriental ones) as multiple eyes, ears, hands or feet which extend their capacity for perception or action: Arist. *Pol.* 1287b29–31 with Newman (1887–1902) on 29; X. *Cyr.* 8.2.11–12; for the idea of the king of Persia as thus endowed with more than human capabilities see above 12.
11 *Lg.* 964d–5b; *Tim.* 69de, 70b cf. *Lg.* 942e; in Arist. *Part. An.* 670a26 the heart is an acropolis. For the fourth-century conception of the rule of the rational element over

the body see below 152–3; whether it was located in the head or the torso remained a matter for controversy, on which see Taylor (1928) on *Timaeus* 44d5; on earlier conceptions of the internal location of consciousness which placed it broadly in the torso see Padel (1992) 12–33. By contrast, in the Middle Ages it was taken for granted that the king was the head of the body politic, as Christ was head of the mystical body of the Church (*1 Cor.* 12.14–27): Kantorowitz (1957) 15, 199–200, 255–6 and *passim*.

12 For the semantics of 'lame' see *LSJ* s.v. χωλεύω 2, χωλός II; Ogden (1997) 33–4 points to the 'link between sure-footedness and legitimacy' in discussing this episode. Diodorus (11.50.4) cites the oracle in a quite different context (475/4 BC) and in relation to the dual hegemony of Athens and Sparta; Cimon reportedly argued that its abandonment would leave Greece lame: Plut. *Cim.* 16.10 = Ion *FGrH* 392 F14 = fr.107* Leurini; de Ste. Croix (1972) 170.

13 Dein. 1.110, Hyp. 5 col.25; soul of the city: Isoc. 7.14, 12.138; D. fr.13.23 (below 175n.57).

14 Of which Padel (1992) gives a highly illuminating account.

15 X. *Mem.* 2.3.18; Polyaen. 3.9.22; Aesop 130 [Perry]. Menenius Agrippa: Liv. 2.32, cf. Dion. Hal. *Ant. Rom.* 6.86, Plut. *Cor.* 6.2–4; for the argument that the fable, memorably elaborated by Shakespeare in the opening scene of *Coriolanus*, goes back to a Greek origin see Nestle (1927). It is indeed surprising that fables based on the body seem not to feature in Greek political contexts, given their effectiveness in communicating with a popular audience: Daube (1972) 130–9, cf. de Ste Croix (1981) 444–5.

16 *arrôstia*: Hyp. 2 fr.10, [D.] 11.14; 'attacks' of disease (*katabolê ... astheneias, prosistasthai*): Pl. *Grg.* 519a; Pl. Com fr.201 [= Plut. *Mor.* 804a]; *sathros*: Hdt. 6.109.5 (though NB above 54 for an alternative interpretation of the word; perhaps both senses are in play); *hupoulos*: Pl. *Grg.* 518e, cf. Thuc. 8.64.5 (below 135n.88); *eklelusthai*: D. 19.224. I exclude *paligkotôs* (Hdt. 4.156.1), *pace* How and Wells (1928) *ad loc.*, since *paligkot-* does not appear in any of the Hippocratic treatises commonly regarded as possibly datable to the fifth century. In later treatises (*Art.* 19, 27, 40, 67, 86(2), 87; *Epid.* 4.20; *Fract.* 11(4), 25, 31; *Loc.Hom.* 43.3; *Mul.* 2.171) the principal notion is of deterioration and malignancy (almost the modern 'complications'), though not gangrene, for which the term is *sphakelizein*.

17 Parry (1969), quotation from p.113, cf. Hornblower (1987) 97, particularly noting Thuc. 2.49.3, for Thucydides' restraint as an artistic rather than a practical choice, and (1991–2008) 1.316–18; at Brock (2000) 26–7 I quoted Hp. *Epid.* 1.2 to point up the contrast.

18 Well discussed in Sontag (1991) 73–87.

19 *R.* 425e–6c, *Ep.* 7 330c–331a (below 172n.37). For fuller discussion of Plato's use of craft analogies, see below 148–52, for medical imagery in particular 150–1, and NB 152–4 and Brock (2006) for the related use of parallel and reflexive corporal images of microcosm and macrocosm.

20 *Grg.* 464b; on the relationship of the doctor and the trainer see below 151–2.

21 Patient should seek doctor: *R.* 489bc; two forms of treatment: *Lg.* 720 with Jouanna (1978) and below 151; *pharmakon* of lying: *R.* 389b-d: for the sense here, close to 'spell' or charm', NB Lloyd (2003) 145–6.

22 Dodds (1959) 210–11; see in general Welcker (1850), a reference I owe to Vivian Nutton. *Laws* 684c is more concerned with training i.e. legislation (below 172n.38) so a fortiori the expectation of pain from medical treatment will be stronger; for doctors justifiably applying coercion cf. *Plt.* 296bc.

23 *Plt.* 293d, cf. 308e–9a, where the same policies are discussed literally; *Lg.* 735d–6a. Conversely, unhealthy bile is said in the *Timaeus* to be 'ejected from the body like an exile from a city suffering from *stasis*' (85e–6a). Plato is aware that purging can go wrong: in the comparison of constitutions and characters the tyrants manage paradoxically to purge themselves of their good elements (*R.* 567c, 573b and NB L. 12.5 for the Thirty's appeal to the language of purity, perhaps not coincidentally). Plato's imagery of purging is part of a wider spectrum of concepts of cleansing and purifying: below 144n.154, 172n.38, 188n.141, and NB Lloyd (2003) 146–8.

24 They also share the more general language of health and disease, and a concern with the vulnerability of the body which *inter alia* reflects the situation of Athens in the fourth century: see below 156–7 for details, and the suggestion that the direction of influence is from philosophy to rhetoric, though it is also the case that the image of the doctor in general is much more frequent in fourth-century comedy (Fantham [1972] 15–16). For a more positive appraisal of medical imagery in the orators see Piepenbrink (2003), who sees it as actuated mainly by principle and a consciousness of a falling-off from the higher standards of the fifth century in the more straitened and threatening circumstances of the fourth.

25 Claim to thanks: Demades fr.64 (below 156, with other examples of self-promotion via medicine); ironic version: D.18.243, reflected in Aeschin. 3.225. Competition between doctors: D. 3.33 cf. *Pro.* 53.4; Aeschin. 3.208.

26 Surgery: [D.] 25.95, cf. D. 18.324 (below 180n.94). 'Hamstrung': D. 3.31, cf. Aeschin. 3.166; mutilation: D. 18.296, where there is a step from illness to violent injury (n.5 above); for the increasing violence of the language of public discourse at this time, see below 163–4. Wiseman (2012) shows how in the deteriorating politics of the Roman republic Cicero likewise came to embrace the image of surgery on the body politic, in other words political assassination (e.g. *Catil.* 2.11, *Sest.* 135, *Phil.* 8.15, *Att.* 2.20.3, 4.3.3); cf. also Fantham (1972) 16–18, 122–3 for his frequent use of medical imagery, which would seem to have been typical of the period, if the recurrent medical imagery in Plutarch's *Pompey* and *Caesar* (and other late Republican *Lives*) is influenced by Asinius Pollio: Pelling (2004a) 322–5; NB also n.38 below. The emperor Claudius, on the other hand, had a weakness for the language of *remedium*: Last and Ogilvie (1958) 485. On Plutarch's political imagery from medicine see briefly Duff (1999) 93; its Platonizing character makes the instances in the *Dion* rather piquant: Pelling (2004b) 94.

27 It also entailed taking the public persona of doctors at face value and turning a blind eye to the shortcomings of their expertise, which indeed they sometimes acknowledged (Cordes 1994, 188–9, Lloyd 2003, 54, 58–9, 149–50, 237–8) as well as to the persistence of sacralized medicine, especially the cult of Asclepios (ibid, esp. 53–61).

28 It should be conceded that Aristotle does not fit this tidy schema: his medical language tends to be rather general and while he speaks in broad terms of 'cure' (*iasthai, iatreia*: *Pol.* 1273b20, 1284b18–19, 1302b20), 'remedy' (*akos*: 1305a32, 1308b26) and 'treatment' (*pharmakon*: 1273b23, 1321a16), this is barely more than the muted vernacular usage (below n.51; cf. *Pol.* 1339b17); he goes into no details as regards treatment and would prefer the lawgiver to establish the constitution in such a way as to obviate any need for it. On concepts of mixture and proportion in Aristotle see below 160–1, 189n.149.

29 Above, 69–70; however, the scope of Theognis' first personal plural is uncertain and need not embrace all Megara.

30 Rulers: Hom. *Il.* 16.384–92, *Od.* 19.109–14, Hes. *Op.* 225–47; Parker (1983) 265–7; below 92. Lloyd (2003) e.g. 5–6, 14–17, 116–19, 236 stresses the persistence in Greek culture of belief in a link between disease and the gods, noting the influence which the narration of the plague sent by Apollo at the opening of the *Iliad* is likely to have had; Parker (1983) 235–56 makes clear that divine visitation may equally be due to caprice, misfortune or anger at mortal disrespect or dereliction of religious duty. Willi (2008) 153–61 argues that etymologically *nosos* means 'lacking divinely granted well-being', hence its extension to other undesirable states such as hunger and lovesickness.

31 A. *Eum.* cf. *Supp.* 625–709, esp. 679–87, where the Danaids' prayers invoking blessings on Argos reverse a previous threat of religious pollution.

32 Parker (1983) 257. This outlook is also in line with the more rational attitude taken by the Hippocratics to the aetiology of disease, especially epidemic disease (Longrigg 1993, 33–46), though even Thucydides uses the language of *loimos* outside the actual description of the 'plague' of Athens (1.23.3, 2.47.3, 54.2-3); for the wider spectrum of popular belief NB Parker (1983) 207–34 and above n.30.

33 Parker (1983) 267–71; Connor (1985), esp. 91–3; nevertheless, magistrates were required to be physically and spiritually healthy, as Parker notes (268).

34 Connor is not so far from this more pragmatic position when he suggests that the doctrine of pollution of the household, i.e. collective guilt, was intended as a restraint on the *oikos* within a still developing polis system (1985, 93–4). For the extirpation of serious offenders from the polis cf. Parker (1983) 45–7, 195–6, 206: as he remarks, 'it is probably true even in cases of sacrilege that the primary public response is one of rage rather than of fear' (196).

35 *Agos*: Parker (1983) 193–6.

36 Parker (1983) 268–9 and NB Yunis (2001) 201, 250, 274 for Demosthenes' forensic tactics in particular; likewise the only two overt references to traitors as sources of divine anger cited by Connor (Lycurg. 1.117, D. 18.296; [1985] 92) come from this period.

37 Most clearly at Hdt. 7.157.2, where the non-Medizers are described as 'the healthy part of Greece'; Eretria with its medizing faction is described as having 'completely unhealthy counsel' and, as we have seen, the term *sathron* in the context of Marathon (6.109.5) may have similar implications. Demosthenes likewise applies disease imagery to support for Philip of Macedon (19.259, 262, cf. 289), though Aeschin.2.177 is more suggestive of internal subversion; cf. 'health and trust' in the context of *stasis* in Pl. *Lg.* 630a. Only in A. *Ag.* 846–50 does Agamemnon appear to apply the image of health and disease to loyalty to himself.

38 [A.] *P.V.* 224, Isoc. 10.34, Pl. *R.* 544c, Plut. *Sol.* 29.5 (= Solon fr.35W). As individuals, tyrants will of course often have been polluted insofar as they were, or were thought to be, guilty of murder. By contrast, by the late first century BC, autocracy had come to be identified with the cure for Rome's ills or the doctor who would administer it: Woodman (1988) 133–4, and cf. Plut. *Brut.* 55[2].1, *Pomp.* 55.3, *Caes.* 28.6, *Cat.Min.* 47.2.

39 Thuc. 2.53, 3.82–3; Hornblower (1991–2008) 1.480 with references to earlier discussion.

40 Prognosis: 2.48.3, 3.82.2, Lloyd (2003) 121–2; medical language: Hornblower (1991–2008) 1.480–1, Swain (1994); Clarke Kosak (2000), esp. 47–8 suggests that *stasis* is a real disease of cities; NB also Kallet (1999).

41 Cordes (1994) 34–5 notes the implicit threat to particular individuals; cf. S. *Aj.* 581–2 for a similarly ruthless resort to surgery (i.e. suicide, in that case).
42 Pi. *P.* 4.271–2, cf. *N.* 3.55 for gentle healing in Pindar; discussion in Marshall (2000) 16–18, noting that Apollo is also the mythical founder of Cyrene as well as a healing god.
43 Thuc. 6.14; below 117, where the possibility of an allusion to the Hippocratic principle *primum non nocere* is noted.
44 Thuc. 6.18.6, with de Romilly (1976), Brock (2006) 355, though Hornblower (1991–2008) *ad loc.* rightly notes that 'ch.14 is explicitly medical, whereas ch.18 is not'; 8.97.2; E. fr.21, from the *Aeolus*; Rechenauer (1991) 296–303 traces specific connections in 6.18 to dietetic theory that the best food is compounded of elements which in their pure and unprocessed state would be noxious to health. For further medical nuances in the 'Sicilian debate' see Jouanna (1980a, b), arguing persuasively that the debate also draws on another contemporary medical controversy, that concerning the appropriate character of change or alteration in treatment; Rechenauer (1991) 353–61 takes this further, comparing the positions of Cleon and Diodotus in 3.37–48, with the implication that the opposition between two models of treatment, one favouring radical change and the other avoiding it even when a regimen is far from ideal, has been taken over into politics by Thucydides.
45 Alcmaeon B4 with Ostwald (1969) 96–106; see further below, 131n.60, also Triebel-Schubert (1984); Schubert (1997) 125–32. Cambiano (1982) 227–36 draws attention to the diversity of models of illness compatible with the model of health as mixture.
46 As I should have recognized in Brock (2000): see further below 189n.149. Plato does display some sense of the organic unity of the body politic at *R.* 462c: Schofield (2006) 215, 218–22.
47 *LSJ* s.vv. μίγνυμι B Ia; ἄμικτος III.1a.
48 NB Welcker (1850: 215–17) for cautious attitudes to surgery and cautery in practice, as opposed to the freedom with which they are deployed as a rhetorical commonplace. We might compare the treatment through diet and exercise, i.e. regimen, applied to an unhealthy Tragedy by Euripides in Aristophanes' *Frogs*: 939–44 with Dover (1993).
49 Neither Alcmaeon's *isonomia* (above 20n.65, below 131n.60) nor *krasis* entailed equality among the elements involved: at the symposium, the appropriate ratio for dilution varied with the quality of the wine, but almost always with wine in the minority: Villard (1988). Aristotle correspondingly reports the observation that different regimens suit different bodies as an argument for proportional equality (*Pol.* 1287a10–16).
50 Sontag (1991) 77, though note Plato's willingness to write off individuals (*Prot.* 325a, *R.* 410a, *Lg.* 735e) and cities (*Ep. 7* 326a; below 172n.37) as hopeless cases and incurable: in fact, he uses *aniatos* ('untreatable', cognate with *iatros*, 'doctor') very largely figuratively and almost always with reference to individual moral health (*Ep. 7* 326a is the one exception), as also the one instance in his works of *anêkestos* ('incurable': *R.* 619a4).
51 That disease could potentially be viewed in such a relatively neutral manner is surely reflected in the very wide use of *nosos* ('disease') and *nosein* ('to be ill') to refer to difficulties of all sorts and *iasthai* ('heal') of their remedies, often in cases where we would more readily think in terms of mechanical malfunction: *LSJ* s.v. ἰατρός II, ἰάομαι I.2, νόσος II; for νοσέω NB Xenophon's allusion to poleis 'sick from crop failures or war' in *Vect.* 4.9. In the public sphere such language can be used of

personal downfall (Pi. *P.* 4.293, Ant. 2.2.13 – the jurors are potential doctors), legal disability due to illegitimacy (E. *Ion* 579, 591, fr.141 (*Andromeda*)) and legal redress (Pl. *Lg.* 918c, 933c, e, *IG* I³ 164.28), as well as of troubles afflicting the state and their resolution: Andoc. 2.9, Isoc. 4.114, 6.101, 12.99, 165, Pl. *Lg.* 919bc. Note also the proverbial advice not 'to cure evil with evil': e.g. A. fr.349, S. *Aj.* 362, fr.77, where 'cure' is variously *iasthai*, *akos*, or *parêgorein*.

6

Leaders and Communities:
the Archaic Period (*c.* 750–480 BC)

Like so many things, political imagery begins with Homer, and as with much else in Homer, its roots extend back in time and away from Greece.[1] Just as Near Eastern kingship seems to have formed the model for the Greek kingship we find depicted in the earliest archaic poetry,[2] so, as we have seen in earlier chapters, the imagery through which it is represented is also very largely derived from Near Eastern models. This imagery was clearly long-established in the oral tradition, since it appears as recurrent poetic building-blocks, as unvarying formulae, or repeated lines or half-lines, or noun-epithet combinations,[3] without any explanatory or persuasive elaboration.

None of this, it may be thought, is very surprising: not only had Bronze Age Greek rulers enjoyed extensive contact with Near Eastern cultures with longer-standing traditions of monarchy, but one can readily imagine that the established monarchic ideology of these cultures would appeal to the upwardly-mobile among these relative kinglets. Yet there are also striking differences. The almost entirely formulaic character of the images, which are never developed in extended simile, suggests that they were not being used in contemporary discourse, in contrast to the individuality of Near Eastern examples, which implies that each one is being devised anew (though no doubt within long-established conventions), nor are they being considered or evaluated, as is plainly the case when the same images re-appear with the resurgence of monarchy in the fourth century BC. Most notable, however, is the absence of the characteristic self-assertiveness of the Near Eastern monarch, who typically speaks in the first person, so that his representation as a good father or shepherd is a matter of self-appraisal; where it is not, it is usually his transmission of the purportedly favourable judgement of a god or gods.[4] This is not what we find in Homer: Odysseus the good father is so designated by his son, or by Athena in disguise or in *propria persona*,[5] and the change of perspective makes a great difference. It is not simply that the image is not self-praise: the fact that it is represented as the verdict of another person implies the basic principle that a monarch can legitimately be externally appraised and that the appraisal need not be positive. Since the king is said to be a good father to those whom he rules, the judgment must be that of his subjects (or at least founded on their experience), but their identity is not yet quite clear: in this case the community is more likely than not the polis, but if my reading of the shepherd image as concerned with military leadership is correct, in other contexts the monarch's association is principally with his followers.[6] However, the Thersites episode in *Iliad*

2, though it demonstrates the existence of dissent,[7] should make us cautious about assuming that the right to judge is as yet open to all (and in all circumstances). On the other hand, Hesiod's fable of the hawk and the nightingale (*Op.* 202–12), in which the hawk dismisses the nightingale's complaint and asserts the folly of trying to rival one's betters, is clearly in some way a coded protest against the *basileis*, to whom it is directly addressed: earlier interpretations plausibly viewed it as a complaint against the law of the jungle, intended to shame the *basileis* and arouse sympathy for their victim(s), or a negative paradigm intended to assert the difference that ought to exist between men and animals,[8] although the trend more recently is to read the hawk as referring to Zeus or the power of Dikê, and hence the fable as a whole as an oblique warning that injustice will meet with retribution.[9]

This, then, is a critique from the margins of the community,[10] yet significant by its very existence, and as with the implicit evaluation of the king as father, it places the ruler in a social context, even if the nature of the family or household is as yet not defined or developed. The implications of the imagery are therefore consistent with the picture widely accepted today of an early archaic society in which social institutions are gradually emerging but still somewhat inchoate, and are in the process of coming to constitute a wider framework within which the 'king' operates.[11] Here, it may be illuminating to consider the Homeric pantheon, which seems to be much more tightly genealogically integrated than its Near Eastern peers: the core divinities who play major roles are essentially organized as two generations of a single family,[12] within which the children of Kronos seem to have a higher status, to judge by the agreed disposition of roles among the males, and from Poseidon's sharp retort to being threatened by his brother (above, 3). It is also significant that, as we have seen (ibid), the prerogatives of the other gods are formally recognized by Zeus: their particular roles (e.g. sun-god, sea-god, love-goddess) are typical of many pantheons, but here they are integrated into a kind of cosmic settlement. The effect of this familial and organizational integration of the Olympians is to tie Zeus into networks and obligations which affect his freedom to exercise his power – he has, as it were, 'to live with these people', so that when his suggestions that he might save his son Sarpedon, or Hector, whom he loves for his piety, meet with the response 'do so – but I tell you, we other gods will not all approve' (*Il.* 16.440–3, 22.178–81), he prudently backs down.[13] Noteworthy, too, are the programmatic expressions of concern at the outset of both epics that his actions in conflict with their wishes will antagonise Hera and Poseidon respectively (*Il.* 1.518–23; *Od.* 1.64–79), and the fact that much of the history of conflict with Hera recorded in the *Iliad* amounts to a 'family quarrel' over his bastard Heracles.

The position of Zeus as lord of the gods thus appears analogous to the position of the *basileus* in the Geometric and archaic periods: Thucydides and Aristotle describe this kingship as hereditary but with 'fixed prerogatives',[14] and though our evidence is sketchy, there does seem to be a widespread pattern of gradual circumscription of the powers of the *basileus*, sometimes extending to his being chosen by election, and/or to a reduction in his term of office from life tenure, as at Athens, where this trend culminates, as quite often, into his fading into a magistrate. In some cases, monarchy was supplanted by an 'oligarchie royale' of the ruling family, as in Bacchiad Corinth or at Ephesus.¹⁵ Other than a finite duration, all these stages of development find an echo to some extent in the politics of Olympus, where Zeus has to negotiate his position among other lesser but still influential figures rather than enjoying the apparently unconstrained power of a Near Eastern autocrat.

The leader is perhaps more overtly associated with the community in imagery which represents him in architectural terms: while description of heroes (or, in one case, the massed Achaeans) as a bulwark or rampart[16] is not strongly figurative, given the physical protection which they provide, and the base reference is to a free-standing wall, there is a stronger sense of integration in the description of the dead Ajax as 'a tower': the exceptional physical protection of Ajax's tower-like shield is extrapolated into an idea of the great warrior as a permanent defensive structure and part of the walls of the polis,[17] a conception which fits well both with the growth of monumental defensive walls in Ionia in the Geometric period and with the argument that walls are a central element in the idea of the Homeric city.[18] It is curious that this imagery clusters on the Greek side; perhaps the prominence of the literal walls of Troy precluded allusion to figurative ones. At any rate, it was left to Pindar to extend the concept to its most natural object in describing Hector as the 'impregnable, steadfast pillar of Troy' (*O.* 2.81–2).[19] Elsewhere the same poet described Athens as 'the support (*ereisma*) of Greece' (fr.76.2), presumably particularly with reference to the defeat of the Persians, for which a Homeric echo would be appropriate. The word can refer either to a pillar or to a prop or stay, and the resonances are slightly different: holding up a structure in one case, holding it firmly in place in the other. The latter is, I think, also the implication of the poet calling the dead Sarpedon *herma polêos* ('support of the city', *Il.* 16.549): although the word is often used literally of one of the stones used to support beached ships, there does not appear to be any specifically maritime reference here, nor is there any indication of the ship of state elsewhere in Homer.[20] In the other instance of this image, when Odysseus says of the suitors 'we have slain the support of the city' (*Od.* 23.121), the reference is evidently to their position as leaders of the community and heads of households.[21]

We can sense an underlying conception of the community here, but the totality of the structure remains only implicit; for a clear and explicit image of the community, we have to wait for the appearance of the ship of state, a century or so after the Homeric epics.[22] If we accept the ancient testimony that Archilochos fr.105 is to be read metaphorically, the conception of some sort of community, perhaps a *hetaireia*, which could be figuratively represented in this way was already established by the middle of the seventh century BC, initially in a military context, and had been extended to a specifically political context around 600 BC in Alcaeus and Theognis (above, 53–4).[23] In its developed form, the image describes a merchantman, but the demarcation between warships ('long ships') and cargo vessels ('round ships') was less clear-cut earlier in the archaic period, and it seems more likely that the ships behind the image in its earliest stages are penteconters, fifty-oared war-galleys which nevertheless had a significant cargo-carrying capacity;[24] these seem to have been the choice of long-distance explorer-traders like the Phocaeans (Hdt. 1.163.2), and were also used by colonial settlers heading off into the unknown, such as the Theraeans who founded Cyrene (Hdt. 4.153, 156.2). Indeed, it is attractive to see the ship of state as the product of an era of extensive mobility in which a handful of ships could literally constitute the whole of a community: Herodotus (1.164) paints a poignant picture of the Phocaeans evacuating their city in the face of the Persian siege, launching their penteconters, putting on board their families, possessions and the moveable property from their sanctuaries, and setting sail in search of a new life.[25]

The referent of the ship in Alcaeus cannot be determined with certainty: it is possible that he means to refer to the polis as a whole, but equally possible that he is only thinking of his own faction.[26] Indeed, a certain indeterminacy may be part of the initial character of the image, especially if the suggestion that it is originally based on a penteconter is correct, since the crew will usually have been men who could both row and fight, and so were prosperous enough to own their own armour;[27] even colonial expeditions normally consisted only of men, who expected to find wives where they settled. Hence the ship of state did not have to take in the polis as a whole, and even when it did, it was perfectly compatible with an aristocracy or oligarchy whose members, though a minority of the population, could identify themselves with the polis.[28] At all events, in the Theognis passage the allusion is quite clearly to the polis as a whole, just as in the case of his metaphor of the body politic (below 92), and in his poetry the ship of state has also acquired a helmsman, even if he is no longer in control. If we are prepared to accept that the Delphic oracle supposedly given to Solon (no. 15 P-W, above 55) is either genuine or goes back to contemporary poetry,[29] that enables us to trace the helmsman back to the very beginning of the sixth century BC, and suggests that the helmsman was on board the ship of state more or less as soon as it was clearly identified with the polis as a whole. The way in which the image of steering likewise comes to be applied to the direction of the cosmos from not long after this time by Presocratic thinkers (above 56)[30] is suggestive of its attractions as a way of expressing the concept of rational authority and direction. Likewise on the political plane the submission of a ship's crew to the authority of the helmsman in view of his skill and expertise will have been an appealing model for the authority of a leader over his followers or over the wider community of a polis. The whole concept of the ship of state could have arisen from elite experience of voyages by sea;[31] even if it did not, it looks highly likely that the rapid rise to prominence of the helmsman was due to their initiative. This is probably the earliest of the images applied to leadership which rest on a concept of professional expertise: these images chime with the aristocratic belief that by virtue of their birth they possessed superior innate endowment and practical ability which is summed up in the label *kalos kai agathos* ('handsome and good').[32]

At the same time, this is an image of considerable persuasive power through the relationship which it implies between leader and followers or community. The particular effectiveness of the figure of the helmsman can best be appreciated by comparing him with the related figure of the charioteer. As we have seen, for literary purposes these images came to be more or less interchangeable, but in fact they are far from being homologous. The helmsman controls the ship, rather than its crew and/or passengers, and while he commands the latter, he does so with their consent, insofar as they have chosen to take passage on his ship.[33] By contrast, the charioteer directly controls the chariot and its horses using the physical constraint of the reins and the goad, so that while he too provides expert direction, he does so in a different mode: here the implication of superiority, of man over beasts, is made more explicit – and indeed, we find appeals to the taming of animals in archaic poetry, most strikingly when Theognis (847–50) exhorts his audience to firm treatment of the empty-headed demos: 'strike it with a sharp goad, and put a galling yoke on it', adding that this will make it the most *philodespoton* ('master-loving') in the world; to put on a yoke himself, on the other hand, would be to accept humiliating submission to his enemies (1023–4). Similar resonances are present in Tyrtaios' description of the Messenians as 'labouring under heavy burdens like asses' (6.1), though their literal subjection to the Spartans makes the simile less pointed, and here the subjugated are directly compared to beasts of burden, an implication not quite spelt out in Theognis.[34] With this imagery we are close to Near Eastern ideas of subjection, expressed in royal inscriptions such as that of Ashurbanipal who 'has made bow to his feet all the other rulers and who has laid the yoke of his overlordship on them' and Cyrus 'whose yoke the kings of all the countries are pulling'; likewise a Babylonian hymn to Ishtar boasts that she has made subject to the king 'the four world regions at his feet, and the total of all peoples she has decided to attach them to his yoke.'[35] The story of Reheboam contains similar elements in the subjects' request to have their yoke lightened, and in the threat that whereas his father has chastised them with whips, he will chastise them with scorpions (*1 Kings* 12.4, 9–11, 14). The whip, more aggressive than the goad, appears in the Delphic oracle warning the Sicyonians of a century of tyranny (no. 23 P-W, from D.S. 8 fr.24), and a warning about tyranny – in this case, that of Phalaris at Himera – is likewise the point of the animal fable which Stesichorus (ap. Arist. *Rh.* 1393b8–22) is said to have told of a horse who, to get revenge on a deer which encroached on his meadow, agreed to let a man put a bit in his mouth and mount him, and found himself a slave (*edouleuse tôi anthropôi*).[36]

The goad and the yoke have a common symbolic role, and the latter in particular was to become the principal image in Greek thinking about Persian domination, overlapping with the imagery of slavery which also figures the overlord as a 'master' (*despotês*).[37] It looks as though Near Eastern precedents are one of the influences here, and it is therefore worth noting that this is not an image which appears in Homer, though presumably available. Another factor, and probably a more significant one, is the importance of horse-rearing and horsemanship in elite Greek culture: the chariot-race is by far the most extensive set-piece in the funeral games for Patroclus in book 23 of the *Iliad*, the four-horse chariot-race at Olympia went back to 680 BC, and chariot-racing was an important feature of the other major games of the festival circuit at which the Panhellenic elite competed and victory in which conferred high status.[38] Furthermore, Aristotle in the *Politics* argues that the first constitution to succeed monarchy was a community formed by the cavalry as the effective fighting force, and makes a connection between wealth, horse-rearing and oligarchy in early Greece.[39] Political imagery drawn from horsemanship is thus a natural development, transferring elite prowess and mastery[40] from animals to their fellow men; the use of 'horsey' imagery in erotic contexts in sympotic poetry indicates that this was a natural way for aristocrats to think about other aspects of their experience.[41]

Viewed from this perspective, the image of the charioteer can be read in part as an extension or variation of the imagery of animal-taming in a muted form which avoids any explicit mention of the use of force or violence while maintaining the implicit concepts of control and restraint, though these are made more purposeful by the new element of guidance and direction towards a goal. That new element is still significant: the imagery of taming is evidently intended for internal consumption, to reinforce elite solidarity, celebrating the fact of their superiority and political dominance through imagery which echoes key elements of their ideology and makes no pretence at any concern for animal welfare – there are no shepherds of the people here.[42] Unlike the simple imagery of taming, however, the figure of the charioteer contains an element of potential justification to an external audience, even if rather on elite terms, so it may not be by chance that it is first attested in the poetry of Solon, in one of the poems written in defence of his reforms. He argues that 'another man who had taken up the goad as I did … would not have restrained the demos' (36.20–2), a passage evidently directed at his critics among the nobility.[43] Similarly in another passage quoted in the same context (6.1–2) he observes that the demos will best follow their leaders if they are on neither too slack nor too tight a rein.[44] Two other characteristic aspects of this image are present here from the outset: the motif of transition or the handing over of power, and the observation that not all charioteers are principled or capable, with the implication that bad driving will lead to disaster.[45] Hence it can also be applied to one particular leader in a sequence or from a choice, either to defend or praise a good one or condemn a bad one. At the same time, the frequency of the motif of the chariot crash, whether in myth (Phaethon, Myrtilos), epic (Eumelos in *Iliad* 23), or tragedy (Orestes) points to a constant awareness of the risks of driving or riding in one, which may arise from external factors such as obstacles or collision, but can also be caused by failure to control the horses. Hence the demos when identified with chariot-horses can be perceived as both an asset and a danger, but in either case it constitutes an inherent part of the polis.

There is a possible indication elsewhere in Solon of another important figuration of the demos, in terms of the elements, which in its developed form represents it as a force of nature, at best irrational and uncontrollable and at worst a threat to the survival of the polis (above, 61). In fragment 12, however, Solon maintains that any upheaval in the sea, that is, in the demos, is due to its being 'stirred up' (*tarassetai*) by the winds, i.e. by powerful or demagogic individuals, and that if left undisturbed, 'it is of all things most just'.[46] This defensive account of the demos as naturally stable, which was to become a literary commonplace, looks like a riposte to prior criticism of the demos from an elite perspective:[47] if so, we can trace back to this date a hostile characterization of the demos in elite circles which retained its appeal to the end of the classical period (below, 159). In a related image (fr.9), Solon describes impending tyranny in terms of a violent meteorological phenomenon, a thunderstorm or hailstorm: again wind as the impetus for political change is identified with 'great men', though here the demos is criticized for the failure to read the weather signs, through lack of understanding (*aidriêi*), which causes it to fall into 'enslavement to a monarch'.[48]

The related identification of the demos with another destructive element, fire (below 120), does not appear in the archaic period, and it is incipient tyranny on Mytilene which is equated with a log about to burst into flame (Alcaeus fr.74): we have only the word 'log' (line 6), but the scholiast gives what is presumably a paraphrase of the line, urging the Mytileneans to extinguish it while it is only giving off smoke, 'lest the light (*phôs*) become brighter'. Here light must imply the glow of a flame, since elsewhere its connotations are always positive, as in the description of the Athenian tyrannicides as bringers of light (Simonides 76D = ep.1 Page). The image of the light of salvation goes back to Homer, and is also found in the Near East.[49]

A certain ambiguity surrounds another force from the natural world, the boulder (*oloitrochon*) with which the Delphic oracle (nr. 6 P-W = Hdt. 5.92 β2) identifies Cypselus: since the rest of the oracle speaks of it falling on 'monarchic men' (i.e. the narrow Bacchiad oligarchy) and bringing justice to Corinth, the immediate implications appear favourable to the Cypselids, but since in Homer the principal signification of the boulder is massive destructive power (e.g. *Il.* 13.137f.), that is likely to form part of the picture, bringing together force (*bia*) with justice (*dikê*). At the same time, the image of the boulder presents this as the operation of an impartial natural force and so depersonalizes it, eliding any consideration of the tyrant's motives or personality.[50]

The elite self-esteem implicit in the images of the helmsman and charioteer is further demonstrated by the propagation of the architectural imagery we have already encountered in Homer. Theognis (233–4) speaks of the noble as 'a citadel and tower (*akropolis kai purgos*) for his empty-headed people', while Pindar styles the tyrant Theron 'bulwark (*ereisma*) of Akragas' (*O*. 2.6):[51] in both cases there is an implicit identification with a Homeric hero, albeit a defensive, collaborative figure like Ajax or Hector rather than a spectacular individualist like Achilles. It is not simply that the leader fights for his people, but that, like a wall or tower, he is a permanent and efficacious protector.[52] Alcaeus develops the concept when he says that 'warlike men are a city's tower' (fr.112.10) and that cities are not stones or wood or the workmanship of builders, but that 'where there are men who know how to protect themselves, *there* are both walls and cities' (fr.426). The extension in the scope of the image is an important one, though we should note that as yet it only includes fighting men: we are still some way from the identification of the city with the whole of its manpower (below 123), let alone its entire population.[53]

A similar though more complex dynamic is observable in imagery drawn from animals. Many of the animals used in such comparisons are drawn from the Homeric menagerie, and by implication with the same agenda of associating members of the elite with the heroes who are compared to charismatic fauna, and particularly with lions.[54] The association is perhaps most clearly seen in the names of the Spartan kings Leon and Leonidas: the leonine nature of the latter is alluded to in the oracle from Delphi presaging his death ('for neither the strength of bulls nor of lions will check the foe head on': Hdt. 7.220.4) and in the stone lion set up at Thermopylae (Hdt.7.225.2). There was of course a natural association between kings of Sparta and lions through their ancestor Heracles, who had killed the monstrous Nemean lion and, perhaps, assumed its characteristics by putting on its skin. The fate of the Troizenian marine Leon (7.180) shows that ordinary people too might be given lion names[55] and that they might be felt to be significant. Elsewhere in Herodotus, lions are associated with tyrants in one oracle addressed to Hipparchus (5.56.1) and another foretelling the birth of Cypselus (5.92 β3), neither straightforwardly positive: in the former case, while one might take the address 'O lion' as a complimentary recognition of Hipparchus' royal status, it is followed by the warning that no wrongdoer escapes punishment,[56] while the latter points to the lion as 'powerful, ravening' predator. Lions are not automatically auspicious but rather ambiguous,[57] a force which may be admirable or destructive depending on how it is directed, and it is conceivable that, as with Cypselus the rolling stone, the oracles were intended to retain and exploit that ambiguity. There is a clear contrast with the oracular description of Alazeir king of Barce as 'the most handsome bull' (Hdt. 4.163.3): as with the association of Leonidas with bulls, as well as lions, in the Delphic oracle cited above, this is a purely complimentary comparison which echoes the comparison of Agamemnon to a bull in *Il.* 2.480, evoking the traditional beauty of heroic royalty.[58] In itself, the eagle is another creature with entirely positive connotations, associated with Zeus and regarded in turn as the king of birds (Pi. *P.* 1.7, *I.* 6.50), which regularly features in Homeric similes, portents and dreams, hence its appearance in hexameter oracles:[59] those associations may be in play in the background of the earlier oracle foretelling the birth of Cypselus which spoke of 'an eagle in the rocks' (Hdt. 5.92 β3), though there is also a clear punning allusion to the tyrant's father, Eëtion of Petra.[60]

A more immediately hostile image is that of the king as predator, already prefigured in Achilles' denunciation of Agamemnon as a 'people-devouring *basileus*' (*Il.* 1.231); Hesiod's talk of 'gift-eating *basileis*' (*Op.* 39, 263-4) likewise implies excessive and transgressive appetites.[61] In archaic poetry, the concept is specifically associated with tyranny: so, adapting Homer's phrase, Theognis refers to a 'people-devouring tyrant' (1181) in a hostile passage that recommends disposing of a tyrant by any means available. Alcaeus twice uses *daptein* ('devour'), a word normally used of carnivores eating their prey,[62] in poems attacking Pittacus: 'let him devour the city as he did with Myrsilus [his predecessor as tyrant]' (fr.70.6-7 cf. 129.23-4). This is an image also found in biblical passages: 'the princes within her (Jerusalem) are like lions growling as they tear their prey' (*Ezek.* 22.25 cp.27); 'like a starving lion or a thirsty bear is a wicked man ruling a helpless people' (*Prov.* 28.15).[63] Very similar is the image, attributed to an imagined critic, of Solon the incompetent hunter or fisherman, who had the prey, that is, the city, in his net, but failed to haul it in and become tyrant (fr. 33.3-4).[64]

Animal imagery also operates at a less exalted level, notably in fables, as we have seen in examples from Hesiod and Stesichorus. Here animals are often associated with a particular characteristic; hence when Alcaeus describes someone who has deceived him in the affair of the Lydians, usually taken to be Pittacus, as like a fox, he is playing on the proverbial cunning of the animal.[65] Solon fr.11.5-6 uses the same characteristic to draw an ironic contrast in familiar terms between the Athenians' cunning as individuals and stupidity en masse, which has caused them to be out-foxed, as it were, by the clever words of a tyrant.

Somewhere between these two registers lies Solon's description of himself as a wolf at bay among hounds: wolves certainly appear in fables, but they also feature in Homer, as does the animal at bay among dogs.[66] The implications of this image have been much debated: in fables wolves have a political aspect, and it has been argued that the wolf here should be associated with tyranny, though this seems at odds with

Solon's apparent opposition to tyranny elsewhere; another reading interprets the wolf as a kind of scapegoat, though there are difficulties here, too.[67] The way in which the image works is perhaps somewhat easier to establish: clearly it is derived from Homer, but at the same time the image has been skewed, a characteristic it shares with Solon's image of himself as holding a shield over both parties in Athens and as a boundary stone (below), thus implying that this is a calculated tactic. In this case, the animal at bay has been changed from a lion or a boar to a wolf, and a lone wolf, though in Homer wolves only appear in packs. Solon alludes to 'gathering strength (*alkên*) from all sides' (26), but the prowess of a wolf is clearly inferior to that of a lion as far as strength is concerned and, as the fables suggest, lies rather in intelligence; on the other hand, wolves are superior to dogs, which here stand for Solon's opponents, now paradoxically united in hostility to him. Evidently Solon is distancing himself from the physical prowess of the traditional Homeric hero, while simultaneously deflating more radically the pretensions of those elite opponents who thought of themselves as lions; nevertheless, in alluding to a stock type of Homeric simile, he suggests that there is something epic about his stance as lawgiver and so heightens the reproach to the Athenians at large.[68]

There is a similar air of paradox to the other two 'Homerizing' images in fragments 5 and 37.[69] In the former, Solon claims that 'I stood casting a strong shield (*sakos*) over both parties and did not allow either to prevail unjustly' (5–6): as commentators have noted, it is impossible to read this image logically, since the warring factions seem to be located simultaneously both inside and outside the shield. In order for it to work, the image surely has to be taken in an impressionistic way which accepts the paradoxical claim that Solon has collapsed the opposition between the two sides into some sort of unity, while at the same time protecting them from harm like a Homeric Ajax.[70] Equally resistant to any concrete reading is Solon's representation of himself as a boundary-stone in no man's land (*en metaichmiôi horos katestên*, fr.37.9–10): rather than a shared civic space, the 'middle' he occupies is a dangerous and contested one – boundaries are what men fight over in Homer (*Il.* 12.421–3) – and one stone will hardly suffice to define a border. One influential reading sees Solon both as setting a limit to faction-fighting and as filling a communal void by marking out for the first time a space for the polis; a more recent interpretation emphasizes the 'cognitive dissonance' between the military character of a no-man's-land and Solon's deliberate inaction, which simultaneously establishes himself as a permanent example.[71] Either way, the image clearly once again trades on Homeric associations while confounding the expectations they create. Clearer in implication, if not syntax, is the preceding metaphor, in which Solon says that another man 'would not have stopped before stirring up the milk and skimming off the cream' (36.7–8):[72] here the cream, a perennial symbol of excellence even in our diet-conscious era, corresponds to the self-assessment of the elite and points to an attempt to conciliate them, as against his 'reproof' to the demos in line 1. The association of superiority with rich food may also appear in the labelling of elites as *pacheis* ('fat ones'): in the past, a fuller figure has tended to be a marker of prosperity, and there is a specific parallel in the 'popolo grasso (or grosso)', the prosperous merchants of mediaeval Florence.[73] At the same time, the image expresses Solon's opposition to stirring things up[74] and to divisive politics.

One image of rule which was to prove highly influential in later periods, that of the king as master, is largely missing in the archaic period. The language of master (*despotês*) and slave (*doulos*) is thinly spread in Homer, and always literal,[75] though the equation of political subjection to a tyrant with slavery appears for the first time in Solon.[76] In the classical period, the image of a monarch as master was to gain a particular negative charge from its association with the Great King of Persia, but this is not clearly attested in our sources before 480 (below 107–10): indeed, it appears to be given a positive valuation in its one appearance, in the so-called 'Song of Hybrias the Cretan' (*PMG* 909.8–10), where the speaker, boasting of the benefits of his military prowess, is made to say that 'all prostrate themselves cowering at my knee and call me master … and great king.' Although scholars have pointed out that the link to Persia is not inevitable, the combination of the titles with the motif of prostration, all of which evoked a strong reaction from later Greeks, is highly suggestive. The date of the poem is likewise uncertain, but it would make sense to place it with the majority opinion in the later archaic period which, if correct, would suggest that there was a brief period after the advent of Persia and before (at the latest) Xerxes' invasion, when it was possible to admire the absolute power of the Great King in somewhat the same way as that of a tyrant.[77]

Around the time of Solon[78] there emerges another hugely significant conception of the community in the idea of the body politic: Solon describes the punishment of Dikê for the crimes of its leaders as coming as a '*helkos aphukton*, an inescapable wound or sore'[79] on the whole city (4.17), which suffers subjection or *stasis*. The idea that a community may suffer misfortunes, including disease, for a ruler's misdeeds is already present in Homer and Hesiod – Solon evidently has the latter specifically in mind here,[80] but Solon takes an important step in conceptualizing the polis itself, rather than the individuals composing it, as the organism affected, and hence as an organic unity, and the sense of unity is enhanced by his perception of the injury to the body as due to divine visitation.[81] There are hints that he might have developed the model further in the use of the language of cure in Plutarch's account, which speaks of his having not applied 'medical treatment (*iatreian*) or surgery (*kainotomian*), afraid that if he threw the city into complete confusion and disorder (*taraxas*), he would not be strong enough to restore her', though this can only be speculation.[82]

Theognis, meanwhile, describes the city of Megara as pregnant, expressing his foreboding that a tyrant will arise 'as a straightener of our evil hubris' (39–40): the image captures not only anticipation (our 'a pregnant pause'), but also a mood of at best uncertainty, and perhaps even a shade of the sinister.[83] In this form the body politic appears not to be entirely inclusive, since the poet's 'our' seems to set him and his *hetairoi* apart to some extent, an effect perhaps enhanced by his figuration of a body which usually has no specific gender as overtly female. On the other hand, they are clearly included in the body implied by his appeal (1133–4) to 'seek a remedy (*pharmakon*) for a growing sore (*helkei phuomenôi*)', though whether that body embraces Megara as a whole is not clear (any more than the nature of the treatment to be applied). Neither Theognis' own elite status nor the Megarian oligarchic regime will necessarily have been an objection to that, however: although at this stage there is no anatomical detail to the body politic, it will always have been natural to regard certain parts of the body such as the head or heart as particularly important and so assume that it was hierarchically organized,[84] and when models of its internal organization emerged they focused on proper balance, and so were perfectly compatible with an elite ideology of proportional equality,[85] while maintaining the essential inclusiveness of the image. The strong association from the outset between disease imagery and political disorder in the form of *stasis* or tyranny suggests a general acceptance of this inclusive and organic conception of the polis as body.

The image of the body politic is mirrored in the conception of the cosmos as a living organism which was developed by Presocratic philosophers in the course of the sixth century; taken with the alternative conception of the cosmos as a political organisation, this suggests both a growing readiness to think analogically of the various levels of existence (body, polis, cosmos) in terms of one another, and an increasing desire to define and describe an order at every level.[86] As we have seen (above 8–10), the cosmic order is characterized by the impersonal working of justice or law, and it is natural to associate this increasingly constitutional conception with the developing political order of the polis and with the political and social ideals expressed in archaic poetry.[87] In addition, it is tempting to think that the analogy will have been reinforced by the perception of a resemblance between the visible periodicity of the physical world and an increasing regularity of procedure and of orderly succession in office-holding in the political one which, like the growing authority of codified law in the judicial sphere, resulted from the work of archaic lawgivers to constrain personal power.[88] The shift in outlook is exemplified by the observation of Heraclitus, a thinker much concerned with law,[89] that 'a people (*dêmon*) should fight in defence of the law as for a city wall' (B44): the image earlier applied to human individuals (above 89) is now transferred to abstract law.

As with any aspect of archaic Greece, the political imagery we have comes overwhelmingly from the elite: rarely do we catch an authentic popular voice, as with the occasional fable.[90] Elite sources bring with them elite values, preoccupations and social forms, and in particular the symposium, the performance context for the poetry which furnishes most of the material discussed above. Even symposiastic games make their mark, in images drawn from board-games like *pessoi*: Alcaeus fr.351 'now he is master, having moved the stone from the holy line' (tr. Campbell) refers to a bold move at draughts (as we would say, 'a last throw of the dice'), apparently alluding to a victory in political infighting. This game naturally lent itself to such comparisons, since one version was called *Polis* or *Poleis*.[91]

Another typical archaic feature is the important role of the epic tradition and in particular of Homer. Given the pre-eminence of the Homeric poems, it is hardly surprising that archaic elites should have drawn on them in constructing their self-representations, both directly and in their imagery.[92] The power of models drawn from myth and, more specifically, the epic tradition can be seen in Alcaeus' use of the story of the impiety of Ajax Oileades and its consequences for the returning Greeks to drive home a political attack on Pittacus: The message is evidently that just as the Achaeans failed to punish Ajax for the rape of Cassandra, and so suffered with him on the voyage home from Troy, so the Mytileneans must take action against Pittacus for some injustice (the broken oaths of frr.129, 306(g), i.e. perjury by the gods?) or face worse trouble later.⁹³ At the same time, as we have seen, Homeric political imagery itself already embodies a degree of concession to the claims of a wider community, however ill-defined, which elites must therefore implicitly have conceded.⁹⁴

The development of imagery through the period reveals further giving of ground: for all that the poetry we have is addressed in the first instance to a select elite audience and maintains the elite stance with its consciousness of superiority, for the most part it tacitly acknowledges the existence and, to some degree at least, the claims of a wider community. Not only are key images founded on models of the community as chariot, ship or body, but the claim to superiority or to a privileged place in the community is obliquely articulated or justified through the imagery in terms of expertise, guidance, protection or the like, rather than baldly asserted, a concession which implies the existence of some form of debate on these issues, and hints at the tone of the voice which we cannot hear directly. Not, of course, that the imagery does nothing to reinforce intra-elite solidarity or to consolidate the demarcation between the 'worst' and the 'best' people, and it generally does so in terms which echo the preoccupations of elites in other areas of their lives, but it is surprisingly rare for it to express overt contempt for or hostility to the demos as Theognis does (above 87, 89).⁹⁵ If anything, there is greater hostility to the tyrant who constitutes at the least a rival for power and at worst a threat to the very position of a community's elite: the stock portrait of the tyrant may be a creation of the fifth century, but we can trace a characterization of him as unprincipled, unnatural or even inhuman back to the time of the archaic tyrants themselves. Alongside this, however, there exists a more ambiguous conception of the tyrant as a force of nature, expressed particularly in oracles, which chimes with a strand of admiration for or even envy of tyranny and implies the possibility of a different evaluation among non-elites of the autocratic exercise of power.⁹⁶

Finally, it may be that we should also look to the elite viewpoint to explain the virtual absence in the archaic period of one of the key political images, the state as a household. Although the actions of the Parian arbitrators at Miletus (Hdt. 5.29; above 25) imply a positive evaluation by elites of good estate management, it may be that in practice this tended to be regarded as essentially domestic (reducing *oikos* to *oikia*) and so essentially women's work,⁹⁷ or else that the growing importance of the polis simply diverted interest and attention away from the smaller sphere of the individual household. Whatever the explanation, and the gap remains something of a mystery given the early appearance of the king as father, it ensured that at least one major field of imagery remained open for development and contestation as the political landscape changed at the end of the sixth century.

Notes

1 I do not mean to imply that I necessarily believe Homer is earlier than Hesiod: it is simply that the oral tradition and its formulaic heritage are much more strongly exemplified in Homer, particularly where kingship is concerned.
2 West (1997) 14–19 sets out the arguments succinctly.
3 Formulae: shepherd of the people (above 43); repeated lines: king as father (above 30:

the first half of 2.47 differs from the other two *Odyssey* passages; *Il.* 24.770 varies the last word but is metrically equivalent); noun-epithet: e.g. *dios Odysseus* x 23 and x 60 in *Od.*, *Hektora dion* x 18 in *Il.*, all at line-end; *Diogenes Laertiadê* x 7 in *Il.*, x 15 in *Od.* in the same position.

4   Above 30; 43. Of course we have to allow for differences in genre, but the image of the king as shepherd is also used in a straightforwardly positive way in Mesopotamian epics such as *Gilgamesh* (I ii), *Etana* (I) and *Erra and Ishum* (IV): Dalley (1989) 52, 190, 308–9, and these were also in circulation at a date closer to our period.

5   As we have the line, that third person is built into it (ἦεν cannot be first person sg.) but one could envisage a first-person version which ended ἦα.

6   For the link between the ruler's behaviour and the community's fortunes see n.80 below; for the early political community as typically composed of the warriors, see Davies (2008) 20–1; Murray (1993) 53–4, also van Wees (1992) 48.

7   van Wees (1992) 83–5 notes that Thersites is represented as a habitual heckler, which implies that 'princes' rights to deference are questioned'.

8   So West (1978a): that the prey is a 'singer' (208) has often been seen as implying a specific link to Hesiod himself.

9   So independently Leclerc (1992) and Nelson (1995), the former suggesting that the fable can be read on two levels, one, superficially encouraging the kings to believe that might is right, undercut by a truer interpretation; NB also Griffiths (1995) 95–6. Dalfen (1994/95) argues from the format of other Greek fables that the moral in this case extends to line 218. Hubbard (1995) identifies the nightingale with Perses, though with similar implications for the audience's perception of the *basileis*. For fables as a vehicle for protest by the oppressed, see Daube (1972) 53–6; for the possibility that Archilochus, who uses animal fables in non-political contexts (frr.172–81, 185–7), used a similar one to Hesiod's to similar effect, West (1978b), and for later animal fables with more specific political morals, below 87, 90.

10 That is, on the standard reading of the world of *Works and Days* as one of subsistence agriculture, though van Wees (2009) 445–52 has recently argued against this; at all events, it comes from a position of political exclusion.

11 Though of course any such picture will be largely based on a historicizing reading of the Homeric poems: see Morris (2001) 68–76, esp. 69–70, 73–6, for a judicious survey of opinion, and van Wees (1992). Morris (1991) 40–3 makes an archaeologically based case for the persistence of some degree of hierarchy through the Dark Ages. Rose (1997) argues *inter alia* (e.g. 162–3, 185, 192) for a disparity between the decline in real authority of the lone *basileus* and his continuing appeal as an ideal.

12 Homer's choice to make Aphrodite the daughter of Zeus and Dione (*Il.* 5.370–4) rather than a by-product of the castration of Ouranos, as in the *Theogony* (188–206), is significant in producing the tidy family structure, though of course there are outliers such as Oceanos and Tethys (*Il.* 14.200–10).

13 The line also appears at 4.29, though the suggestion there of a diplomatic solution to the Trojan War is apparently simply intended to provoke Hera (4.5–6). Van Wees (1992) 120–1 and n.118, 139 and n.149 highlights the way in which Zeus, like human *basileis*, issues threats of violence; I would want to point to the fact that although the power of Zeus remains potentially truly terrible, <u>actual</u> violence involving him is confined to the poems' past: note in particular how he meets Athena's response to his threats at the beginning of book 8 with the same reassurance that he is 'not serious'

as he does in retreating from the suggestion that he might rescue Hector (8.39–40 = 22.183-4), and his reference to controlling Hera verbally (5.893). Van Wees (1992) notes other concessions to Olympian public opinion at 145 and n.161; Zeus likewise shows respect for other powers such as Night (*Il.* 14.261).

14 Thuc. 1.13.1, Arist. *Pol.* 1285b2-23, and cf. Plato's historical sketch of constitutional kingship in the Peloponnese at *Lg.* 684a2-b2.

15 For early monarchy see Carlier (1984), particularly the overview at 485–501, with a helpful tabulation, and his sketch of developments in this period in the conclusions (503–14) at 506–10; note also his response to the very sceptical views of Drews (1983) at 503–5. On Athens, see 359–72 and Rhodes (1981) 65–79, 97–101; for 'royal oligarchy', Carlier (1984) 496: his other examples are Basilid Erythrae and Penthelid Mytilene.

16 *Il.* 1.283-4 (Achilles), evoked at Pi. fr.52 f.85; 3.229, 6.5, 7.211 (Ajax); 4.299 (massed infantry).

17 *Od.* 11.556; Callinus 1.20 recycles the Homeric image and its resonances in the context of the hoplite phalanx, calling on the Ephesians to defend their polis, but the 'stout-hearted man' need not be a *basileus*. For Ajax' shield see especially *Il.* 7.219-24 with Kirk (1990) *ad loc.*, and compare his comment on 6.5: 'he is the great defensive fighter'; Sophocles appropriately picks up the image in his *Ajax* (159, 1211–13). The army as a whole can also form a defensive tower (*purgêdon*): 13.152, 15.618 with van Wees (1992) 320 n.32 (cf. 12.43 in a simile, of hunters, and *purgos* in 4.334, 347 of a contingent in close formation). Tower imagery, which initially suggests depth of protection at least as much as height, is extended to denote eminence in general, and then, given the Greek sense of its dangers, pride and excess: Page (1938) on E. *Med.* 526, Bond (1981) on E. *HF* 238.

18 Briefly, van Wees (1992) 28–9; extensively explored by Scully (1990), esp. 81–99; see also, more generally, Ducrey (1995), Camp (2000).

19 On the detail of this passage and the later history of the column/pillar image see Fatouros (2002); it is equally at home in *oikos* contexts, e.g. A. *Ag.* 897–8 (interestingly, West (1997) 570–2 on this passage does not cite any specific Near Eastern parallels for the column image), E. *IT* 57; on columns and other architectural images in antiquity, see more generally Thomas (2007) 17–21, 53–5, and for Roman Republican usage, in which *columen* oscillates between 'ridgepole' and 'roof-peak', Fantham (1972) 45–6. On the funerary associations of the column and the implication of <u>loss</u> of support, NB Vermeule (1979) 69.

20 Below n.22, *pace* Janko (1992) *ad loc.*; the ship of state does not seem to feature in Near Eastern literature either, apart from the Old Testament (West 1997, 531–2), which is not surprising given the environment and the self-identification of kings with land warfare. Chantraine (1968) s.v. suggests that the unifying root meaning to the varied senses is simply 'stone'.

21 Note that the phrase appears in a different position in the line (and to slightly different metrical effect) in the two cases, which suggests that it is being used creatively.

22 'Homer' uses 'helmsman' metaphorically of a charioteer ('Homerus' fr.20 Davies, perhaps imitated by Ennius (l.465 with Skutsch 1985); compare Pollux I 98 for the reverse image as a poetic commonplace, and the juxtaposition of the two at *Il.* 23.316-8), but the association is clearly limited to steering and direction, and neither vehicle is linked with the community – it is also suggestive of the conceptual convergence of the two activities that the word *kelês* can mean both 'racehorse' and

'yacht'. The later interchangeability of the images is indicated by the use of *euthunô* and *apeuthunô* ('steer') both of chariots and ships (e.g. Ar. *Av.* 1739, Aeschin. 3.158); note also 'shipwreck' applied to chariot crashes: S. *El.* 730, 1444, D. 61.29; Plato juxtaposes the two images with reference to philosophical debate at *Prt.* 338ab. There is a lovely modern example of the conflation in Flaubert's *Madame Bovary* (part 2 ch.8) – the speaker is a politician: 'ce roi … qui dirige à la fois d'une main si ferme et si sage le char de l'État parmi les périls incessants d'une mer orageuse'. In other contexts related to elite activities, Pindar applies both images to the trainer (*N.* 6.60, *I.* 4.78), and Alcman (fr.1.92–5) links the trace-horse and the helmsman with the chorus-leader.

23 Since suggested dates for 'Theognis' range from 640 to 540, there is a potential margin of error of half a century either way; even if one adopts the position that the Theognid corpus accumulated over that period, as well as achieving circulation beyond Megara (Nagy 1985, 33–6), one is no nearer dating any particular passage which lacks internal evidence. However, as far as the major fields of imagery are concerned, a degree of imprecision is inevitable, since it is prudent to regard the poets writing in the fragments which happen to have survived as witnesses to concepts which may have been in circulation for some time, rather than as treating the earliest datable instance as the moment of creation. Despite the inevitable difficulties – particularly the paucity of material for much of the sixth century – and uncertainties, I believe (*pace* Morris 1996, 26) that we have to make the effort to read the archaic literary sources diachronically: otherwise, we flatten out what must have been a dynamic process to a static and tidily schematic picture (and leave the developmental pattern in the material record as our model by default).

24 The use of penteconters for such expeditions was first suggested by Humphreys (1978) 166–8; lack of clear demarcation of ship-types: van Wees (1992) 245, Snodgrass (1983) 16–17, dating the advent of the 'round ship' in art to 'the last quarter of the sixth century'; the trireme seems to be a relative rarity before the later sixth century – note the upgrade from penteconters of the Samian tyrant and freebooter Polycrates *c.* 525 BC (Hdt. 3.39.3, 44.2). On the cargo capacity of the penteconter see Morrison and Coates (1986) 30; more general account in Casson (1971) 43–65, with 65–6 on 'merchant galleys'.

25 For the extent of mobility in this period see Purcell (1990).

26 Gentili (1988) 213 has no doubt that 'the constant meaning is *city*', in line with his consistent allegorical reading, which takes in other passages which refer to a ship, but without any overt indication of political allusion (frr.73, 306i col. II V); others (e.g. Bowie 1986, 17) assume that the poem evokes the experience of Alcaeus' *hetaireia*; so also Lentini (2001), who reads the personified ship of fr.73 as representing the *hetaireia*; for this approach cf. Rösler (1980) 115–48, though he interprets the ship of fr.73 as the majority of Mytileneans, weary of *stasis* (115–26); Cucchiarelli (2004).

27 Prosperous in relative terms, at least, even if that armour was limited to shield, spear and helmet; van Wees (1998) 363–6 draws attention to the stores of arms held by rich men which would enable them to arm followers, though presumably they would not constitute a *hetaireia*.

28 On the ambiguity of references to the city, see Irwin (2005) 108; Levine (1985) argues that the symposium is seen as a microcosm of the polis in the poetry of Theognis; for the symposium as symbolically constituting the world, Davidson (1997) 44; as a sea voyage, *id.* 44–5 and n.11 for further bibliography, to which add Wilkins (2000) 238–41 and now Corner (2010), esp. 364–9.

29 The oracle, from Plut. *Sol*. 14, is accepted as authentic by Parke and Wormell (1956) but rejected by Fontenrose (1978) 290, though he does not explain why he excludes Solon's poetry as a possible origin. The exhortation to 'sit in the middle of the ship' is suggestive of a link with Solon's later self-presentation (Silk 1974, 122 and below 90–1), though Irwin (2005) 228 n.65 emphasizes Plutarch's association of the lines with tyranny. That implication is clearer in the other oracle to Solon, nr.16 P-W, which speaks of the city 'listening to a single herald', and here the link to Solon's own poetry (fr.1.1) is also clear.

30 Lloyd (1966) 272–4: the earliest attested instance in Anaximander will fall in the first half of the sixth century, the next, in Heraclitus, *c*. 500 BC.

31 For the regularity of freebooting see van Wees (1992) 208–10, 213–17, 244–8 (Homer), 257–8 (archaic reality) and (2007) for archaic Attica; also de Souza (1999) 17–26.

32 Donlan (1999) remains the best account of Greek aristocratic values: on *kalos kai agathos* see particularly 129–34, dating the emergence of the phrase to the fifth century; further extensive discussion in Bourriot (1995) 113–22. In the classical period the ideology comes to be more fully articulated in terms of intelligence and education: see (e.g.) Morawetz (2000) 15–47.

33 This is clear for the developed ship of state, figured as a merchantman; on van Wees' account (2007), the crew of a pentecontor will likewise have chosen to make the voyage, though in any case their reliance on the helmsman will normally have been distinct from any obligation to the commander. In later examples, the point is sometimes made more explicitly in terms of a ferryman and his passengers (e.g. Aeschin. 3.158).

34 Yoke and goad do not in themselves identify the animal(s) in question, since they are as compatible with horses drawing a chariot as with oxen (below n.43); where there is no more specific indication in the context, the toil and drudgery of oxen might be more naturally suggested when oriental rulers are said to 'yoke', though Atossa's dream in A. *Pers*. 181–99 of Xerxes yoking two women representing Europe and Asia to his chariot shows that the identification should not be automatically assumed.

35 Pritchard (1969) 297, 314, 383 respectively; further parallels in West (1997) 519–20, (2007) 420. According to Diodorus, Sesoöis of Egypt gave a literal demonstration of this image (1.58.2 cf. Tzetzes *H*. 3.38f.). However, Near Eastern imagery of yoking is not automatically positive for the ruler: the Cyrus Cylinder records that Nabonidus 'destroyed his (people) with a merciless yoke' and that the Babylonians '(had suffered) a yoke unsuitable for them' (§§ 8, 25, tr. Brosius).

36 The anecdote also appeared in the fourth-century history of Philistos: *FGrH* 556 F6 with Jacoby *ad loc*.

37 The one possibly archaic instance of this image is in 'the song of Hybrias the Cretan' where the speaker's self-identification with the Persian king is a positive one (see below 92): the shift in the main application, and so in the resonances of this imagery, is likely to have followed closely on the Persian conquest of Ionia in the 540s, but the effect does not clearly appear in our sources (mainly Herodotus) until the fifth century – there is perhaps a hint in Xenophanes' rejection of any hierarchy among the gods (A32) on the grounds that it was wrong for any of them 'to have a master (*despozesthai*): NB B22 with Murray (1993) 261 for his recognition of the coming of the Persians as a watershed.

38 *Il*. 23.262–538, followed by a stewards' enquiry at 539–652. Note Morgan (1990) 90, 141 on horses and chariots in early material remains at panhellenic and other

sanctuaries. Equestrian contests at crown games: Miller (2004) 75–82; at Athens: Kyle (1987) 185–90.

39 *Pol.* 1297 b16–22, 1289 b33–40 with Newman (1887–1902) on b39; cf. 1321 a8–11.

40 In historical times the victor came increasingly to be a wealthy horse-rearing 'owner', while the drivers were often slaves or professionals, although in some cases the chariot was still driven by the victor himself or by a relative or associate (Lefkowitz 1984, 40–2, Golden 1998, 82–3, 118–23, 169–70; 2003, 34), which will have allowed the elite to continue to identify with the epic model in which heroes drove their own chariots, as at Patroclus' funeral games or Orestes' purported fatal drive at Delphi in Sophocles' *Electra* (698–756). On this latter passage see OKell (2004) for the persistent appeal of success in hippic competitions.

41 For equestrian imagery in erotic contexts both hetero- and homosexual, see Thgn. 257–60, 952, 1249–52, 1267–70, Anacr. frr.360, 417, Ibyc. fr.287; compare Thgn. 1357–8 for yoke imagery in an amatory context, again with a Near Eastern parallel: West (1997) 523.

42 After Homer, there is no instance of the image in the archaic period in a political context: Anacr. fr.348 applies it to a patron goddess, and in the early classical period Pindar *O.* 6.60 is a clear Homeric echo (above 44).

43 *Pace* Irwin (2005) 228–9 (following Catenacci 1991, 85–7), I am dubious that at this date there is any necessary association between the goad and tyranny: apart from this passage there are only three instances of *kentron* in archaic poetry, two referring quite neutrally to its use in driving a chariot (*Il.* 23.387, 430, with the cognate verb at 23.337 and cf. *kentores* = 'drivers': *Il.* 4.391, 5.102); in the other case, cited above, it seems to me highly unlikely that Theognis is commending tyrannical behaviour as such. The resonances of goad and yoke are rather different after the advent of the Persians (above, nn.34, 37). This is not, of course, to deny that tyranny is prominent elsewhere in Solon's poetry.

44 For this sense of ἀνίημι 'let slip' see *LSJ* s.v. II.1a *fin* and cf. Plut. *Per.* 11.4; NB also Wilamowitz-Möllendorf (1893) II 308, Loraux (1984) 206 n.30. The context in which these passages are to be read is supplied by [Arist.] *Ath.Pol.* 12, citing both and further related excerpts (below, 90–1).

45 The motif of 'handing over' implies a perception that it is important to maintain control, even if the process may miscarry: compare e.g. S. fr.683, Pl. *R.* 566d, and see further below, 121; the image of the charioteer's loss of control forms a memorable conclusion to Virgil's first *Georgic* (1.512–14).

46 On the interpretation of the image see Gentili (1975), (1988) 44–5; later examples include Plb. 11.29.9–10, 21.31.6f.; Liv. 28.27.11, 38.10.5 (*vulgata similitudo*). There is also a suggestive parallel in Herodotus 7.16α1, where Artabanus applies the same image to the nature of Xerxes, undermined by association with bad men: given that both he and Solon (in book 1) function as 'Warners', one wonders if some sort of intertextual relationship is at work. For other instances of 'stirring up' in Solon's imagery see below 91.

47 The concept of the dual nature and dangerously deceptive calm of the 'sea-woman' in Semonides (7.27–42) is suggestive here, as noted by Vlastos (1946) 66; Fränkel (1975) 228 n.21; Noussia-Fantuzzi (2010) 320–1. *Pace* Mülke (2002) 228, I find it more natural to apply the image to the demos than to the polis as a whole: the parallels which he cites from the *Iliad* (2.394–8, 9.4–7) describe the Achaeans as a crowd, not a community. If the allusion is to the demos, it is also less likely that there is a link to ideas of cosmic justice here (as Noussia 2001 *ad loc.* suggests).

48 Noussia (2006) 140–6 has a good discussion of the persuasive character of analogies from nature; she also notes the implicit exclusion of any divine causation.
49 On Greek imagery of light see Tarrant (1960), esp. 181–3; on the association of light with salvation or rescue, see Fraenkel (1950) on A. *Ag.* 522 (below 112) and for Near Eastern parallels, West (1997) 253, cf. 574, 577. The Great King of Persia is often said to have been surrounded by a radiant nimbus of kingly glory, the *Hvarena* (also rendered *Khvarnah* or *farnah*): Dvornik 1966, 84–7, though 'it is not uncontentiously clear … that the concept is attested *as such* in any Achaemenid era document or context' (C. Tuplin, pers. comm.); certainly the Persian king was associated in symbolic and religious terms with the sun and fire (Briant 1996, 259–63), an idea echoed in Aeschylus' *Persae* (Harrison 2000, 78–9, 82). That kind of association of light with the glory of monarchy finds some kind of echo in Pindar's description of Xenocrates, brother of the tyrant Theron as 'light of the Acragantines' (*I.* 2.17), as it does later in Roman imperial coinage and other propaganda (Thomas 2007, 66–7) and early mediaeval iconography (Kantorowicz 1957, 61–5, 78–82). The portent of the sacrificial pots boiling over that prefigured the birth of Peisistratus (Hdt. 1.59.1–2) perhaps also suggests an association between tyranny and fire, though in a more ambiguous way: Lavelle (1991) 318 notes the implication that it is Peisistratus' destiny to be tyrant.
50 So there is a difference from Solon fr.36.15–17, as well as a resemblance (Irwin 2005, 224–6). There is also a riddling allusion to Cypselus' birthplace, Petra (Parke and Wormell 1949, 138), as also in the reference to the 'eagle in the rocks' in no.7 (so How & Wells (1928) *ad loc.*): these allusions point to a post-event invention, though presumably within Cypselus' lifetime (so e.g. Forrest 1966, 111, Salmon 1984, 186–7, 191). The extended analysis of McGlew (1993) 61–74 brings out the ambivalence of the oracles, which he associates with the inherently violent character of tyrannical justice and Delphic reservations about autocracy.
51 Strictly speaking this belongs to the classical period (the ode is dated to 476 BC) but, as often, Pindar is reflecting the persistence of elite values established in the archaic period.
52 Compare Callinus 1.20, where the reference is specifically military (and more overtly Homeric).
53 Rightly noted by Kearns (1990) 338. Longo (1974) has a good discussion of the extension of the image from the lone hero to a wider group in the context of the emerging polis while retaining its primary signification of defence.
54 'The image of the lion to represent the fierce force of kings is conventional and could be described as a fixed piece of the "portrait" of the king': Pucci (1998) 51 n.7; NB West (1997) 246–7, 388 for Near Eastern parallels.
55 Allowing for some uncertainties of dating, I count some 53 archaic and classical instances of Leon and 15 of Leonides/-as across vols.1–5A of the *Lexicon of Greek Personal Names* (and so across the Greek world) together with a Leonikides, a Leonike and a Leonumos.
56 Noted by McGlew (1993) 83–4.
57 I postpone to the following chapter (118) the most conspicuous case, the dream of Agariste, since its specific reference is to Pericles. For the ambiguity of lions even in Homer, see Lonsdale (1990), esp. 39–70, on lion similes; Wolff (1979).
58 This is another Homeric image with Near Eastern parallels: West (1997) 243–4. A bull (or its head) appears on the archaic coinage of Sybaris, Croton with Sybaris, Eretria and Lydia, in the latter case together with a lion, which features alone on those of Miletus, Samos and Sardis; boars appear winged on coins of Samos and

eagles on those of Acragas (but wolves not at all). In a later period one might compare the Delphic oracle presaging the death of Philip II: 'the bull is garlanded...' (D.S. 16.91.2-3).

59 Similes: *Il.* 17.674, 21.252, 22.308, *Od.* 24.538; portents: *Il.* 8.247, 12.201f., 13.822, 24.315, *Od.* 2.146, 15.161, 20.243; dreams: *Od.* 19.538f.; for the eagle as ruler of birds in Assyria see West (1997) 540.

60 Silk (1974) 193 n.2. On eagles see further below 118.

61 See Pulleyn (2000) on *Il.* 1.231, citing Eide (1988), for this reading, and for Hesiod, West (1978a) *ad loc.*; readings of the fable of the hawk and the nightingale which align the *basileis* with the hawk (above 84) would complement this association. Strictly speaking, the 'predation' involved in gift-eating is a kind of parasitism; West (2007) 422 cites Hittite and Vedic parallels for the 'eating' of bribes.

62 e.g. *Il.* 11.481, 16.159, 23.183: in the last case the verb is also applied zeugmatically to fire, which provides a conceptual link to that image of the destructive tyrant (above 88-9). There are similar implications of destructiveness, though more specifically directed against the elite, in the object-lesson of the ears of corn given by Thrasybulus (Hdt. 5.92 ζ2-η1), if that goes back in substance to the archaic period, as plausibly argued by Forsdyke (1999) 364-5, highlighting the implication of anti-elite hostility: for full discussion see below, 143n.142.

63 Though note that the tyrant is not yet Plato's werewolf (*R.* 565d-6a, below 179n.82, 187n.134), since he is not figured as eating his own kind. Vox (1984) 120-1 on the bestial greed of the tyrant is suggestive here, if overstated.

64 On the form of the net and its alternative uses, see Mülke (2002) 342-3; for the net's association with tyrants, Vox (1984) 97 – note especially the oracle at Hdt. 1.62.4 (where the specific reference to tunny-fishing highlights the intelligence of Peisistratus the fisherman: Lavelle 1991, 317, 321-3) and Cyrus the fisherman at 1.141.1-2; Catenacci (1991) 88-9. However, net imagery appears in an erotic context at Ibycus fr.287.1-4: compare Thgn. 949-50 (= 1278c-d) for a similar image of a predatory animal, linked to others from warfare and chariot-racing: hunting is at home in the symposium.

65 Fr.69.6: for the identification with Pittacus see Page (1955) 231-3; Griffiths (1995) 89, 93 underlines the unheroic character of the fox, never mentioned by Homer. Cf. the fox-dog (i.e. the Paphlagonian) in a mock oracle at Ar. *Eq.* 1067-8 with Neil (1901) *ad loc.* On Alcaeus' use of proverbs see further below, n.91.

66 Solon fr.36.26-7; wolves in fables: Irwin (2005) 252-6; the closest parallel for the animal at bay is *Il.* 12.41-2, cf. 11.548-9, 17.281-3, 657-64.

67 Wolves and tyranny: Irwin (2005) 248-61, though Loraux (1984) 207 notes the conflict with Solon's overt rejection of tyranny; scapegoat: Anhalt (1993) 134, but NB Stehle (2006) 93 n.41, noting that the scapegoat moves away, outside the community.

68 Relation to Homer: Irwin (2005) 245-6; my reading of the wolf broadly follows Mülke (2002) 395-7: for the wolf and the lion cf. A. *Ag.* 1258-9 (but the wolf is *gennaios* for Aristotle, *HA* 488 b17), and for wolves' superiority to dogs, A. *Supp.* 760-1; wolves tend to get the better of dogs in fables (n.66 above). Irwin (2005) 260 n.174 astutely notes that Solon's opponents have also been turned into unheroic bitches. Reproach: Martin (2006) 164: '[t]he message conveyed ... that this is not the way things should be'; cf. Stehle (2006) 94 for the note of anger. Plut. *Sol.* 23.3-4 reports that Solon offered a bounty for wolves and their cubs, against which the Athenians have always been battling, so evoking a wolf will also have linked the image to real life.

69 Loraux (1984) 202, 206–7 notes the resemblance between the three images in their Homeric and paradoxical character and their emphatic placement at the end of passages of self-justification (though we cannot be sure that any of them marks the end of a poem – indeed, the last line we have of fr.37 is incomplete).
70 Stehle (2006) 97 puts it nicely: 'when the two ideas are combined the shield turns into a Möbius strip, for in order to make the same image convey both ideas the speaker must pretend that the outside of the shield is simultaneously its inside'; cf. 96 for the evocation of the tower-shield of Ajax. Martin (2006) 163–4 suggests that the paradox 'retains the association of protection, but eliminates the notion of battle'.
71 The first reading is that of Loraux (1984), esp. 211–13, who sees a contrast with the multiple *horoi* of the Eupatrids in fr.36.6; she also notes (208 n.36) that real *horoi* may speak in the first person. For the second, see Martin (2006), esp. 166–71, summarising Solon's 'metaphorical message' as 'copy me, do not take up arms against one another, respect this eloquent rock' (170).
72 Commentators dispute whether *gala* or an implied *dêmon* is the object of *antaraxas* (Noussia-Fantuzzi 2010, 492–4, Mülke 2002, 405–6), but the broad sense is the same in either case. It is suggestive that *piar* occurs in the *Iliad* only in the simile of a lion at bay at 11.550, 17.659 (NB n.66 above) in the sense 'fat (i.e. choicest one or part': Hainsworth 1993 on 11.550) and otherwise at *Od.* 9.135, *hAp.* 60 and *hVen.* 30; here it might properly mean 'butterfat' (Salmon 1997, 68), but the implication remains the same.
73 Donlan (1999) 129–30 assumes the term is pejorative (and Alcaeus' abuse of Pittacus as 'Pot-belly' [frr.129.21, 429] makes clear that not all fat is good), but it is used apparently neutrally by Herodotus 5.30.1 (Naxos), 6.91.1 (Aegina), 7.156.2 (Megara Hyblaea) cf. 5.77.2 and LSJ s.v. πάχης (the word can also mean 'sturdy', 'solid', but that does not seem an effective slogan); of course, what began as self-praise could be given a more pejorative edge in egalitarian Athens: Ar. *Eq.*1139, *Vesp.* 288, *Pax* 639 (but NB 1170 'and then I become fat', on which Olson (1998) remarks 'a positive development in a world where extra calories were scarce').
74 Compare the undesirable stirring up of the sea in fr.12.1 (above 88); Archilochus uses the same verb, *tarassô*, in his maritime metaphor at fr.105.1 and it is applied to civil disorder in Thgn. 219. In the fifth century, the imagery of 'stirring up' is negatively associated with Cleon (below 132n.68, 138n.118).
75 And Homer barely uses the common Near Eastern image of kings themselves as servants of the gods (only *Od.* 11.255 comes close, but a *therapôn* is of relatively high status: 'a non-kinsman of noble, but dependant status', according to West in Heubeck, West and Hainsworth 1990 on *Od.* 1.109; NB also Stagakis 1966): contrast (e.g.) Pritchard (1969) 275, 277, 281, 289, 298, 307 (Assyrian and Neobabylonian), 315–16 (Cyrus), 334, 337 (Akkadian) for kings addressing a god as 'my lord' or 'the lord'.
76 Fr.9.3–4, cf. fr.11.4 with Brock (2007) 209–10; on the resonances of *monarchos* here, NB McGlew (1993) 65–6.
77 See Tedeschi 1991 for bibliography and discussion, especially 184–5 for the arguments against a Persian link (cf. Willetts 1962, 317–23) which he nevertheless regards as '*molto plausibile*' and 124 for an agnostic position on the date (Page 1965 65 proposed a fifth-century context); note also his suggestion that the speaker's grandiloquent self-advertisement became somewhat humorous when the poem became adopted in wider sympotic use (122–4). There is perhaps a similar deliberate hyperbole in the use of *turanni-* words applied to women in erotic contexts at Anacreon fr.449 and, apparently, Archilochus fr.23.20 (for this interpretation see

West 1974, 118–20); with the preceding military image in lines 18–19 compare Thgn. 951, which follows the hunting image cited in n.64.
78 Since the other earliest witness is Theognis, there is the same uncertainty concerning priority and absolute date as for the ship of state (above, n.23).
79 Recent discussions tend to follow the assertion of Adkins (1985) 118 that at this date *helkos* can only mean 'wound', but he seems to have overlooked Thgn. 1134 (below), where *phuomenôi* surely excludes that sense; NB also Irwin (2005) 181 n.71, suggesting that a reminiscence here of the silent diseases of Hes. *Op.* 102–4 ought to keep both senses in play. I would see Solon as giving more prominence to the sense of disease, while exploiting the ambiguity of *helkos* to imply the culpability of the leaders: see above 69 and n.5 for the implications of imagery of deliberate wounding.
80 Irwin (2005) 155–98 discusses the relationship of Solon fr.4 to Hesiod in depth. Community's fate linked to justice of rulers: Hom. *Il.* 16.384–92, *Od.* 19.109–14, Hes. *Op.* 225–47 with West (1978) 213, Parker (1983) 265–7; West (2007) 422–4 notes parallels in Vedic and north European poetry. For later periods see above 73–4.
81 This might encourage us to regard the injury as disease, given the model of infliction of disease from outside by a divinity (typically Apollo, as at the beginning of the *Iliad*); otherwise, sickness in the body politic tends to arise from internal causes (above 73–6), while gods, particularly Apollo and Artemis, normally inflict death rather than wounding: see the good brief discussion in Graf (2009) 9–10, 14–18.
82 West prints the passage as fr.33a: Mülke (2002) 347–9 is dubious on linguistic grounds that any of Solon's words survive, though the underlying idea might derive from his poetry; Noussia-Fantuzzi (2010) 423–5 is cautiously more positive. Cp. Plutarch's phrase 'cure (*iasaito*) his desire for tyranny' in *Sol.* 29.5, West's fr.35, though both Mülke (2002, 360–1) and Noussia-Fantuzzi (2010, 425) are sceptical that it goes back to Solon.
83 There is a variant at 1081–2 which overtly labels the expected tyrant 'a man of hubris, a leader of harsh *stasis*': renaming the tyrant 'for what he "really" is' (Irwin 2005, 227 n.63) may help aristocrats cope, but removes none of the force of the image.
84 As in the Delphic oracles to Argos and Athens from just before the Persian wars (Hdt. 7.148.3, 140.2–3; above 70); compare the synecdoche of 'heads' for 'men' in Homer and Hesiod (*Il.* 11.55, Hes. fr.204.118) and *kephalê* for various individuals (*Il.* 8.281, 18.114, 23.94; Hes. *Sc.* 104); so too Pindar can call the Emmenid tyrants of Akragas 'the eye of Sicily' (*O.* 2.9–10, cf. *P.* 5.55–7, of the Battiads; *LSJ* s.v. ὀφθαλμός IV). Fables based on the body (on which NB Daube 1972, 130–9), though none appears to be of so early a date (Adrados 1999–2003, I 398–409) tend to emphasize diversity of function within the bodily unity (e.g the stomach, the eyes, the feet).
85 Below 114, and for conceptions of the body in political terms see Brock (2006); Harvey (1965) shows that, though retrojected to Solon (121–2; Plut. *Sol.* 14.2), the concept of proportional equality only develops in the fourth century, although its antecedents go back to Homer (101–2).
86 Cosmos as organism: Lloyd (1966) 232–41; as state, above 8–10, Lloyd (1996) 210–29.
87 Lloyd loc. cit (n.86), prefigured by Vlastos (1947), (1953); Seaford (1994) 220–8 elaborates a contrast between Anaximander and Heraclitus, developing the arguments of Vernant (e.g. 1982, 119–29) which emphasize the impact of the new civic space of the polis.
88 For examples of periodicity in early law, note the monthly meetings of the Spartan assembly stipulated in the 'Great Rhetra' (Plut. *Lyc.* 6.2), perhaps imitated by Solon

(Rhodes 1981, 154), and the *boulê dêmosiê* in the law from Chios (*ML* no.8C) and the ban on serving as *kosmos* twice within ten years at Dreros (*ML* no.2).
89 Cf. fr.114: 'all human laws are nourished by the single divine law. For it has as much power as it wishes, and is enough for all, with something to spare' (tr. Lloyd).
90 Griffiths (1995) assesses what we do have.
91 On the various board games called *pessoi* see Kurke (1999b), (1999a) 254–74 (a little fuller); Hansen (2002) reconstructs the variant called *Polis*; for images from *pessoi* in general, see Collard 1975 on E. *Supp.* 409–10a. Kurke characterizes them as 'games of order', linked with a symbolic civic order, and suggests that Alcaeus 'bitterly and dismissively characterizes his opponent as (merely) a pretend king in a board game' (258); I am inclined to follow Porro (1994) esp. 367–8 and Lelli (2006) 49–51 in linking the image to games played in the symposium – cf. frr.306 (i) II. 30–1 and 306B, both again with proverbial overtones: in particular, the numerous vase-paintings of heroes playing *pessoi* (Kurke 1999a, 270) could as easily be seen to link these games, like *kottabos* and dicing (Kurke 1999a, 278–95, to be read with Fisher 2001, 195–6, 357–61), with the elite world of the symposium (and NB Kurke 1999a, 265–7, omitted from *id.* (1999b), for a suggestion of more democratic or oligarchic versions of *pessoi*). There is also a link to a proverbial expression for 'risking all' (Kurke 1999a, 257–8; cf. Hansen 2002, 10 for 'playing city/-ies' as proverbial) which is probably the specific reference here; while there is no implication of sharp practice (since these are games with clear structure and rules), there does seem to be an overtone of cleverness (cf. E. *Supp.* 409 and A. *Supp.* 11–12 with Bakewell 2008) rather than honest achievement. Alcaeus employs another proverb in fr.344: 'this I know for certain, that if a man moves gravel, stone not safely workable, he will probably get a sore head' (cf. Sapph. fr.145); the idea of a fool's labour which brings trouble to the labourer might have been applied to Pittacus' *aisymneteia*, though as often there is no context from which to make deductions. Lelli (2006) 23–70 discusses Alcaeus' fondness for proverbs, though that should not surprise us: the game of *eikones* ('Comparisons') played at symposia (e.g. Ar. *Vesp.* 1308–13 with MacDowell 1971, *Av.* 804–6 with Dunbar 1995, Pl. *Smp.* 215a, X. *Smp.* 6.8–10) points to the appeal of the pithy, well-turned phrase in these circles.

A related mystery is the popular song *PMG* 869 'grind, mill, grind, for Pittacus too grinds who rules over great Mytilene': it could conceivably mean that Pittacus really did do his own grinding (so Carlier 1984, 460–1), which might have been inappropriate or demeaning (NB Arist. *Rh.* 1411 a23–4 for figurative mills), or might refer to 'grinding the faces of the poor' (or rich), or to a claim by Pittacus to have ground his enemies small, or, perhaps most likely, the reference might be obscene (NB Campbell 1982–93 *ad loc.*), but decision is impossible.
92 Irwin (2005) 22–9, 35–62 offers a subtle discussion of the use of Homer in elegiac exhortation poetry.
93 S262 (= 298 in Campbell 1982–93), the so-called Cologne Alcaeus, with Lloyd-Jones (1968), esp. 128–9, 136–9, who emphasizes the link with the epic cycle.
94 For uncertainty as to the extent of the community, see above 86 and n.28.
95 This relative homogeneity in the imagery makes it difficult to square with the influential model (Morris 1996) of two traditions in archaic poetry, an 'elitist' and a 'middling' one: on the one hand, there is from the outset an acknowledgement of a wider community which gains definition over time, though a useful element of ambiguity as to its extent remains, even for the body politic, the most naturally inclusive model; on the other hand, elites continue to use imagery to distinguish

themselves from ordinary people, often drawing on the resources of epic to do so (cf. the acute discussion in Irwin 2005, 55–62 of the ideology of exhortation elegy). A lack of clear distinctions in imagery between genres might also be seen to support the view that associates almost all archaic poetry with the symposium.

96 For the development and date of the stock view of tyranny see Lewis (2004); Connor (1977) discusses the potential for admiration of tyranny, for which NB also Irwin (2005) 238–9, while Salmon (1997) makes a case for a more positive view of the archaic tyrants in action. Irwin (2005, e.g. 203–4, 275–6) rightly argues that the demarcation between tyrants, law-givers and sages is not straightforward – Pittacus is a key figure here.

97 As in Meno's definition of female excellence at Pl. *Men.* 71e, though Xenophon's *Oeconomicus* shows that a broader outlook was perfectly possible.

7

Democracy and Autocracy: The Fifth Century (c. 480–404 BC)

The two developments which exerted the greatest influence on classical political imagery, the rise of Persia and the emergence of democracy, both belong to the archaic period, but their impact only appears in literature after 480. Thereafter, in political imagery as in ideology at large, they become increasingly interlinked through the growing predominance of Athens in our sources; often they are linked through the motif of tyranny, with which Persia was frequently aligned, especially after the Marathon campaign of 490, which sought to restore Hippias as a Persian puppet, and Xerxes' attempt at the wholesale subjugation of Greece a decade later.[1] That motif is one element in the formation of the complex of images of slavery or subordination to a master with which the rule of the Great King of Persia[2] came to be associated. As we have seen (above 92), when the idea of slavery is first used figuratively by Solon, it is associated with tyranny, and the language of slavery and freedom continues to be regularly used in that context through the classical period (below, 157–8). It was natural to extend this language to Persia: not only was the Great King as absolute monarch a tyrant writ large (whether Greek or Lydian), but since his control over the Greeks of Asia was exercised through tyrants in their *poleis*, he was as much 'Tyrant of Tyrants' as 'King of Kings'.[3]

The other element which contributes to the developed image of the Persian king as master is Greek perception of Persian royal ideology. It is clear that there existed a feudal relation between the King and even his most exalted subordinates, which was denoted by the term *ba(n)daka*: in Greek sources this is largely simplified into an antithesis between the Great King, the one free man, and his subjects, who are slaves, no matter what their status. What is less clear is whether this is the result of genuine misunderstanding or deliberate misrepresentation, or (perhaps most likely), some combination of the two.[4] The association of the titles 'Great King' and *despotês* in the 'song of Hybrias' combined with the mention of obeisance (above 92) suggests that the perception of the Persian king as overlord had already become established in the archaic period,[5] and there is a hint in Xenophanes A32 that such terminology was already coming to be used pejoratively (above 98n.37). That outlook comes sharply into focus in Aeschylus' *Persians*, produced in 472, less than a decade after Xerxes' invasion, in an exchange between the Persian queen Atossa and the chorus of Persian elders concerning the Athenians (241–2):

— What shepherd (*poimanôr*) is set over them and is master of (*epidespozei*) the host?
— They are not called any man's slaves or subjects.

The queen's naïve assumption that Athens is like Persia is transparently (to our eyes) set up for a rebuttal which forms part of a sustained contrast between the democratic Athenians and their barbarian opponents,[6] in a way that shows that by this date both the stock view of Persia and its location in a wider antithesis between freedom and democracy and barbarians and autocracy are firmly established; it would not be surprising if the Athenian experience at Marathon had given an impetus to the process even before the advent of Xerxes, and the sophistication and subtlety of the play's ideological presentation implies an extended period of gestation.

The same play provides evidence for another element in the figurative representation of Persian subjection, the imagery of animal-taming, here represented by the motif of the yoke. In the parodos, the chorus speak of the army's mission to 'put a yoke of slavery on Greece' (50), and, after news of the disaster at Salamis has reached them, they express their fears for the Persian empire 'now that the yoke of might is undone' (594).[7] Xerxes' ambition is also symbolized in Atossa's dream of his attempt to yoke together the two women who represent Europe and Asia (181–96), and his literal yoking of the continents by the bridge across the Hellespont (68–72, 722, 736):[8] the Athenians captured and dedicated the cables from that bridge, so they will have had a permanent physical reminder of that act of *hybris*.[9] Furthermore, since the image of yoking and taming was at home in the Near East (above 87), it was natural for it to take on a particular association with the threat of subjugation from that quarter.

By the second half of the fifth century we find this group of images firmly entrenched in tragedy and historiography. Herodotus applies the imagery of the control of animals to Persian conquest of external subjects in a way that implies that it has become almost standard usage: Persian kings are said to 'tame' (*hêmeroun*) their enemies both authorially and by their victims, as well as by Persians themselves, and submission is referred to as 'bowing one's neck to the yoke' (*hupokuptein*).[10] Likewise Xerxes says of the proposed complete conquest of Greece 'and so both those who have wronged us and the innocent will bear the yoke of slavery' (7.8.γ3). In a similar way, the claim of Euripides' Helen that 'everything among barbarians is enslaved except one man' (E. *Hel.* 276) encapsulates the stock view of Persian monarchy at the same time as extending it to a dramatic setting in Egypt, though this does not inhibit her from using the same idea to flatter and deceive the Egyptian king Theoclymenus ('do not be a slave to your slaves, lord', 1428). The same ideology can be applied to entirely non-Greek contexts: in the Euripidean *Rhesus* 410–1, Hector speaks of handing over the Thracians to the rule of Rhesus as slaves, though when Timotheus in his dithyrambic *Persae* makes a Persian refer to Xerxes as 'my master' (115–16, 152) it is presumably simply realistic, just as *despotês* is frequently used in Herodotus as a term of address for the king of Persia.[11] Herodotus too extends the use of language originally used of Persia to a wider sphere: *despotês* and *despoina* ('mistress') are applied also to Lydia *à propos* of the Gyges and Candaules episode,[12] to Egypt, where Amasis is said to have overthrown 'his master' Apries (3.1.4) and, most strikingly, to the former subordination of Persia to Media: in 1.115.2 Cyrus addresses Astyages as 'O master', and the herdsman and his wife describe Astyages and Mandane as 'our masters' (1.111.2, 112.3) while at 1.91.6 Cyrus' father is said to have been living with his 'mistress', inasmuch as his wife Mandane was a Median princess rather than a Persian.

That distinction brings us to a new element in Herodotus' use of the image, the application of the language of mastery and servitude to the control of an imperial power over its subjects. Here the term 'master' refers to the ruler as overlord, either from his own perspective ('Your master Cambyses, Psammenitus, asks you...': 3.14.9), or the conquered (Croesus addresses Cyrus as master at 1.90.2; cf. 5.18.3). During the account of Darius' Scythian expedition, the title is nicely made the object of a contention which brings out its implications: Darius calls on the Scythian king to fight, or else acknowledge his master and submit (4.126), and is met with the riposte that the Scythian king acknowledges as his masters only Zeus and Hestia 'queen of the Scythians' (4.127.4 cf. 128.1); however, when the Scythians exhort the Ionians at the Danube bridge to abandon Darius, they describe him as 'your former master' (4.136.4). Equally revealing is Xerxes' address to the Hellespont in which he identifies himself as 'your master' (7.35.2) before he has it whipped. Earlier, after his defeat at the hands of Cyrus, Astyages reviles Harpagus for having made the Medes slaves instead of masters and the Persians masters instead of slaves (1.129.4). That introduces the other side of the coin, the perception of subjection to an external power as a form of slavery: in Herodotus, this most frequently concerns Persian control, as in the formulas which mark the first 'enslavements' of Lydia (1.94.7) and Ionia (1.169.2, 6.32), but we also find it applied to the subjection of the Medes to Assyria (1.95.2) and, as we have just seen, it is also used of the Persians themselves in relation to Media (1.126.5). Hence the Persians themselves can perceive that reversal of roles as 'liberation' (1.126.6, 127.1, 3.82.5),[13] while those subjugated, like the Medes, become 'slaves'.[14] Although Herodotus sometimes reports literal enslavement in the wake of Persian conquest, he uses a different terminology in these cases,[15] and it is clear that the *douleia* at issue here is figurative and carries significant ideological implications.

It is not only the subjects of the Persian empire who are figured as slaves: as we have seen, fifth-century Greeks perceived all the subjects of the Great King (and, by extension, other oriental monarchs) as his 'slaves'.[16] Whether or not this belief was correct, this conception is applied in Herodotus in a quite pointed manner in contexts which imply that it reflects, or is believed to reflect, Persian ideology. Thus Artemisia in advising Xerxes labels as his slaves not only allies such as Egyptians, Cyprians, Cilicians and Pamphylians (8.68.γ), but even Mardonius, the king's cousin and brother-in-law and son-in-law of Darius (6.43.1, 7.5.1), who is to serve as deputed supreme commander after Xerxes' withdrawal (8.102.3). When the Samian Syloson similarly describes Maiandrios to Darius as 'our slave' (3.140.5), he is presumably again fitting his expression to the ideology of his audience. By extension, when the Persians pursuing the fugitive doctor Democedes demand that the Crotoniates surrender him, they describe him as the King's 'runaway slave' (*drêpetên*, 3.137.2), and Dionysius of Phocaea is made to reflect that Persian outlook when he warns the Ionians before the decisive battle of Lade that their choice is 'to be free men or slaves, and runaway slaves at that' (6.11.2).[17] So too the Scythians scorn the Ionians after their failure to act against Darius on the Danube as 'slaves that love their master and do not run away (*adrêsta*)' (4.142). This ideology may also help to explain the Persian dismissal of Cambyses as 'a master ... because he was harsh and contemptuous' (3.89.3): the point would be that Cambyses overstepped the mark by making his status as master too literal a reality in his treatment of them.[18] By contrast, the house of Otanes alone is 'free', because it is not subject to the King's authority, but only to the laws (3.83.2–3).[19]

It accords with this conception that Kings of Persia should be styled not merely as rulers of their land, but as its possessors, both in the speeches of subordinates and in their own pronouncements.[20] We also find on a number of occasions the phrase 'the King's house' used with reference to the Persian empire, which seems quite likely to draw on Persian conceptions, since not only is it found in later Greek sources, but we also find the phrase 'great favour will be laid up in store for you in the King's house' in lines 15–17 of the letter of Darius to Gadatas, even if the Greek versions involve a degree of over-simplification of what was in practice a rather more complex relationship between the King's house and the empire at large.[21]

The suggestion that Herodotus is here to some extent reflecting actual Persian thinking gains some support from indications of a sensitivity to other aspects of Persian ideology such as the emphasis on personal prowess in royal inscriptions, which is reflected both in the text of an inscription of Darius reported by Herodotus which styles him 'best and fairest of all men' (4.91.2) and in his remark after enumerating the Persian forces that 'for looks and stature none was more worthy than Xerxes to hold this power' (7.187.2); the ideal of the king as exceptional among men also finds an echo in the attribution to him of more than human power and reach by Alexander of Macedon (8.140.β2).[22]

Greek experience of Persian rule, then, very probably coloured by some degree of awareness of actual Persian ideology, will have been one strand in Herodotus' use of the imagery of servitude and subjection: the other must have been the association established by Solon half a century earlier than the coming of the Mede between slavery and tyranny.[23] For Herodotus this link is so firmly established that he can apply it even to constitutional monarchy (and its removal) outside Greece: thus the Egyptians can be described as 'liberated' after the cessation of monarchy in Egypt, even though it was replaced by the limited monarchy of the twelve kings (2.147.2), while he describes their acceptance of Amasis' rule as pharaoh by saying that he 'induced the Egyptians to agree to be slaves' (2.172.5). More frequently, however, the imagery of freedom is used to refer to the overthrow or absence of tyranny in Greece, especially at Athens, but also with reference to Samos after Polycrates, Miletus in the Ionian Revolt and Selinos in Sicily. Conversely, Maiandrios is made to speak of Polycrates 'acting as master of men like himself', and Herodotus says of the Athenians' military lethargy under the Peisistratids that they 'deliberately fought badly because they were working for a master'.[24] Particularly noteworthy are those editorial passages where Herodotus equates freedom with opposition to or rejection of tyranny and alleges that those who laid down tyrannies voluntarily were motivated by justice (*dikaiosunê*).[25]

In tragedy the image is used to colour the presentation of rulers who are tyrants, or show tyrannical traits. In Euripides' *Heracles*, Lycus is a stock tyrant, and it is natural that he should advertise himself as *despotês* of the Thebans (141–2) and refer to them as 'slaves to my tyranny' (251); the chorus' reply indignantly repeats the offending image (258, 270, 274). Similarly, Pentheus at his most unsympathetic refuses to come to terms with the Theban bacchantes with the reply 'How? By being a slave to my slaves?' (E. *Ba.* 803).[26] Likewise in *Phoenissae*, Eteocles, who has just invoked *Turannis* as the greatest of the gods (506) exclaims 'When I can rule, shall I ever be a slave to him [sc. his brother Polyneices]?' (520);[27] and an unknown speaker in Sophocles fr.85 (*Aleadae*) faces the same dilemma, musing that it might be better to have control of his enemies even at the price of impiety rather than obey others as a slave, while elsewhere we meet the more general proposition that anyone attending on a tyrant is his slave (fr.873). Conversely, the removal of a tyrant is equated with freedom, notably in Aeschylus' *Choephoroi*, where Aegisthus is, like Lycus, a usurper.[28] The same imagery naturally also appears in the *Prometheus Vinctus* to describe cosmic tyranny – not, surprisingly, that of Zeus, but rather that aspired to by the Titans before him (208) and then what will follow him (927, 930), though the implication is that his part in the sequence is the same.[29] This concept of the king of the gods is echoed in Euripides' *Heracles*, in the hero's attack on the 'baneful tales of poets' and his denial that any god 'is master of another' (1344), rebutting Theseus' consolation that even gods 'have defiled one another for the sake of tyranny' (1317–8).[30]

A similar role is played by the image of the yoke: as we have seen (above 87), such imagery was already associated with Near Eastern autocracy as well as with tyranny in the archaic period, and those associations have now effectively fused together. In the *Prometheus*, a play suffused with imagery of yoking and taming,[31] Io describes the compulsion on her father to cast her out of his house as 'the bridle (*chalinos*) of Zeus' (671–2), so reinforcing the portrait of Zeus in the play as a tyrant. In Aeschylus' *Agamemnon*, Aegisthus meets the resistance of the Chorus to his new regime with the threat that the disobedient will be yoked to a heavy yoke and 'softened' by hunger (1639–42):[32] here again the language of taming contributes indirectly to the portrait of Aegisthus and Clytemnestra as tyrants. Sophocles uses the language of control of animals in a more oblique and suggestive way. Sometimes he puts it in the mouths of rulers who are shortly to come to grief: in the *Antigone*, Creon complains that 'some men ... muttered against me, tossing their heads in secret, and would not keep their necks duly (*dikaiôs*) under the yoke' (290–2), and later he warns Antigone menacingly 'I know that wild-tempered horses are made docile by a little curb (*chalinôi*)' (477–8), while Aegisthus, warning the Mycenaeans of the futility of resistance after Orestes' purported death, bids them 'accept my bit (*stomia*)' (*El*. 1462). Agamemnon in the *Ajax* makes a similar remark to Creon's: 'A big-ribbed ox is still kept straight on the road by a little goad (*mastigos*)' (1253–4); it is tempting to see an echo of the famous Homeric image of Ajax as an ass driven by beating out of the cornfield (*Il*. 11.558f.), but with the heroic reminiscence undercut to emphasize the king's petty authoritarianism. Here, though within the play the official standing of the Atreidae is not suspect or contested, the resonances of their language serve to characterize them negatively in a way that undercuts their pretensions to heroic leadership.[33]

There is a degree of ambiguity even to some images which in the archaic period have had positive implications. Oedipus' first words in Sophocles' *Oedipus Tyrannus* are 'Oh children', and the implication that he was thinking like a father attracted favourable comment from the scholiast; however, all the fifth-century parallels are in Near Eastern contexts: the chorus in Aeschylus *Persae* addressing Darius as 'father' and Atossa as 'mother', and the description of Croesus and Cyrus as fathers in Herodotus.[34] Furthermore, as with the Homeric precedents, in all these cases the image is used by someone else, but Oedipus is implicitly styling himself as a father, which again is closer to Near Eastern practice. Similar concerns surround Agamemnon's self-presentation as doctor (A. *Ag.* 848–50, quoted above 75): although health is an unarguable good, his readiness to resort immediately to the most radical methods of treatment was surely meant to provoke some anxiety in the audience.[35] Behind the king's words lurks the suspicion of disloyalty which he intends shall meet its just reward; elsewhere, the suspicion is of tyranny, which Oedipus expresses in describing Creon, whom he suspects of trying to supplant him, as 'a palpable robber (*lêstês*) of my kingship (*turannidos*)' (S. *O.T.* 535). A few lines later he ridicules Creon's attempt 'to hunt kingship (*turannida*), which is caught with numbers and money' (540–2): here what was implicit in the former passage becomes overt, echoing the imagery of hunting with which would-be tyrants are described in archaic poetry in a way which is suggestive of Oedipus' state of mind and his attitude to his royal status.[36]

It is not, of course, that the images of the king as father or doctor in themselves had acquired negative connotations, but rather that the attitude of fifth-century democratic Athens to monarchy was complex and conflicted.[37] Athens had good kings in her own past, notably Cecrops, Erechtheus and Theseus, and they and their like could appear on stage as such, while in many other plays kings could form part of the background assumed as normal for the heroic past without being problematized, as long as their status remained in the background;[38] however, in the cases just surveyed, the effect of the imagery is by characterizing them to draw attention to the status of tragic kings as kings. That in turn could have aroused negative feelings in the audience at what might have seemed presumption in arrogating to themselves roles and responsibilities which in a real-life democratic context would be assigned by a political process, and that was more likely, I think, when the images clashed with competing democratic versions of the field of imagery (the state as household, the body politic).[39]

For confirmation that images such as these retained their positive valuation we can turn to Pindar, more or less the only exponent of a positive presentation of monarchy in the fifth century.[40] He clearly feels no embarrassment at describing Hieron, tyrant of Syracuse, as a father or a steward, even if the implications are more specific and muted than in Homer,[41] or having the mythical Iamus ask for *laotrophon timan tin'* ('the honour of feeding a people', that is, as a *poimên laôn*; *O.* 6.60).[42] In other images that echo Homeric usage and that of archaic sympotic poetry, rulers are compared to bulwarks, to radiant light and to an eagle.[43] Elsewhere, Pindar elaborates concepts which first appear in the archaic period: in *Pythian* 4 he appeals to the image of the body politic in calling on Arkesilas IV of Cyrene to cure the disease of *stasis*, though with a markedly different tone from that of Aeschylus' Agamemnon: 'you are a most opportune healer, and Paian honours you with the light of salvation. One must tend an ulcerous wound by applying a gentle hand' (270–1).[44] This is an ode in which the contemporary political context is unusually conspicuous in an epilogue which pleads for the restoration of an exiled Cyrenean with the aid of a diverse array of political images.[45] First comes a reference to a felled and mutilated oak-tree which still reveals its quality, whether put on a fire or made into an architrave (263–9): that is most readily connected with the exiled Damophilos, bereft of rights and possessions, but might also allude to the whole city,[46] as the succeeding medical image presumably does, since the word *polin* appears in the line which follows it ('for it is easy to shake a city...' 272). Here, however, the word *seisai* ('shake') suggests a building shaken by an earthquake (which would pick up the motif of the tree as architrave), or perhaps a ship being rocked, and the idea of the ship of state is certainly in the background with the mention of a helmsman two lines later, though this is not an mortal ruler, but a god (274).[47] Medical and maritime imagery recurs with reference to the exile's personal suffering in the final section, where he is also compared to Atlas in bondage supporting the heavens (again with a reminiscence of the tree image). The artfulness with which the various images are interwoven is plain, and the passage is even more artful if, as recent commentators tend to agree, the poet is feigning a plea for a return which has already been granted, highlighting the clemency which he affects to solicit.[48] At the same time, the way in which he frames the appeal necessarily gives more attention than he usually does to the relationship between ruler and community.[49] The reference to guiding 'the host with a just rudder' in an ode for Hieron is a little different, measuring the ruler against an abstract standard, though a call to him to act with generosity is also couched in maritime imagery (*P*. 1.86, 91–2), but the phrase 'pilotings of cities' at the end of the tenth *Pythian* (10.72) is intended simply to exalt the position of the Aleuadai. Overall, there is a noticeable disparity between the frequency and variety of Pindar's maritime imagery and the infrequency and conventionality of instances with political applications.[50]

That disparity is all the more marked if we contrast Pindar's practice with the prominence of political maritime imagery, and of the helmsman in particular, in Attic tragedy. The earliest instance is in Aeschylus' *Persians* (656), where the chorus says that Darius 'steered the host well'.[51] In this case, however, the image suffers no guilt by association with Persian monarchy, as we can see from its use five years later to characterize positively the Theban king Eteocles in *Septem*, expressing his sense of duty in his own words and his responsibility as seen by others; the figure of the helmsman is complemented by the image of the storm-tossed ship which evokes the danger to the city. The same note of dependence on the helmsman is struck by Jocasta in Sophocles *O.T.* 922–3; on the whole, though, the figure of the helmsman, or his position on the helmsman's bench, comes to be used more as a generic expression for monarchic rule.[52] Given the risks of seafaring and human fallibility, an awareness of the danger of shipwreck is certainly present in some passages.[53] A fragment of Sophocles (683 [*Phaedra*]) alludes in the same way to the dangers to the chariot of state when 'a chattering man with a wicked goad in hand has charge of the city'[54] and indeed even the figure of the helmsman is not inherently a positive one: we find it applied to the new regime of Zeus in the *Prometheus* (149–50),[55] while in the *Agamemnon* Aegisthus as the new helmsman looks down with contempt from his bench on the chorus as mere rowers (1617–18):[56] the distortion of the metaphor into a crude expression of superiority serves only to underline the usurper's lack of kingly qualities. It is not that the figure of the helmsman cannot be used negatively, but that it need not be: in the majority of instances the resonance is at least neutral and generally positive. The explanation is not clear, but it might be suggested that this was a field of imagery where, in contrast to those mentioned earlier (above 112), there was no specifically democratic version in competition:[57] it may be that fifth-century Athenians were sufficiently disposed as a maritime people to respond positively to the broad concept of the ship of state that they were able to tolerate the figure of the helmsman, by now firmly entrenched, as an essentially neutral model for leadership.[58]

The other key influence on fifth-century political ideology and its expression, democracy, has already been visible in the imagery we have examined so far, though only as the implied antithesis, defined by opposition to monarchy, particularly in its negative forms as tyranny or oriental autocracy.[59] When one turns to the positive expression of democratic ideology, this is less immediately conspicuous than one might have expected. We can observe the continued development of constitutionalist thinking in cosmology, in Empedocles' account of the cosmos as ordered by a regular succession of equipollent powers and by 'decrees of the gods' (above 6, 8) and in the similar conception of the body in political terms, in which health is dependent on a balance between the various elements, and the monarchy of any one of them causes disease. This conception first appears in Alcmaeon of Croton (B4), probably in the first half of the fifth century, and is also found in a number of early Hippocratic treatises.[60] We should note, however, that the underlying principle here is one of *isonomia*, a term which indeed is first attested in the Alcmaeon passage, and it is now recognized that the key resonance of that term is precisely constitutionality, as opposed to absolute monarchy: in itself, it is as compatible with oligarchy as democracy.[61] The same, I think, can be said of the figuring of the tyrant and (increasingly) of *stasis* (civil strife) as diseases of the body politic, the symptoms of which will be no less painful in an oligarchy than in democratic Athens.[62] We can also locate theorizing like that of Empedocles and Alcmaeon within a broader tendency to think about the cosmos in ever more specific political terms which is exemplified both by the elaboration of the politicized pantheon to embrace assemblies, votes, assessors and the rest of the apparatus of procedure, not to mention an array of personified powers, and by increasingly circumstantial accounts of the process by which the pantheon came to be established.[63] In the latter case particularly, the elaboration in 'realistic' contemporary detail credited to Epimenides and Stesimbrotus also demonstrates that, whatever their status in an earlier period, these analogies were by now being used in a thoroughly conscious and calculated way, and the wide geographical spread of this material is also invaluable in demonstrating the currency of this political mode of thought across the Greek world.

The field of imagery which the Athenian democracy does appear to have made particularly its own is the comparison of the state to a household. I have argued in examining this image in detail (above ch.2) that the Athenians developed this image in two directions: the first articulated the relationship between politicians and the demos at large through analogies with various kinds of service, while the second set out a familial model which substituted for the earlier hierarchical model a relationship based on fictive kinship between the citizens on the one hand and the polis on the other. Given its importance, the evolution of the analogy between house and state is surprisingly difficult to trace in detail: not only is it virtually absent from archaic sources (above 94), but rather than gradually emerging, it materializes in the second half of the fifth century as a virtual commonplace in the terminology of *oikonomia*, *oikein* and *dioikein* (above 25). The rationale for the analogy – or at least one rationale

– is most clearly expressed in Aristophanes' fantasies of rule by women, *Lysistrata* and *Ecclesiazusae*: in both plays, their capacity for competent administration (*tamieuein*) is cited as justification for putting the affairs and resources of Athens in their hands.[64]

The language of administration and guardianship appears in other, earlier comic contexts, notably in *Knights*,[65] and the very scenario of that play, set in the household of a personified Demos, implies a further development in the analogy, the representation of politicians as servants of the demos, even though we have to wait until the fourth century for explicit statements of this ideology.[66] Instead, what we have is a further elaboration which critiques the operation in practice of the ideological principle by drawing attention to the shortcomings in the service which the demos receives. Paphlagon, the current favourite servant of old man Demos, who stands for the leading demagogue Cleon, deploys a variety of underhand machinations to maintain his position, in particular a pandering to Demos' desires which reduces him almost to the condition of an invalid.[67] In the dramatic scenario, he can only be displaced by a rival who uses the same techniques even more effectively; however, in the final round of the contest, in which the gratification of the demos is literally realized as feeding him, the challenger, the Sausage-seller, reveals the extent to which Paphlagon has been keeping the lion's share of benefits for himself. The charge that politicians starve the people is echoed when Aristophanes compares them to niggardly wine-stewards and likens the demos to agricultural labourers for hire.[68] Such imagery not only expresses a belief in the corruption of politicians, but also implies the subordination of the demos, which has to look to them for sustenance and hence has lost the economic autonomy on which genuine freedom depends: indeed, the two elements come together in accusations, especially in the fourth century, that the demos is being tamed like an animal by such techniques.[69] There may also be a specific concern with the diversion of the resources of empire from the demos, a preoccupation which is prominent in the agon of *Wasps* a couple of years later, though the persistence of starvation imagery into the fourth century (and so after the loss of Athens' empire) indicates that this is not an integral element of the concept. Furthermore, the willingness of Demos to accept and indeed encourage this treatment hardly reflects well on him, so while the criticism of comedy is chiefly directed at the politicians, it is certainly not confined to them.[70]

There are connections between the figure of the politician as servant and another image which comes into view around the same time, the politician as lover of the demos, since the same words, *therapeuein* and *therapeia* ('care [for]') can be applied positively to the activities of both; equally, behaviour designed to court favour can easily slide into, or be represented as, simple gratification or even 'pandering' (*kolakeia*).[71] It looks as though the language of erotic love entered Athenian politics in the celebrated passage in Pericles' Funeral Speech of 431/0 (Thuc. 2.43.1) in which he calls on the Athenians to 'gaze daily on the power of the city and become her lovers (*erastas gignomenous autês*)'. Interpretation is complicated by uncertainties with the sources: on the one hand, what we have is not a transcript of Pericles' speech but a *post eventum* version constructed by Thucydides; on the other, the presentation of rival demagogues as lovers of the (personified) Demos is evidently satire, but its precise nature is impossible to grasp with certainty. However, given that we know from Aristotle that Pericles had a gift for striking imagery, it is quite plausible that our metaphor is authentically Periclean, and since we also know of other instances of Cleon aping the language of Pericles, it is by no means impossible that we have here another such case.[72]

If this is correct, then this is one of the rare cases when we can not only locate the invention of a new political image precisely in time, but also identify the individual responsible. Pericles' objective in deploying this image has been the subject of much recent debate:[73] it seems clear that he seeks to inspire his readers to enter into a positively engaged and personal relationship with the city[74] which in some way reflects the dynamics of an idealized homosexual relationship in which reciprocity plays an important part, with the *erastês* courting his beloved by appropriate behaviour and offerings, and receiving his reward from the beloved.[75] Insofar as such relationships were, or were perceived to be, typically an elite pursuit, the image would function as part of a wider process of assimilating all members of the audience – and the demos at large – to the elite and aligning them with its values.[76] It might also be seen to function rhetorically by prompting the audience to abandon purely rational calculation and respond to their instincts and to passion,[77] and that passion also distinguishes the relationship with the city from the rather different dynamic created by figuring the polis or the land of Attica as a parent (below 155), which implies a more moderate and reflective emotional bond and, though also reciprocal, emphasizes gratitude, duty and the repayment of obligations.[78]

In Aristophanes' *Knights* we find that this image has been taken over and personalized into an individual claim to an intimate and exclusive relationship with the demos: the Paphlagonian and the Sausage-seller present themselves as rivals (*erastês* and *anterastês*: 732–4; cf. 1163) for the affections of Demos, and court him with a range of techniques designed to win his favour. In a later passage (1340–4), the Sausage-seller, now triumphant, makes it clear that they are not the only ones to have deployed this particular appeal, which he now associates with deception (though of course his honest courtship automatically shows up his rivals as frauds). It has been argued that language which expresses an emotional association with the demos in more measured terms, through adjectives such as *philodêmos* and *misodêmos*, which first appears in our sources in the 420s, in fact entered Athenian politics at exactly this time, with the ascendancy of Cleon, and might indeed be due to his initiative.[79] We cannot be sure that Cleon did in fact claim to be the demos' lover – the comic poet might be deliberately exaggerating from use of more moderate terminology[80] – though the passage in *Acharnians* a year earlier which associates the same sort of language with the Thracian king Sitalces[81] suggests that it was in the air at this time, so the development is not out of the question for a politician who could style himself 'the watchdog of the people'.[82]

Furthermore, we should note that while we are desperately short of literary sources for the preceding quarter-century, there are indications in inscriptions that language which evaluated virtue and affection in terms of the interests of the demos was already becoming established around the middle of the fifth century, and it would not be surprising if Pericles' striking turn of phrase itself built on a developing trend in the language of public discourse.[83] We should remember, too, that Pericles had not always been the Olympian figure portrayed by Thucydides;[84] more generally, this shift in language and ideology is in keeping with the increasing radicalization of the democracy after Ephialtes, and once language in which leaders identified themselves with the interests of the people on both a practical and an affective level became established, one would expect a degree of escalation over time, given the competitive character of leadership at Athens.

If the image of the 'lover of the demos' could therefore paint for the audience a picture of the politician as utterly devoted to them, it had its attractions for the speaker also: not only did it assert a claim to an exclusive relationship with the demos which, if established, would permanently thwart the efforts of rival leaders, but it may also have allowed him to rationalize his service to the demos in more attractive terms, not as a mere servant, but as an active citizen male writ large, a 'real man' (*anêr*), in the jokey language of comedy.[85]

Elsewhere in fifth-century Athenian imagery the ideological pre-eminence of the demos is by implication more absolute. While the helmsman of the ship of state features widely in tragedy, as we have seen, he does not appear in any other genre. Herodotus can make Miltiades express in his speech to Callimachus before Marathon the fear that *stasis* may strike Athenian will to resist and shake it apart like a squall falling on a vessel (6.109.5), perhaps locating the threat outside the vessel in response to the immediate threat of Hippias and the Persians and the possibility of a fifth column,[86] but that seems to be unique in fifth-century prose. It is revealing, too, that maritime imagery is very thinly spread in comedy: apart from a reference to the ship of state in *Wasps* which points to its status as a rhetorical commonplace, we find only allusions in *Frogs* to that ship as storm-tossed, with reference to the upheavals towards the end of the Peloponnesian war.[87] Clearly, such language could only be used with a high degree of generality: not even a Pericles would have dared to lay claim to Mao's soubriquet 'The Great Helmsman'.

Again, the concept of the body politic is firmly established and exemplified in references to its suffering from the sickness of *stasis*,[88] and here too comedy suggests that it had become commonplace.[89] However, outside high poetry the figure of the doctor appears only once, in the argument of Nicias, appealing to the *prytanis* of the assembly to put the question of the Sicilian expedition to the vote for a second time, that in so doing he 'will be the physician of the city when it has deliberated badly' (Thuc. 6.14). Its uniqueness makes this a more striking metaphor than has often been supposed, and the attribution of such implied authority to an individual, against the ideological trend, stands out as a potentially risky strategy, emphasizing the degree to which Nicias is going out on a limb here in his opposition to the expedition, as with his request, contrary to precedent, for an *anapsephisis*; however, that risk may well have been largely defused by the fact that the prytanis is an ordinary man, selected by lot, whose formal standing lasts only for a day,[90] and who is therefore in no position to capitalize on any reflected eminence, and the image is then perhaps softened by generalization in the following clause, which implicitly aligns the ethics of office-holding with the Hippocratic principle of helping, or at least not harming.[91] By contrast, the imagery with which Alcibiades ripostes (6.18.6–7) draws on contemporary medical ideas of mixture and regime, alluding obliquely to the body politic as a unity.[92]

Another virtually absent authority figure is the teacher, who appears only in a passage of Sophocles' *Philoctetes* (385–8) which points to the danger that bad teachers may mislead when a city or army belongs entirely to its rulers. It would seem that at this date schools were still not common and the status of teachers was perhaps not high, but the principal explanation must be that the Athenians shared the belief expressed by Simonides that 'the polis teaches a man', as the discussion of civic education in Plato's *Protagoras* makes plain, and so the role of educator was not to be monopolized by any individual.[93]

Similar preoccupations can be seen at work in the use of animal imagery in the period, which in many ways exemplifies the developments I have so far outlined. As we have seen, even in the archaic period a certain ambiguity surrounded lions, for all their majesty, and it comes very much to the fore in the fifth century, especially in the dream of Agariste, the mother of Pericles, that she gave birth to a lion (6.131.2; cf. Plut. *Per.* 3.3).[94] What is striking here is precisely that we are given no indication of how to respond to the ambiguity: Herodotus has certainly chosen to include the anecdote, which may well have come to him from the Alcmaeonids, but the way in which he leaves it without comment and followed by a marked pause[95] serves if anything to emphasize the way in which he leaves open its implications. That is rather less the case for a later Alcmaeonid lion image: Aeschylus' famous image of the lion's whelp which destroys its owner when full-grown (*Ag.* 717–36) is plainly alluded to in Aristophanes' *Frogs* 1431 in the mouth of his Aeschylus with reference to Alcibiades, and the advice to tolerate his ways does not undo the implied condemnation of his destructive nature.[96] This is not to say that the positive evaluation of lions disappeared: when the Paphlagonian in *Knights* (1037–43) deploys with reference to himself an oracle foretelling that a woman 'will bear a lion in holy Athens', that is obviously intended to reflect favourably on his stature and prowess, though it is also blatantly presumptuous, as is his attempt a few lines later (1051–3) to associate himself with the hawk, Apollo's bird, beset by envious crows; while he is presumably aiming to strike a Pindaric tone, the audience is more likely to pick up the connotations of rapacity.[97] Bird of prey imagery is acceptable for individuals in tragedy like the two Atreidae in Aeschylus' *Agamemnon*, who are like vultures at 49 and symbolized by eagles in the portent at 113–15,[98] but in comedy it should properly be reserved for the Athenian demos at large, in the celebrated oracle which described Athens as an eagle soaring in the clouds.[99] The fact that the eagle was thought, rightly or not, to be associated with Persia was no obstacle to its acting as emblem of the imperial city.[100]

Things are rather different in the case of an important new animal image, the watchdog of the people. Here Aristophanes' persistent canine representation of Cleon – notably as the Dog in *Wasps* – surely confirms what the Paphlagonian's self-identification with a dog in the oracle-contest implies, that this was an image Cleon created for himself.[101] Assuming that this is correct, it strengthens the impression we have already gained of a rapid development in the language of politics in this period, and supports the suggestion that Cleon personally played a significant creative role in this. In its workings the image of the watchdog is in fact quite similar to the lover of the people: while accepting a degree of subordination, it lays claim to a special and familiar relationship with the demos which emphasizes loyalty and trust, and adds an additional implication of protection, not so much of the person(s) of the demos as of its assets and interests, which was not otherwise easy to strike in a context of imperial democracy.[102] Even though it was wide open to comic distortion in terms of theft, barking or yelping, or even perversion into Cerberus the hound of Hell,[103] it evidently retained an appeal for democratic politicians down to the end of the classical period (below 156).

While it may have been positive for individual politicians to be represented as dogs, that did not hold true for the demos at large, and when the jurors are compared to dogs trained through hunger by the demagogues to be set on their enemies with a hiss, or the demos as a whole is said to have torn apart like hounds those accused by the demagogues of treason, the implications are the very negative ones that the demos has been tamed by politicians who are able to manipulate it by the establishment of conditioned reflexes, whether by drip-feeding jury-pay or by the use of political slogans, into acting as its masters wish.[104] Here the comic use of animal imagery is particularly pointed; elsewhere it offers generic criticism of the demos' intelligence and independence in comparisons to sheep and to cuckoos and bustards, proverbially gullible birds.[105] In the same way, comparisons with animals are regularly used to abuse politicians: apart from the mentions of greedy gulls and voracious whales, suggestive of peculation, which we have already noted (above 136n.97),[106] there are allusions to various politicians as monkeys which, as well (doubtless) as being satisfyingly abusive, suggest the deceit and trickiness of monkeys and a willingness to resort to 'shameless antics and flatteries' to obtain their objectives.[107]

The implication of sharp practice also underlies much of the imagery which describes political competition in terms of sport, especially that drawn from wrestling. Such imagery is used several times in *Knights* to describe the contest between the Paphlagonian and the Sausage-seller: the latter is 'professionally' advised to oil himself so that he can slip out of his opponent's slanders (491-2),[108] and the chorus speak of his opponent as 'gripped round the middle' (388) and urge their man 'don't let the fellow go, now that he's given you a hold' (841-2). Likewise in *Frogs* the chorus intercedes for those who were 'thrown by Phrynichus' wrestlings (*palaismasin*)' and 'slipped' (689-90), that is, in the machinations of the oligarchs in 411, and Plato Comicus not only uses *diaklimakisas*, the technical term for a wrestling move, to refer to the removal of an opponent, presumably political, but associates it with a winning move in the board game *pessoi*.[109] The tone is similar when this imagery is used in tragedy: Prometheus anticipates the overthrow of Zeus by a rival wrestler, the implications being of active violence, while in Sophocles 'the wrestling which is good for the city', in other words Oedipus' struggle for the city in seeking Laius' murderer, is implicitly contrasted with the unseemly political battle between him and Creon.[110] There may also be an athletic colour to a couple of general references to 'contests': when Otanes withdraws from competition for the throne of Persia he says 'I will not compete with you', while the reference to political struggles as *agônes* in Thucydides, linked as it is to *stasis*, suggests more violent rivalry.[111] The only exceptions to a specific sporting focus on wrestling, with its violence and chicanery, are two allusions to the track, both referring to oratory: when Eupolis speaks of Pericles outstripping the orators by his rhetorical prowess, like a crack sprinter, he suggests a clean victory on merit; so too in

Knights the proposer of a popular motion could easily outstrip his opponents and be gone.[112]

The pretensions of politicians, and of Pericles in particular, were also deflated by a series of comic attacks in the form of mythological burlesque which satirized him as 'the Olympian'. It is impossible now to tell whether the label itself was a comic invention mocking his power or aloof demeanour, or a perversion of a more favourable evaluation of his pre-eminence or of his thunderous oratory; although the most prominent figure in these attacks was Cratinus, who seems to have had a particular antipathy to Pericles, the motif is attested for such a wide range of other comic poets that it clearly became common currency, even if it started with him. The personal character of the satire is evident not only in references to the unusual shape of Pericles' head, but also in the way in which his relationship with Aspasia is incorporated in references to her as a divine or mythic consort such as Hera, Helen or Deianeira.[113] By contrast, Cleon is depicted as a Typhon or a multiform monster, and the comic poet claims the heroic role of a Heracles for himself, just as Plato Comicus wishes for an Iolaus to cauterize the politicians who grow like Hydra's heads.[114]

Comedy's criticism of politicians and the demos through imagery operates very largely within the normative framework of democracy, functioning as internal critic to police the ideologically appropriate behaviour of either party, and the relationship between them. At other times, however, we can catch echoes of a more thoroughgoing critique of democracy from a hostile standpoint, notably in the comparison of the demos to elemental forces of nature. This is a field of imagery which goes back to the archaic period but becomes rather more prominent in the fifth century. The comparison of the demos to water is particularly marked: Herodotus has Megabyzus, the Persian advocate for oligarchy in his 'Constitutional Debate', compare the political behaviour of the demos to a river in spate (3.81.2) since it 'rushes into affairs without thought and sweeps things before them', while the Spartan Lampito in *Lysistrata* terms the demos a 'drain'.[115] The comparison of the demos to the sea, stirred by the winds, continues in the anonymous iambic passage quoted above (61), and this equation was to persist in anti-democratic rhetoric in the fourth century.[116]

The storm-wind also appears independently in Euripides, associated with 'violent fire' as an elemental force that cannot be controlled while its emotion is raging: one has to run before it until it slackens of its own accord.[117] By extension, fire can also describe stasis, which can be fanned by unscrupulous politicians.[118] Indeed, it is a moot point whether imagery drawn from the elements as such is ever positive: Agamemnon is associated (though primarily in a domestic context) with thirst-quenching water, shade or warmth in Clytemnestra's hyperbolic and somewhat orientalizing welcome, but none of these evokes the power of the element in question. In Sophocles, Oedipus is said to have acted as a fair wind for Thebes, or supplied her with a fair wind, but while the image is prima facie favourable, given the notorious instability of the wind of fortune, and the fact that from Homer onwards it is the business of the gods to supply fair winds, it is tempting to think that the audience was meant to feel some misgiving, as with other apparently positive imagery associated with him (above 111).[119]

Elsewhere, the character of the demos and its need for control is expressed through comparison with horses. Plutarch reports a comic fragment which describes the effect on the demos of the freedom which Pericles gave it: like a horse, it became insolent and would no longer obey but bit Euboea and jumped on the islands. That control of the demos-horse is desirable is suggested also by a fragment of the sophist and oligarch Antiphon which uses the word *euêniôtata*, 'most obediently to the rein'.[120] Both the congruence of all this imagery with elite imagery of the archaic period and its internal consistency are encouragement to believe that what we are hearing is an authentic antidemocratic voice, even when it appears in the context of literature sponsored by the democracy.[121]

It is therefore a little surprising to encounter the image of the chariot of state not only in Sophocles (fr.683), where the specific concern is with the risk posed by the bad charioteer, but also in comedy, where we find two passages which foreground the motif of the handing over of the reins: in *Knights* Demos speaks of handing over 'the reins of the Pnyx' (1109) to whichever suitor treats him better, while in *Ecclesiazusai* Blepyrus expresses his fear that if the women 'take over the reins of the city' (466) men of his age may be compelled to give sexual favours by law. Since both passages are concerned with a radical change of regime in a context of fantasy, it would be unwise to suppose that the image was unproblematically positive for democrats: we are dealing with scenarios which begin from the existing constitutional regime but solve its problems by recourse to new leadership. It may be that in such contexts the ideological sensitivities of a democratic audience were reduced and they were more receptive to the associations of the image with expert and responsible direction, in rather the same way that, as we have seen, the figure of the helmsman could be positive in contexts which did not relate directly to contemporary politics.[122]

Athenian political imagery, then, is certainly willing to accommodate images for leaders and politicians but, as we have seen, in doing so it tends to exert fairly firm control over them, as one might expect given the ideological hegemony of the demos.[123] It is rather more surprising from the same perspective how much less prominently the community and the demos feature in such imagery: in particular, given the ideological association between Athens' empire, naval power and the radical democracy,[124] one might have expected to find a version of the ship of state based specifically on the trireme. In practice, this would seem to have been a case where the accumulated weight of tradition was simply too great to shift: even if such a development was theoretically possible, both the entrenched prominence of the helmsman before the emergence of democracy, and the fact that the detailed model of the ship of state appears to be based on a merchantman militated against it in reality.[125] The other possible model from the military sphere, the hoplite phalanx, was more controversial: not only was it essentially at odds with the ideology of radical imperial democracy, but insofar as membership of and identification with hoplites were aligned with more conservative political positions, it could have been perceived as implying a challenge to that ideology:[126] some degree of popular antipathy may be suggested by the fact that terms for military leadership are applied to rulers and leaders only in the heroic context of tragedy.[127] At the very least, inasmuch as its appeal to the whole community would have been based on extrapolation from the actual experience of a defined minority (as indeed would also have been the case for the putative 'trireme of state'), it must have been a less attractive prospect for Athenian authors.

Towards the end of the century we do encounter some new images which suggest a concern with the constitution and unity of the citizen body. One notable instance is Lysistrata's image drawn from wool-working, which offers a specific application of female domestic expertise to the male world of politics.[128] It begins simply on an international level as a proposal to 'disentangle the war' (567–70) and then moves with increased complexity to the domestic scene (574–86): first the city must be cleaned of sheep-dung, and then the *mochthêroi* ('scum, riff-raff') must be beaten out and the burrs removed, the conspirators and office-seeking cliques carded out and their heads (i.e. leaders) plucked off. After this, the common goodwill must be combed into a basket, mixing in everyone, including metics, foreigners, state debtors and Athens' colonies, which are described as scattered scraps from the fleece, and the wool turned into a ball of yarn and woven into a cloak for Demos. Despite the detail, the image is essentially quite general and inclusive: the only groups specifically excluded are anti-democratic political activists – audience members are left free to identify their own bêtes noires as dung and riff-raff – and the violence implied in their handling is only imaginary, if momentarily gratifying, while the cloak to cover everyone (compare contemporary talk of 'big tent politics') is surely meant to evoke the *peplos* woven for Athena to which the female semi-chorus will shortly allude in the parabatic debate (642).[129]

Rather different is the coinage image in the concluding stanza of the parabasis of *Frogs* (718–37). This takes its cue not from the dramatic scenario but from recent numismatic history, and is rather more specific in its reference: here a distinction between traditional upper-class political leaders and their arriviste rivals is underlined by a contrast between the genuine and tested silver coinage and the recently issued 'counterfeit' silver-gilded bronze issued as an emergency measure. As well as trading on the widespread idea of bad men as counterfeit, Aristophanes more originally puns on the ruddy colour of the copper to insinuate that the leaders he is disparaging are of foreign birth and servile status.[130] Although different in character, the two passages can nevertheless both be seen to respond to the stresses put on the community by the political upheaval which followed the Sicilian disaster, and perhaps specifically the pressures caused by severe loss of manpower.[131]

Some degree of tension is also implied by Alcibiades' characterization of the body politic in terms of the Hippocratic concept of mixture (*xugkrathen*) in the debate before the Sicilian expedition (6.18.6), which is clearly intended to emphasize unity in a conciliatory manner in response to Nicias' appeal to the older members of the assembly. The idea must have been in circulation for a decade or so, since Euripides made a character speak of 'a *sygkrasis* (blend)' of rich and poor some time in the 420s;[132] what is new here, apart from the blend's consisting of three elements, is the way in which the image is inclusive while clearly not being egalitarian: 'the inferior, the middling and the really rigorous' are evidently not meant to be regarded as on a par with one another, nor as existing in the same proportion in the demos, yet each has by implication something to contribute.[133] That tone might encourage us to read Thucydides' judgement on the regime of the Five Thousand, that it was 'a moderate *xugkrasis* with respect to the few and the many' in the same vein: the image does not have to imply that the regime gave equal rights or power to either side, but it does suggest that by having regard to the interests of both it offered an inclusive solution to the tensions between democrats and oligarchs in 411, if a regrettably short-lived one.[134]

Perhaps the most clearly articulated image of the community is to be found in Nicias' speech before the decisive battle at Syracuse, where he identifies the city with its men (7.77.7): although this harks back to passages in archaic poetry, it is far from being a cliché. I suggest that it more specifically evokes the situation of Athens before Salamis, and Themistocles' evocation of the Athenians as a potential new city. Whereas Alcaeus compared fighting men to a city's walls (above 89), Themistocles equated the Athenian fleet of 200 ships with a potential polis and homeland (8.61–2, esp. 61.2): given that the Athenians had been forced to evacuate Attica, the future of the polis, whether re-established there or relocated elsewhere, lay in its deracinated population and its fleet in particular. The fact that there is the same antithesis between the sacked city of Athens and the 'safe bulwark (*herkos asphales*)' constituted by men suggests both that the sentiment in Herodotus is authentically Themistoclean and that it struck a chord. In Nicias' speech, however, there are no longer any ships, since it comes after the Athenians have been defeated in the Great Harbour of Syracuse and forced to retreat by land, and so the focus is entirely on the men of the expeditionary force, but Nicias' words are surely intended to evoke that earlier isolation of Athens' finest hour, and to underline, not without pathos, how things have changed.[135]

If this reading is correct, it strengthens the impression we have already gained from tragedy in particular that the conception of themselves which the Athenians expressed through political imagery was profoundly affected, like so much else, by the experience of the Persian wars.[136] Indeed, in a sense that influence comes full circle through the century, as we see the imagery which originally described Greek-barbarian relations increasingly extended to cover relations between Greek poleis.

By the late fifth century, the imagery of slavery came to be applied to relations between Greek poleis, especially under the Athenian empire, the classic instance being Thucydides' observation in his account of the Pentekontaetia that Naxos 'was enslaved contrary to established practice' (1.98.4): clearly this is not the treatment meted out later to Scione or Melos, cases which became emblematic of Athenian brutality, but something figurative, a constraint on liberty more keenly felt given the development of the concept of freedom by this date.[137] Although the image is often found in rhetorical contexts in Thucydides it is also clearly firmly established in his own thought, since it is already found in the 'Archaeology', in the observation that at an early date weaker communities 'submitted to slavery to the stronger ones' (1.8.3) in the pursuit of gain. In the conference at Camarina, Hermocrates uses the language of master and slave of Ionian submission to both Persia and Athens so as to draw a pointed association between the two.[138]

The implication that Athens had become a *despotês* to rival the King of Persia was underlined by the Peloponnesian War concept of 'the tyrant city'. In what seems to be its original form as anti-Athenian propaganda, this is a natural extrapolation of the imagery of slavery: if Athens is taking away the freedom of other poleis, then she is behaving like a tyrant (or a barbarian monarch), hence the Corinthian denunciation of Athens to representatives of the Peloponnesian League at Sparta as *turannon polin*.[139]

The dramatic date is 432, though the same image is attributed by Plutarch to the political opponents of Pericles (*Per.* 12.2) in the context of his building programme, which if authentic would imply that the image was already in use in Athenian domestic politics a decade or two earlier.[140] In this context the image is still critical of the empire and congruent with the well-known Athenian ideological antipathy to tyranny as the antithesis of democracy expressed in much of the imagery studied in this chapter.[141] A further instructive instance is the object-lesson given by Thrasybulus tyrant of Miletus to Periander tyrant of Corinth by decapitating the tallest ears of corn in a field: although evidently originally aristocratic in origin, in Herodotus' retelling it has come to signify an attack on the whole polis, represented in the image by the economic damage to a productive crop, and the image is used in the same form by Euripides, though combined with the pathos of the plucked flower (*k'apolôtizêi neous*).[142] By contrast, when Cambyses' sister-wife makes a similar point about her brother's destructive career as king of Persia by tearing all the leaves off a lettuce, she assigns the damage done to 'the house of Cyrus' (3.32.3–4), that is, to the patrimony of the Achaemenids.[143]

This consistency in classical Athenian imagery concerning tyrants makes it all the more striking that the figure of the tyrant becomes internalized and almost embraced in debate within Athens about her empire. In Pericles' final speech, he is made to say that Athens' empire is like a tyranny, the acquisition of which is felt to be unjust and which would be dangerous to relinquish (2.63.2). Whether or not one reads the first element as concessive ('whatever the rights and wrongs...'), the second point is, I think, the essential one: Athens has a tiger by the tail and, as Solon said about tyranny (Plut. *Sol.* 14.8), there is no way out. Later speakers in Thucydides are more direct: Cleon makes the identification between empire and tyranny directly (3.37.2), while the Athenian envoy Euphemos equates tyrant and imperial city in their concern for self-interest and security (6.85.1). In each case the principal note struck is one of wary self-interest: the comparison does not necessarily imply a positive evaluation of tyranny, but the use of such a strongly ideologically loaded word to drive home a realistic view of the world is hardly less striking for that.[144] In fact, a passage in Aristophanes' *Knights* does suggest that popular culture in the Archidamian War did find room for a perception of the tyrant's position as enviable: the chorus compliment Demos on his fine *archê*, since all men fear him like a tyrant (1111–14), and his rejuvenated self is hailed as king of the Greeks (1330, 1333).[145] Here again, to be feared is not necessarily morally good, but it inspires envy and admiration. This passage is also important since it strongly suggests that the image is not simply invented by Thucydides as part of his interpretation of the Athenian empire.[146] It may remain debatable whether the Athenians embraced a positive evaluation of the empire as tyranny, but clearly they did not disavow the identification either.[147] In its hostile form the image traded on Sparta's reputation as an opponent of tyranny and chimed with Spartan propaganda of liberation before and during the Peloponnesian War;[148] perhaps the Athenians responded with a grudging acceptance of the role thus wished on them.

Even if we may doubt whether non-Thucydidean Athenians were quite as blunt as he makes them, or that they ever aired the tyranny comparison except in debate among themselves, we have to accept that they appear to have made no effort to develop any more appealing or affective image for their relationship with their allies and subjects. The same is true of other aspects of that relationship, in which the Athenians appear deliberately to have promoted asymmetry, as in their manipulation of grants of honours so that they were, as far as possible, always donors and never recipients, so denying the allies the satisfaction of conferring *charis*.[149] Likewise religion, though it did offer the opportunity of participation, did so in a distinctly unilateral manner, and also served as an expression of Athenian power, particularly in the combination of ceremony and architecture on major ritual occasions.[150] Indeed, it has recently been suggested that the self-presentation and self-advertisement of the Athenian empire through visual means is one of the respects in which it draws on the model of Achaemenid Persia; one might add in this context that Achaemenid monarchs strikingly depart from the tradition of imagery in Near Eastern royal inscriptions in favour of direct statement of their prowess and greatness.[151]

In its turn, the Athenian attitude to the presentation of their empire is of a piece with their attitude to democracy: notoriously, there is no explicit statement of democratic ideology in our sources.[152] Nor do they seem in the fifth century to have done much to promote democracy by indirect means: the personification of Demokratia does not appear in art until 403, and Demos appears, together with Athena, only in 421/0, and only twice in the fifth century, in both cases on document reliefs.[153] The same is true of Athenian political imagery, as we have seen: there is no image which expresses the centrality of the demos and its power within the Athenian political system, although the character of imagery and its patterns of occurrence are often predicated on its pre-eminence. Perhaps the closest we come to the presentation of ideology through imagery is in the treatment of law, most conspicuously in Aeschylus' *Eumenides*, where it is compared to pure water which should not be sullied by mud (694–5)[154] and to a wall or breastwork (*eruma*: 701), guard (*phrourêma*: 706) and fortress (*poleôs phrourion*: 948); in the same vein Gorgias' Palamedes numbers among his inventions 'written laws, guardians (*phulakas*) of justice'.[155] Indeed, by about the turn of the century Law has itself come to have status of a king (above 10).[156] The centrality of law and justice to Athenian thinking legitimates ideas of protection which are very largely excluded from the discourse of politicians' relationship with the demos: hence Alcibiades could call himself 'guardian of the constitution' (*phulax ... tês politeias*: [Andoc.] 4.16),[157] and a sophistic author can even put forward the argument that the rule of a tyrant guards and holds in trust law and justice.[158] Furthermore, the democratic system can itself become the basis for imagery: in [Andoc.] 4.7 the speaker calls on his audience to be 'fair and impartial presidents (*epistatas*) over our speeches, and all of you to act as archons concerning them', equating the citizens conducting the ostracism with the magistrates responsible for it, and urging them to accept the same responsibility.[159] Aristophanes goes further, invoking Nikê in terms of factional politics as 'comrade (*hetaira*)' who sides with (*stasiaizei*) the chorus against their enemies, though here again it is the activity of politics which forms the basis of the image.[160]

The paucity of imagery which expresses the ideals of democracy is, like the absence of any explicit statement of democratic ideology, a puzzle for which it is hard to provide a proper explanation: perhaps the evident success of the system on an everyday level, underlined in the fifth century by the imperial power with which it was natural to associate it, obviated the need to explain or justify it.[161] It is also frustrating, doubly so because of the dominance of Athens in our sources: it is difficult to believe that the democracy in, say, Samos would have failed either to articulate its merits or to set them out in the appealing trappings of imagery, and differences in circumstances might have been reflected in presentation. In the fourth century, the ideological entrenchment of the system was even stronger after its resurgence following two episodes of suppression, but we shall see from the picture painted by the imagery of the period that this was not the whole story.

Notes

1 One might expect the link to have been made earlier, given that Persian-sponsored tyrants were a feature of Ionia from the 540s: its absence is most likely to be due to the paucity of contemporary sources for the later sixth century, though the relative lack of personal animus against the tyrants deposed at the beginning of the Ionian Revolt is noteworthy (Hdt. 5.38). For the widespread development of democracy in the last quarter of the sixth century, and very probably in some places earlier than at Athens, see Labarbe (1972), O'Neil (1995), Robinson (1997).

2 In classical usage he is usually *basileus* without the definite article, the ultimate monarch (*LSJ* s.v. III).

3 In practice the interaction of Greek tyrants with Persia was a complex business: see Austin (1990). Since the Persians tended to work with and adapt the constitutional status quo when they extended their empire (Young 1988, 42–3, 103–5, Briant 1996, 82–3, 87–96), subjects in other parts of their empire were not ruled by tyrants, but our classical Greek sources show no awareness of this fact.

4 Missiou (1993) argues that *doulos* essentially renders correctly the implications of Persian *ba(n)daka* (cf. Cook 1985, 224 n.1), while noting that the terminology was 'ideologically useful to the Greeks' (391); Briant (1996) 507, 524, cf. 335–7, 791–2 suggests that the choice of *doulos* as the nearest equivalent to render *ba(n)daka* brought with it an element of distortion; Tuplin (2007a) 57 points to a Greek desire to 'mock their tormentors' by suggesting that they too were slaves, combined with a tendency to think in terms of polarities, which implies a degree of more wilful misrepresentation, though some Greeks, notably Xenophon, were capable of greater insight (below 157–8). Cyrus may style himself 'master' in the Cyrus Cylinder (so Pritchard 1969, 316; Brosius 2000, 10 has 'lord'); also relevant is the issue of whether Evagoras would make terms with Persia as king to King or *doulos* to *despotês* (D.S. 15.8.2–3 with Stylianou 1998 *ad loc.*). NB [Arist.] *de Mundo* 398ab for the Persian king as model of remote supreme majesty.

5 It is hard to know how much weight to place on the phrase Γαδάται δούλωι in Darius' letter to Gadatas (*ML* 12.3–4), given the protracted and probably irresoluble debate over its context and authenticity (on which see most recently Tuplin 2009). Even if it is, or derives from, an authentic document of Darius, we cannot know who did the translation or at what date, though the Persian administration certainly contained Greek-speakers: Lewis (1977) 12–15.

6 Hall (1989) ch.2, esp. 57–60, 93–8, Goldhill (1988), Harrison (2000) 76–91, all with attention *inter alia* to the language of accountability, on which NB Roberts (1982) 5.

7 Note also the phrase *desposunoisin anankais* ('under the compulsion of masters') a few lines earlier at 587, and the Chorus' invocation of Darius as *despota despotan* ('master of masters') at 666. Raaflaub (2004) argues that it is precisely at this time that the image of slavery is complemented by that of freedom (58–101, esp. 60–5, 100–1; contrast 27–8).

8 On yoke imagery (and related images including hunting and fishing) in this play see Fowler (1967) 3–9, Pelling (1997) 6–7 and n.21 for further bibliography; Hall (1996) on 50 suggests that the idea was literally presented on stage through Atossa's chariot and Xerxes' wagon, cf. Taplin (1977) 75–9.

9 Hdt. 9.121; scholarly opinion is divided as to whether the dedication was at Athens or in the Athenian Stoa at Delphi: see Flower and Marincola (2002) *ad loc.*

10 *hêmeroun*: 5.2.2 (authorial), 4.118.5 (speech of the Scythians), 7.5.2 (speech of Mardonius); *hupokuptein*: 1.130.1, 6.25.2 (authorial), 6.109.3 (speech of Miltiades).

11 Hdt. 3.34.2, 35.4, 62.3, 5.105.2, 7.5.2, 9.1, 38.1–2, 147.3, 8.68.α1, β1, 88.2, 100.2, 102.2, 118.3, 9.111.3, 5, 116.3; on the resonances of 'master' as against 'king', NB Dickey (1996) 90–8. In the same way, Gorgias' Palamedes is made to equate defection to the Trojans with exchanging freedom for slavery (B11a.14).

12 1.8.3 *bis*, both in speech (once in the vocative), 11.4 again *bis*, once in speech and once in the narrative voice and 91.1, attributed in indirect speech to the Delphic oracle.

13 Persian 'liberation' from Media: cf. 1.126.3, 127.1, 210.2*, 3.82.5. Otherwise the language of *eleutheria* is by far most commonly used with reference to Persian subjection (asterisked passages contain an antithesis with *doul-* language): 4.136.4, 137.1, 139.2, 5.49.2–3, 109.2–3, 116*, 6.11.2, 109.3*, 6, 7.51.1*, 139.5, 178.2, 8.132.1, 9.45.2–3*, 60.1*; in this context, *eleutheroô* can mean 'protect against subjection' as well as 'liberate' (7.157.2; cf. Hyp. *Ag. Diondas* 137v 2, 176v 17, 175r 15 for the same language applied to the Macedonian threat) and *katadouloô* 'allow to be subjected' (8.144.4). *eleutheros* can also mean 'independent', as at 1.6.3, 3.65.7 (Cambyses speaking of Persia), 7.111.1 (~ *hupêkooi*), 8.140α1.

14 'Slavery' of Medes: 1.120.5, 129.3–4, and cf. 4.118.4, of Persian subjection to the nomadic Scythians (1.103–6, 4.1). Again, the image most frequently appears with reference to Greek subjection to Persia: besides passages cited above, 1.164.2, 169.1, 170.2, 174.1, 6.12.3, 44.1, 106.2, 7.102.1, 108.1, 168.1, 235.2, 8.22.1, 142.3, 9.90.2; however, it can also be applied to non-Greeks: 3.19.1 (Carthage escapes it), 88.1 (Arabians escape it), 4.93 (Thracian Getai), 6.45.1 (Brygoi), 7.1.3 (Egypt), 8.116.1 (Bisaltai). The image regularly appears in the mouth of Persians with reference to both individuals and peoples: 7.8β3 (Aristagoras), 9.2, 39.1, 8.100.3, 5, 101.3, 102.2 (Artemisia is the speaker), 9.48.2; particularly striking is the reference to Pelops as slave of Xerxes' ancestors (7.11.4). Clearly Herodotus regards this as part of Persian ideology: it is emblematically expressed in the antithesis between rule and slavery to others in the work's final sentence (9.122.4) and expressed in those terms by the Ethiopian king at 3.21.2; note also the editorial remark that Xerxes' divisional commanders accompanied the expedition 'as slaves like the rest of the troops' (7.96.2), where the focalization seems to be Persian, though many of the editorial instances cited above are more neutral. The outlook is not exclusively Persian: the Royal Scythians are credited with the same perception of all the other Scythians (4.20.1), and note also 1.27.1, where Bias or Pittacus applies the same image to Croesus' treatment of the Ionians.

15 *andrapodizô* and cognates: e.g. 1.161, 3.25.3, 6.19.3, 101.3 (cf. 94.2, 119.1 and

3.147.1), 7.233.2, 8.126.2; note also the specialized term *sagêneuô* (3.149, 6.31) for the Persian 'netting' of islands.

16 Further instances at E. *I.A.* 1400-1, fr.719 (*Telephus*), Hp. *Aer.* 16.4-5, 7, 23.5-8: note esp. the claim in the last passage that 'their spirits are enslaved' (*hai psuchai dedoulôntai*, §7 with Brock 2007, 211-12).

17 Note also the threat to enslave (*andrapodizesthai*) the Crotoniates (3.137.3) in reprisal which, like the threats to make the sons and daughters of the Ionian rebels into eunuchs and slave-women just before Dionysius' speech (6.9.4), underlines the ideological divide.

18 For the argument that this label, like that applied to Cyrus as 'father', is likely to reflect Persian ideology, see Brock (2004a) 174-5. The same may be true of the third comparison, the labelling of Darius as *kapêlos*: the disparagement of his interest in money is in line with Cyrus' appraisal of Greeks trading in the agora (1.153.1-2), itself an echo of the horror of dishonesty and debt which Herodotus attributes to the Persians (1.138.1; NB Cyrus' use of retail commerce [*kapêleuein*, 1.155.4] to neutralize the rebellious Lydians; so also Cook (1985) 224.

19 We should note, however, that this is editorial commentary which is doubtless also intended to make an ideological point further underlined in the later dialogue between Xerxes and Demaratus, where the antithesis drawn is between freedom and autocracy (102.1, 103.3-4, 104.4); the same is true of the speech of the Spartans Sperthias and Boulis to Hydarnes (7.135.3).

20 'your land': 7.5.2 (Mardonius), 9.116.3 (Artayktes); 'my land': 1.87.3 (Cyrus), and extended by assimilation to the mythical Proteus in Egypt (2.115.6).

21 Hdt. 5.31.4, 6.9.3, 7.194.2, 9.107.1 cf. 8.102.2-3, and the same idea may well underlie the reference of Cambyses' sister to 'the house of Cyrus' (3.32.3; below, 124). Cawkwell (1981) 72 suggested a Persian origin, comparing Thuc. 1.129.3, 137.4 and Philochorus *FGrH* 328 F149; on the Gadatas letter see now Tuplin (2009) 165, and on the Persian realities Briant (1996): 485-6. Cambyses can thus regard the Ionians and Aeolians as <u>inherited</u> (*patrôoi*) slaves (2.1.2).

22 The ideology of the king's personal prowess is expressed most clearly in Darius' second inscription at Naqš-e Rustam (DNb; Briant 1996, 226-44, esp. 237-9); the concept of more than mortal reach is hinted at in DNa §4: 'the spear of a Persian man has gone far ... a Persian man has given battle far indeed from Persia' (tr. Brosius 2000). For the presentation of Persian (and other oriental) kings as exceptional, even more than mortal, see above 12.

23 fr.9.3-4 (above 88, 92). Herodotus could even have had the specific passage in mind, given his knowledge of Solon's poetry (Chiasson 1986) and the fact that Peisistratus is one of the major case-studies of Greek tyranny in his work.

24 Athens: 1.62.1, 5.55, 62.1, 2, 63.1, 64.2, 65.5, 78, 91.1, 2, 6.109.3, 6, 123.2, cf. Ar. *Lys.* 1155; Samos: 3.142.4, 143.2; Miletus: 6.5.1; Selinos: 5.46.2. The language of slavery is rarely applied to Greek tyrants in Herodotus, but note 7.154.2 (Hippokrates) and 6.22.1 ('slavery to the Medes and Aiakos'), and allusion to Athenian rescue of the Herakleidai from slavery at the hands of the Myceneans (i.e. Eurystheus: 9.27.2 with 8.142.3). Polycrates: 3.142.3; note the contrast with oriental rulers who are, or try to appear (often through the institution of elaborate ceremonial: 1.98-100) different from their subjects (above, n.22). Athenian military lethargy under a tyrant (5.78) is echoed in the rationale offered by some Greek writers for oriental military inferiority (e.g. Hp. *Aer.* 16.1, 23.5-8; cf. Arist. *Pol.* 1285a16-29, 1327b20-33). It is important to note, however, that the word *despotês* is not automatically negative, and can denote

legitimate control or ownership, as in Archilochus' allusion to the 'spear-famed masters of Euboea' (3.5; cf. Pi. *P.* 4.52–3) or quite commonly of patron deities (e.g. Bacch. 11.117, 13.95, E. *Hcld.* 771–2, so also Hdt. 4.127.4 of Scythian Hestia (above), and cf. 1.212.3 (the sun as *despotês* of the Massagetae) and Pi. *N.* 1.13, fr.36 (the first of Zeus, the second of Ammon as 'master of Olympus'). See Brock 2006, 213–14 for further extensions of figurative mastery; hence Pindar's styling Medea 'mistress of the Colchians' (*P.* 4.11) may be read as entirely neutral.

25 Freedom as absence or rejection of tyranny: 1.62.1, 3.143.2; abdication 'just': Maiandrios (3.142.1); Cadmus of Cos (7.164.1).

26 NB Dodds (1960) xliii, Seaford (1996) 47 for tyrannical traits in Pentheus.

27 Diggle (OCT) brackets the line, but it is retained by Mastronarde (Teubner) and Craik (1988); Mastronarde (1994) *ad loc.* notes how the context brings out the negative potential in *turannis*, a term which can be used neutrally in tragedy.

28 A. *Cho.* 809, 863, 1046: the 'light of freedom' in the first two passages might be meant to evoke Simonides' description of the Athenian tyrannicides (above 89), though light is one of the important complexes of imagery and symbol in the play: see Garvie (1986) *ad loc.*, also n.43 below.

29 Note, too, how the assertion of Kratos that 'only Zeus is free' (50) implies oriental despotism: Griffith (1983) appositely cites E. *Hel.* 276 (above, 108).

30 Theseus' view is in line with the fifth-century tendency to read the Hesiodic succession-myth in contemporary political terms (above 4–5); with Heracles' response compare the view of Xenophanes (above 98n.37).

31 Griffith (1983) 21 gives a good brief summary.

32 The contrast with the well-fed trace-horse (*seiraphoros*) is a useful reminder that yoking imagery can refer to co-operative effort: cf. the comparison of Odysseus to a loyal *seiraphoros* in this play at 842 and the description of the Atreidae as 'the two-throned yoke' at 44 and, more generally, Cimon's famous image of Athens and Sparta as yoke-mates, recorded by Ion of Chios (Plut. *Cim.* 16.10 = Ion *FGrH* 392 F14 = fr.107* Leurini).

33 Compare the attitude of Menelaus, that at least he can control a dead Ajax (1067–9), where *pareuthunontes* might possibly evoke control of animals, though it most probably refers to a child (Stanford 1963 *ad loc.*; Garvie 1998 offers both possibilities); NB Stanford (1963) xlv–xlix and n.64 for the 'lowering of tone' in these scenes. On Creon's imagery of animal taming NB Goheen (1951) 26–35, though he reads it as suggestive rather than straightforwardly negative. Also worth noting is the word *zeuxileôs*, cited from Sophocles (fr.133.6) by the lexicographers, who gloss the word as 'yoker of the people' or 'he beneath whom the peoples are yoked' (Hsch. ζ127, Sud. ζ36): since the play in question was the *Andromeda*, it seems likely that the expression was used of a non-Greek ruler (NB *tôi Lubikôi* in l.7 and cf. n.121 below).

34 Oedipus: S. *OT* 1, cf. 6, 58, 142, and for the problems of interpretation in this opening scene see above 39n.32. Darius: A. *Pers.* 664 = 671; Atossa: A. *Pers.* 215; Croesus: Hdt. 1.155.1–2; Cyrus: Hdt. 3.89.3; fuller discussion above, 30–1, and on the king as father in Homer see 83. One possible use in a Greek context is Pi. fr.105, on which see 30 and below.

35 Indeed, this is one of the earliest medical images to feature the doctor: contrast the approach expected of Arkesilas by Pindar a few years earlier in *Pythian* 4.270–1; fuller discussion at 75 above.

36 As with 'murderer' in the previous line, the hyperbolic expression also undermines

the charge (though Aeschines [2.253] uses *lêstês* of Demosthenes' monopolization of politics – an actor's unconscious reminiscence?). Given the echoes of archaic poetry, this may be one of those contexts in which the ambiguities of *turannos/-is* are in play: 'who is more like a tyrant here?' On the association between tyrants and the use of nets for hunting or fishing, see above 101n.64.

37 Braund (2000) explores the complexities of the fifth-century Athenian relationship with monarchy.

38 Plays involving 'good kings', on the other hand, often (though not invariably) highlight the king's constitutionality, as with the Argive Pelasgus in Aeschylus' *Suppliants* and Demophon in Euripides' *Heracleidae*, or seek to accommodate it within a democratic framework, as in the case of Theseus in Euripides' *Suppliants*; Easterling (1997) 34–5 highlights the 'subtle indeterminacy' (34) in Sophocles' construction of a 'democratic' king Theseus in *O.C.*

39 For the contrast with the ship of state see below, and more generally 117, 121.

40 Hornblower (2006) discusses Pindar's ideas about monarchy and their later influence; there is also Bacchylides, whose political imagery is extremely sparse.

41 Father: fr.105, *P.* 3.71; steward: *P.* 1.88, and also of the Libyan king Battus at *P.* 5.62: above, 26.

42 As Gildersleeve (1907) rightly noted *ad loc.*

43 Bulwark: Theron of Akragas (*O.* 2.6; above 89); light: Xenocrates, Theron's brother (*I.* 2.17, above 100n.49) and Arkesilas of Cyrene, on one reading of *P.* 4.270 (e.g. the translations of Bowra, Farnell, Lattimore, Sandys; *contra*, Braswell 1988 *ad loc.*); otherwise of Agamemnon at A. *Ag.* 522–3, E. *Hec.* 841; eagle: Arkesilas of Cyrene (*P.* 5.111–12), the comparison being specifically in regard to boldness.

44 Pindar alludes to gentler methods of healing such as incantation alongside surgery at *P.* 3.47–53 (and cf. *N.* 3.55 for gentleness in medicine): for discussion see Hornblower (2004) 67–71, though he is doubtful whether Pindar was personally committed to such methods of healing the body politic.

45 For the historical context see Carey (1980), Braswell (1988) 1–6.

46 Braswell (1988) 361 argues for a more limited reference to Damophilos, Carey (1980) 145, 151–2 for possible reference to the city as well; both agree that the image evokes Homeric comparisons of fallen warriors to felled trees. Silk (1974) 144–5 comments on the gradual intrusion of the underlying personal reference into the allegory, which adds 'emotive nuance'.

47 Braswell (1988) on 273 argues that *epi chôras autis hessai* could mean either 'set in place again' or 'put on an even keel again', thus linking the two conceptions.

48 Carey (1980) 148, notes that the feigned plea is dramatic and avoids servility; Braswell (1988) 5–6.

49 Hornblower (2006) 156 observes that Pindar does not praise one-man rule uncritically, and appears to celebrate its fall in *Olympian* 12, which begins with an invocation of Zeus Eleutherios, probably alluding to the freeing of Himera from the tyrant Thrasydaios, and perhaps to the later fall of the Deinomenids (Barrett 1973; Raaflaub 2004, 61, 89–90, 106 is more equivocal); *eleutheria* is likewise associated with constitutional government, as opposed to tyranny, in *P.* 1.61–2: Raaflaub (2004) 90, 205–6. In Pindar's advice to 'bear lightly the yoke on the neck' and not 'kick against the goad' (*P.* 2.93–6) the yoke and goad are not to be associated with tyranny (Catenacci 1991; above 99n.43), but rather emphasize his counsel of '*willing* acquiescence in the laws of the universe' (Carey 1981 *ad loc.*), and is to be aligned with the use of yoke imagery for divine will or fate, as at *hDem.* 216–17

with Richardson (1974) *ad loc.*, who compares the Pindar passage; cf. E. *Ba.* 795 with Dodds (1960) *ad loc.* for additional parallels, inc. *Acts* 26.14 (whence our 'do not kick against the pricks') and Fränkel 1950 on A. *Ag* 218 for the 'yoke of *anagkê*'. Very similar is the acceptance of service or slavery to the gods, which the disparity in power between mortals and divinities makes inevitable: Brock (2007) 215. Such passages make it clear that while the yoke and goad may be commonly associated with punishment and servitude (Allen 2000, 86–7, and cf. Griffith 1983 on [A.] *PV* 108), this is not automatically the case.

50 On Pindar's maritime imagery see Péron (1974), who discusses these passages at 110–13: *Pythian* 10 is an early poem, from 498 BC
51 By means of the sail, strictly speaking (above 64n.22), but the implication is the same: this and other passages cited below are discussed more fully above, 55–6.
52 Eteocles: A. *Th.* 2–3, 208–10 (duty), 62–4, 652 (responsibility); Kirkwood (1969) argues that he is vindicated as helmsman, since Thebes is preserved, despite the disastrous outcome for the house of Labdacus. Later helmsmen: S. *Ant.* 994, E. *Supp.* 473–4, 879–80 and cf. the bow-watcher in S. fr.524 (*Polyxena*); helmsman's bench: E. *Ion* 595, *Pho.*74–5 and cf. A. *Supp.* 345.
53 E.g. S. *Ant.* 994, E. *Supp.* 879–80, and cf. also the implied wrecking of the ship of state at 507–9 noted by Radt (1970) 345: the *locus classicus* is Plato's elaboration of the image in the *Republic* (488a–9a; 58 above). In a related passage in E. *Andr.* 471–5, 479–82 images from monarchy and seafaring are used in parallel to illustrate the argument that divided authority is undesirable.
54 Though *kôtilos*, 'chattering' or 'persuasive', suggests a politician, in line with other fifth-century use of the image (below 121).
55 The thought may be influenced by imagery of Zeus and other cosmic helmsmen: Griffith (1983) *ad loc.*, A. *Ag.* 182 with Fränkel (1950) *ad loc.* and above, 64n.31.
56 For the interpretation see Fränkel (1950) *ad loc.*
57 There was (e.g.) no 'trireme of state' (above 59–60).
58 Hence in due course it could be applied to democratic politicians (below, 156).
59 The idea of Greek, and especially Athenian democratic, self-definition through polarity in reaction to an 'Other' is well-established: see in particular Hall (1989) on tragedy and Hartog (1988) for Herodotus.
60 Alcmaeon B4 with Ostwald (1969) 96–106; see 97–9 for Alcmaeon's dates, and NB above 20n.65, 81n.45; Hp. *Nat.Hom.* 4.2, *VM* 16.1, 8; in the Hippocratics as in Alcmaeon the elements are commonly referred to as *dynameis* or said to 'hold power' (*dunasteuein*): Brock (2006) 353–5. Not all medical writers accepted this model: the author of *Breaths* exalts Air as a *dunastês* (*Flat.* 3, 15), while in *Regimen* Fire is described as controlling and 'steering' (*kubernai*) everything (*Vict.* 10), albeit within a broadly constitutionalist framework: Brock (2006) 356.
61 E.g. Raaflaub (1996), esp. 143–5, 153; *isonomia* is praised in the aristocratic sympotic context of the Athenian *skolia* (*PMG* 893, 896) and associated with moderate oligarchy at Thebes in Thuc. 3.62.3.
62 Herodotus speaks of oligarchic Miletus in the mid-sixth century as 'gravely sick with *stasis*' (5.28) and even of affairs being 'swollen' in Persia around the time of the overthrow of the usurping Magi by Darius and his co-conspirators (3.76.2, 127.1; above 77n.8); NB nn.86, 88 below.
63 For the politics of Olympus see above, 6–8; for the politicized succession-myth, 4–5.
64 Ar. *Lys.* 493–5, *Eccl.* 210–12, cf. 600; Henderson (1987) *ad loc.* draws attention to the extent of economically productive activity in the *oikos* (on which NB also Brock

65 *ouk eti emoi tamiueseis* ('you shall no longer be my steward'): *Eq.* 947-8; *epitrepô/ epitropos*: *Eq.* 212, 426, 949, 1098, 1259; for the ambiguities of this language see above, 27.
66 Above 26-8; the dearth of fifth-century oratory from domestic political contexts must be an important factor. On the domestic allegory in *Knights* see above, 26-8.
67 His identity becomes clear with the mention of leather-tanning (Cleon's business) at 44 and the succeeding character sketch: his name could be due to a pun on *paphlazô* ('boil', 'bluster': 919) and/or the contemporary prominence of a Paphlagonian eunuch at the Persian court (Lewis 1977, 21). Machinations: 46-70; for his nurse-like services see above 28 and n.19. On flattery cf. n.71 below, and for the blurred line between *therapeia* and *kolakeia*, above 28-9 and below 155; *therapeuein* (59, 799, 1261) is the *mot juste* for courting political favour (Neil 1901 on *Eq.* 59, Thuc. 1.9.2, Isoc. 2.16, 9.46) as well as a lover's devotions (Pl. *Smp.* 184c4).
68 Meal scene: *Eq.* 1151-1226, especially the revelation at 1211-23; compare fr.699 (wine-stewards), *Vesp.* 712 (olive-pickers), above 28; *krousidêmon* in *Eq.* 859 also carries implications of giving short measure (Neil 1901 *ad loc.*). In *Eq.* 213-6, the Sausage-seller's trade is applied to his prospective new career in politics, which is described in terms of cooking: apart from puns on *dêmos*, which can also mean 'fat' (cf. *Vesp.* 40-1), and *hupoglukainôn* ('sweetening'), the principal idea is that of stirring things up (214-5, cf. *kirnantes* in fr.699 and, for the motif, 66, 251, 309-10, 358, 363, 431, 692, 840, 902, *Pax* 654), also alluded to in the reference to Cleon as a pestle and mortar (*Eq.* 982-4 cf. *Pax* 265-70) and the comparison with fishing for eels (*Eq.* 864-7; for mud cf. 309): NB nn.118, 154 below. Wilkins (2000) 196-7 notes implications of violence in *Eq.* 213-16; NB more generally 173-201 on the theme of food in the play.
69 On the character and ideology of hired labour in classical Athens see de Ste Croix (1981) 114-17, 179-86, Cartledge (1993) 148-9, Cohen (2002) 100-1 (all with further bibliography); see also above 29 and below 119.
70 Hesk (2000b) 289-91, Scholtz (2007) 59-70 on 1111f.; the same might be said to a lesser extent of *Wasps* (so Sommerstein 1983, xvi-xviii); the implication that the demos is behaving immorally is less typical of oratory, which focuses mainly on judgment and responsibility.
71 Cf. n.67 above and references there; on flattery in *Knights* see also Scholtz (2007) 54-9, esp. 55 n.43 for parallels with the Flatterer in Theophrastus' *Characters* (plucking out grey hairs, offering a cushion).
72 Periclean imagery: Arist. *Rh.* 1365a30-33, 1407a2-6, 1411a2-4, 15-16; since Pericles left no written speeches, these striking phrases must have survived through oral tradition. For this possibility NB Gomme in Gomme, Andrewes and Dover (1945-81) on 2.43.1, and *id.* on 3.40.4, for 'Cleon's borrowings from Perikles in Thucydides', also Hornblower (1991-2008) on 2.43.1 and 61.2; more generally, Connor (1971) 119-34, esp. 119-22, and cf. 97 n.14; Cairns (1982) 203.
73 Monoson (1994), Wohl (2002) 30-72, Ludwig (2002), esp. 319-76, Scholtz (2007) 21-42.
74 Formally speaking, *autês* could refer either to the city or its power, both being feminine singular nouns, and recent commentators have tended to regards both senses as being in play together (Wohl 2002, 57 and n.61; Scholtz 2007, 38), but the dynamic would be rather different in the two cases: since power is essentially

abstract, the desire would presumably be simply to possess it, as in Hdt. 3.53.4, where tyranny is said to have many *erastai* in a sharpening of the common use of the verb *eran* of the desire or lust for tyranny (e.g. 1.96.2, 5.32; E. *HF* 65–6, *Rhes*. 166, fr.850 [*erôs*] – cf. the chorus' denunciation of Bdelycleon as *monarchias erasta* in Ar. *Vesp*. 474 and NB n.83 below, also 184n.117 for Pl. Ep.8 354c4 (hunger)); the personified polis much more readily suggests a personal and affective relationship.

75 So Monoson (1994), 254, 262–5 and especially 267–9: she highlights the motif of the *kalliston eranon* ('fairest contribution') of death in battle, but emphasizes that this is not the only possible service to the city as beloved (cf. Ludwig 2002, 165–7 on the liberality released by *erôs* for the Sicilian expedition), and that the city's desire for it is properly controlled. Wohl (2002) 55–62 lays much more emphasis on death in battle as ideal, despite *asphalesteron* in 2.43.1, while Ludwig (2002) 335–8 links the desire for honourable death with the self-regarding desire to be loved by the beloved. Wohl denies that the colouring of the implied relationship is necessarily homosexual (2002, 63 n.73), but that surely better suits the idea of romantic love in this period, and also implies a more equal relationship between the parties, as opposed to the perceived subordination of female to male: Rosen (1997) has some illuminating discussion of the implication for power relationships of figuring poleis as female. On this view, the polis becomes ambiguous in gender (Rosen 1997, 166 notes that 'the Athenian polis in literary sources ... seems to transcend gender categories'), though on either reading the members of Pericles' audience occupy the position of the sexually dominant adult male citizen (Monoson 1994, 255–7 with references there). Demos is normally portrayed as a mature bearded male (*LIMC* s.v. nos. 43–6, 53–6), though in the earliest instance (no.42, of 421/0) he is youthful, while Demokratia, like Athena, is female (but not attested before 403: *LIMC* s.v., Commentary). The female identity of Athens could be used disparagingly: Plutarch tells us that Pericles' enemies decried his building programme as dressing up the city like a vain and pretentious woman (*Per*. 12.2).

76 Hubbard (1998) argues strongly for the centrality of class dynamics in Athenian homosexuality, though this has been challenged, at least for the later fourth century, by Fisher (2001) 58–62. For Pericles' rhetorical strategy, see (e.g.) Loraux (1986) 180–92, Wohl (2002) 36–46; Monoson (1994) 257–8, 269 also plays up the inclusiveness of the image.

77 Scholtz (2007) 37–42; Wohl (2002) 62–72 argues that the Athenians are supposed to fall in love with Pericles himself.

78 Cf. Ludwig (2002) 333; Monoson (1994) 266 notes the absence of the parent motif from Pericles' speech.

79 Connor (1971) 99–108; further references in Brock (1991) 165 n.25: such language is prominent in those speeches of Lysias which rake over the events of 411 and the régime of the Thirty such as those against Agoratus (13. 1, 10, 13, 93) and for Polystratus (20. 2, 8, 9, 17, 19, 20, 27 cf. 12.49 [Eratosthenes]; 25.7 [Subverting the Constitution]; 31.18 [Philon]). It is interesting, too, that Thucydides puts such an expression in the mouth of his Sicilian demagogue Athenagoras in a speech which contains the most explicit statement of democratic ideals in the work (6.36.1).

80 Scholtz (2007) 46–51 notes that in oratory such language is always attributed to a speaker's opponents, and canvasses the idea (51 n.33) that it may be precisely such critiques by Cleon which are parodied here.

81 He writes '*Athênaioi kaloi*', i.e. 'I fancy Athens' on the walls: 143–4 with Olson (2002) for the derivation from homosexual amatory language.

82 Below 118. There are further hints that Cleon had a memorable turn of phrase: the word *gerontagogein* ('tend in old age') is used in *Eq.* 1099 with reference to the Sausage-seller's care of Demos in a line derived from a fragment of Sophocles (fr.487 [*Peleus*]); it is an intriguing coincidence that apart from another Sophoclean passage (*O.C.* 348), it is only attested from a comic fragment attacking Cleon (*Com. Adesp.* fr.740) which is twice cited by Plutarch (*Nic.* 2.3, *Mor.* 807A): could these passages go back to an actual event, perhaps an injudicious off-the-record remark? Another such coincidence is the association of the verb *ephoran* ('watch over') with Cleon in *Knights* 75 and Eupolis fr.316.1; cf. the Paphlagonian's claim not to miss anything that happens in the polis at *Eq.* 862–3, which elsewhere he is made to elaborate with recherché metaphors from woodworking (461–3 with Neil 1901). An additional complicating factor is the pin-up status at this time, reflected in the joke at *Vesp.* 97–9 (with MacDowell [1971] *ad loc.*), of the real-life Demos, the son of Pyrilampes, on whom see also Cartledge (1990): it is probably he, rather than the personified demos, who was represented on stage (Eup. fr.346) as rebuking a matchmaker for recommending base suitors (so KA *ad loc.*; contra, Nightingale 1995, 188 n.44).

83 Whitehead (1993) 43–7, citing *IG* I³ 17 for the Sigeians, traditionally dated to 451/0; for the parallel development of the language of virtue 'towards the people/polis', see Brock (1991) 164. However, there is a growing body of opinion that this inscription should be down-dated to some time in the Peloponnesian War: most recently Rhodes (2008) 501, 504 [418/7(?)]; Papazarkadas (2009) 77 [407/6]. If that is accepted, the earliest document cited by Whitehead (44 n.24) in which the formula 'good man/ men towards the demos/polis of the Athenians' is reliably attested is *IG* I³ 65, of 427/6 (it is restored in *IG* I³ 43, of c.435–27). However, we should note that the oath prescribed for the Colophonians in the Athenian settlement for Colophon contains the clause 'I will love th[e demos of the Athenians]' (*IG* I³ 37.47); the conventional date is 447/6, maintained by Rhodes (2008) 501, 505, though Papazarkadas (2009) 70 again favours a lower date, 427/6. It is attractive to associate the striking and I think unparalleled language with what we take to be Cleon's, and place the decree during his ascendancy; indeed, by systematic down-dating we could link all this language together as a single movement in the 420s, but on balance it still seems plausible that it was a development which gathered pace gradually. Recent commentators on Thuc. 2.43.1 draw attention to A. *Eum.* 852 with Sommerstein (1989), though there is a big difference between the broad language of desire in the verb *eran* (cf. E. *Pho.* 359, where Mastronarde 1994 sees homesickness as the key element, and NB Nielsen 2004, 57 n.55 for the *patris* as object of love) and the metaphor of the *erastês* (above n.74): the grammatical variation defamiliarizes the expression, as also with *phileso* for *philos esomai* in the Colophon decree. We should also note that Thucydides makes Pericles call himself *philopolis* (2.60.5), if that is not an anachronism. On the history of the language of *erôs* see Ludwig (2002) 121–53; note also Yatromanolakis (2005), who traces the language of affection and desire for the polis back to Homer and down to Aelius Aristides' love affair with Smyrna. Philodemos appears as a personal name at Athens as early as 530–20 BC (*LGPN* II s.v. = *IG* I³ 1255) and a further half-dozen times in the fifth century.

84 *Ath. Pol.* 28.2 makes him leader of the demos, opposed by Thucydides son of Melesias, the leader of those variously labelled 'well-born' (*eugeneis*), 'distinguished' (*gnôrimoi*) and 'prosperous' (*euporoi*); Connor (1971) 119–28 has a good discussion of Pericles as proto-demagogue.

85 *Eq.* 179, 392, 1255, picked up tongue-in-cheek in Pl. *Smp.* 192a; Socrates takes

issue with the 'manliness' of politics at *Grg* 500c (see Dodds 1959 *ad loc.*). It should be noted that this sense of *anêr* is not confined to politics (*LSJ* s.v. IV) nor within politics to democracy (Hdt. 3.134.2, X. *Cyr.* 5.5.33 [monarchy]; Thphr. *Char.* 26.2 [oligarchy]); Gov. Schwarzenegger's mockery of opponents as 'girlie-men' shows that the discourse remains current in contemporary politics. Recent scholarship has tended to be preoccupied by the implications of the demagogue's active status; Wohl's psychoanalytic reading focuses on the sexual aspects in a somewhat lurid manner: (2002) 80–92; also Monoson (1994) 255–7, 269–70, Scholtz (2007) 43–4, 51–9.

86 In the next sentence the word *sathron* might continue the image with an implicit reference to 'something rotten' in the fabric of the ship of state, but more probably involves a slide into the related image of the body politic (in either case with a further implication of moral corruption): above, 78n.16. For a couple of possible rather general characterizations of the polis as ship in Thucydides, see Smith (1918) 246.

87 Ar. *Vesp.* 29, *Ran.* 361, 704; above 57.

88 In prose, besides Hdt. 5.28 (above n.62), note also his use of the language of 'health' to denote loyalty to the Greek cause in 480 (6.100.2, and perhaps 109.5 [above n. 86], 7.157.2). Thucydides attributes to Thasian oligarchs in 411 a perception of the oligarchy sponsored by the Athenian revolutionaries as 'festering' (*hupoulou*), i.e. unsound or phoney (8.64.5).

89 Bdelycleon begins his speech in the agon of *Wasps* with the mock-formal exordium 'it is hard ... to heal a long-standing disease which has become innate in the city' (650–1): the reference is presumably to a mania for judging not unique to Philocleon (so Sommerstein 1983 *ad loc.*; NB previous attempts to cure him at 118–24) rather than to the jury system.

90 Like Socrates at the trial of the generals after Arginusae (X. *HG* 1.7.15 with Krentz (1989) *ad loc.*, *Mem.* 1.1.18, 4.4.2; Pl. *Ap.* 32b, *Grg.* 473e–4a), though the *prytanis* here remains anonymous.

91 NB Hornblower (1991–2008) III 337; Rechenauer (1991) 352–3 provides further Hippocratic parallels.

92 Above 81n.44.

93 On schooling at Athens see Beck (1964) 72–141, esp. 72–80 (development to the end of the fifth century) and 111–14 (status of *grammatistês*); Simon. fr.90W; Pl. *Prot.* 322d–3a, 327e–8a; inasmuch as Protagoras hailed from Abdera, not Athens, we might infer that this view of education was more generally accepted in Greece, though Socrates directly challenges it at Pl. *Ap.* 24c–5c. Just as Protagoras compares the laws themselves as models of behaviour to outline letters (Pl. *Prot.* 326cd), they are described as 'guide-lines of just...' (*kanones tou dik...*) in what is either a political pamphlet or comic fragment of the later fifth or early fourth century (*PHeid.* 182 [Gigante 1957] = *Com. Adesp.* fr.1094, lines 15–17).

Although craft analogies are, as we have seen, largely absent from fifth-century Athens, kingship is itself represented as the highest craft (*technê*) at S. *OT* 380, *Phil.* 138 (with Webster 1970). Otherwise, there is Gorgias' obscure joke (A19) that the *dêmiourgoi* were makers of Larissaeans, presumably a pun on the two senses of the word, 'magistrate' and 'craftsman', and perhaps alluding to some particular political context which now eludes us; the 'crafters of citizens (*tôn politôn ... dêmiourgoi*) in an anonymous comic fragment *(Com. Adesp.* fr.245) are generally taken to be poets, a more original variation on the common identification of poets as teachers.

94 Of which a striking diversity of views have been taken, from strongly positive (Dyson 1929) to equally strongly negative (most recently, McNellan 1997); for a judiciously

guarded evaluation, see Thomas (1989) 270–2. By contrast, the dream of Philip II that he sealed Olympias' womb with a seal bearing the device of a lion (Plut. *Alex.* 2.4) evokes Achilles and Heracles, both ancestors of Alexander: Hamilton (1969) *ad loc.*
95 For this concept NB Brock (2003) 7 and n.11.
96 Cp. Plut. *Alc.* 16.2–3, and 2.2–3 for Alcibiades biting 'like a lion'; the reference of Callicles, a rather similar figure, to the taming of lion cubs at Plato *Grg.* 483e may hint at some sort of historical association lurking in the background.
97 He evokes envious crows in an earlier mock-oracle at 1020; in Pindar they appear at *O.* 2.86–8, *N.* 3.82. For the rapacity of the hawk NB Hes. *Op.* 203–12 (above 84), Pl. *Phd.* 82a and Epicrates fr.2.4; Cleon/Paphlagon is likewise identified with a greedy gull (our 'gannet') at *Nub.* 591 and *Eq.* 956 (by implication, though the reference is then diverted against Cleonymus) and a voracious whale at *Vesp.* 35.
98 The sinister implications of the portent do not oblige us to take a negative view of the eagles themselves, which remain regal birds (Plato has Agamemnon reincarnated as an eagle in the myth of Er: *R.* 620b), as (despite northern prejudice) are vultures (which in fact were not always clearly distinguished by the Greeks from other large raptors: Arnott 2007 s.v. Aigypios): compare the Homeric similes at *Il.* 16.428–30 and *Od.* 16.216–18 cited by Fraenkel (1950) *ad loc.*; indeed, Homeric influence is likely to be a factor here, as also on oracular language. In the fifteenth-century *Boke of St Albans*, vultures were ranked above eagles in the falconry hierarchy, to be flown only by emperors. Bird of prey imagery later in the trilogy certainly enhances the status of those to whom it is applied: the description of Orestes and Electra as 'children of the eagle-father' (*Cho.* 247, 258–9) is part of the rehabilitation of Agamemnon after his death, though the picture is complicated by patterns of imagery, particularly that of the eagle and snake, the latter not being automatically negative (applied to Orestes at *Cho.* 549–50, 928 ~ 249, 1047; Lebeck 1971, 13–6, Garvie 1986 on 249).
99 At *Eq.* 1011–2 Demos asks for 'the one about me which I enjoy, how I'll become an eagle in the clouds', though the Paphlagonian only abandons self-glorification and deploys it at 1086–7; it is also mentioned in fr.241 (*Daitalês*) and *Av.* 977–9, where the oracle-seller tries to offer a version to Peisetairos for the new city of the birds (useful note in Dunbar 1995 *ad loc.*); Parke and Wormell (1956) nr.112 give the text and testimonia.
100 In A. *Pers.* 205–10 the eagle as symbol of Persia is put to flight by the hawk: Harrison (2000) 74 and n.50; for the association in later thought between its keen eyesight and the ability to withstand the light of the sun, see Goodenough (1928) 82–3. Another Persian symbol, the 'king bee', is applied to Xerxes in *Pers.* 126–9: for discussion see below, 160.
101 For the Dog in *Wasps* (891–930) see esp. 895 (with MacDowell 1971), where he is assigned to Cleon's deme, Kydathenaion; in *Knights* note especially 1017–9, 1023–4.
102 There may by contrast be an ironic reference to Hyperbolus as a makeshift shield in *Peace* 686 (so *LSJ* s.v. περιζώννυμι: '*put* him *on* as a defence', though Olson (1998) takes the passage to refer to dress, 'as if Hyperbolus were an odd bit of cloth, snatched up in an emergency'. For the watchdog as 'protective yet subservient' see Christ (1998) 149–50. On the resonances of the word *prostates* see below, n.127; otherwise fifth-century politicians are restricted to claiming to defend ideals and values such as the constitution (below 125): contrast Aristotle's presentation in the fourth century of monarchs as guards (*phulakes*) of property (*Pol.* 1310b40–11a1, 1314b17).

103 Theft: Ar. *Eq.* 1025–6, 1031–4, *Vesp.* 904, 914, 928, 971–2 (note that this is equally true of the other dog, Labes [834–6, 910–11, 958–9]); barking or yelping: *Vesp.* 929–30, cf. *Eq.* 863 – Cleon's voice was notoriously loud and grating: e.g. *Ach.* 381 with Olson (2002), *Eq.* 137 with Neil (1901), [Arist.] *Ath.Pol.* 28.3 with Rhodes (1981); compare Eup. fr.220 (*Poleis*) for the demagogue Syracosius yapping at the *bema*; Cerberus: *Eq.* 1030, *Pax* 313–15 with Olson (1998) cf. Pl. Com. fr.236: note how Aristophanes transfers the adjective *karcharodôn* ('jag-toothed') to his description of Cleon as monster in *Vesp* 1031 = *Pax* 754. The comic dog also fawns on his master: *Eq.* 47–8, 1031. An apparent caricature of Cleon on a Corinthian cup as a sphinx with canine aspects is a hint that this satire might have percolated outside Athens: Brown (1974). More generally, Mainoldi (1984) 143, 152–60, 179–80 discusses the ambiguities that still attach to dogs after they are figuratively domesticated in the post-Homeric world of the polis.
104 *Vesp.* 704–5 (for *ton tithaseutên* 'the tamer' cf. *tithaseuousi* 'they tame' in D. 3.31), *Pax* 641; for taming imagery see above 87, 111, below 159. There is also a conceptual link to the motif of the bad servant (above 115, below 159).
105 Ar. *Vesp.* 32, 34, cf. *Eq.* 264, *Nub.* 1203; the claim in *Vesp.* 955 that the dog Labes is 'capable of taking charge of many sheep' implies the herding of a passive demos. In *Ach.* 598 Dikaiopolis credits the election of Lamachus to 'three cuckoos', the number implying that those involved were also a very few fools: Sommerstein (1980), Olson (2002) *ad loc.*, D. 18.149; Pl. Com fr.65.3, Taillardat (1962) 256. Bustards: *Com. Adesp.* fr.209. Of a very different character is Theras' image of leaving his son as a sheep among wolves (Hdt. 4.149.1), which recalls the vulnerability of livestock to predators in Homeric similes. Such animal imagery, reinforced by that of Plato, continued to be deployed by critics of democracy in later ages: Roberts (1994), Index s.v. 'animals and animal imagery'.
106 Cleon is described as stealing the people's honey (*blitteis*) at Ar. *Eq.* 794, so by implication as a drone parasitic on the productive bees (cf. Pl. *R.* 564e, below 187n.134).
107 *Ran.* 708 with Dover (1993) and bibliography there, to which add McDermott (1935), 1085, fr.409 (*Nêsoi*); Phryn. Com. fr.21.1–2; *Com. Adesp.* fr.310 cf. *Eq.* 887 ('monkey tricks'); quotation from Stanford (1958) on *Ran.* 1084–5; abuse: political (e.g. D.18.242) and other (e.g. *Ach.* 120, 907 with Olson [2002]).
108 The word in 492 is *paidotribikôs* 'like a trainer'; *diabolas* 'slanders' in 491 is punning for *dialabas* 'holds' – the same play on words appears at 262.
109 Pl. Com. fr.132 (*Presbeis*); cf. Cratin fr.61.3, and on *pessoi* see above 104n.91. Aristophanes' application of wrestling imagery to the struggles of Thucydides son of Melesias in court in *Ach.* 704, 710 is related, but must be particularly due to his family's wrestling tradition (Olson 2002 on *Ach.* 703, citing the 'brilliant ... detective work' of Wade-Gery 1932, 208–10); similar is the anecdote that when asked by Archidamus whether he or Pericles was the better wrestler, Thucydides replied that whenever he threw him, Pericles would prevail by using his rhetorical skills to persuade the spectators that he hadn't fallen (Plut. *Per.* 8.5; cf. Plutarch's own wrestling image in 11.1). For wrestling in reality see Poliakoff (1987) 23–53 – violent in modern terms (27–30) but less so than boxing or pankration (23) – and NB 134–47 for the potential for more positive figurative use.
110 [A.] *P.V.* 918–21: for Zeus as metaphorical wrestler cf. *Ag.* 171; S. *O.T.* 879–81: for the antithesis between good and bad *palaismata* (cf. good and bad forms of strife at Hes. *Op.* 11–26) see Long (1978), Winnington-Ingram (1980) 190–1; even if

Creon in reality has no political ambitions, Oedipus believes that he does and reacts accordingly.
111 Hdt. 3.83.2 *humin ouk enagônieumai* (the same verb is used authorially at 3.83.3); Thuc. 6.38.3 (Athenagoras is talking about politics at Syracuse). Wrestling terminology is used in comedy of disputes (Ar. *Ach.* 571, *Nub.* 1047, *Ran.* 469, *Eccl.* 258–60) and chicanery (*Nub.* 434, 792) and can also be applied to philosophic argument (Pl. *R.* 544B with Adam 1902; Rutherford 1995, 113–14); compare the use of athletic metaphors for historiographical polemic: Marincola (1997) 220 n.17.
112 Eupolis fr.102.1–3 (*Dêmoi*), Ar. *Eq.* 1353; compare the metaphor of starting a race for the beginning of a contest: *Ach.* 483 with Olson (2002), *Eq.* 1159–61, *Vesp.* 548.
113 For details, see above, 13.
114 Typhon: Ar. *Eq.* 511; monster: *Vesp.* 1030–6 = *Pax* 752, 754–9 – Aristophanes credits himself with 'a Heraclean spirit' at *Vesp.* 1030 = *Pax* 752; hydras: Pl. Com. fr.202.
115 Ar. *Lys.* 170: the word *ruachetos* occurs only here, but is glossed by the ancient lexicographers as *ho reôn ochetos*, 'the flowing drain/pipe'; NB Taillardat (1962) 386–7; NB also above 61. The representation of a disorderly crowd in terms of wind and water goes back to the *Iliad* (2.144–8, 9.4–7; Moulton 1977, 38–42); for a leaderless crowd compared to water out of control in Mesopotamia, see Frankfort et al. (1946) 203. This was another image which influenced later critics of democracy: Roberts (1994) 115–6 with n.29 (Plutarch), 141 (Bodin), 182–3 (John Adams, quoting Rollin: 'is this government or the waves of the sea?'). The French Revolution is compared to a storm by the aristocrat Gauvain at the guillotine in Victor Hugo's *Quatre-vingt-treize* (quoted by Sontag 1991, 81).
116 Iamb. *Adesp.* 29D; cf. D.19.136 (below 159). Pindar's labelling of democracy as *ho labros stratos* ('the boisterous host': *P.* 2.87) is suggestive in this context, since the adjective 'is used of wind and sea': Hornblower (2006) 152–3; it is also used of fire in E. *Or.* 697 (below).
117 E. *Or.* 696–701; there are echoes of both in *Hec.* 606–8 ('anarchy stronger than fire') and, more obliquely, 533 ('made the mob calm [*nênemon*, lit. windless]', i.e. silent).
118 Ar. *Ran.* 359–60, followed in 361 by a maritime image of the storm-tossed polis; similarly, in Cratinus fr.95 political agitators are apparently referred to as shirts of Nessus i.e. inflammatory, while in Ar. *Eq.* 430–1, 511, 691–2, Cleon is the wind which stirs up (*tarattôn*; above 132n.68) land and sea and forces opponents to take in sail (432–3, 436–7, 440–1; contr. 756–62); Edmunds (1987) 1–16 is a stimulating discussion of Cleon as stirrer-up, though I feel that he focuses too exclusively on the ship of state. The torrent image is also often applied to his voice: Ar. *Ach.* 381, *Eq.* 137, *Vesp.* 1034 = *Pax* 757, fr.644, Pherecr. fr.56.3.
119 A. *Ag.* 899, 966–72: on the oriental character of the 'panegyric metaphor-strings' see West (1997) 570–2; S. *O.T.* 695 (*ourisas*): for the fair wind of fortune cf. *Phil.* 855, E. *Ion* 1509, S. *Tr.* 815 (ironic), and for its instability, E. *HF* 216 with Bond (1981) *ad loc.*; in this case, the depiction of Thebes as a ship in distress at the beginning of the play (*O.T.* 22–4, cf. 46, 51 and above 64n.26) will increase the audience's misgivings here. Gods supply winds: e.g. Homer *Od.* 2.420, 4.520, and cf. the formula *Dios ourôi* ('a fair wind from Zeus': *Od.* 5.176, 15.297, *hAp.* 427 cf. *Il.* 14.19). Element imagery seems to be difficult to apply positively on a human level apart from light, which is not associated with the demos as such.
120 Com. *Adesp.* fr.700, cited in Plut. *Per.* 7.8: see Stadter (1989) *ad loc.* for the likely context c. 446 BC and the implication that the horse is a sexually aroused stallion; it has been suggested, a little fancifully, that the bearded man struggling to control

a spirited horse on the Parthenon frieze (West viii.15) was similarly meant to suggest the difficulties of government, and perhaps specifically those of Pericles: Ashmole (1972) 122–5, Stewart (1996) 80. Antiphon B70: the gloss on the word reads 'obedient to the reins: the man who is gentle, moderate and not disruptive; the metaphor is from horses': compare Plato's use of the adjective in the conservative context of the *Laws* (730b6, 880a7).

121 Similar ideology may lie behind the name of the Eurypontid prince of Sparta Zeuxidamos (Hdt. 6.71); the names Echestratos, Archidamus, Agesipolis and Agesilaos (with which cf. the *lawagetas* of the Linear B tablets) make the same point of firm control in a more literal and overt way (though names in Ages- and Hege- could also carry overtones of military leadership, as perhaps at A. *Pers.* 765 where Medos is first *hêgemôn stratou* in Persia; cf. also the Homeric *agos* [below, n.127]). *Hêgemôn* and *hêgemônia* are widely used in a neutral way of monarchy (Pindar uses the more original *hagêtêr anêr* when he wants to emphasize the leadership motif at *P.* 1.69) and by extension can be applied in an equally neutral manner to Persian imperial power (Hdt. 3.65.6, 7.8.α1, 9.122.1 – note the zeugma with kingship in the last passage) and leadership of Greek leagues (Thuc. 1.95.1, 120.1, 3.10.6, 6.76.3, 82.3): Thuc. 5.16.1 is unique in using the word of political power in general (and has been suspected: Hornblower [1991–2008] *ad loc.*). Timotheus strikingly employs the word of the Spartans as a whole (fr.791.206–7), probably with reference to their control of Sparta as *homoioi* rather than to their post–403 hegemony (so Hordern [2002] *ad loc.*, who suggests however that 'the compliments may be ironic').

122 Note also instances of the verb *euthunô*, which can describe the steering both of chariots and of ships (above 96n.22): A. *Pers.* 773, S. *Ant.* 178, E. *Hec.* 9, all of monarchic direction; in E. *Supp.* 418 and 442 (*euthuntêr*), the terminology is deployed in political polemic.

123 Ober (1989) has been particularly influential here.

124 e.g. Forrest (1975); Strauss (1996); Ceccarelli (1993) takes a more sceptical line.

125 See above 59–60 for a detailed discussion. Boedeker & Raaflaub (1998) 422–3 n.35 remark on a similar rarity of warships and naval warfare in fifth-century Athenian art and Neer (2002) 162–7 describes more specifically how ships disappear from Athenian vase-painting just when the navy becomes politically significant, to be replaced by more oblique visual allusions to sea-power.

126 Political rivalry is often perceived behind the championing of the rival claims of service in the Persian wars of sailors (Salamis) and hoplites (Marathon, Psyttaleia): Fornara (1966), Podlecki (1966) 12–14, van Wees (1995) 157–62, Harrison (2000) 97–100; Pelling (1997) 9–12 is more cautious on the 'battle of the battles'. Osborne (2000) 28–40 argues for the sectional promotion of hoplite values in art; continuing tension is suggested by the stress in the oligarchic revolution of 411 on hoplite service ('those best able to contribute with bodies and money': [Arist.] *Ath. Pol.* 29.5, 33.1; Thuc. 8.65.3 (putting money first), 97.1 cf. X. *HG* 2.3.48. Raaflaub (1994) 138–42 makes the case for a more general ideological marginalization of thetes in comparison to hoplites, while Liddel (2007) 282–7 argues that 'only hoplite activity would be universally accepted as a full disbursal of civic obligations' (285), though his focus is on the later fourth century: in the fifth century the proportion of Athenian citizens of military age serving as hoplites was probably around a third (Pritchard 2004, 209 and n.8).

127 And (again) in Pindar: *promos* (A. *Ag.* 200, 410, *Eum.* 399, *Supp.* 905, S. *O.C.* 884, E. *Hcld.* 670, *Tr.* 31, *Pho.* 1244, *I.A.* 699, *TrGF Adesp.* fr.668.5; perhaps equivalent

to *promaxos*: Fraenkel (1950) on *Ag.* 200); *aristeus* (E. *Med.* 5, *El.* 22, *Ion* 416, *Pho.* 1226, 1245, *I.A.* 28, *Rh.* 479; Pi. *P.* 9.107) and *agos* (A. *Supp.* 248, 905, E. *Rh.* 29; Pi. *N.* 1.51), all of which are Homeric, and *harmostôr* (A. *Eum.* 456 [a *hapax*]). Similar is the substitution of *stratos* for *laos* in Aeschylus (*Pers.* 241, *Eum.* 566 [NB Sommerstein (1989) for the implications here], 569, 668, 683, 762, 889, frr.47a.2, 281a.24) and Pindar (*O.* 5.13, 11.17, *P.* 1.86, 2.46, 87, 10.8, *N.* 8.11, 10.25, fr.52 k.44 cf. *P.* 11.50): the virtual confinement of this usage to these two authors (there are isolated instances in S. *El.* 749, perhaps a Pindaric echo, given the Pythian setting, and *Trach.* 795) suggests that it may chiefly be archaizing poetic colour.

It is not clear to what extent the term *prostates* (and cognates) retained military implications (*pace* Connor 1971, 110–15): while it could be used in contexts where the sense of protection was strong (e.g. A. *Sept.* 408, 798), in many other contexts that sense appears faded, notably as the technical term for a metic's patron (alluded to in tragedy at A. *Supp.* 963–4, S. *OT* 411; in comedy at Ar. *Pax* 683–4, with punning reference to the political *prostates* Hyperbolus: Olson 1998 *ad loc.* and NB also *Ran.* 569; for the word's associations with patronage see Millett 1990, 33–6). The word is quite widespread outside Athens as a title for an office-holder, generally the chairman of a decision-making body (Corcyra: Rhodes with Lewis 1997, 163, and more widely in the Hellenistic period: *ib.* 637 s.v. Chairman; Davies 2000, 245–53 (esp. 252 on *prostateia* of the Chaones at Thuc. 2.80.5); Schaefer 1962, 1289–92; note also Hdt. 2.178.3, of the overseers of the Hellenion at Naucratis). At Athens, it goes from being 'the standard word for a political leader' (Rhodes 1981 on [Arist.] *Ath. Pol.* 2.2; E. *Hcld.* 206 (of a monarch), 964, *Supp.* 243, *I.A.* 373, frr.194, 774; Ar. *Eccl.* 176 [and perhaps *Pl.* 920; cf. *Vesp.* 419]; cf. Hdt. 1.59.3, Thuc. 3.82.8) to becoming almost a formal title for the leading politician: E. *Or.* 772, Ar. *Eq.* 1128 (the earliest example), *Pax* 684, Hdt. 3.82.4, Thuc. 2.65.5, 11, 8.65.2 (cf. 3.70.3 [Corcyra], 6.35.2 [Syracuse]). It is true that Thucydides uses *dêmou prostatai* in the plural (3.75.2, 82.1, 4.46.4, 66.3), but these refer to other poleis, and plurals are used with reference to Athens only in rather general periphrases (3.11.7, 6.28.2, 89.4, 6, though NB Aeschin. 2.176 for two named leaders; L. 13.7 uses the plural, but the sequel refers only to Cleophon); otherwise, the plural generally means 'leading men' (Hdt. 4.79.5, 6.74.1, 9.41.3, Thuc. 8.17.2, 81.1, 90.1). I suspect that, rather like our 'champion', it came to combine implications of eminence, leadership and advocacy as well as protection, which varied in prominence according to the context: most of these nuances are present in Herodotus' use of the word for monarchs (1.127.1, 5.23.2 cf. 3.36.2, 134.2), and the perception of leader as champion is also there in Darius' account at 3.82.4 of the leader of the demos who will put an end to the prevailing corruption. Similarly, in Thuc. 8.89.4, though *prostatês tou dêmou* is mainly used in the technical sense, it also carries 'the much more positive sense of the champion who achieves the restoration of government by the δῆμος' (Andrewes *ad loc.* in Gomme Andrewes and Dover 1945–81).

While there is no imagery based on the phalanx as a whole, we do find occasional evocations of the experience of combat within it in the use of the words *parastatês* and *paraspistês*, the man who stands beside one to mean 'comrade' or 'champion', though usually in the context of action (e.g. A. *Pers.* 957, S. *Ant.* 671 with Jebb 1891, citing the use of the word in the ephebic oath [*R&O* 88.7], E. *Hcld.* 88); properly figurative usage tends to refer generally to support (Dicaiogenes fr.2 [children]; *TrGF Adesp.* fr.14) and only comes close to a political image in 'champions of justice' (E. fr.295 [*Bellerophon*] – or 'supporters at a trial': Collard, Cropp and Lee [1995] *ad loc.*). Imagery from weapons is rare, and negative: A. *Ag.* 483 with Fraenkel (1950), *Cho.* 630 with Garvie (1986), [A.] *P. V.* 405, cf. E. *Hec.* 9.

128 Cf. 27 above on women as stewards; however, Dorati (1998), who locates the image in a wider discourse of gender roles and stereotypes, sees it as exemplifying the women's inability to think politically like males. Moulton (1981) 49-58 considers this and the coinage image in *Frogs* (below) from a poetic perspective, noting the interplay between domestic and political elements (55-6) and the way in which the image takes off from the verb *tarattô* (565, 567; above n.118). Lane (1998) 164-71 compares this image of weaving with that in Plato's *Statesman* (below 161), highlighting the gendered aspect, the model of 'simple unity' it represents, and the minimal attention given to the actual process of weaving (169).

129 Evocation of the *peplos*: Henderson (1987) p. 141; for the image of clothing as protection cf. 1155-6. Wool-grease is a symbol of unpleasant disorder at Ar. fr.415, and wool-dying is evoked as an emblem of female competence at *Eccl.* 215f. Eup. fr.104 offers a rather different clothing image in which young whippersnappers nonchalantly let the generalship trail to their ankles like a cloak (cf. D. 19.314), which might have a specific reference to Alcibiades: Denyer (2001) on Pl. *Alc I* 122c1.

130 He also slightly complicates matters by making reference in 720 to the emergency golden coinage of 406 (Dover 1993, 281-2, Kurke 1999a, 306-8), though the essential antithesis remains clear. Kurke (1999a) 325-7 notes how the differentiation between types of coinage here departs from a general tendency to use coinage *tout court* as a metaphor for legitimacy and integrity (cf. 309-14 on the use of the language of scrutiny (*dokimazein*) and assay (*basanos*) of both coinage and people). The language of forgery and counterfeiting (*kibdêlos* and cognates) is already applied to character in Theognis (117-24, 965-7; Kurke 1999a, 53-5) and is applied to sycophants at Ar. *Ach.* 517-8 (with Olson 2002 *ad loc.*; cf. *Plut.* 862, 957). Hence Medea can draw a contrast between the testability of coinage and the inscrutability of human worth (E. *Med.* 516-9 with Page 1938), and Creon can present office and the laws, in other words political activity, as the touchstone (*entribês*: 177, *LSJ* s.v. 1) of a man's judgment and moral character.

131 The emergency mobilization of slaves and numerous members of the upper classes to crew the fleet at the battle of Arginusae in 406 (X. *HG* 1.6.24) is prominent in *Frogs* 33-4, 190-2, 693-705, the last passage coming just after the allusion to 'Phrynichus' wrestling' (above 119) and ending with an evocation of the storm-tossed ship of state (above 117). Strauss (1986) 70-86, 179-82 has argued that the thetes suffered particularly heavy casualties in the later stages of the Peloponnesian War, which may have a bearing on the political complexion of the audience for *Frogs* in 405; on the play's politics and the reception of the parabasis in particular see Arnott (1991), Dover (1993) 69-76, Sommerstein (1993). McGlew (2002) 163-70 contends that Aristophanes is sincere in commending the oligarchs' rehabilitation, but only on condition that they abandon their political pretensions: if this is correct, his presentation of them in terms of elite values (gold, wrestling [above n.109]) will assist in setting up those pretensions to be undercut.

132 Fr.21, from the *Aiolos*, which must have been earlier than Ar. *Nub.*, which alludes to the plot (1371-2), while metrical arguments also suggest a date in the mid-420s: *TrGF* V p.162.

133 de Romilly (1976); NB also Jouanna (1980a, b) for the suggestion that there may be an allusion in 6.18.7 to current medical controversy concerning change or alteration in treatment, and above 75. Wohl (2002) 195 and n.54 suggests that there may also

be play on different medical senses of *hesychia* (6.10.2, 18.2, 6) as restorative rest and lassitude.

134 8.97.2. For the persistent controversy over the regime of the 5000 see Hornblower (1991–2008) on this passage. Incidentally, even if the image were a sympotic one, from the blend of wine and water, it would not be egalitarian, since the typical ratio was around two to five, and the appropriate mixture varied according to the wine in question: Villard (1988).

135 Rood (1998) 196 makes the comparison with Themistocles and notes the absence of walls and ships here; the idea of the priority of men over property appears elsewhere (S. *OT* 56–7, E. fr.828; Macleod 1983 compares Pericles' argument for the evacuation of Attica in 432: Thuc. 1.143.5; Hdt. 8.100.2 is related but lacks the element of community) but given the particular resonances here Connor (1984) 202 is surely wrong to label the passage 'trite' and a 'cliché'. The association of this form of the image with Themistocles goes back to Smith (1907), who also notes the variant association with Sparta, a famously unwalled polis, as well as later Roman examples. NB Camp (2000) 47–50 for the persistence in the classical period of walls as a constitutive element of the polis.

136 Harrison (2000) 71–2 highlights the impact of the evacuation of Attica on Athenian ideology. That sense of themselves as embattled makers of their own destiny might perhaps provide a context for the striking application of the epithet *polissouchos* to the Athenian people in Aeschylus (*Eum.* 775, 883, 1010; above 16n.23). Compare the observations of Parker (1996) 186–7 on the impact of 'the struggle against Persia' on fifth-century Athenian religion. Constantakopoulou's discussion of the conception of Athens as island (2007, 137–75) is also suggestive here, and could help to explain Athenian ideological isolationism (below 124–6).

137 Full discussion in Raaflaub (2004) 118–32; on use in rhetorical contexts in Thuc. see 129 and n. 55, and NB a typically incisive paragraph already in de Ste Croix (1972) 36. Scione and Melos: e.g. X. *HG* 2.2.3, Isoc. 4.100. Wohl (2002) 181–4 argues that the intensification of the master-slave antithesis into a choice between rule or slavery makes the Athenians prisoners of their own rhetoric (and cf. 184–8 for the inescapable tyranny of empire [below]).

138 Thuc. 6.77.1: the ethnic contrast between enslaved Ionians and free and autonomous Dorians perhaps also evokes images of the Ionians as servile (above 109) as well as the reality of subordination.

139 Thuc. 1.122.3, 124.3, in the second case emphasized by use of the article. Full discussion with a review of earlier bibliography in Tuplin (1985), who emphasizes the relative rarity of the image of imperial tyranny; NB also, more recently, Mitchell (2007) 141–9; Sancho Rocher (1994) argues that the image was invented by Thucydides as part of his analysis of the exercise of power.

140 That is, after the transfer of the treasury of the Delian League to Athens in 454 BC and before the ostracism of Thucydides son of Melesias c.443 (see Stadter 1989 on *Per.* 14.3): the charge could derive from Stesimbrotus or comedy (see Stadter 1989, lx–lxx on Plutarch's contemporary sources for Pericles); Powell (1995) makes a good case for authenticity, and see also Kallet (2003) 134–5.

141 Hence the identification of freedom with democracy: Thuc. 8.68.4, 71.1 and perhaps already 6.56.3 (NB Hornblower 1991–2008 on 8.68.4 for the reckoning of liberty from 510), though here the antithesis is with oligarchy, to which the language of slavery comes therefore to be extended ([X.] *Ath.Pol.* 1.8, Thuc. 6.40.2), while oligarchs can be labelled as tyrants. This becomes common in the early fourth

century with reference to the Thirty (below 183n.111), but we already find a plurality of tyrants in the mid-fifth century in the Erythrai decree (*IG* I³ 14.33), presumably 'those who have taken refuge with the Medes' (l.27), thus encouraging the association.

142 Hdt. 5.92.ζ2-η1; E. *Supp*. 448-9. For the destruction of value in the image see Felton (1998) 43-5 and n.15, who notes that in Roman versions of the image referring to Sextus Tarquinius (Livy 1.54.5-8, Ov. *Fast*. 2.701-8, Dion. Hal. *Ant. Rom*. 4.56) flowers (usually poppies – whence our 'tall poppy syndrome'?) substitute for ears of corn; see also Forsdyke (1999) 365-8 for the shift of focus to the polis as a whole, and particularly 367 for a suggestion of puns alluding to the citizen body (*astachus* ~ *astos, lêion* ~ *laos*). Michelini (1978) esp. 42-4 points to 'docking' as a cure for *hybris* in vegetation, but there is surely something perverse about the concept in these cases. The flower motif evokes reminiscences of the Homeric image of a fallen warrior as a drooping flower (*Il*. 8.306-8, uncomfortably echoed at E. *Supp*. 714-7; cf. Sappho fr.105c and imitations at Cat. 11.22-4, V. *Aen*. 9.435-7), but the shift from the domain of warfare and the implication of arbitrary selection adds a discordant, sinister note to the pathos. The image re-appears in Aristotle: below 193n.175; Felton (1998) 50-2 also discusses parallels in rabbinic texts.

143 On the Persian conception of the 'King's house' see above 110.

144 Though a little later on, Pericles observes that envy and hostility are the natural concomitants of empire in a way that echoes the argument of Periander for tyranny (Hdt. 3.52.3; cf. Pi. *P*. 1.85). Kallet (2003) 120 sees Pericles' warning as specifically directed to the Athenian *apragmones* (political quietists) in his audience.

145 I agree with Tuplin (1985) 358 that the reference must be to the empire (though NB n.148 below), but am doubtful that *kalên g'echeis archên* is ironic, since in that case it is hard to see how the antithesis between that and his domestic political competence works; rather, I think the *ge* takes the popular self-congratulation as read ('your empire is, of course, fantastic') before undermining it. There is a similar mild debunking of popular pretensions when Philocleon is made to boast that his judicial *archê* is as great as any kingdom (*Vesp*. 548-9 cf. 575, 587).

146 The pattern of a bold image that first appears in the mouth of Pericles and is then taken up by Cleon which we have already encountered (above 132n.72) is suggestive, as is the fact that the comic passage falls during Cleon's ascendancy, but no more than that.

147 The issue is thoroughly debated in the papers collected in Morgan 2003. In particular, Kallet (2003) and Henderson (2003) argue for the possibility of a positive valuation by the demos of its power as (quasi-)tyrannical – Henderson (157) appositely quotes Huey Long's 'Every man a king, but no one wears a crown.' This line of argument goes back to Connor (1977); *contra*, see now Raaflaub (2003), esp. 77-82.

148 Thuc. 1.18.1, 2.8.4 with Hornblower (1991-2008). Bernhardt (1987) is highly sceptical that Sparta ever had a principled opposition to tyranny and argues that the idea arises from hostile Athenian propaganda which contrasted Sparta's past and present policies, perhaps even before the Peloponnesian war; however, that idea (regardless of its actual historical validity) would seem to fit more naturally into the context sketched here, and the fact that the Spartans are made to speak of 'liberation' rather than specifically of 'tyranny' (Bernhardt [1987] 277, 288) is less significant given the complex of associations surrounding the former term by this date.

149 As argued recently by Low (2007) 233-51, esp. 242-51.

150 Brief surveys in Meiggs (1972) 291–305, Parker (1996) 141–51; for cult as the expression of power, see especially Jameson (1994) on the depiction of sacrifice on the sculptures of the Athena Nike parapet on the Acropolis.
151 Raaflaub (2009), esp. 107, 110–11. For the style of Achaemenid royal inscriptions one might cite the opening of Darius' Bisutun inscription: 'I am Darius, the Great King, king of kings, king of Persia, king of lands...' (DB §1) or his funerary self-appraisal at Naqš-e Rustam (DNb), e.g. §9: 'as a horseman, I am a good horseman; as a bowman, I am a good bowman, both on foot and on horseback; as a spearman, I am a good spearman...' (tr. Brosius 2000).
152 The classic statement is Jones (1957) 41; which is not to say that no attempt can be made to piece it together: e.g. Raaflaub (1989), Brock (1991).
153 *LIMC* s.vv. Demokratia (Alexandri-Tzahou); Demos (Alexandri-Tzahou) nos. 42 (Eleusis, 421/0) and 43 (Athens, 410–08) = Athena (Demargne) nos. 606, 608 – both beardless (above n.75); Athena also appears without Demos, but with a personified Samos, on the stele bearing the grant of honorary citizenship for the Samians (no. 607) of 405 BC. It should be noted, however, that not all scholars would accept that personifications of Demos appear at all before the early fourth century: see Glowacki (2003), esp. 462–6; in the fourth century Athena appears five times on document reliefs between 375/4 and 322–17 (nos. 609–13) and Demos eight times between 398/7 and *c.* 320 (nos. 44–6, 53–7), including twice with Demokratia. The cult of Demokratia is only reliably attested for 333 BC, but might go back to 403/2 (*LIMC* s.v.), though Hansen (2008) 21–2 argues that it goes back earlier than 430, if not indeed to Cleisthenes; as he notes, there was a shrine of Demos and the nymphs before 450. One of the earliest attested images of Demokratia was a negative one, the depiction of Oligarchia setting fire to her (or her hair? Cf. Ar. *Lys.* 1216–22) with a torch on the funeral monument for Critias (DK88 A13; Bultrighini 1999, 316–9; see Webster 1954, 18 for making personifications forceful or violent to enhance their persuasiveness). Less seriously, some time in the fourth century the comic poet Heniochus describes two women, Demokratia and Aristokratia, who throw the personified cities of his chorus into confusion (or stir them up: *taratteton*) and cause them to get drunk and misbehave (fr.5; Olson 2007, 126–8).

For other, more oblique political personification in this period see Smith (1999), Stafford (2000) 173–97. On mythological aspects of 'official art' at Athens see Castriota (1992), and on the relationship between democracy, empire and the arts more generally, the essays collected in Boedeker and Raaflaub (1998), especially Hölscher (1998) on 'political monuments'; in their 'reflections and conclusions', the editors remark on 'the apparent absence of specifically democratic themes in Athenian art' (325–31, quotation from 326). The Athenians seem to have given prominence instead to actual events (e.g. the tyrannicides, the Persian wars), to a newly constructed mythological past (authochthony, Theseus) and to monumental expressions of power and wealth (above all, the Parthenon and the rest of the Acropolis complex).
154 Sommerstein (1989) on 693–5 judiciously summarizes the scholarly debate on 'the most controversial passage in *Eumenides*' (p. 216) and plausibly suggests that 'the poet has deliberately left his precise meaning obscure' (p. 218) where the specific political content is concerned. For the image we can consider the comparison of a foreign marriage to muddy water (*tholerôi*) at E. *Supp.* 222–3 (with Collard [1975] *ad loc.*; the contrast between clear and muddy water appears in an erotic context at Thgn. 959–62, and the clear water of a desirable citizen population is contrasted with

the water of 'torrents' to be excluded at Pl. *Laws* 736b (with England [1921]). More generally, there are similar resonances to the imagery of 'stirring' which surrounds Cleon: above n.118.

155 Gorg. B11a.30. Earlier in the trilogy it is Agamemnon who is the (fallen) guardian (*Ag.* 1452) and, probably, the chorus who in his absence consider themselves the 'lone-guardian bulwark (*monophrouron herkos*) of the Apian land' (*Ag.* 256: so Denniston and Page [1957] against Fraenkel [1950] *ad loc.*, though perhaps the image might be deliberately ambiguous, applied prima facie to Clytemnestra, and actually to themselves). This is in line with the restriction to tragedy of the use of the imagery of protection with reference to individuals (cf. n.127 above on military imagery): so in Sophocles Oedipus was 'a tower against death' for Thebes (*thanatôn ... purgos*: *OT* 1200–1) but by the end of the play it is Creon who is the only guardian (1418). The transfer of these images to the court here is in line with the movement from the individual to the communal in the trilogy. In *TrGF Adesp.* fr.646.12 *kl]einês eruma patras* the reference is apparently to the Macedonian people (10) rather than their kings (so Kannicht-Snell *ad loc.*); A. *Pers.* 859–60 might also refer to laws as towers (*nomi(s)mata purgina*) but other interpretations are possible, and the text is in any case irremediably corrupt: see now Garvie (2009) *ad loc.*

156 And can be personified as an agent: Hdt. 7.104.4, Ant. 3.1.1 (cf. E. *Supp.* 312–3, Andoc. 1.9; L. 1.26, 34–5); this develops markedly in the fourth century (below 166). The Boule is personified only in the fourth century (*LIMC* s.v.: of the four instances only one is securely datable, to 323/2).

157 Admittedly this is on the account of an opponent, but the attack is based on the inconsistency between his democratic rhetoric and his actual behaviour, not the rhetoric itself (for which cf. Isoc. 8.53).

158 Above 27 – though the Anonymous Iamblichi is of course not necessarily an Athenian author; on his thinking on law see Ostwald (1969) 92–4, and on the question of identity 92 n.1; on a more positive note, he also speaks of the desirability of law and justice 'ruling (*embasileuein*)' in men (6.1).

159 As Edwards (1995) *ad loc.* observes.

160 Ar. *Eq.* 589–90; *stasiazei* suggests a particular focus on rival choruses rather than just favour for their own, though the knights' participation in real warfare is prominent in the stanza as a whole. For an interest in procedure we can compare the depiction of the process of voting with *psephoi* on almost a dozen vases from the early fifth century, at a time when democracy and its procedures are a relative novelty: Spivey (1994). Something of the same kind perhaps applies to the bean (*kuamos*) used in the sortition process, particularly for the Boule (Thuc. 8.66 with Hornblower 1991–2008, 8.69.4, decree *ap.* Andoc. 1.96; also Hdt. 6.109.2, Ar. *Av.* 1022), and interestingly exported to the Athenian-sponsored democracy at Erythrai *c.* 450 BC (*IG* I³ 14.9): when the personified Demos is labelled 'bean-chewing' (Ar. *Eq.* 41), there is something symbolic about the adjective, as Neil 1901 remarks *ad loc.*

161 So Cartledge (1998) 394, reporting the suggestion in Brock (1991) 169, though he offers as alternatives the possibility of democratic antipathy to theorizing and to writing. Compare the remark of Boedeker and Raaflaub (1998) 326 on the late personification of Demokratia, that before 404/3 'there was no need for such tangible reaffirmation of the precise constitutional concept'.

8

Orators and Philosophers: The Fourth Century to Alexander (*c.* 400–322 BC)

From one perspective, the year 404/3 marked the triumph of Athenian democracy, which emerged from a second episode of oligarchy even more ideologically entrenched, and stronger in practice for a more realistic appreciation of where threats to it lay.[1] That perspective is, as we shall see, reflected in the persistence of imagery which expresses democratic ideology such as that based on the model of the polis as household. Yet just as recent scholarship has tended to highlight the ways in which democracy in the fourth century differed from the radical version of the previous century,[2] there are distinct differences in the character of fourth-century political imagery, above all in the handling of the imagery of authority figures. That change is driven by two interlinked processes: the resurgence of monarchy as a serious constitutional option, and the emergence of clearly articulated political thought. The return of kings and dynasts to the political stage naturally drew attention back to appropriate images, which in many cases went back to Homer, but had been marginalized or problematized in the previous century, at least at Athens. Yet the thinkers who reached for them were clearly conscious that it was not sufficient to recycle the heritage of epic and archaic poetry: not only are Plato, Xenophon and Isocrates preoccupied with the nature of authority and the search for the ideal ruler or constitution, but we can also see in their works an effort to articulate the rationale behind the expression of authority through images and to distinguish between those images, and their implications.

As far as our sources go,[3] then, this is a fourth-century development which could be seen as a counterpoint to the steady-state Athenian democracy and an indication of alternatives elsewhere, yet it is highly likely that its origins lie earlier, in the latent opposition to radical fifth-century democracy. For one thing, we do not have to wait until the fourth century for examples of effective monarchs: the figure chosen by Polus in Plato's *Gorgias* (470d–71d) as the type of the all-powerful autocrat, Archelaus of Macedon, came to the throne in 413 (and was dead by 399); Evagoras, eulogized by Isocrates, seized power at Cypriot Salamis in 411, and Dionysius at Syracuse in 406.[4] Most conspicuously, the Athenians will have had to acknowledge from 412, if they had not done so earlier, that the king of Persia was no longer a figure to be contemptuously dismissed, but a major player in Greek affairs, as he was to remain until the triumph of Alexander.[5] We can therefore reasonably suppose that intellectuals will already have started to take an interest in monarchs and monarchy in the late fifth century. The same is true of the elaboration of authority figures such as the helmsman, the doctor and the shepherd. Reading the dispute between Thrasymachus and Socrates in the first book of the *Republic* about the ruler as shepherd (above 45), one has the sense of tuning in to a debate which has been going on for some time, and by the middle of the century the various images for rulers have become a standardized repertoire, almost a tool kit, to judge by the question of the Athenian in the *Laws*: 'What sort of ruler do the gods in fact resemble? Or rather, what rulers resemble them? … What about drivers of competing teams of horses, or steersmen of boats in a race? … Or we might compare the gods to commanders of armies. Again, it could be that they're analogous to doctors concerned to defend the body in the war against disease, or to farmers…, or to shepherds.'[6] However, this typology is the product of a process of evolution which I believe can be traced back to the late fifth century, and specifically to Socrates. The images themselves of course go back much further, and preceding discussion of them has brought out the latent implication of skill (above [e.g.] 94):[7] what appears to be new is a much sharper and more overt focus on knowledge, expertise and skill as essential for the practice of politics, both in leadership and decision-making, and the expression of this belief through analogies with a wide range of practical skills which are for these purposes substantially assimilated to one another.

The emphasis on politics as a *technê* ('craft' or 'skill') is not likely to be peculiar to Socrates, since the sophists were characterized as a movement by teaching, and a number of them had interests in politics,[8] but there is little indication in the admittedly scanty fragments of their works of the use of this kind of analogy.[9] Socrates, on the other hand, is well-attested as having frequent recourse to analogies from craftsmanship, often in humble forms such as shoemaking, tanning, metalworking and fulling. The methodological difficulties of recovering any aspect of Socrates' teaching from the works of his disciples Plato and Xenophon are notorious, but it is not, I think, necessary to take a position on the 'Socratic Question' to argue that there are strong indications that this is an authentic aspect of it: first of all, the consensus between the two in presenting him as using the same kinds of images;[10] secondly, the characterization of this as a consistent and notorious feature of his argumentation;[11] thirdly, Xenophon's highlighting of the use of one such comparison to criticize democratic election by sortition as typical of the kinds of charges levelled at him at his trial in 399;[12] fourthly, the same author's anecdote in which his use of an analogy from animal husbandry roused the anger of Critias and Charicles during the rule of the Thirty, which ought to be authentic, or at least plausibly representative of his manner of speech;[13] and finally the adoption of this kind of analogy by his pupils in their own works.[14] If this attribution is sound, it follows that the reappraisal and elaboration of the imagery of expertise has its origins in informal debates in the latter part of the fifth century, and since Socrates was evidently conspicuously active by 424/3, the date of Aristophanes' *Clouds*, it need not have been a response to the fallibility of democracy of which the Sicilian disaster was clear proof.[15] Indeed, it was arguably not inherently anti-democratic, since its principles amounted to a critique of political leaders of all stamps, as well as of mass popular decision-making; nevertheless, its attractions for critics of democracy are patent, and its positive espousal of expertise in leadership offered more purchase to advocates of minority regimes, particularly if they were not concerned to think too hard about the philosophical implications.[16]

The ways in which this imagery was elaborated in the fourth century are most clearly visible in the treatment of the model of the state as household.[17] The keynote of the fifth-century imagery of domestic management (*oikein, dioikein, oikonomia*) had been administration, and indeed that version, with the associated implications of competence, honesty and service, persisted in the democratic discourse of the fourth century (below 154). However, fourth-century intellectuals shifted the focus to authority and to the figure of the householder, and the analogy between the two spheres is made explicit in the assertion that there is a single art of rule, so that expertise is transferable between them.[18] The firm establishment by this point of the lexical usage bridging the two spheres[19] doubtless made it easier to assert that what was in question was essentially the same activity, the only difference being one of scale, but the principal attractions of the householder as the model of the authority figure were, I think, his ubiquity, and the fundamental importance of his role: since effective running of the *oikos* was a pre-requisite for the survival of the polis and its inhabitants, the authority of the householder could likewise be regarded as fundamental and natural, always operative and not requiring explanation or justification.

The domestic model had two further advantages: first, since the householder could readily be identified with a father, it added an affective appeal to his role, while at the same time furnishing a justification for the application of sanctions or punishment when necessary,[20] and secondly, since the householder would normally also have legal control of his property, it justified a ruler's authority over the resources of the state and his right to use them as he judged best, a step which was quite at odds with democratic ideology, and would probably have been impossible to take in the preceding century.[21] The two strands instructively appear in reverse order in the peroration to Xenophon's *Hiero*, when Simonides advises the tyrant, who will take it for granted that the state is his to dispose of as he pleases,[22] to think of his fatherland as a household, and hence of his relations with citizens and friends in familial terms, and to outdo them all in benefactions: if the state is his household, he has an obligation to preserve and increase it, and likewise he should display not only the authority, but the affection and concern of a father.[23] However, Aristotle completely rejected the household model for his own theoretical reasons: first, the *oikos* was not parallel to the polis, but rather a less-developed subsidiary component of it, and secondly (and more importantly), the nature of the authority exercised by the householder differed even between different members of the household (wife, child, slave) according to their intellectual capacity, and for the same reason the authority exercised in the political sphere by a man ruling his peers was distinct from all of these. He does accept a father's control over his children as a model for monarchic authority, but distinguishes that from the familial relationships appropriate to the other constitutions in which he is in practice much more interested in the *Politics*.[24]

The suitability of the household as the master-image of 'rule' becomes clearer if we consider the other images for authority which fourth-century intellectuals deploy. The closest to the householder as an analogue of essential but benign control is the shepherd, but we have already noted that this image was much more controversial, since the difficulty that the relationship entailed some degree of exploitation was readily perceived,[25] which necessitated the setting out of a rationale which would mitigate or justify it, though this was certainly far from impossible (above, 45–8). It also shared with other imagery of control over animals the implication of an essential difference in nature between ruler and ruled: that was not a problem when it was applied to the relationship between gods and men,[26] but made it less suitable for contexts of constitutional rule, and hence it was more easily applied to more authoritarian regimes, such as the Persian monarchy of Cyrus, and in the military sphere, where the divide between commander and troops was more readily accepted as a given.[27] This is probably the main reason why it plays a less central role in Plato on the human plane: in the *Statesman* it is deployed temporarily and heuristically, as a model of ruling which is ultimately discarded.[28] In the *Republic* it appears early on (343–5), precisely because the ambiguity over its aims and objectives offers Thrasymachus a purchase, which the doctor does not, to highlight issues of knowledge and justice and enable Socrates to insist on the centrality of the welfare of the flock (i.e. the ruled) even in this contentious case. Thereafter the model of the Guardians as shepherds does linger in the background to the middle of the dialogue, as one might expect given their superiority, though what is particularly at issue is the relationship between shepherds, watchdogs and flock.[29] In some ways, herding imagery is most easily deployed as a negative paradigm, as in Socrates' comparison of the Thirty to bad herdsmen who had made their charges fewer and worse, mentioned earlier, or the more extended analogy between Pericles and other great Athenian statesmen and keepers of horses or cattle who have allowed their charges to become savage instead of tame, to their own harm (*Grg.* 516), since in these instances questions of ends can be left in the background.[30]

These weaknesses were not a feature of the doctor or the helmsman, two figures which particularly appealed to Plato[31] as types of the expert practitioner within society, to whose authority their fellow men should defer precisely because of their superior knowledge[32] and expertise: hence they appear even before the shepherd in the *Republic* as the types of the expert practitioner of a skill who exercises it in the interest of his subject and of those in his charge.[33] As with household management, these are pre-existing images with an obvious appeal which are now articulated much more explicitly: in highlighting the importance of knowledge here, Plato lays a particular emphasis on politics as a specialized skill, but he also brings out the need for the expert practitioner to overcome obstacles which may prevent the community from reaching its goal, or threats which could jeopardize its health or survival. In either case, the appeal of the image is increased by the implication of an essential objective shared by both parties but which only the expert has the necessary understanding to attain, the health of the body or safe arrival at the destination of the voyage, either of which therefore requires willing acceptance of his authority.[34]

The implications are nevertheless somewhat different: the doctor's judgement as to what treatment will restore health provides a charter for intervention which no sane man will gainsay, while on board ship, what is important is obedience to the helmsman's orders, even though these may be reinforced by sanctions if necessary.[35] Behind this lies a further distinction: since it is not the helmsman's business to set the destination, his role is concerned with means rather than ends,[36] but the doctor is treated as the judge of what constitutes health as well as how it is to be achieved, and it is more or less taken for granted that any patient will be unhealthy to start with.[37]

That is made explicit in cases where he is paired with the trainer, who is to the healthy body as the doctor is to the sick one, while the comparison of the individual doctor to a judge hints that the treatments prescribed for a polis will have a moral aspect too, and explains both why treatment is so much more prominent in Plato than in earlier medical imagery, and why he highlights the more radical and painful aspects – surgery, cautery and purging.[38] A distinction in character is perhaps also indicated in those passages where Plato considers dysfunction in civic seafaring and medicine: the famous parody of the ship of state in the *Republic* (488a–9a; above 58) satirizes the pretensions of popular leaders in laying claim to a role which they do not understand and aggressively maintain cannot be taught – that is, the distinction is between the job done properly, as a craft, and badly, because founded on ignorance; in the *Gorgias*, on the other hand, the doctor is opposed to the pastry-cook and the confectioner, the former a practitioner of a true art, which may cause pain to do good, and the latter two practitioners of a knack which panders to its objects and gratifies rather than conferring genuine benefits:[39] the doctor *qua* doctor does not make mistakes, just as Thrasymachus avers (R. 340de). Finally, whereas seamanship is palpably a skill exercised in practice,[40] medicine could potentially be codified in writing, as the growing Hippocratic corpus was demonstrating by Plato's time:[41] hence it lends itself to an exploration of the distinction between the codification of knowledge as principles or rules and its application in practice. So in the *Statesman* Plato acknowledges the possibility that a trainer or doctor could write down instructions for their charges, but points out that generic instruction and legislation are poorly adapted to variations between individuals and unable to adapt to changing circumstances, unlike the expert in person. Furthermore, legislation entails compulsion; in the worst case, written codes could actually impede the truly knowledgeable practitioner,[42] though Plato goes on to acknowledge their value for laymen. So in the *Laws* he draws a distinction between two kinds of doctor, the slave-doctor who treats slaves generically and without explanation on the basis of experience, and the true doctor who uses his understanding to engage with individuals.[43] Here Plato's doctor is starting to anticipate the Hellenistic concept of the monarch as embodying law in his person (below 166); meanwhile, his rational expertise allows him to make use of falsehood.[44]

The trainer comes into his own when the focus narrows from the polis to politicians, and the concept of politics as a specialized skill combines with the established image of politics as a contest (above 119): the logical conclusion is the need for serious training on the part of Socrates' protégés, and particularly that of Alcibiades. In Plato's *Alcibiades I* Alcibiades starts out from the belief that since his opponents in Athenian politics are untrained amateurs, there is no need for him to train, since he will defeat them by superior nature (119b), and the function of the argument in the dialogue is to convince him that he needs special training to prepare him for politics (132b);[45] similarly, in Xenophon's defence of Socrates, Alcibiades is said to have neglected to train properly for politics because of his easy superiority (*Mem.* 1.2.24).[46] The antithesis between amateurs and professionals is given a different spin in *Mem.* 3.7, where Charmides is criticized for refusing to enter politics like an athlete who could win honour for himself and his city but refuses to compete; he replies that competition with the masses (*plêthos*) is difficult, and Socrates in turn points out that as a trained expert he has nothing to fear from amateurs. However, the analogy is not limited to democracy, and finds a more general validity when Isocrates advises Nicocles that just as monarchy is the supreme contest with the supreme prize, so the monarch must have a mental mastery superior to the physical excellence of the athlete (2.11 cf. 13, 51); similarly, Aristotle reports claims that the legislator Onomacritus 'trained (*gumnasthênai*)' in Crete (*Pol.* 1274a25–7).[47]

The other fundamental consequence for Plato's imagery of his belief that the exercise of authority should be based on reason is his commitment to a model of parallelism between macrocosm and microcosm at the levels of body, polis and cosmos: given that knowledge and virtue are constants, the structures of power relations must be analogous at each level, and are, or should be, administered on the same basis by one universal art of rule.[48] In one sense this kind of analogical thinking goes back to Homer and Hesiod and their conception of the social and political organization of the gods as mirroring that of mortals. That traditional model is still in play in the fourth century, though Isocrates hedges his bets on its reality in appealing to the kingship of Zeus as validating earthly monarchy, and Plato himself sometimes makes use of it.[49]

However, more directly influential is the Presocratic elaboration of the model of cosmic authority, which comes to express a principle of rational direction (above 9–10), to which Plato quite frequently alludes, notably in the figurative language of helmsmanship,[50] though in later works he tends to depersonalize his sole ruler and to refer to it as 'reason' or 'soul'.[51] At the other end of the scale, in the course of the fifth century medical writers developed a conception of the body as organized on political principles. As we have seen, the earliest such model for which we have evidence, that of Alcmaeon of Croton, imagined bodily health as dependent on a proper, though not necessarily equal, balance between the constituent humours, which are described as 'powers', disease being the consequence of the 'monarchy' of any one of them. A similar conception and terminology are to be found in some Hippocratic treatises, though it is not the only possible model, and we also encounter, as in Presocratic cosmology, proponents of a single element as supreme power;[52] the parallel drawn between different levels of order is made explicit in Democritus's description of man as a *mikros kosmos* (B34).[53]

In Plato these ideas come together in a distinctive form: the concept of a directing reason is combined with a simplified model of the individual as consisting of two or three elements, of which the rational one is, or ought to be, in control. The claim to rule founded on the priority of reason is reinforced by the identification of the ruling element with the soul, which being divine is prior to, and of a superior nature to the body, just as gods are superior to mortals, and so entitled to rule.[54] It may be that the basic principles behind this again go back to Socrates, since we find the same kind of thinking attested in Xenophon, who in *Mem.* 4.3.13–14 moves from reference to an unnamed divinity, 'organizing and maintaining the whole cosmos' and administering (*oikonomôn*) matters invisibly, to the human soul which 'partakes of the divine and patently rules (*basileuei*) in us', for all that it too is invisible. Certainly the principle of rule by a rational element is widespread: Isocrates asserts (15.180) that no-one would deny that soul is 'more fitted to lead (*hêgemonikôteron*)' than body, and the concept is firmly established in Aristotle's thought, from biology to ethics,[55] but it also appears in less elevated contexts. The author of the Demosthenic *Erotic essay* ([D.] 61.37-8) commends the cultivation of intelligence (*dianoia*) on the grounds that this directs (*hêgemoneuousan*) all human affairs, and that all physical and material goods are its slave and overseen by it, and ps.-Demosthenes can even support a closing appeal to jurors to uphold the laws by citing the direction of the whole cosmos, the divine and the seasons by law and order (*nomos kai taxis ... dioikein*: [D.] 26.27). To some degree, this conception is paralleled by a hierarchical conception of the physical body as ruled or overseen by the head, though the Greeks' imperfect grasp of physiology and the persistence of a dispute as to where the seat of consciousness was to be located limited its impact.[56]

The level of order which is least prominent in this binary analogy is the polis, at least in Plato: others speak of the *politeia* as the soul of the city, but he refuses to accept this move.[57] Instead, he deploys a tripartite model (the 'political analogy') in which the internal organization of the polis mirrors that of the individual: this is initially presented as a means of obtaining a clearer view of justice in the individual (*R.* 368c-9a), and the establishment of the tripartite structure proceeds from city to individual, the implication being that the individual soul will function in the same way.[58] This builds on Plato's distinctive move in articulating his basic analogical model, namely the identification of the directing principle with the rational soul, yet even from this perspective the polis stands apart from the rest of the system as not being animate: instead, when Plato turns to specifics in Books 8 and 9, the characters of the individuals who correspond to the different constitutional types and the developments which they undergo are themselves described in political terms.[59]

Again, the argument begins from the polis: the four imperfect types of constitution are enumerated alongside the ideal 'aristocracy' (544cd), and then it is stated that there must be five corresponding types of individual (544d6-e6). The sequence of decline[60] is then analysed, first in the constitution and then in the equivalent individual (545bc), in terms of the relations between the three elements. First the timarchic man hands over authority in himself (*tên en heautôi archên*) to the spirited element (550ab); the oligarchic man dethrones this and establishes desire and love of money as a Persian king who 'enslaves' the other elements (553cd; above 8). With the transition from oligarchy to democracy we come much closer to contemporary realities, and the account of internal political change becomes more detailed and circumstantial, characterized as a civil war between necessary, oligarchic passions and unnecessary democratic ones. After the initial democratic coup (559de),[61] both internal factions will depend on support from external sympathisers: if the remonstrances of the man's family are successful, the oligarchy will regain control, kill some of the rival desires, exile others and restore the status quo (559e-60a). However, if the exiled democratic passions are allowed to increase and breed in secret, they will seize the citadel, empty as it is of any garrison of wisdom and good education. It will then be too late to reinforce the economical element in the man's soul, since the gates to it will be barred, or even to negotiate; good qualities will be arbitrarily redefined and exiled (560ad), and the way will be open for a life of anarchy, dictated by the same unquestioning enthusiasm for equality as in the democratic city, though some of the economical passions may return and force some degree of restraint (561a8-b2).[62] The final sketch, the tyrannical man, moves away somewhat from political reality (unlike the corresponding constitutional outline), inasmuch as the supreme passion is implanted as tyrant and leader of the idle passions (572e–3a), though the killing or expulsion of decent opinions and feelings and its attendance by a bodyguard and supporters from outside (573ab) conform to the pattern in the tyrannical polis.[63] At the close of this section, Plato reconnects the two sides of his analogy by describing the fate of tyrannical individuals in the world: they will become bodyguards to a tyrant, or mercenaries, or if they are numerous they will set up as tyrant the most tyrannical of their number.[64] The elaboration of this image[65] and of its analogue, the conception of the body as a city in the *Timaeus*,[66] imply that Plato found the more complex model of political interaction particularly illuminating for the intricacies of human psychology, even if analogies with actual constitutions only describe men as they are, rather than as Plato believes they ought to be.[67]

At this point, with political realities once again to the fore, it will be convenient to bring Athenian democracy back into the picture. The common perception that the democratic regime essentially picked up from the point at which it had been interrupted by the Thirty is encouraged by much of the political imagery associated with it: the politician as servant, the politician as lover and the watchdog of the people, to name but three, reappear as if nothing much had changed since the time of Cleon. Indeed, it is only now that we encounter the orthodox statement of the democratic model of the household: it is the orators who deploy the language of service to express the ideal relationship between politician and demos.[68] Applied to themselves, it can strike a note of self-deprecation, but is more frequently developed in an implicit antithesis between the speaker, who adheres to this code, and his opponents, who have made themselves masters instead of servants, while reducing the demos to servitude.[69] That charge recalls the scenario of Aristophanes' *Knights* (above 115), and we find it similarly elaborated in charges that the food which should sustain the demos is being hogged by politicians who resemble greedy nurses or selfish guests at a pot-luck meal (*eranos*);[70] in this last case, the image, which occurs elsewhere in the orators, carries implications of unsociability and failure to demonstrate appropriate reciprocity.[71] While the character of this form of political service varies according to the use made of the image, there is an unambiguously pejorative implication in the allusions to wage-labour which become widespread in the oratory of the later fourth century as a convenient label for corruption, whether among Athenians or, more typically, with reference to foreign policy and, above all, dealings with Macedon, whose supporters could be represented as hirelings lacking the independence of a proper citizen.[72] To a considerable extent, this imagery, and the related language of retail commerce,[73] must reflect the diminished position of an Athens obliged to negotiate and to place considerable reliance on diplomacy, rather than operating from a position of superior power; the increased complexity of Athenian foreign policy and the greater frequency of failure also made mutual recrimination and infighting more likely. The introduction of money and commerce into this figurative discourse also engenders a lurking suspicion of prostitution, at least where the interactions of politicians are concerned. As we have seen, one cannot prostitute oneself to the demos: that explains why the positive figuration of the politician as lover of the demos remains current, even if it typically appears in our sources as the sort of thing other speakers are likely to say.[74] However, there could be a further factor at work here: the persistence of another image of more or less the same vintage, the demagogue as watchdog of the people, makes one wonder whether there was perhaps a repertoire of stock images of leadership validated by their origins in the heyday of imperial democracy. If so, then the good old days were regarded as the time of Cleon at least as much as the age of Pericles.

In the *Gorgias*, Plato pointedly takes issue with the conception of the politician as servant and lover.[75] As we have seen (above 26, 115), the two are linked linguistically through the terms *therapeia* and *therapeuô*, which can denote service and a lover's attention, as well as referring to treatment by a doctor and the courting of political favour, and, as with all the language of service, can be evaluated negatively as well as positively. Plato pushes hard at this weak point: first, Socrates is made to argue that rhetoric, here regarded as essentially a tool of politics, is no more than a kind of pandering, lacking a foundation in knowledge and aiming only at gratification without regard to consequences, equivalent to cookery as opposed to medicine (above 151). Then the aspiring politician Callicles is said to be the lover both of the Athenian demos and of Demos the son of Pyrilampes, forced to follow his inconstant loves through every change of stance, incapable of resistance, and hence of adhering to any standard of truth.[76] The implication of subordination is reinforced when Socrates argues that the only way to win favour with a lover or a demos is to become as like them as possible, not just superficially, but in nature.[77] Thus the politics of gratification is fundamentally opposed to any possibility of change or improvement: the politicians of the past, whom Callicles chooses to follow in ministering to his love's desires, have simply given the demos what it wants and so ruined its health.[78] Clearly in this thoroughgoing demolition of democratic politics Plato has one eye on Aristophanes' treatment of the same issues in *Knights*,[79] but the critique is sharpened if we appreciate that the images with which he takes issue were still current in the discourse of many a real-life Callicles when he was writing.

Plato engages in a more nuanced manner with the other side of the democratic household metaphor, the state as a family. Again, it is in fourth-century oratory, and particularly in funeral speeches and related public rhetoric, that we get a clear view of a conception of Athens as a family in which citizens are, by virtue of the myth of autochthony, all siblings and children of Attica or of the Athenian polis and its institutions:[80] they were thus bound to the polis by the same obligation to love, support and defend it as individual children had towards their parents.[81] Plato sometimes draws on this model in passing, notably in Socrates' philosophical commitment to the Athenians as his kinsmen,[82] and he makes more substantial use of it in the *Crito*, where the Laws claim that Socrates is both their offspring and slave,[83] and that they are therefore entitled to deference and obedience, and *a fortiori* should be immune from violence at his hands to an even greater degree than parents. Here, though, he strikes a somewhat different note in the emphasis on submission (or persuasion), and the usual implication of an affective bond is lacking, replaced by a construction of the relationship as more or less contractual.[84] He similarly puts his own spin in the *Republic* on the myth of autochthony, which he hijacks to form the basis of the Noble Lie, though here the affective aspect is of central importance, and a little later he extends the language of the earth as nurse and mother to the whole of Greece as against the wider barbarian world.[85] Neither Plato nor the democrats have any use for the image of the king as father of which Xenophon and Isocrates are fond, though for rather different reasons: the aspects which made it problematic in the fifth century persist in the fourth, despite Athens' increasing engagement with real-life monarchs, while for Plato the fact that fatherhood is at once nearly universal and, though a hierarchical relationship, not founded on knowledge, rules it out of court.[86]

When we turn to the imagery of democratic leadership, the picture is again a complex one. In the fifth century, though the ship of state becomes a commonplace image of community, the figure of the helmsman is confined to tragedy, and no individual in the real world is allowed to lay claim to the position (above 117). The commonplace persists in the fourth century,[87] but matters are very different: orators regularly represent themselves as in charge of the ship of state, and indeed the orthodoxy of the claim is illustrated by the way in which, in the aftermath of defeat by Macedon, the foundering of the polis can give rise to denunciations of an opponent's helmsmanship.[88] Similarly, Demades claims that a politician deserves pardon for ignoble policies if he is 'governing the shipwreck of the polis' (fr.17). This self-representation probably developed earlier in the century, since Plato's satire on the ship of state seems intended *inter alia* to mock the pretensions of democratic politicians.[89] It is tempting to see another deliberate appropriation in Plato's characterization of his Auxiliaries as watchdogs or sheepdogs,[90] since that image too clearly retained its currency in democratic discourse: ps.-Demosthenes ridicules Aristogeiton's claim to be the 'watchdog' of Athens, arguing that he does not bite those whom he accuses of being wolves, but does consume the flock he claims to be protecting, and is therefore subject to the penalty he himself invokes on such rogue sheepdogs (25.40 cf. 26.22). On the other hand, Demosthenes himself had no objection to the image, since he is said to have likened himself and his party to watchdogs given up by the sheep to the wolves, or rather the lone wolf (*monolukos*) Alexander (fr.11.2).[91]

It is more difficult to judge the nature of the relationship when we come to medical imagery. As with the helmsman, there is a striking shift in the way in which orators use such imagery, bringing the doctor into the democratic arena[92] and, like Plato, giving greater prominence to treatment than in the previous century. The comparison of politicians to doctors is made both explicitly and implicitly: Demades (fr.64) says that politicians, like doctors, should not be blamed for the disease, but thanked for their treatment, while Hyperides implicitly compares the two in contrasting the destructive behaviour of certain individuals with the need of cities for greatest care at times of crisis, like sick bodies (2 fr.10), and Demosthenes draws an analogy between doctors and lawgivers.[93] Ps.-Demosthenes endorses radical intervention in treatment, too, saying that Aristogeiton must be disposed of by cautery or surgery, like a cancer or ulcer.[94] Oratory and philosophy also have in common much of the more general language of health and disease: the equation of *stasis* with disease and the identification of loyalty with health and its opposite with disease.[95] They also share a concern with the links between disease and stress, a new development which is doubtless due to the more uncertain political environment of the fourth century: in one version, the focus is on the body's vulnerability and consequent need for care at times of stress, while another looks to the stress of sickness to reveal inherent weakness.[96] It is tempting and, I think, plausible to suggest that in this case some of the similarities are due to influence from the theoretical writers on practising politicians: while we have to be careful not simply to fall into assumptions on the basis of the chronology of the sources, the most natural rationale for the way in which the doctor's role is articulated in the fourth century is a philosophical one, and that is where we find it at its most detailed; moreover, this is the only authority figure of which Plato neither challenges nor subverts a democratic version.[97]

The new-found capacity of rhetors to present themselves as helmsmen and doctors implies that the demos allowed their pretensions considerably greater scope than in the era of Pericles and Cleon,[98] and that conclusion is encouraged if we turn to sporting metaphors. These continue to centre around wrestling, and again frequently with the implication of underhand behaviour: Demosthenes complains that the demos allows speakers too much scope for 'tripping and trickery' (18.138), and Dinarchus accuses Deinias of 'giving the laws a throw' (fr.9.3 Conomis).[99] What is new is a broader focus on the contest itself, in which the speaker and even his audience are felt to be engaged themselves: so Aeschines begins by warning that Demosthenes will use 'judicial wrestling' but then, shifting his image, says that the jurors must face up to Demosthenes all day long, like boxers in the gymnastic contests jockeying for position, not letting him out of the ['ring' of?] charge of illegality but (shifting the image again, to hunting) lying in wait for him, they must drive him into the toils of the discussion of illegality.[100] In the same vein, earlier in the speech he urges the Athenians to look on themselves as 'organizers of political games' (*agônothetas politikês aretês*) and to ensure that the prizegiving (i.e. the crowning) is fair, if they want to attract contestants; the implication is that any politician is a competing athlete, and that indeed is what Demosthenes calls himself.[101]

One has more of a sense of the sharing of neutral ground when Plato's characters resort to the language of freedom and slavery which had already become commonplace in the fifth century and remained current in the fourth, where the pattern of application in common parlance hardly varies. The association with autocracy, typically labelled 'tyranny', persists: the king of Persia is, as he has been from the time of Aeschylus' *Persians* at the latest, master of subjects who are all, even the most exalted, his slaves.[102] That image slotted neatly into the burgeoning rhetoric of panhellenism, painting the enemy as both alien to Greek values and inherently vulnerable, something which we also find in Xenophon.[103] Elsewhere in the same author, however, there are passages which appear to reflect an accurate appreciation of the vassal status of Persian nobles: when in *An.* 1.9.29 and 2.5.38 Artaxerxes lays claim to the weapons of the Ten Thousand as the property of his late 'slave' Cyrus, that might be no more than a literal representation of an ideology by which all the assets of a vassal derive from the King, as in 2.3.17 the *douloi* are presumably the followers of Tissaphernes and other Persian nobles. Similarly, in the *Cyropaideia* Cyrus refers to his satraps and subjects as *douloi* (8.1.43, 6.13) as does Cyaraxes (5.5.9), and conversely the kings of Media and Assyria are referred to as *despotes* (1.3.18; 5.3.6).[104] Something of the same kind may be true of Ctesias: at the battle of Cunaxa he depicts a Persian officer inveighing against Cyrus the Younger 'hoping to overthrow your master … who has millions of slaves better than you', and elsewhere he has Cyrus' brother appointed as *despotês* of Bactria and the other lands of which he is governor.[105]

In a striking development, Demosthenes extends this imagery to Philip, whom he represents as a *despotês*, while Antipater and Parmenion are reduced to servants; similar imagery is applied to contemporary tyrants with Macedonian connections, perhaps to create the implication that the resemblance to Persia extends to the patronage of tyranny.[106] Certainly the perceived threat from Macedon to the liberty of Athens and other poleis accounts for a substantial proportion of instances in which the imagery of freedom and slavery is applied to independence and subjection in inter-polis relations,[107] though it is also used with reference to Athens in the fifth century and Sparta and Thebes in the fourth, as well as Persia;[108] however, since 'freedom' had now entered the formal language of diplomacy, the image of slavery may have lost a little of its bite.[109]

In a domestic context, the identification of tyranny with servitude is by now entirely commonplace,[110] and the development of interest is the increasing willingness to use the same language of other regimes. We have seen that oligarchy was beginning to be associated with slavery towards the end of the fifth century: in the early fourth century this tendency becomes general, particularly with reference to the regime of the Thirty at Athens, though we also find it retrojected in the orators to the earlier and broader oligarchy of the Four Hundred.[111] Increasing readiness to label oligarchy as slavery implies a general belief that democracy was the only constitution which constituted freedom: hence, for example, Demosthenes' consistent antithesis between democracy and oligarchy in his speech *On the liberty of the Rhodians*,[112] and Plato's casual assumption in the *Republic* that oligarchic rulers are referred to as 'masters' and in turn refer to their subjects as 'slaves'.[113] Demosthenes goes even further in his speech against Timocrates, extending to oligarchy the charge against oriental tyranny that it makes its subjects 'unmanly and slavish'.[114] Indeed, by now oligarchy can actually be described as 'tyranny': this is again most frequently attested for the Thirty, and was doubtless intended to imply a lack of legitimacy and of respect for law or their subjects.[115]

In this context the label 'tyranny' has almost ceased to be figurative, and comes close to collapsing the two constitutional forms into a single antipole to democracy, but it is also widely used as an image for arbitrary and unaccountable power:[116] in particular, Plato builds on earlier personifications of passions and other powerful influences on human psychology to develop the concept of the tyranny of passions within his political psychology of the individual,[117] which in turn coheres with the application of the language of slavery, mastery and freedom to self-control and its absence.[118] In fact, that language too is coming to be used very broadly of control, often with little clear moral implication, in a way that suggests that it was losing some of its impact.[119]

That is certainly not true of the image of the tyranny of the demos which, given the ideological antithesis between the two constitutions, is both plainly figurative and distinctly pointed.[120] Although in its early stages in the late fifth century the resonances of this concept are ambiguous and difficult to pin down (above 124), by this stage it has become broadly pejorative,[121] but it is more than a reflex anti-democratic slogan:

the almost paradoxical suggestion that the majority is capable of unjust domination of the minority is carefully and occasionally almost gleefully worked out.[122] Plato exploits the motif in the *Gorgias* to undermine further the image of the politician as servant: as a *despotês*, the demos is no better than a tyrant, and whatever his pretensions, the attention which the *rhêtor* pays it can never rise above servility. We can see from Xenophon that this viewpoint was well-established among opponents of democracy, to the point that poverty could be regarded as a blessing in disguise, if it meant freedom from slavery to the commands of the demos and its imposition of tribute,[123] though he presents it as open to the riposte that those who exercise power are more free and less servile than those who do not.[124] In part, the negative variation achieves its effect by expressing the relationship through nouns which highlight issues of status rather than verbs describing the activity which, as we have seen, are less clear-cut in their implications and so open to interpretation.[125]

Here we can see opponents of democracy constructing a response to a persuasive representation of a central tenet of democratic ideology, though it would not be surprising if its origins went back a generation earlier than the first surviving attestations. The shift in the character of our sources also provides us with a clearer view of the persistence of deeper-rooted expressions of anti-democratic prejudice that stress the irrationality of the demos and its need for firm control. Demosthenes alleges that Philip's Athenian advisers compared it to the sea for instability, inconstancy and inscrutability, shifting at random like the waves, while Isocrates compares Athens to a torrent (*cheimarrous*).[126] Aristotle intriguingly suggests the possibility of a populist alternative when he remarks that with people as with water, a greater volume is less easily polluted or corrupted (*adiaphthorôteron*: Pol. 1286a31–3), though the observation seems to be his own. We have already registered reflections of the model of animal-taming with reference to shepherding and the household (above 115, 150); Plato also alludes to another variant when he speaks in the *Statesman* of installing the statesman in the chariot of state and handing over the reins to him and when he canvasses the charioteer as one possible model for the rule of the gods in the *Laws*, though he can also employ the image negatively of the new tyrant in the *Republic*, or the increasingly accident-prone politicians of fifth-century Athens.[127] In fact, he seems agnostic on the possibility of taming the demos, at least for non-philosophers: the image of the 'large and powerful animal' (*R.* 493a-c) which, even if not specifically political, emphasizes the inscrutable animality of the demos, is picked up a little later in the image of the philosopher in politics as a man in a den of beasts (*thêria*: 496d), though the demos can equally well be viewed as a lethargic if fine horse in need of a gadfly (*Ap.* 30e). For democracy, of course, all this is anathema, and the thought that other politicians are making the demos tame to the hand, like a caged animal, outrages Demosthenes.[128]

One particular animal image which arguably belongs here is the beehive. *Prima facie* the bee's status as a social animal would recommend it as an image of community, but in practice Greek bee-imagery concentrates either on leadership (the 'king' i.e. queen bee) or on social problems (drones).[129] Xenophon does the former in a Greek context, comparing the Elean democrats flocking to their leader Thrasydaios to a swarm of bees, although with no implication beyond the picture of followers crowding round the leader and the consequent magnification of his importance,[130] but the queen bee is more frequently associated with Persian kings. Already in the fifth century Aeschylus had by implication likened Xerxes to a queen bee followed to Greece by a vast swarm which has left Susa deserted.[131] In the fourth century the image seems to have provoked some contention: Plato rejects the model of the king bee as natural-born and acknowledged ruler, at least for the real world,[132] but Xenophon makes positive reference in the *Cyropaideia* (5.1.24) to the belief that the king bee was of a different nature from the bees it ruled: the speaker, Artabazus, says that Cyrus seems like a born king no less than the king bee, which the bees obey voluntarily, all attending it wherever it stays or goes, through the strength of their desire to be ruled by it. It has long been suggested that this was a Persian idea, in as much as it is in accord with the Persian belief in the superior nature of the ruler, and more recently it has been argued that the Persians may well have identified themselves with bees, in which case Aeschylus anticipated Xenophon in the reflection of authentic Persian ideas.[133] On the other hand, in his account of constitutional and individual types in the *Republic*, Plato does develop the idea of drones as anti-social and subversive exploiters, which becomes a running but increasingly prominent and developed subsidiary image in the passage from oligarchy through democracy to tyranny: it is to be noted that here no king bee is mentioned, and the drones have a multiplicity of leaders, one of whom exploits his position as *prostatês* to make himself tyrant.[134]

One striking new development which seems to spring from elite values is the appearance of imagery drawn from art – specifically, from music and the plastic arts. Notwithstanding the prominence of cultural aspects in Athenian public life, it is only now that we encounter analogies between art and politics,[135] and their character is quite distinctive: they are confined to philosophical writing, though unlike much of such imagery, they are not (contrary to what one might expect) primarily concerned with the exercise of *technê*. They seem instead to rely on a quasi-aesthetic judgement of the degree to which perfection is approached and of proper proportion, and as such lend themselves to the justification of the principle of proportional equality and of inequality in political contexts: harmony in music depends on a specific mathematical ratio, while in art what matters is the relationship between the disparate parts of the body.[136] Aristotle puts this point most clearly *à propos* the 'virtue' of a constitution, comparing the need for moderation to the avoidance of extremes in representing facial features, and he likewise observes that growth in a polis as in a body must be in proportion to avoid damaging constitutional change.[137] Plato concentrates more on the legislator as creative artist, which allows him both to introduce the idea of a model (*paradeigma*), the Form of the Good, from which the philosophic legislator will work,[138] and on the way in which he will work on the material to arrive at the desired result: the verb which he often uses for this process, *plattô* ('mould') implies that the ruled will be entirely passive, like clay,[139] and suggests that he envisages the legislator mainly as a sculptor,[140] though terminology from painting sometimes intrudes.[141] Painting is a particularly good analogy for the endless process both of repairing damage to the picture and, even more, of striving to bring it closer to perfection (*R.* 501a-c, *Lg.* 769a-c). For Aristotle, too, legislators are craftsmen (*dêmiourgoi*) and their work can be more or less 'polished (*glaphuros*)'.[142]

Like his artistic imagery, Plato's musical imagery links in to key ideas in his thought, particularly in the *Republic*, in which the notion of harmony plays a significant role. Socrates defines the cardinal virtue *sophrosunê* (self-control or discipline) as a kind of harmony (*harmonia, sumphônia*) which consists in an agreement between the constituent elements of state and individual as to which of them is to rule (430e, 431e–2a, cf. 591d); the order which this creates, with the three elements performing their proper roles, is the essence of justice (442cd, 443c-e). Musical imagery thus supports the political analogy and, since it is also a feature of the cosmos, the parallelism between microcosm and macrocosm.[143] In the *Laws* this harmony is equated with knowledge and is a prerequisite for the exercise of power, and its absence is folly and 'dissonance' (*plêmmeleia*).[144] Aristotle, in his musical as in his artistic imagery, is concerned with a balance between extremes, so that a harmonious constitution is one that achieves a mean between slackness and excessive tautness; the difference here is that he seems to show some preference for a defective regime which errs on the side of tension (*suntonôteran*), rather than being too slack (*anieisthai*).[145] There are also some instructive allusions to pipe-playing, which he regards as a distinctive *technê*: hence he identifies the ruler, as the possessor of expertise, with the piper and the ruled with the pipe-maker.[146] The Aristotelian *Oeconomicus* reports a similar comparison of the relationship between commander and troops to that between piper and chorus: such passages make it easy to understand why Xenophon values the chorus as a model of order (though not in specifically political contexts) but it does not form the basis of any democratic imagery.[147]

There is a degree of continuity between these artistic images and the image of weaving in Plato's *Statesman*:[148] weaving too involves the expert manipulation of raw material which is itself furnished by subordinate crafts, and the application of expertise in the combination of disparate elements,[149] which makes it inclusive but not necessarily egalitarian.[150] On the other hand, its ubiquity as a feature of the Greek household removes any potential taint of the banausic (insofar as Plato was concerned by that) and by assimilating it to *oikonomia* increases its suitability as an analogue for a universal art of rule, and Plato takes that further by removing the gendered aspect which was so marked in the Aristophanic image; he also devotes much more attention to the process of weaving itself, as opposed to the preparation of the wool.[151] The central aspect of weaving here is the diversity and complexity within the unity which it creates by binding together elements which are complementary but not self-sufficient, though the fact that it is the product of a collaborative process is also important, as is the function of clothing as a form of protection.[152] In the *Laws* the image is put to a slightly different and less generous use: the magistrates are compared to the tough, tested warp, and the rest of the citizens to the softer and more pliant woof.[153]

If imagery drawn from the arts is confined to philosophy, the evidence is much more widely spread for another of the major developments of the fourth century, the burgeoning use of military imagery. As we saw, in the fifth century such imagery was surprisingly infrequent, and restricted almost entirely to tragedy and to the figurative use of words for leadership (above 121). While this usage continues to some extent into the fourth century,[154] it is far outweighed in volume and interest by two new kinds of military imagery: the language of station, duty and obedience (*taxis*) and of personal warfare (*polemein*). The language of *taxis* is particularly noteworthy, as it is common to Plato and to the orators: it is attested earlier for the former, and indeed, if Plato's attribution of it to Socrates is not anachronistic, must actually go back to the end of the fifth century, but his usage of the image does not seem distinctively philosophic, and it is more likely that both Plato and the orators are reflecting a more general innovation in Athenian public discourse: Plato himself is capable of echoing the popular view of the laws and constitution as a *taxis*.[155] In fact, at the most general level, to denote the ancestral policy or behaviour of a state, the image is not confined to Athens: in his *Archidamus* Isocrates has his speaker appeal to the Spartans not to allow the city 'to abandon the position in which our fathers stationed her' (6.93); the image of desertion would obviously be a potent one for Spartans. In the same way, Demosthenes can call on the Athenians not to abandon 'the post of valour' won by their ancestors;[156] by extension, the orator can identify democracy as their ancestral constitutional post and dilate on the implications: just as the military deserter is deprived of citizen rights and communal privileges, so the oligarch, the political deserter, should be deprived of the right to advise the city; as it is, the stipulation to have the same friends and enemies is applied in diplomacy, but patently neglected where Athens' politicians are concerned (15.32–3). The orators also refer to a citizen's duty as *taxis*: the earliest instance is in Lysias, where Philon's failure to support the city at the time of the Thirty is treated as aggravated desertion,[157] but it can also be applied to the duty to give truthful evidence, or for jurors to hold their position as defenders of the democracy, ashamed of deserting.[158]

More commonly, the image is applied to choice of policy within Athens. Demosthenes regularly uses it to describe his own policy choices, with the implication of courage and resolution, often in a dangerous stance of loyalty, or to refer to a policy maintained in a time of crisis. By contrast, Aeschines initially took up the *taxis* of hostility to Philip, a position from which he subsequently 'treacherously deserted (*êutomolêse kai proudôke*)'.[159] Aeschines returns the insult with references not only to similar shifts in policy, a 'desertion' revealed by scrutiny of public records, but also to the more literal desertion of Demosthenes' post in the city after Chaeronea, following on from his physical *lipotaxia* at the battle itself. The image is also applied by Demosthenes to the policy choices of others and was evidently so used by other speakers; naturally, that means that his opponents marshal themselves with Athens' enemies.[160] The strong emotional and legal pressure to hold one's position in the battle-line made *taxis* and the associated ideas of courageous obedience and treacherous desertion a powerful image.[161] Demosthenes' denunciation of Aeschines shows that it is a short step from desertion to treachery, and the further step to mercenary service is easily made if one adds the monetary element: pseudo-Demosthenes gives his discussion of the Macedonians' mercenary politicians a clever twist by suggesting that they are 'bodyguarded' (*doruphoroumenoi*) by Macedonian garrisons, bodyguards being a characteristic of tyrants.[162]

Battle-line imagery, then, is applicable to both foreign and domestic politics; the idea of warfare *tout court* is not surprisingly confined to internal affairs. The earliest instance seems to be in Theramenes' defence speech, where he is made to say that he is 'at war' with extreme democrats;[163] this may be intended as a riposte to Critias' denunciation of him as a traitor and hence worse than a simple enemy, and it is noteworthy that he expresses his opposition to extreme oligarchs with the softer *enantios eimi* ('I am opposed to'). Demosthenes makes the same assertion of his relationship with the pro-Macedonians, and he attributes the same expression to Meidias and other politicians; the image is also employed by Isocrates and Aeschines, who also predicts with mild ridicule that one of Timocrates' supporters, a general, will 'make a raid (*katadromên*)' in his defence.[164] On the whole, though, the intended implication is clearly a favourable one, to lend glamour to what might otherwise be seen as tedious and self-serving infighting, by dressing it in the clothing of warfare.[165]

Military imagery naturally suggests protection, and here again we find politicians making claims that would have been impossible for their fifth-century predecessors. Dinarchus alludes to Demosthenes' claim in *de Corona* to have 'fenced round' (*perikecharakômenên*) Athens with his counsels, but in that speech Demosthenes, though drawing a contrast with his literal activities as overseer of the fortifications, still claims to have fortified Athens with military assets – arms, cities (i.e. allies), strongpoints, harbours, ships, horses and men. Aeschines likewise reports Demosthenes' claim to have fortified the city with 'brazen and adamantine' walls, meaning his alliance with the Euboeans and Thebans, and Demades also claims to have fortified Attica metaphorically by 'the city's security (*têi tês poleôs asphaleiai*)'.[166] Beyond the particular circumstance of Demosthenes' service as overseer of fortifications in 337/6 BC (D.18.112–19, Aeschin. 3.17–23, 236), the stress on resources is a further reflection of Athens' straitened circumstances, and even if the talk is of metaphorical fortifications, it is notable that the image of men as the essential protection of a city appears only once, in Lycurgus' speech against Leocrates, where the defendant's physical desertion makes it particularly apposite.[167] Instead, as we shall see shortly, the language of guarding and protection is transferred inwards to the machinery and personnel of the democracy. In the same way, too, the architectural imagery of bulwarks and props once applied to individuals now comes to be used of the social structure of the polis and the crucial importance of its integrity: for Plato in the *Laws*, unwritten laws are like carpenters' props (*ereismata*), the failure of which causes catastrophic collapse, while in the *Statesman* a purely written constitution is a shaky though surprisingly resilient foundation (*krêpis*), just as in the view of Demosthenes the absence of truth and justice is for Philip's power; hence the vital role of those elements which hold the city together, like a building, a body or a ship.[168]

Warfare between politicians is one element in a strain of increasing violence in the political language of fourth-century Athens which we can detect also in animal imagery. Politicians now routinely refer to one another as 'wild beasts' (*thêria*) or 'brutes' (*knôdala*), just as sycophants are abusively compared with 'a small menagerie'.[169] The perception of particular animals also comes to be contested: against the watchdog of the people, we have bad dogs who bite, like Idrieus, who Androtion said was dangerous when off the leash of prison; earlier, Thrasyboulos had undermined the pretensions of the Thirty by pointing out that, so far from the Spartans being an asset to them, they had handed over the former oligarchs to their victims like dangerous dogs tied up in a wooden collar.[170] Hyperides drew a similar distinction between good and bad examples of a creature, comparing rhetors to snakes, some of which were venomous, while others, like the 'brown snake', ate other snakes; the defensive tone acknowledges a negative popular perception which is reflected in the Aesopian fable of the fox who declines an offer to remove his fleas, on the grounds that at least that lot, being already sated, are not sucking much of his blood.[171] On the other hand, Aristotle puts a positive spin on another fable, that of the lions and the hares ('where are your teeth?') as germane to the position of the ideal monarch.[172] Demosthenes was similarly violent in his medical imagery, accusing the 'crop of traitors' of 'hack[ing] off the limbs of their own countries' and calling the demos 'hamstrung' (*ekneneurismenoi*, lit. 'with sinews cut'); Aeschines' attribution to him of the phrase 'the sinews of the demos have been cut through' is thus entirely plausible.[173] Also reported there are a very similar image from viticulture – 'the shoots of the demos have been cut away' – and two from carpet-making: 'we are being stitched up like a mat (*phormorraphoumetha*)' and 'certain people are threading <us> like needles into tight spaces'.[174] In fact, horticultural imagery in the fourth century tends somewhat to the sinister, and although we find positive mentions of the figure of the farmer or gardener, all is not necessarily well in the garden: Socrates suggests ironically that he is being weeded out by Meletus, and Aristotle picks up the anecdote of lopping off the tallest ears of corn as an object-lesson for tyrants, and for other regimes too. Furthermore, what grows may not always be desirable: for Plato, tyranny is a baneful plant, while orators regard opponents and their proposals as the seed and root of trouble.[175]

For all their ideological differences, there is one point on which the philosophers and Athenian public speakers are in complete accord: the central importance of Law or laws. *Nomos* had already come to have the status of a king by the turn of the century (above 125), and its ideological predominance increased even further in the course of the fourth, so much so that it transcended earlier controversies to become a king, a master, and even a god.

For Athenian democrats, the concept of law naturally extended to include the constitution and those who made it work. Thus it was natural, for example, to transfer the language of protection and guardianship to the laws and to those who applied them, the jurors and magistrates, though the role of the latter is perhaps envisaged as a deterrent vigilance.[176] By now, politicians too might claim to be guardians against illegality and guardians of the constitution or of the democracy, though in all these passages such claims are reported sceptically, and ps.-Demosthenes points out that it is such self-appointed watchdogs who really need watching.[177] The military colour of *phulax* and *phulattô* has faded here, to be replaced by broader notions of security and a new specific implication of scrutiny and oversight.[178]

The centrality of democracy as a frame of reference encouraged the figurative use of its terminology and institutions, a practice which had begun to appear by the end of the previous century and is widespread in fourth-century oratory. So, for example, Isaeus is credited with the aphorism that the greatest 'liturgy' was to live an orderly and sober life, while the title *chorêgos* has become generalized to mean one who backs or funds politicians, usually with the implication of corruption. It is revealing that a number of such cases refer to financial administration, which underwent a series of reforms in response to Athens' chronic budgetary difficulties: Demosthenes applies the image of the symmory system to Athenian politics, which he suggests is now run by organized consortia similar to those existing for taxation purposes.[179] Another key principle is accountability: Demosthenes regularly applies the idea of the *euthuna* system to more general concepts of accountability, often to draw a contrast between accountable rhetors, especially himself, and post-eventum critics and sycophants or the unaccountable Philip, and similarly he appeals to the jurors to act as *logistai*, assessors at an audit.[180] Aeschines for his part claims that the laws are acting as supporting speakers for him (*sunêgoroi*).[181] Contrariwise, the institutions of the democracy come to be described in figurative terms: for Demosthenes in *De Corona*, the herald's proclamations are 'the common voice of the fatherland', Demades referred to the theoric fund as the 'glue (*kollan*) of the democracy, and Aeschines called the *sanidion*, the whitened board on which the disputed decree and the relevant laws were inscribed in *graphai paranomôn*, the measuring-rod (*kanôn*) of justice.[182]

Demosthenes may also reflect contemporary concerns, both financial and legal, in his use of the imagery of counterfeiting. In his speech against Timocrates, he attributes anachronistically to Solon the concept that while silver coinage is the medium of private transactions, laws are the common currency of the city, and that therefore penalties for debasing or counterfeiting this public coinage should be correspondingly more severe, since though states have survived debasement of their coinage, none has survived debasement of its laws. Here law is treated as having an absolute worth corresponding to what we would call the 'gold standard' of the highly-prized Athenian silver coinage; that concept is played on in a slightly different way when he suggests that the assembly should assay speeches like coinage or weigh up individual politicians in the bankers' scales, and the conceit of the juror as assayer (*argurognômôn*) is echoed in Aristotle's *Rhetoric*. Demosthenes' denunciation of Leptines for having made Athens 'counterfeit and untrustworthy', in revoking immunities from liturgies previously granted, is more in line with earlier imagery which applied the language of counterfeiting and assay to individual character.[183]

In all this, the democracy for all its ideological predominance is a touchstone or a point of reference, not an agent: that status is reserved for *Nomos*, which comes to be personified in various ways.[184] Like those who implement them, the laws can be represented as guardians and as preserving (*sôizein*) the city and its citizens; here the personification is limited, but in other images the personified laws are much more active, as rulers of the city or the motive power that drives the institutions of the democracy. Equally, the laws can be represented as a disembodied prosecution, as in Apollodorus' speech against Neaira, or as having imposed the due penalty on an adulterer, or as forming a triumvirate with the prosecutor and the democracy in cases of *graphê paranomôn*. Indeed, the laws can be represented as legislating in themselves, moved by their zeal for what is just and good.[185] In an appropriate context, however, law may be personified as almost passive: in his speech *Against Meidias* (21.223–5), Demosthenes represents the laws' strength as resting in their maintenance by the jurors, whose sovereignty is reciprocally generated by the power of law, rather than in a capacity for active intervention, since they are only 'inscribed letters'; thus the laws are seen in this case as a victim in need of assistance.[186]

Nevertheless, this passage looks anomalous when compared with the presentation of the laws within the framework of Athenian democracy, and even more so when compared with the depiction of law or laws as kings: Plato puts in the mouth of the tragic poet Agathon the phrase 'laws, the kings of cities', and Aristotle credits almost the same words to the rhetorician and sophist Alcidamas, while Plato himself writes that salvation comes 'when law becomes supreme king over men'. Law can even become a tyrant, or like one: Demades observes that the best democracy is that in which all fear the law like a tyrant, adding aphoristically that while for slaves compulsion serves as law, for free men the law compels. For the sophistic proponent of the rule of nature, however, law is illegitimate constraint, and so Plato represents Hippias as describing law as 'tyrant over men', doing many violent deeds against *phusis*.[187] As a monarch, whether king or tyrant, law is readily figured as a master (even more so as a god: see below): hence it becomes increasingly uncontroversial to speak in terms of servitude to the laws, an idea which we find frequently in Plato and Aristotle. Xenophon expresses the same idea in a more nuanced manner when he describes Agesilaus as 'doing service to the laws' (*tois nomois latreuôn*), using a verb often applied to dutiful service to the gods; the conception of rulers submitting to a higher authority looks forward to the somewhat paradoxical Hellenistic concept of monarchy as 'distinguished slavery'.[188]

We can also see in the convergence of law and monarchy, combined with the insistence of the philosophers on ruling as a matter of skill, the foundations of another key concept of Hellenistic ruler theory, the idea that the king embodies law (*nomos empsuchos*): the earliest allusion to ideas of that kind is to be found in Xenophon, who in the *Cyropaideia* attributes to Cyrus the belief that, while men are improved by written laws, the good ruler is 'a law with eyes for men, because he is able not only to give commandments, but also to see the transgressor and punish him'. It is not surprising that we should encounter the notion first in a Persian context, since their belief in the inherent natural superiority of their kings also prefigures philosophic contemplation of the ideal king or statesman.[189]

The final step is the apotheosis of law and of the ruler, which in the light of prior developments seems almost over-determined. The personification of forces capable of affecting human behaviour physically, like wine, or psychologically, like love, was by now a well-established process: these are typically characterized as *turannoi* or *dunastai*, minor powers with a tendency to arbitrary behaviour (above 7–8), and there had been something of this in some earlier personifications of Nomos as the somewhat arbitrary 'king of all' in Pindar, or as a 'master (*despotês*)' comparable to an absolute King of Persia.[190] Now, however, the description of law suggests something closer to an established divinity, as when Plato describes the ideal constitution as divine, and submission to the laws as submission to the gods.[191] If law merits such reverence, then it is natural to regard those who create it as something more than mortal, hence Plato's reverential allusions to Lycurgus, and his description of the Nocturnal Council in the *Laws* as 'godlike' can be viewed in the same light; likewise his proposal to heroize the Guardians in the *Republic* after their death assimilates them to the founders of colonies and implies a foundational aspect to their activity. At the same time, his readiness to style them 'saviours and defenders', titles more usual for gods, is in line with an increasing willingness to confer divine honours on living individuals and to credit them with superhuman characteristics.[192]

That process reaches its culmination in Alexander. Callisthenes' flattering description of the sea on the Pamphylian coast with its rollers recognizing Alexander as its (new) master (*anakta*) and performing a sort of *proskynesis* clearly evokes the description of Poseidon being greeted by the denizens of his realm in the *Iliad*: the implication is that the Macedonian king is no local divinity, but, like Plato's divine Nomos, something akin to one of the Homeric pantheon.[193] In itself that is a startling enough step, but Anaxarchus' comparison of Alexander to Zeus with Justice seated beside him (Plut. *Alex*. 52.2-4; above 14) goes even further, effectively combining the image of the king as god and that of the king as embodying law. As an authentic god, the king embodies law, and as embodied law he is godlike, even divine: power, legitimacy and divinity collapse into one another in the unique person and situation of Alexander, and from that singularity will emerge the new world of the Hellenistic kings.

Notes

1   For the author of the *Ath.Pol.* (41.2), this is the point at which the Athenian constitution achieves its final form: Ober (1998) 352-3 with references in n.2. Osborne (2003) offers a stimulating discussion of the changing status in the late fifth century of tyranny and oligarchy as threats to democracy.

2   E.g. Rhodes (1980), Hansen (1989), though NB Eder (1998) for a model of more gradual evolution.

3   The shift in the character of those sources requires acknowledgement at the outset: the prominence of philosophic writing is one aspect of a more general dominance of prose texts, which includes a much greater volume of oratory, at the expense of drama, where we have little comedy, and still less tragedy, and of verse in general.

4   Both Archelaus and Evagoras had supported the Athenians during the Peloponnesian war and been honoured by them (*IG* I³ 117 = *ML* 91; *IG* I³ 113) – indeed, Evagoras was probably also awarded Athenian citizenship at this time: Rhodes & Osborne (2003) 52-3; Dionysius was admittedly largely unsuccessful before 404, though he might have benefited from association with Athens' nemesis Syracuse (on which see Thuc. 7.55, 8.96.5).

5   Hence Plato not only acknowledges Greek fear of Persian power (*Lg.* 685 c6-7), but has the oligarchic man establish wealth in himself as a Persian monarch with all the trappings (*R.* 553c7-8), and treats the Great King as the type of the fortunate man in *Grg.* 470e4-5, *Apol.* 40d7-e2, *Euthyd.* 274a6-7; cf. also the account of Persian wealth at *Alc I.* 123bc, Cyrus and Xerxes as models for Alcibiades' ambition (*Alc I* 105c5-6), Callicles' choice of the invasions of Xerxes and Darius as instances of the unfettered exercise of power (*Grg.* 483d – though these are poor historical exempla: Ober 1998, 200) and Darius as lawgiver (*Phdr.* 258bc, *Lg.* 695cd, *Ep.* 7 332ab). This might be another Socratic preoccupation: Antisthenes, like Xenophon, wrote a work centred on the elder Cyrus (Rankin 1986, 143-4), for whom NB also Pl. *Lg.* 694a-5b, in a passage of suggestive polemic, and Isoc. 9.37-8.

6   Pl. *Lg.* 905e-6a (tr. Saunders). Compare Socrates' reference to 'the likenesses to which we must always compare our kingly rulers… the noble steersman and the doctor who is "worth many others"' (*Plt.* 297e7-11 tr. Rowe): in the *Statesman* Plato

works through a range of comparisons, beginning with the model of the shepherd (261d–8c), then the doctor (from 293b) and gymnastic trainer (from 294d), and helmsman (from 296e) and also alludes to the charioteer (266e8–11). Xenophon likewise juxtaposes father, teacher, doctor and helmsman in the context of military discipline at *An.* 5.8.18–20. Cf. Pender (2000) 111–14, 118–48 for such 'metaphors working together' (though the combinations are not necessarily the same) to describe the gods, and on mixed metaphor in the *Republic* see Tarrant (1946) 29–30.

7   And we have also registered a strand in oligarchic imagery which highlights the irrationality of the demos (above 61, 120); in ps.-X. *Ath.Pol.* the demos is explicitly disparaged as ignorant (1.5, 7) and mad (1.9). Aristotle offers a critique of the craft analogy at *Pol.* 1281b38–82a23.

8   de Romilly (1998) 217–25; Protagoras is credited with drafting the legal code for the Athenian-sponsored colony at Thurii: Guthrie (1962–81) III.1, 263–4 (and see 262–9 for his political thought more generally).

9   Plato's attribution to Protagoras of a myth in his *Protagoras* is a possible exception, but all aspects of his presentation of the sophists require very cautious handling.

10 Compare the surveys in Brickhouse and Smith (1994) 5–10, 163–6 (based on Platonic instances) and Vlastos (1994) 96–9 (drawn from Xenophon).

11 Pl. *Grg.* 490c8–491a3, especially e9–11: ' "you're always saying the same things, Socrates" "Yes, and about the same things, too, Callicles" '; *Smp.* 221e4–6; X. *Mem.* 4.4.6.

12 That argument, which is regarded as characteristically Socratic by Aristotle (*Rh.* 1393 b4–8) also appears in the *Dissoi Logoi* (7; probably to be dated around the end of the fifth century: Robinson 1979, 34–41), somewhat elaborated, and combined with prudential consideration of the risk that the lot will select enemies of democracy. Isocrates, however, is careful to deploy only the latter argument in the *Areopagiticus* (7.23).

13 X. *Mem.* 1.2.9, 32–8: note especially Critias' warning to 'keep away from the cobblers, carpenters and smiths' at 37.

14 Note also the use of the doctor and helmsman images by Antisthenes: frr.15.8, 185–6, Rankin (1986) 25, 139, who suggests that craft analogies became 'agreed areas of reference' and 'basic "counters"' in dialectical argument (ibid. 141), though Lloyd (1966) 292–4 remarks on the disparity between the use of such imagery in Plato and Aristotle and their disdain for actual craftsmen. For an anonymous 'socratising' fragment see xviii n.12.

15 That is, it could be roughly contemporary with the beginnings of explicit criticism of democracy in pseudo-Xenophon's *Athenaiôn Politeia*: Ober (1998) 14–15 (though note that Hornblower 2000 has argued for a fourth-century date).

16 Socrates' political sympathies: Guthrie (1962–81) III.2 89–96 is still a sensible overview; Vlastos (1994) argues that he was fundamentally democratic, while Brickhouse and Smith (1994) 163–4 note that his positive allusion to banausic craft activity is unlikely to have appealed to an elite audience (as Callicles' impatience in the passage cited at n.11 indeed implies), and suggest (164–6) that he was equally critical of all existing constitutions, and Wallach likewise concludes that Socrates' 'political orientation ... is indeterminate' (2001, 92–119, esp. 116–19; quotation from p.118) . However, even if Socrates was not himself specifically opposed to democracy, he had in practice made available some powerful weapons to those who were. The commitment of Socrates to oral debate in public (Ober 1998, 174 n.37) also represents an exception to what is often seen as a link between a culture of writing

and criticism of democracy: e.g. Steiner (1994) 186–241 esp. 220–7 (at 216 she excludes Socrates as uncategorizable); Ober (1998) 45–8, who notes the exception (45 n.60) without exploring the point.

17 In what follows I am not specifically concerned with articulating the approaches of individual authors (for a sketch centred on Xenophon see Brock 2004b) and although for practical reasons I focus particularly on philosophical writers, my agenda is only incidentally philosophical. In particular, I am not attempting to give an account of Plato's political philosophy (on which see recently Schofield 2006), or of his use of imagery (discussed by Pender 2000; 2003), or even of his political imagery from a philosophic perspective (Bambrough 1956 is still fundamental here; also Louis 1945, Jackson 1988), all of which lies beyond my competence (the same goes for Aristotle, though his more sparing use of imagery makes the issue less prominent). Rather, my aim is, within a picture of fourth-century political imagery as a whole, to examine the working of Plato's imagery in itself and to set it in the broader context of earlier and contemporary usage. Again, to make my coverage as full as possible, I have tended to include material from works of debated authenticity such as *Alc. I* (on which see Denyer 2001 14–26) and *Ep. 7* (see Schofield 2006, 13–19 for a recent summary of the debate with extensive bibliography), but this should not be taken to imply an informed judgment on my part, and more expert readers are at liberty to discount such material if they wish, though I do not think the argument would be substantially affected.

18 Pl. *Plt.* 258e–9c; X. *Oec.* 13.5, 21.2, 10, *Mem.* 4.2.11: above 25–6. It follows that this is not exclusively a masculine prerogative, hence Socrates' injunction that Ischomachus' wife should administer her household 'like a queen' (X. *Oec.* 9.14–15); at *Mem.* 3.9.11 Xenophon notes that in wool-working women exercise authority over men because of their knowledge of the craft.

19 Above 36n.4.

20 Above 31: Plato emphasizes the parental right to control (*archein*) at *Lg.* 690a, while Xenophon (*An.* 5.8.18) and Aristotle (*Pol.* 1315a21) look to the father-child relationship to justify and palliate punishment where necessary. In this form such imagery not only combined the two strands in the imagery (household, family) which had been kept apart hitherto, but also tapped into the Homeric resonances of the king as father which had been rather under-exploited in subsequent literature (above 111–12).

21 Most overtly stated in Isoc. 2.19, 21 (above 32): contrast Pindar's use of the language of stewardship (above 26). The Persian conception of the empire as 'the King's house' (above 12, 110) might well have been one countervailing factor for fifth-century Athenians, but the concept would have been controversial in any case: see above 23n.91 on S. *Ant.* 738.

22 That proprietorial attitude is expressed in Hiero's earlier comparison (6.15–16) of his citizens to a fine horse of which he is afraid, lest it cause him fatal harm, and so would be hard put either to use or to kill. Cyaxares similarly compares Cyrus' winning over of his subjects to diverting the affections of a man's dogs, attendants or wife (*Cyr.* 5.5.28–30), while Isocrates echoes the undertone of animal-taming in the observation that men, like dogs or horses, can only be properly ruled by one who loves and takes pleasure in them (2.15); in both these cases, too, monarchy is the regime in question.

23 *Hiero* 11.14 (quoted above, 32). For the positive characterization in Xenophon of the ruler or leader (Greek as well as non-Greek) as father, see above 31; note the similar

sharpening of the language of friendship (*ou monon philoio an*) to that of desire (*alla kai erôio*) a little earlier (11.11 with Gray 2007 *ad loc.*) and NB Gray's rebuttal of ironic readings of these aspects of the *Hiero* (212–13) and now in Gray (2011), *passim*.

24. The universal model of rule is firmly rejected at *Pol.* 1252a7–16 (cf. 1253b18–20); mastery over slaves is distinguished from statesmanship at 1255b16–20 and the different kinds of authority exercised by the head of the household over slaves, children and wife distinguished more fully at 1259a37-b17 (cf. 1278b30–1279a2). In discussing the development of the polis in *Pol.* I.ii, he uses the verb *basileuein* of authority in the household in a way that implies that it is an early evolutionary stage (1252b19–27, cf. 1255b19), but when he identifies a fifth, total form of monarchy with household authority, it is presumably that of the ideal king (1285b29–33 with Robinson 1995, 52–3). Analogies between different familial relations and constitutional forms are elaborated in the *Nicomachean Ethics* (1160b22–61b10; above 34); NB also n.86 below.

25. Plato himself trades on this in the unflattering portrait which Socrates draws in the *Theaetetus* of the ruler in the eyes of the philosopher as a kind of herdsman 'milking' (*bdallonta*) his subjects, as well as rendered uncivilized by his environment (*Tht.* 174de). Blondell (2005) 27–8 discusses the social marginality of herdsmen, though I think that this is the only passage in political imagery where capital is made of it.

26. Pender (2000) 108–110, 119–23; the problem of the ruler's being of a different species is highlighted by the myth of the rule of Kronos in the *Statesman* (274e–5c; cf. *Lg.* 713de): Blondell (2005) 31, 38–9, 43 and above 46.

27. X. *Cyr.* 1.1, 8.2.14, cf. Pl. *Lg.* 694e–5a (above 47–8). In X. *Mem.* 3.2.1 Socrates expounds the duties of the general in terms of the Homeric epithet *poimena laôn*, and indeed specifically of Agamemnon, which lends some support to the interpretation advanced above (43), and suggests that Homeric reminiscences were being consciously exploited. Aristotle likewise cites Homer's characterization of Agamemnon as shepherd at *EN* 1161a12–15, with reference to friendship in monarchy (the king cares for his subjects so that they do well), laying his emphasis on affection instead of authority: Pakaluk (1998) 122.

28. Lane (1998) 40–6, Blondell (2005) 23–44, also Miller (1980) 43–54, who sees a problematic association with autocracy as well; additional difficulties with the image include the lack of specialization and differentiation of a proper art. Lane (40) observes that the methodology here means that herding (Plato uses a more neutral language [*agelê*] which covers a range of animals and indeed birds) is more than just an analogy. Blondell (54–5) notes that the shepherd is retained in a subsidiary role in the dialogue's later model, weaving, as supplier of the raw material.

29. Blondell (2005) 26–7. The Guardians as watchdogs should protect the flock from external attack rather than behaving like wolves themselves (415e–16e; cf. the accusation levelled at the Romans by a Dalmatian rebel that their governors are 'not dogs, or shepherds, but wolves': Dio 56.16.3), obey the rulers as shepherds of the polis (440d) and guard the herd (451cd; but *agelê* is used of the Guardians in the sense 'pack' in the analogy from stock-breeding at 459de, on which NB Halliwell 1993, 17); canine imagery also at 466a, 537a, 539b. The tripartite arrangement here of course coincides with Plato's psychology. At *Lg.* 735b the Athenian, discussing the selection of citizens for the new foundation, speaks in terms of purging the herd of 'unhealthy and inferior stock', again underlining the herdsman's absolute control of inferior species (and the concept is pursued in terms of medical purging and pure

water: above 72, 144n.154). A further attraction for Plato is the etymological link between the vocabulary of herding (*nomeus, nomeuô*) and that of law (*nomos*) – the verb *nemô* ('dispense', 'inhabit' 'manage' 'pasture') covers both fields: Pender (2000) 109, *Laws* 714a with England (1921) on 714a1; cf. *Plt.* 295e. This tactic is picked up and elaborated by the author of the pseudo-Platonic *Minos* (317d–8a, 321b-d), who makes a link with the Homeric formula *poimena laôn* at 321b10-c2.

30 Though talk of wildness and tameness and the introduction of horses in the *Gorgias* passage hint at the overtones of control in earlier imagery of animal-taming, as does the mention of the charioteer at 516e3–7.

31 Though Xenophon too links the doctor and helmsman as examples of leaders to whose superior understanding men will voluntarily defer in their own interest (*Cyr.* 1.6.21), and in *Mem.* 3.9.10–11 the helmsman is joined with the farmer, doctor and trainer as models for the deference to true expertise which ought to operate in ruling; cf. also *Mem.* 4.2.5 for the doctor as the type of expert who must be trained by experts, and NB also n.6 above. The Persian empire is described as 'steered by the *gnômê* (will/judgement/wisdom)' of Cyrus at *Cyr.* 1.1.5, significantly echoed at 8.8.1. Bad doctors are also compared to bad helmsmen at Hp. *VM* 9.4.

32 Schofield (2006) 136–93 argues that 'two very different conceptions of knowledge in politics are in play' (138) in Plato, one practical and 'architectonic', the other truly philosophic; however, I find it difficult to discern any clear distinction between the two in his usage of imagery.

33 *R.* 341c–2e; in fact it is Thrasymachus who is made to appeal first to the expertise of the doctor as defining him (340d2–3), so setting up Socrates' elaboration. Note that horse-training is briefly slipped in as a parallel at 342c4–6, perhaps to prepare the ground for the next section as a less problematic example of control of animals than shepherding. The doctor and helmsman are joined as types of the skilled practitioner in Plato's fantastical democratization of their arts at *Plt.* 298a–9d, where he imagines them being selected by lot (298c5–9); note, though, that wealth, the oligarchic touchstone, is similarly excluded as a criterion for helmsmanship at *R.* 551c2–6. The crucial need for understanding (*nous*) when a doctor or helmsman exercises power is the point of the paired images at *Alc I* 134e–5a. See also Cordes (1994) 138–69 for discussion of Plato's medical imagery, esp. 140–52 for political imagery.

34 The point is made explicitly with reference to the helmsman and the doctor at *R.* 489b5-c3; Aristotle too distinguishes the helmsman and doctor from the despotic authority of a master which is mistakenly regarded as statesmanship (*Pol.* 1324b29–33), while at 1278b40–1279a21 he cites the trainer, doctor and helmsman as examples of those who rule for the benefit of others while belonging to the same community and benefiting indirectly, thus fitting his model of ruling and being ruled in turn. In this they can be clearly distinguished from the slave-master, but the status of household management is less clear-cut in this regard (1278b37–9).

35 Xenophon highlights the importance of discipline on a storm-tossed ship at *An.* 5.8.20, and Aristotle makes a similar point about the dangers even of small errors to a weak body or a badly-crewed ship (*Pol.* 1320b33–21a1), so that the worst constitutions require the greatest precaution. Plato appeals to the idea of constant peril at sea in establishing a standing committee of the Nocturnal Council in the *Laws* (758ab), in an image which slides from 'watching' (*phulake*) to the more explicitly military 'guarding' (*phrourein*). The essentially interventionist character of the doctor image is presumably the reason that while the image of the helmsman is very commonly applied to the role of the gods and cosmic direction in Plato

(Pender 2000, 110–11, 240; and other authors: above 64n.31), that of the doctor only appears once, in *Lg.* 905e9–10, where it is rapidly assimilated to ideas of protection through the doctor's role in the 'war' against disease: Pender (2000) 139–43.

36 That the helmsman is essentially a facilitator is acknowledged in *Grg.* 511b–12b, where his capacity to save lives is advanced as a parallel for oratory. At *Euthd.* 291cd the mistaken notion of the kingly art as directing the other arts is described precisely in terms of helmsmanship (*kubernôsa*), the point underlined by allusion to the maritime image applied to a human monarch at A. *Sept.* 2–3: Bambrough (1956) 105 notes the difficulty that pursuing the helmsman image to its logical conclusion implies that in that case he 'is not content to accept the fares of his passengers or the fee of his master, and then to conduct them where they wish to go, but ... insists on going beyond his professional scope by prescribing the route and the destination as well as the course by which the route can best be traversed and the destination most suitably reached.'

37 Paradoxically, this state of affairs can justify the philosopher's disengagement from politics. In *R.* 425e–6c Plato compares a society – by implication, democratic Athens – to a patient on whom it is pointless to try the specific cures of ad hoc legislation (which he also compares to amputating a Hydra's head: 426e8) until he reforms his way of life, a change to which Athens, with its laws against alteration of the constitution, is inherently opposed (contrast Plut. *Lyc.* 5.3 on that legislator's complete change of regimen for Sparta), and in the *Seventh Letter* he justifies his refusal to intervene in Athenian politics in very similar terms (*Ep. 7* 330c–1a): the first course in treating an invalid is to advise him to change his way of life, and if he refuses, only a fool will persevere in his attempts. So too with a government: if it is orderly, and requests advice, by all means give it, but to comply with a government that opposes change with the threat of death and enforces compliance with its desires is unmanly (and Plato had already judged all existing constitutions incurable: 326a). Likewise in the *Republic*, just after the satire on the ship of state (489bc), he asserts that it is for the patient to seek out the doctor, not vice versa; the principal theme of this section is the obstacles to the true philosopher's engaging with society (for the burlesquing of 'mastery of animals' imagery in the picture of the 'large and powerful animal' [493a-c], see below 159).

38 Doctor and trainer: *Cri.* 47b, *Prot.* 313d, *Alc I* 131a, *Grg.* 504a, 517e, *R.* 389c, *Plt.* 295b-e, *Lg.* 684c, 720e, 916a): at *Grg.* 464bc Plato makes it explicit that the trainer is to the healthy body what the doctor is to the sick one, corresponding to the legislator and the judge; the analogy between doctor and judge is elaborated in the account of the painful but therapeutic character of punishment in 477e–80b: cf. *Lg.* 728c, 854e, 862bc, and for the metaphor see Pender (2000) 199–206. Painful treatment: e.g. *Grg.* 456b with Dodds (1959) on b4, 521e–2a, cf. *R.* 564bc (excision in the hive) and above 72; purging: *Plt.* 293d (cf. 308e–9a for a literal parallel), *Lg.* 735d–6a, above n.29 (and for other 'cleansing' imagery in Plato cf. below n.141; even training is expected to be painful: *Lg.* 684c. It follows from Plato's perception of the sickness of real-world constitutions that the trainer rarely appears directly in political contexts (but see below): *gymnastikê* tends to serve as a side-kick to *iatrikê* rather than an independent concept. Plato's identification of the doctor with the judge brings to the fore a moral aspect that is at most latent in earlier medical imagery (above 73; compare a moralizing use of helmsman imagery at *Clit.* 408ab.

39 *Grg.* 463a–5e, 500b, e–501a, 517c–9a, 521a–2a (the last passage imagining Socrates

the doctor arraigned by a pastry-cook before a jury of children); Plato is here attacking the democratic model of service (below, 155).

40 'Just as a steersman, always watching out for what is to the benefit of the ship and the sailors, preserves his fellow-sailors not by putting things down in writing but offering his expertise as law' (*Plt.* 296e–7a2, tr. Rowe).

41 NB Hornblower (2002) 187–97 on 'system-building and treatise-writing [and] professionalism' (184) in this period, with particular reference to warfare.

42 *Plt.* 295d–300a: seafaring is included, as a much more clear-cut case than medicine, to underline the fatuity of subjecting experts to a democratic legal framework in 298b–9d, where there is also a clear echo of the caricature of the ship of state in the *Republic* (above 58).

43 *Lg.* 719e–20e, 722e–3a, where the underlying issue is whether laws should simply be prescriptive or include an explanatory preamble; the image reappears in the context of penal legislation at 857c-e (cf. the law as loving and thoughtful parent at 859a). On the medical model for preambles (or 'preludes') see Yunis (1996) 217–23, with an emphasis on the contrast with the authoritarian doctor of the *Gorgias*; Schofield (2006) 84–6, who notes that the demarcation between the two classes of doctor is almost certainly Platonic invention (97 n.99): indeed, Jouanna (1999) 112–16 observes that while Hippocratic doctors may have had assistants, these were not considered doctors themselves, and that Hippocratic doctors treated slave and free alike.

44 *R.* 389b-d. Aristotle cites the licence of Egyptian doctors to vary the prescribed treatment after a specified interval as a parallel for the superiority of the expert ruler to law, but in the following chapter queries the validity of the craft analogy and makes the countervailing case that even in such cases written rules can serve to prevent deliberate malpractice and errors of judgment due to emotion (*Pol.* 1286a9–14, 1287a32-b3). At *Rh.* 1375b20–25 he recommends litigants whose case is supported by the law to use the stock argument that it is not advantageous to outwit a doctor: here the authority of the law is identified with that of the doctor, but without reference to writing.

45 And, reintroducing the medical theme, inoculate him against its dangers: what he learns will be *alexipharmaka* ('antidotes': 132b2).

46 Although Xenophon alludes briefly to the related figure of the teacher (above n.6; similarly, at *An.* 2.6.12 the troops of the harsh disciplinarian Clearchus regard him as children do their teacher, with respect but no affection or loyalty), he does not feature in Plato, for whom he would presumably not function as an analogy.

47 The aristocratic overtones of the image are pointed up by the way in which the idea of politics as an *agôn* (contest) with prizes for the individuals who participate comes to be particularly associated with election to the Spartan *gerousia*: X. *Lac. Pol.* 10.3, D. 20.107, Arist. *Pol.* 1270b24–5; cf. Plut. *Lycurg.* 26.1. Xenophon also compares the ephors to judges at games (*Lac.Pol.* 8.4) in terms of their authority and close supervision, and it may be the capacity for authoritative action and judgment which underlies the use of *brabeus* ('umpire') for rulers in Aeschylus (*Pers.* 302, *Ag.* 230, and NB Kannicht [1969] on E. *Hel.* 703); Homer uses another word for umpire, *aisumnêtêr* (*Od.* 8.258), to mean 'prince' at *Il.* 24.347: cf. *aisumnai* 'rules' in E. *Med.* 19 and Arist. *Pol.* 1285b25–6 for *aisumnêteia* as elective tyranny such as that of Pittakos. That last case brings to the fore the further aspect of due adherence to a specific code of rules, which is clearly present, combined with the implication of informed adjudication, when Aristotle compares the juror to an umpire (*brabeutês*:

Rh. 1376b19–20): cf. the appointment of a referee (*rhabdouchon kai epistatên kai prutanin* as well as *brabeutên*) for the discussion in Pl. *Prot.* 338ab, and for the word *brabeutês* see also E. *Med.* 274 with Page (1938), *Or.* 1065.

48 On this kind of analogical thought in Plato see esp. Lloyd (1966) 220, 225–6 (cosmic rule), 254–7 (world as a living creature), 389–403 (analysis of analogical arguments).

49 Zeus as king: Antim. fr. 3, D. 35.40, Aristodicus *FGrH* 36 F1, Aglaosthenes *FGrH* 499 F2 (above 18n.39), partly rationalised in Isoc. 3.26 (above 6); so Herodorus (*FGrH*31 F30) gives an account of Prometheus in which he is a king of the Scythians, bound for failing to feed his people. Plato makes Zeus the supreme ruler at *Cra.* 396a8, *Criti.* 121b, *Phdr.* 246e, and speaks of the rulers in Hades at *Cri.* 54b (cf. Isoc. 9.15: Aiakos as *paredros* of Pluto and Kore); the myth of judgment in *Grg.* is based loosely on the traditional succession of Kronos and Zeus (523ab) and the myth in *Plt.* on the Hesiodic tale of the Golden Age (268ef.). Plato also imitates fifth-century practice in personifying Eros as a tyrant (*R.* 572e–3b): on the tyranny of passions see further below 158, and for Eros as unruly divinity cf. Aristophon fr. 11 (above 7); a weaker personification is Isocrates' characterization (3.9 = 15.257: above 7) of Logos as *hêgemôn* ('leader').

50 For helmsman imagery in the Presocratics, see above 64n.31. In Plato, this imagery, often employing the verb *(dia)kubernan*, covers a range of powers from traditional divinities to pure abstractions: so at *Smp.* 187a medicine 'is steered' by Asclepios and the tyrant Eros (above n.49) *diakubernai* the soul (*R.* 573d4–5; cf. *Smp.* 197b3 [Zeus], e1 [Eros]). The next step is the divine rulers in myths: *Plt.* 272e3–4, 273c3, d6-e1, *Ti.* 42e3, *Criti.* 109c2–4; cf. *theos* (God) at *Lg.* 709b7–8 (and NB already Antiph. 1.13 for Dike as helmsman; Menander fr.372 reflects the popular view of a world steered by Tyche), while at *Phil.* 28d8–9 Socrates speaks of 'reason and intelligence' (*noun kai phronêsin*); note also n.36 above for the refusal to assign the same role to the kingly art in *Euthd.* 291cd. The assimilation of levels of organization through the language of 'steering' extends to the microcosm (and appears already in Hp. *Vict.* 10.3, of fire as the directing bodily principle [above 131n.60]: use of the same verb at *R.* 590d6 and 591e3 helps to assimilate rule of reason in the city and individuals. Isocrates too applied this metaphor at the microcosmic level, describing the soul as the helmsman of the body (fr. 37 = Apophth. δ3 Blass; also attributed to Menander: fr.1100K = Comp. Men. et Phil. III 57–8 Jaekel, whence perhaps a similar instance in Latin: Ter. *Hec.* 311); Antiphanes uses the verb of the circulation of the blood (fr. 42).

51 Reason: *Ti.* 48a, *Phil.* 28d; Soul: *Lg.* 896de, 897c, and cf. the world-soul of *Ti.* 34bc; note also the rule of the sun and the Good at *R.* 509d (cf. *epitropeuein* of the sun at *Cra.* 413b4–5; this word and cognates are also applied to divine/cosmic rule at *Cra.* 412d, *Phil.* 28d, *Tht.* 153a; to rule of knowledge: *Plt.* 304c – and hence of statesmanship: 304c–5e), the ordinances of the Demiurge at *Ti.* 42de, and the passing reference to 'our king' at *Lg.* 904a6; also Lloyd (1966) 220, Pender (2000) 106–7, 239. For cosmic monarchy in Plato and its antecedents see above 9–10, and compare Aristotle's restatement of the principle in *Metaph.* 1076a3–4, backed up by a Homeric quotation (above 9).

52 On Alcmaeon B4, see above 20n.65, 81n.45, 131n.60. The language of *dunamis/-iai*, *dunastês* ('potentate') and *dunasteuô* ('hold power') are found in Hp. *Nat.Hom.* 4.2, *VM* 16.1, 8, 17.2, 19.4–5, 20.4, 6, 22.1, 24.1, *Aer.* 12.4, while the author of *Breaths* is a proponent of the monarchy of air: *Flat.* 3 (quoted above 7), 15; all this material is treated more fully in Brock (2006) 354–6.

53 Democritus also speaks of the 'bodily tabernacle' (e.g. B37, 187, 223, 288) and draws

pictures of the mind and senses at odds (B125) and of the body taking the soul to court (B159). The simpler binary model of a ruling and a subject element and the debate over the location of the former are foreshadowed in places by the Presocratics: Anaximen. B2, Alcmaeon A8, Emp. A30, B 105, Philolaus B13, Democr. A105, Antiphon B2.

54 Soul is entitled to rule as prior: *Ti.* 34bc, *Lg.* 896b, 967d, *Epin.* 980de; as divine: *Phd.* 79e–80a, *Lg.* 967d cf. 726–7a; as rational element: *Phd.* 94b, *R.* 441e, *Lg.* 875cd, *Epin.* 983d; as divine and rational: *R.* 590d; rule of soul more generally: *Clit.* 407e, *Phlb.* 35d, 64b, *Alc. I* 130ac; Pender (2000) 171–2. This also introduces an ethical dimension, at least implicitly, since the superiority of soul is in part moral: cf. the pre-eminence of *sôphrosunê* in *Chrm.* 173a, 174de.

55 It is consistent with Isocrates' more muted formulation that he goes on to say that the role of soul is to take counsel (*bouleusasthai*) and that of body to carry out (*hypêretêsai*) its decisions. For Aristotle, knowledge (*epistêmê*) is authoritative: *APo.* 76a16–18; superiority of soul and mind: *de An.* 410b12–14 cf. 429a18–20; soul commands body: *MA* 703a37-b1. The basic principle is often nuanced: in *Pol.* 1254b5–7 he states that soul rules body as a master, but reason controls the appetites in a kingly or constitutional manner; in *Top.* 129a10–16 reason is said to command *normally*, and likewise in *EE*, while maintaining the normative position that one should live in accordance with reason in all things (1249b7–13 cf. 1219b26–20a2) he addresses the problem of the individual's failure to heed reason (1246b8–12). So too in *EN* he asserts that the part which chooses is dominant (1113a6–7), and that the faculty which creates also governs (1143b33–5; hence prudence [*phronêsis*] cannot be in authority [*kuria*], but only at most a steward [*epitropos*]: 1145a6–9, cf. *MM* 1198b9–20) but a later passage appears agnostic on whether this is specifically *nous*, and if so whether it is actually divine (1177a13–16).

  The political organisation of the individual does not always work smoothly: the self-willed man disobeys his internal *hêgemôn* (*MM* 1203b8–9) and views his desires as decrees (*psêphismata*: *EN* 1151b15–16) and a man without self-control is like a state which doesn't observe the good laws it passes (1152a20–4); there can even be *stasis* in the soul (1166b19; cf. Isocrates' dictum that evil thoughts must be banished from the soul like the *stasiastês* from the well-ordered city [fr.31]).

56 The head is master of the body (*Ti.* 44d) and most authoritative, as seat of the senses (*Lg.* 942e; cf. 961d, adding reason and the soul, and 964d–5b for an analogy between the two types of Guardians and the senses and intelligence located in the head); by the same logic, the front of the body as the location of perception is superior to the rear (45a). At *Ti.* 90a the head, being the highest part of the body, is closest to heaven. By the same logic, Aristotle makes the heart an acropolis (*PA* 670a26) and locates the soul in an *archê* there (e.g. *MA* 701b25, 29, 702a37): for the controversy, see Brock (2006) 353, 356–7. The tendency to impose hierarchy seems to have been a strong one: for physiological 'sovereignty' see the note of Farquharson (1912) on Arist. *IA* 706a20.

57 Isoc. 7.14: 'the soul of the city is nothing else but the *politeia*, which has as much power as intelligence (*phronêsis*) in the body', echoed almost verbatim at 12.138; Demosthenes is credited with the sentiment that laws were the soul of a city because without them it would perish like a body without a soul (fr. 13.23; cf. his identification of laws with a city's character (*tropous*): 24.210). Similarly Aristotle reports the argument that the rule of law is the rule of God and reason (*Pol.* 1287a28–30). In his parodic funeral speech (*Mx.* 238c1) Plato does call the *politeia*

'nourishment (*trophê*)', but doubtless with his eye on commonplaces of democratic rhetoric. The term *politeia* in such contexts can include social organization as well as formal constitution: Bordes (1982); hence Aristotle observes that the *politeia* is 'a kind of way of life (*bios tis*) of the city' (*Pol.* 1295a40–1).

58 First the three elements in the soul corresponding to the economic class, Auxiliaries and Guardians are identified (434d–441c), then the hypothesis that it will therefore function in the same way is tested and confirmed (441c–2d) and validated by example (442d–3c); justice is further identified with good household management and harmony (443d) and injustice with ill-health (444c-e). For a helpful discussion of the 'political analogy' see Annas (1981) 109–52 esp. 146–51.

59 In other words, this is principally an exercise in psychology (Annas [1981] 294, 305): man is like a city, but not the other way round (in contrast to the physiological conceptions of the *Timaeus*: Brock 2006, 351–2, 358), except for the seizure of the acropolis within the democratic man at 560b. Arguably this is unsurprising, since the analogy is introduced as aimed at getting a clearer view of justice in the individual; note also the introduction at 552c of a subsidiary image, bees, which as social insects lend themselves to description of politics (though they can themselves also be 'politicized': below n.129).

60 Schofield (2006) 106–7 is doubtless correct to insist that formally this is not strictly a linear process, but it nonetheless reads that way: this is partly because of the structuring of the sequence of individuals as a generational narrative of a family, but also because of Plato's language (e.g. the use of *ex* and *meta* at 544c5–6, 550c8–9 and the image of the slope at 568c9-d1).

61 In another compact and suggestive subsidiary image, the bad companions are described as *aithôsi thêrsi*, 'tawny beasts' (559d9): *aithôn*, which appears only here in Plato, hints at the lions of Homer.

62 There are shades of Thucydides' analysis of *stasis* at this point, esp. 560d–1a ~ Thuc. 3.82.4; for the likelihood of direct influence: Pohlenz (1913) 247–52, esp. 252, McDonnell (1991) 191–2. The motif of *stasis* in the individual is established early, at 352a; cf. 440b, e, 442cd, 444b, 586e, 603d; so too in an inversion of the stock image (below n.95) the sick body 'is at odds with itself' at 556e. For Plato, the city hit by *stasis* actually becomes two cities (551d), an idea echoed by Aristotle (*Pol.* 1310a4–5) and by Cicero *à propos* the impact of Tiberius Gracchus (*Rep.* 1.31); Catiline combined Plato's ideas to give the state two bodies (ap. Cic. *Mur.* 51). Schofield (2006) 203–27 emphasizes the centrality of unity to Plato's thinking in the *Republic*.

63 It is the man's bad companions, described as 'wizards and tyrant-makers' (572e4–5) who bring in the passion, though use of the word *prostatês* (572e6, 573b1) recalls the earlier picture of the development of a popular leader into a tyrant (esp. 565d1–4, e3). Bodyguards: 573a8, e7, 574d7 – the madness which performs this service is imported (*epaktou*: 573b4), just as the tyrannical individual may take service abroad (n.64). On the tyranny of passion see n.49 above and see further 158 below.

64 Bodyguards or mercenaries: 575b; most tyrannical as tyrant: c4–5; note the phrase 'like a city' already at 575a3, likewise the closing of a circle by the linking of the tyrant's family and fatherland (*mêtrida te ... kai patrida*) at 575d.

65 Note subsequent casual references to the internal *politeia* (579c, 590e–1a, 608b), and a final brief allusion to the image in Book 10 to justify the exclusion of the poet from the ideal city because he precipitates an internal coup d'etat against reason (605b cf. 606d).

66 *Ti.* 69c–70b; Brock (2006) 351–2.

67 But in the political analogies of the *Laws* he reverts to a binary opposition between reason, naturally fitted to rule, and emotion, 'like the demos and masses of a city' (689ab; cf. 863e–4a for an antithesis between the tyranny of passions in the soul and the just rule of reason). Plato of course has other models besides the polis for the tripartite soul, most notably the chariot in *Phdr.*
68 *Diakonein, therapuein, hupêretein, epimeleisthai*: e.g. D. 18.311, [D.] 50.2, Aeschin. 3.13, 15, Hyp. 5 col.30; above, 26. Note how Isocrates' lip-service to this ideal helps to camouflage the highly conservative project of the *Areopagiticus*: 7.26, cf. 12.146; Ober (1998) 278–80.
69 Self-deprecation: Yunis (2001) on D. 18.206; demos enslaved: e.g. D. 2.14, 3.30–1, 22.54f., [D.] 13.31, cf. Aeschin. 3.3; compare the charge that opponents are like ungrateful liberated slaves (D. 24.124).
70 Nurse: Democrates fr. 1 Baiter-Sauppe = Arist. *Rh.* 1407a8–10; *eranos*: Aeschin. 3.251 (above 28). Isocrates 4.76 ascribes to the politicians of the past the orthodox respect for public property; compare Aristotle's advice to tyrants to present their handling of public funds as stewardship (above 28), in contrast to theoretical treatments of the monarch as householder (above 31–2). Analogous is Demosthenes' accusation that the 'crop of traitors' gave away their countries' freedom to Philip and Alexander 'like a drinking present' (*propinô*: 18.296; for the behaviour in reality see 19.128, 139): the implication of physical self-indulgence and moral laxity is here combined with the implication of associating with the enemy at symposia as boon companions. However, in 3.22 the charge is that the interests of Athens have been 'pledged away' to the demos for the sake of short-term gratification, though the language attributed to the guilty politicians ('What do you want? What shall I propose? How can I gratify you?') brings us back to the model of politician as (bad and irresponsible) servant.
71 On the *eranos* (either a communal meal or, later, a contribution to an interest-free loan) and its ideology of reciprocity and mutual friendship, see Millett (1991) 153–9; for selfishness at an *eranos* meal, cf. Thphr. *Char.* 30.18. The image is quite widely applied to civic behaviour: in one version, jurors are encouraged to assess like fellow-contributors whether a defendant makes the proper contribution of lawful behaviour ([D.] 25.21–2; the image is a little more general in D. 21.101 [with MacDowell (1990)], 184–5, and cf. the image of the liturgy, below 164); more specifically, the appropriate contribution may be to the city's defence, often of one's life: Thuc. 2.43.1 (above 133n.75), Ar. *Lys.* 648–55 (on which NB Vannicelli 2002, arguing for a deliberate echo of Pericles), Lycurg. 1.143, cf. X. *Cyr.* 7.1.12; there may well be an association here with the particular use of the image with reference to returning due care to parents: E. *Supp.* 361–4 with Collard (1975) on 363, D.10.40; Millett (1991) 289 n.11; Aristotle draws on this to justify the reciprocity of being ruled when young and then ruling when mature (*Pol.* 1332b38–41). Liddel (2007) 141–3 brings out the potential complexity of the image, noting that while an *eranos* can be viewed as 'a public-spirited and voluntary contribution to the reciprocal exchange-relationship between individual and *polis*', it is also possible to emphasize the obligation of reciprocity arising from an ongoing relationship.
72 With reference to foreign policy: (e.g.) D. 15.32, 18.33, 19.316 (Philip or other foreigners hire politicians; [D.] 7.7 hyperbolically posits this of jurors); D. 9.54, 10.19, 18.21, 149, 19.29, 68; Aeschin. 3.86, 220; Din. 1.15, 28, 3.12 (politicians as hirelings); the two are combined in Demosthenes' scathing dismissal of Aeschines' claim to guest-friendship with Alexander (NB Yunis 2001 *ad loc.*). Likewise within Athens a politician may take a wage: D. 24.14, 25.37 (in the latter case from Philip's partisans)

or be hired: D. 24.67, 51.22; comprehensive references on both: above 38n.22. Demosthenes uses the image of retail commerce (next n.) more frequently in 19 (*F.L*), that of wage labour significantly more often in 18 (*Cor.*), presumably because the latter speech takes a longer-term view.

73 According to which politicians, particularly those opposed to Demosthenes, are said to have sold (*pipraskein, apodidosthai*) something (the people, the city, the city's interests, freedom, affairs, defences, etc.), usually to Philip of Macedon; it is particularly prominent in *F.L.*, as in the celebrated denunciation of Philocrates: 'he would go round shopping for whores and fishes with the money for which he sold the city's interests (*pragmata*)' (19.229); cf. D. 18.23, 28, 46–7, 177, 19.28, 90, 121, 133, 141–2, 149, 178, 180, 207–8, 253, 300, 329, 334, 343 (the peroration); cf. generally 9.38–40 and, for such imagery applied to internal politics, 23.201. However, the charge was not unique to Demosthenes, and could even be turned against him: Aeschin. 3.66, 92–4, 226, Din. 1.88, Pytheas fr. 3B-S; also [D.] 7.17, 11.18 (external affairs); [D.] 25.46, Din. 2.1, 3.12 (internal). Less common is the inverse form, which represents Philip as purchasing these same commodities: D. 9.9, 18.32, 47, 247, 19.133, 300, Aeschin. 3.66, 91, Hyp. 5 col.15; Arist. *Rh.* 1410a17–20 cites a non-Athenian example; for the capacity of monarchies to do this cf. Isoc. 3.22. On this commercial vocabulary for bribery, see Harvey (1985) 84–6, and cf. the image of the scale (*trutanê*) unbalanced by money in D. 5.12, 18.298; Theramenes' contemptuous reference to 'those who out of poverty would sell the city for a drachma' (X. *HG* 2.3.48) looks with its implication of treachery like a precursor to such imagery, though with a rather different ideological slant.

74 Isoc. 12.141, D. 3.24, *Pro.* 53.3 [D]. 26.23, 58.30, Din. 3.22; Scholtz (2007) 46–51. For the near-absence of political prostitution and pimping see above 29 and n.23.

75 Ober (1998) 190–213 offers a stimulating reading of the *Gorgias*; see also Yunis (1996) 117–61; Schofield (2006) 63–72; Scholtz (2007) 127–35.

76 Two loves: *Grg.* 481d1–5; for Demos see above 134n.82. With 481d–2a compare Socrates' fear that Alcibiades will become *dêmerastês* ('besotted with the demos') and be corrupted, though for all its superficial attractions, if he sees it naked he will know it for what it is (*Alc. I* 132a with Denyer 2001).

77 513ac: strictly speaking this is a social point rather than a moral one, since Socrates admits the possibility of change for the better, but in the context it is bound to take on a moral aspect (as well as undermining Callicles' plans for mastery: 484a); Socrates has already compared the life of endless gratification commended by Callicles to that of a catamite (*kinaidos*: 494e4).

78 See esp. 521a for two kinds of *therapeia* with 38n.24 above: Callicles chooses *diakonein* (521a8); politicians of the past: 517b; in X. *Mem.* 2.6.13 Pericles is said to have charmed the city into loving him; rhetoric and its political application equivalent to pandering (*kolakeia*): *Grg.* 463b1, 517a5–6 with Dodds (1959) *ad locc.*, 521b1, cf. *Alc I* 120ab; for *kolakeia* as a derogatory label for a lover's behaviour see *Smp.* 183b1, 184c1 and NB Nightingale (1995) 50–1; ruinous gratification: *Grg.* 518e–9b, cf. *R.* 426c. The representation of the demos as children is perhaps gentler in its implications than Aristophanes' characterization of it in *Knights*, but does impute to it the inability to make sound judgements for itself. *Therapeia* is also ambiguous in Isocrates: see Morgan (2003) 185–9 for a stimulating discussion.

79 Nightingale (1995) 187–90 has a good discussion, particularly on the shared assimilation of gratification to feasting. Plato also had *Knights* in mind in the

Republic: the rare word *anterastai* (*R.* 521b5) echoes *Eq.* 733 (otherwise only once, in a general sense in Aristotle *Rh.* 1388a15); see n.89 below for another clear echo.
80 Above 32–3; Plato plays this theme straight in his own funeral speech, the *Menexenus* (238e–9a, cf. 237e).
81 There is a subversive version of the familial image in comedy in Antiphanes fr. 194, where one speaker deliberately misinterprets the riddle of the writing tablet (feminine) and her children as referring to the city and her children, the politicians: for text, commentary and translation, see Olson (2007) 200–3, 441.
82 *Ap.* 30a; cf. Meletus telling tales on Socrates to the city as mother (*Euthphr.* 2c) and the tyrant who turns werewolf through kindred murder (*R.* 565e); similar comparisons, promoted by the family narrative, in the political analogy in books 8 and 9: *R.* 548b, 568e–9c; above, 33.
83 *kai ekgonos kai doulos*: 50e3–4; the triad 'begotten, raised, educated', on which the claim rests, appears just before at e2 and again at 51c8–9; at 51e5–7, however, 'parents and rearers' is supplemented by 'and because you agreed to obey us' (see next note).
84 Argument *a fortiori*: 51a7–b3; but the language of consent which comes to predominate derives from Socrates' choice as an adult to reside in Athens: 51e1–4, cf. 52a7–8, c1–2, d2–e2, 53a5–8, 54c3–4. Likewise 'slave' implies that a very different fictive relationship (though a legitimate one: below 166) is playing a part in the argument. However, *pace* Liddel (2007) 139–41, I would see this contractual and 'authoritarian' strand as peculiar to the *Crito*: elsewhere the impetus to the obligation behind the parent-child analogy is supplied by its affective character, and more generally by the firm embedding of *charis* and reciprocity in Greek society, both of which would lead those concerned to internalize it.
85 The Noble Lie is well discussed by Schofield (2006) 284–309, who emphasizes the way in which Plato uses the affective power of its familial character to give the Guardians a non-philosophical commitment to the ideal city; on the element of autochthony, see 223–4. The earth is 'mother and nurse' in the Lie at 414e, and of all Greeks at 470d7–8, in the context of the argument that war between Greeks amounts to *stasis* (ibid. 207); cf. also the image of the quarrelling brothers at *Lg.* 627b–8a, which springs from the principle that citizens are kinsmen (*suggeneis*) and offspring of the same city (627b3–4).
86 King (or general) as father in X. and Isoc.: X. *Cyr.* 8.1.1, 44, 2.9, 8.1, *Ages.* 1.38, 7.3, *An.* 5.8.18, 7.6.38; Isoc. 2.19, 21; above 31. There is a partial exception to the democratic aversion to father imagery when Demosthenes inverts the standard topos to make all citizens parents of the polis (10.40–1; above 33). Plato does employ the father image for human-divine relations (Pender [2000] 104–6 and 238–9 for references); on the human plane, on the other hand, he explicitly points to the failure of fathers as teachers, especially where politics is concerned: *Men.* 93a–4e, *Prt.* 319d–20b, *Lg.* 694c–5e. As we have seen (above n.24), Aristotle accepts the analogy between king and father as legitimate for true monarchy, but does not consider it applicable within the polis; note also the comparison between the affection of father towards son, god to man and natural ruler to subject at *EE* 1242a32–5, and *EN* 1180b4–7 for a familial image for the acceptance of the authority of law and custom.
87 Allusions to the ship of state in Demad. frr.13, 29 (cf. fr.17 [below] and frr.42–3, 56, 63 for his evident fondness for maritime imagery); D. 9.69; more developed versions at D. 18.281, fr.13.16, *Ep.* 1.8: on all these passages see above 57 and n.35.
88 D. 19.250; Aeschin. 3.158, rebutted in D. 18.194 (above 57 and n.37). There is an

echo of the philosophic view of the helmsman, though with a democratic twist, in ps.-Demosthenes' observation (*à propos* Aristogeiton) that whereas the mistakes of the individual sailor have small, local consequences, those of the helmsman-politician are large and general, and consequently such men must be subject to stringent control (26.3). Wooten (1978) discusses the exculpatory shift in Demosthenes' maritime (and medical) imagery in the wake of Chaironeia; indeed, Ronnet (1951)159–60 observes that his figurative language evokes defeat far more often than victory.

89   He also has a comic precursor in mind, to judge from the characterization of the Demos as 'somewhat deaf (*hupokôphon*)', copied from Aristophanes' Demos (*Eq.* 43, noted by Nightingale 1995, 188 n.44; Aristotle too echoes the word at *Rh.* 1406b35–6). Critias' denunciation of Theramenes for constant changes of course (X. *HG* 2.3.31) provides an instance of the helmsman as leader at the end of the fifth century (for which cf. Odysseus' self-characterization as helmsman at Antisth. fr.15.8), though not in a democratic context: Usher (1968) 132 suggests that this image, and Xenophon's version as a whole, derive from the original speech (though Gray 1989, 183–4 takes a sceptical view of the possibility that the speech is authentic).

90   This is another image prominent in comedy, too (above 118–19), though it also does significant philosophical work as 'alienating' (Schofield 2006, 227–8) and as an instance of the combination of spirit with knowledge (ibid. 39–40), as well as forming part of another tripartite schema (above n.29); on their function as guards see below n.178.

91   Plutarch also credits Demosthenes with this self-depiction (*Dem.* 23.5); the antithesis between dog and wolf is found also in Plato (*R.* 415e–6a, *Lg.* 906d). The image persisted even later: Thphr. *Char.* 29.5 with Diggle (2004). With the watchdog's barking (*hulaktein*) compare the application of the same verb to the fifth-century politician Syracosius in Eup. fr.220, where 'yaps' perhaps catches the tone better. For further negative dog imagery, see below 163.

92   It is in fact in oratory that we finally encounter the phrase *to tês poleôs sôma* ('the body of the city'): Dein. 1.110, Hyp. 5. col. 25, both in prosecutions of Demosthenes, perhaps not coincidentally.

93   [D.] 26.26; cf. Demades' comparison of jurors to doctors in their need for understanding (fr.24 and cf. the analogy between an unjust argument and eye disease in fr.26). For Demosthenes' ironic variant, making Aeschines a doctor wise after the event (D. 18.243, reflected in Aeschin. 3.225) see above, 72.

94   [D.] 25.95, cf. D. 18.324 for expulsion of the 'incurable'. More gentle therapy underlies his comparison of the theoric distributions to inadequate invalid food (above 73); here the food imagery mirrors the idea of politicians feeding the demos in a niggardly manner (above 154).

95   *Stasis* as disease: Pl. *Mx.* 243e, *Plt.* 307d, *Lg.* 628cd, 744d (and cf. 758cd for the Guardians 'healing' revolutions; by inversion, disease can now be seen as *stasis*: Soph. 228ab, *R.* 556e, *Ti.* 82a, 85e–6a), [Arist.] *Ath.Pol.* 6.4, 13.3, Arist. *Pol.* 1273b18–24, 1284b17–22; Isoc. 12.99, 165, D. 2.14, 9.12, 50; more generally of disorder: D. 9.39, and of the oligarchic drones (*R.* 552c cf. 563e, 564b; Pelletier 1948, esp. 145–6) in the political analogy, where the tyrant is the 'ultimate disease of the city' (544c), and internally diseased himself (579e), just as for Protagoras the man without the social virtues will not only be a disease in the city (*Prot.* 322d), but personally incurable (325a). Plato also applies *phlegmainein* ('inflammation') to political disorder in early

Sparta: *Lg.* 691e–2a, cf. the 'disease of kings' at 691a and *Ep.* 8 354b; more generally, *R.* 372e, and note *ouden hugies* ('nothing sound') of the philosophic appraisal of real-world political action at *R.* 496c. Loyalty: Pl. *Lg.* 630b; D. 8.36, 19.289; treachery: D. 19.259 and 262, cf. Aeschin. 2.177.

96 Vulnerability: Pl. *R.* 556e; Hyp. 2 fr. 10 (cited above); sickness reveals weakness: D. 2.21, imitated at [D.] 11.14; Demosthenes develops the idea in a stinging passage in *De Corona*, where he observes that Aeschines, like bodily ills, only surfaces in times of trouble (18.198), contriving also to insinuate that Aeschines' disloyalty is a long-standing problem. The underlying concept may also explain Demosthenes' use of medical terminology for Athenian lack of preparation: 3.31, 9.35, 19.224 (and contr. identification of success with health: 18.286); similarly, the Athenians are asleep in 10.6, blind in 18.159, 19.226. On medical language in D. see further Wooten (1979).

97 We have sufficient oratory from the first half of the century (see Ober [1989] 341–9 for details and a handy tabulation) to suggest that it is significant that almost all the instances cited above date from the 340s or later, i.e. after Plato's death, while the appearance of medical imagery also in Xenophon (nn.6, 31 above) and Antisthenes (n.14 above) may indicate that this was another aspect of the Socratic heritage. Not that politicians always make things better: Pl. Com. fr.201 implies that contemporary politicians disagree with Demos and make him feel sick; he asks for a feather and a bowl because he wants to be sick, while another figure is called a 'disease (*nosos*)'; for Demos as the speaker and interpretation see Plut. *Mor.* 801AB; for the date (380s) Olson (2007) 220.

98 There may well be a connection with the suggestion that the period after the Social War sees 'a growing valuation of the importance of political expertise': Liddel (2007) 248–50 (quotation from p. 248): for the reforms to financial administration of Eubulus and Lycurgus, greater specialization in the generalship and the pursuit of efficiency in this period, see Rhodes (1980) 312–15, 321–2.

99 Plato similarly makes Gorgias argue that rhetorical skill must be exercised responsibly, like that of the boxer or wrestler (*Grg.* 456c–7b); for the association between the two skills see above 119 and Gera (1993) 68 n.142.

100 Aeschin. 3.205–6; in the earlier speech against Timarchos he makes a similar point in terms of horse-racing, telling the jurors that they must 'drive him down the course' (1.176), perhaps with the implication that his evasions will be less cunning and more obvious. Ober (1989) 282–3 notes Aeschines' fondness for athletic imagery, which he suggests was intended to imply that Aeschines was 'the sort of man who spent a good deal of time in gymnasia and so naturally used athletic turns of phrase': the whole section (280–92) on aristocratic values and democracy is relevant here, though I am less convinced than he is that democratic ideology is straightforwardly dominant by this date.

101 Aeschin. 3.179–80; D. 61.48 (*agônistês … tôn politikôn*). Demosthenes 15.30–1 compares Athens as a whole to an athlete obliged to take on two contests, against internal as well as external enemies, and so is unable to achieve anything without a struggle (*akoniti*, lit. 'without [the] dust [of the arena]').

102 Master: Isoc. 4.90, 127; D. 15.27, Aeschin. 3.132 (note the echo of Hdt. 7.8.γ1–2); slaves: Isoc. 4.150–1, 5.139, drawing on the sophistic view of the influence of constitutional forms on character and temperament (above 128n.124) to talk down the power of Persia as a whole (cf. the more generally environmentalist passage at 7.74 and Arist. *Pol.* 1285a19–22, b2–3, 23–5, 1328b27–9); D. 9.43, 14.31–2, 15.15,

23; the same rhetoric is echoed in Plato's mock funeral speech (*Mx.* 239d–40a). Andocides extends the image in referring to the rebel Amorges as 'the king's slave and a runaway' (3.29; see above 109 for earlier instances). Hence it also becomes a topos that the giving of earth and water amounts to slavery: Arist. *Rh.* 1399b11–13; doubtless the same ideology underlies the purported advice of Aristotle to Alexander (fr.658R) to treat Greeks like a leader (*hêgemonikôs*) and barbarians as a master (*despotikôs*) like animals or plants.

103 In *HG* 6.1.12 (a speech attributed to Jason of Pherae) and *An.* 3.2.13 (where Xenophon himself is the speaker) the idea is deployed as a proof of the military impotence and consequent vulnerability of the Persian empire; cf. *HG* 3.1.21, 4.1.35–6 for the standard Greek view of the position of even eminent Persians; so too the contrast which Cyrus himself draws between the freedom of his Greek mercenaries and his own prosperous but servile status (*An.* 1.7.3) might be considered a *topos* calculated to appeal to his audience. In the *Laws* Plato makes a general contrast between the maximal freedom of Athenian democracy and the servitude of Persian monarchy (697c, 698a, 699e, 701e, 757a) after a golden age of imperial freedom under Cyrus (694a).

104 His application of the term *hupêretês* to Cyrus' aides de camp in *Cyr.* might also be the product of a search for a less loaded term to reflect the position of *ba(n)daka* (see esp. 8.4.29 for the rich rewards reflecting their status; also 2.4.4, 5.3.52, 4.18, 6.2.13, 3.14, 29, 7.1.38, 2.2–3, 5.18, 39, 8.5.13). See also Petit (2004) on *An.* 1.6.4–11 for arguments that Xenophon genuinely understood Persian 'vassalité'. The enigmatic passage in *An.* 2.5.23 in which Xenophon has Tissaphernes speak of 'wearing the tiara upright (i.e. being king of Persia) in one's heart' also looks likely to rest on an unusual awareness of Persian protocol: Brock (2004b) 255; for the underlying complexities of this Greek perception of (apparently) Median ceremonial see Tuplin (2007b).

105 Ctesias *FGrH* 688 F19, F9.8.

106 D. 1.4, 18.235; the same word is applied by Hypereides to an unspecified Macedonian king (6.20); the word for the service done by Antipater and Parmenion, *diakonein*, is also applied to the servile relation of Arthmius of Zelea to the Persian king (D. 19.69, 9.43; cf. 9.32 for 'slaves' of Philip deputing as *agônothetai*). Tyrants: [D.] 17.8 (Macedonian support); particular case: D. 9.66 (Eretria), Din. 1.44; cf. also Hyp. 2 fr.1, 2.8, 10, where Philip and the Macedonians are characterized as 'tyrants', and 6.39, where Leosthenes and his men are praised as superior to the tyrannicides Harmodius and Aristogeiton for having overthrown the tyrants, not just of Athens, but of all Greece (i.e. Antipater and the Macedonians).

107 D. 1.23, 2.8, 6.25, 8.46, 59–60, 62, 9.22, 26, 56, 59, 70, 10.4, 25, 61–2, 64, 18.46, 47, 65, 72, 203, 208, 295–6, 305, 19.81, 112, 259–61; [D.] 7.32, 11.4; Lycurg. 1.50, 60, 149, fr.12.1 Conomis; Din. 1.19; Hyp. 6.24–5, 34, fr.27 Jensen, *Ag. Diondas* 137v 2, 176r 3 and cf. 175r 15–16: 'to endure slavery under [the pro-Macedonian] Demades'.

108 Athens in the fifth century: L. 2.56, Isoc. 4.80, 104, D. 18.205, Lycurg. 1.104, X. *HG* 2.2.23 ('the beginning of freedom for Greece'), Pl. *Mx.* 242ac, [Arist.] *Ath.Pol.* 24.2, Arist. *Rh.* 1396a17–19 ('enslavement' a stock criticism of Athens); and generally: D.18.100, X. *HG* 2.4.20; Sparta (with particular reference to the decarchies and the seizure of the Theban Cadmeia): L. 2.59–60, Isoc. 4.127, 7.65, 69, Din. 1.38, X. *HG* 3.5.12–13, 5.4.1, 7.1.44; Thebans: D. 8.74, X. *HG* 7.5.1, 3; Persia: L. 2.59–60, 33.6, D. 14.31–2, 15.3, 15 (Mausolus), X. *HG* 3.1.3, 16, 21, 4.8.2; also Isoc. 9.56, 68, D.20.69 (Evagoras and Conon as liberators), X. *An.* 7.4.24, 7.29 (subjects of Seuthes); Pl. *Plt.* 308a (consequences of excessive moderation or courage).

109 The principle of freedom and autonomy is spelt out in the charter of the Second Athenian League: *IG* II² 43 = R&O no. 22.9–11, 20 cf. *IG* II² 126 = R&O no. 47.16–17; [D.] 7.30, 17.8, building on the principle of general autonomy established by the Peace of Antalcidas (X. *HG* 5.1.31); the fuller formula appears already in X. *HG* 3.1.20 with reference to events in 399 BC and in Athens' alliance with Chios of 384 (*IG* II² 34 = R&O no. 20.20–1). Demosthenes deploys the formula to amplify the slavery-freedom antithesis at 1.23 and 18.305 (and the effect is gained by implication at [D.] 7.32, 17.8), and Xenophon likewise makes the same point editorially about the Spartans at *HG* 5.4.1; the concept is already present in Thucydides, though not explicitly formulated: 2.72.1, 3.10.6, 46.5, 4.86.1, 5.27.2, 6.77.1, 84.3, 8.64.5; Ostwald (1982) 35–41, Raaflaub (2004) 149–60.

110 Of the Peisistratids: Isoc. 16.25, Lycurg. 1.61; of Euphron at Sicyon: X. *HG* 7.3.8; of Athenian anti-tyranny legislation: Lycurg. 1.125; of tyranny in general: Pl. *R.* 344b, 563e–4b, 569a, 575d, 576a, 577c, Arist. *Pol.* 1314a7–9, 19–21, cf. 1324a35-b3. Plato inverts the image in his extended analysis of the condition of the tyrant in terms of a hypothetical slave-owner (578d–9e), beset by fears and external pressures which render him a prisoner and the slave of his own slaves. Here, as usually in fourth-century political imagery, the common perception of the tyrant's position as desirable is assumed but undermined; positive images for tyranny are rare, and seem to be associated only with Dionysius I of Syracuse, who is reputed to have been told that tyranny was 'a fine shroud' (i.e. worth dying for: Isoc 6.44–5; cf. D.S. 14.8, 20.78, identifying the speaker as one Heloris; Plut. *Mor.* 783D), and, by the historian Philistus, that one should not leap down and escape from tyranny on a galloping horse, but should rather be dragged off it by the leg (*FGrH* 556 F59/T4).

111 Of the Thirty: L. 2.61–2, 64, 12.39, 73, 94, 97, 13.17, 14.34, 18.5, 24, 27, 28.13, 31.26, 31–2; Isoc. 16.37, Lycurg. 1.61; X. *HG* 2.3.24, 4.17 (but in Andoc. 1.99 *edouleues tois triakonta* means 'you were the lackey of the Thirty' and is a purely personal insult); of the Four Hundred: Andoc. 2.27; Lys.12.67); of both revolutions: L. 12.78; Isoc. 20.10. Liberty is identified with the establishment of Athenian democracy at L. 2.18, Isoc. 10.35 (in the latter case credited to Theseus: cf. the same idea and language at E. *Supp.* 352–3); hence Phormisius' proposal to limit the franchise also threatens enslavement: L. 34.2.

112 D. 15.15, 17–20, cf. 20.107–8, Isoc. 8.125; Demosthenes draws a similar contrast in the *Leptines* between the voluntary honours conferred by a democracy and those of tyrants and oligarchies received 'from one's master' (20.15–16). Democritus' alignment of democracy with freedom and oligarchy with slavery (B251) probably dates from the later fifth century and, since he hailed from Abdera in Thrace, which may also have been a democracy (Lewis 1990), implies that the concept was by no means confined to Athens.

113 *R.* 463ab: compare his concern that the Guardians should not turn into 'masters' (416b, 417b; 590cd appears at odds with this, but NB Schofield 2006, 273–4 and n.119 below for the 'mastery' of reason), and the presentation of Spartan-style timarchy (547c); at *Mx.* 238e the image is used of tyranny and oligarchy indifferently, while at *Lg.* 712e–3a all existing constitutions are said to entail the slavery of the ruled.

114 D. 24.75; above, n.102. The opposition in this passage between oligarchy and the rule of law also implies that oligarchy resembles tyranny in ruling by whim or private law.

115 L. 12.35, X. *HG* 2.3.48, 4.1, *Mem.* 1.2.56, Polycrates ap. Arist. *Rh.* 1401a34–6, [Arist.] *Ath.Pol.* 41.2; earlier, Critias is actually made by Xenophon to argue that for

their own safety the Thirty must behave tyrannically (*HG* 2.3.16). More generally, Theramenes is made to apply the adjective *turannikos* to men of extreme oligarchic sentiments (2.3.49); otherwise such language is applied to the fifth-century Athenian view of oligarchy (Isoc. 4.105), to the pro-Spartan oligarchy at Thebes after the seizure of the Cadmeia (5.4.1–2, 9, 13, 7.3.7), to the harmosts and decarchies of the Spartan empire (L. 2.59, X. *HG* 3.5.13, 6.3.8) and, more tendentiously, the democratic party at Corinth during the union of Corinth and Argos (*HG* 4.4.6; NB n.122 below). For the figurative language of tyranny in the fourth century (and earlier), see further Tuplin (1985) 366–75.

116. The slave-doctor of Plato's *Laws* is like a tyrant because he stubbornly (*authadôs*) imposes his will (720c, 722e), just as spoilt (*truphôntes*) young men do to their lovers (*Men.* 76bc). Closer to political reality, Polus perversely expresses admiration of accomplished speakers who are like tyrants because they can kill, rob or exile whom they please (*Grg.* 466bc): the same point is made in a more moderate way in the *Phaedrus*, where orators are said to be 'like kings' and 'kingly' (*basilokoi*; 266c). Demosthenes picks up the motif of 'issuing orders' (*epitattein*) in his critique of the dysfunctional nature of contemporary Athenian politics with reference to the behaviour of its leaders (2.30).

117. The motif of freedom from the passions as masters is introduced very early, at *R.* 329cd, and the internal tyranny of the passions is developed at length in the 'political analogy' (e.g. 553cd [the 'Persian king' analogy: above 153], 572e–3b, 577d) and the expression appears elsewhere (*Phdr.* 238b [cf. e], *Lg.* 863e). Plato makes an explicit link to the earlier characterization of Eros as a tyrant (573b, 575a): see above 8 for earlier instances relating to Eros and the symposium (drink is also mentioned at *R.* 573bc and *Phdr.* 238b), and 7 for Eros as unruly divinity. Political power can of course also engender *erôs* as desire (*R.* 521b; above n.79), and the desire for tyranny can be assimilated to other physical desires, as in the remark attributed to Jason of Pherae that he felt hungry when he was not tyrant (Arist. *Pol.* 1277a23–5; *erôs* and hunger appear together at Pl. *Ep.* 8 354cd); that in turn links in to the perception of the tyrant as indulging his appetites without restraint (e.g. Wohl 2002, 220–3, 241–7; popular belief that the tyrant enjoys greater pleasures of all kinds is foregrounded as the initial premise of X. *Hiero*); see also next note.

118. In a political context, slavery to pleasure is contrasted with ruling servants: Isoc. 1.21; rule yourself as well as subjects and do not be a slave to pleasure: 2.29; a good ruler leads his pleasures, not vice versa: 9.45; the worst ruler is the one who cannot rule himself: fr.40; the free and truly kingly man is not ruled by any pleasure: Pl. *Alc I* 122b; contrast Democr. B214: some men are masters of cities, yet slaves to women; on slavery to pleasure in general see Brock (2007) 211–13. For slavery and freedom in relation to self-control and virtue see (e.g.) X. *Mem.* 4.5.2–5, Pl. *Phdr.* 256b, *Lg.* 863d, for rule and obedience *Grg.* 491de, *R.* 389de (and cf. the internal war of *Lg.* 626e); in the *Republic* the cliché 'master of oneself' is elaborated in terms of the rule of the better element, i.e. the rational element in the tripartite soul, so that 'ruling oneself' amounts to justice (430e–1b, 443d): hence the philosopher is 'most kingly and king of himself' (580c).

119. So the rule of soul (above n.54) is expressed as *despozein* (Pl. *Phd.* 80a, 94de, *Lg.* 726; cf. *despotis* [*Ti.* 34c], *despotoun* [*Ti.* 44d]) and the position of the body or passions as *douleuein* (*Phd.* 80a, *Lg.* 726); for *douleuein* of submission to authority see *R.* 653d, *Lg.* 701bc, *Ep.* 8 354de, all with reference to democratic ideology, and cf. Arist. *Pol.* 1274a17–18 (lack of right to election and scrutiny would be slavery), 1297a2,

1317b10–13 (but 1311a19–20, 1313b7–9 refer to tyranny, and cf. 1295b19–22, of the dysfunctional city split between rich and poor). Such language can be used positively, of the acceptance of authority (*Lg.* 762e), shading into the imagery of the mastery or kingship of law (below 166), in contrast to the sophistic perception of *nomos* as enslaving *phusis* (*Lg.* 890a, cf. the tyranny of law: below 166 and n.187). The broad identity of *despozein* and *archein* is also implied by statements that the art of rule is the same in political and domestic contexts (above 25–6). Philemon, in the characteristic philosophizing mode of fourth-century comedy, extends the idea into a universal principle, that everyone is slave to someone or something else: the speaker, a slave, has a master, while the Athenians are slaves to *nomos*; others are slaves to tyrants, who in turn are slaves to fear; mercenary commanders serve satraps, who serve kings, who serve the gods, who are subject to necessity (fr.31 [*Thebaioi*]). The effect of universalizing the concept is both to blunt its impact and to remove any stigma attaching to it.

120 As is the image of imperial tyranny, which is deployed in an unambiguously negative manner both by Demosthenes of the Spartan empire (20.70; see above n.108 for Conon as liberator and n.106 for the tyrannicides as a point of reference) and by Isocrates with reference to Athenian naval imperialism in the *de Pace* (8.89–115 cf. 15.64), in contrast to a lawful and kingly hegemony modelled on the Spartan monarchy (8.142–4): Davidson (1990) 31–2, 35–6; Tuplin (1985) 359–61.

121 Isocrates' claim that in the ancestral democracy it was held that the demos should have electoral and judicial power 'like a tyrant' (7.26) or 'which the most fortunate of tyrants have' (12.147) is superficially positive, but may be deliberately double-edged: when Aeschines presents a version of this thought, he carefully says that that in a democracy the private citizen 'is king (*basileuei*) through law and vote' (3.233); in his warning not to give these up, the word *dunasteia* ('power') must be used in a neutral sense, since the warning not to give up the (figurative) strongpoints (*ischura*) of the democracy to the few (234) hints at the physical occupation of Athens by the Thirty (who are mentioned in 235) and the Four Hundred before them.

122 The classic passage is the amusing dialogue between Pericles and Alcibiades preserved by Xenophon (*Mem.* 1.2.40–6); there is a tantalizing suggestion that the idea might have appeared in tragedy at *TrGF Adesp.* fr.656.7(]*ochlos turan*[, perhaps from a fifth-century satyr-play). Plato makes varied use of the concept: discussing constitutions in *Plt.*, he airs the idea that the mass may rule by force (291e–2a; cf. *Lg.* 627b for the domination of a just minority by an unjust majority), while in *Grg.* Socrates forces Callicles to realize that the Athenian demos will be his tyrant-like master (513a2 with Dodds 1959; cf. 510d), but earlier Callicles' objection to democracy is that it facilitates the enslavement of individuals of superior *phusis* by the feeble masses (492ab cf. 484a). The image was not confined to Athens: Xenophon ascribes it to opponents of the brief Corinthian democracy of the early fourth century (*HG* 4.4.6), though there is some blurring together of internal and external politics, since the desired liberation and salvation is both from democracy and from Argive control.

123 X. *Smp.* 4.45, 4.32: the mention of the discredited concept of *phoros* (tribute) in the latter passage may hint at the imperial 'tyrant city' (above 123–4, though NB Tuplin 1985, 351–2 for a different view), *Mem.* 2.1.9; above 30. For Plato see the previous note.

124 *Mem.* 2.1.10–12, 8.4; above 38n.26.

125 Typically *doulos* and *despotês*, though *oiketês*, the word used by Aristippus in *Mem.*

2.1.9, is also most frequently applied to slaves (*LSJ* s.v.); by contrast, nouns such as *tamias* (steward) and *hupêretês* (servant) refer to activity and, while implying subordination, do not necessarily denote a particular status: Brock (2007) 209–10.

126 D. 19.136: at 314 he imputes to Aeschines anti-democratic views which regard the current state of affairs as 'rough water (*kludôna*) and madness'; Isoc 15.172, and cf. Pl. *Ep. 7* 325e2–3 for the dizzying flux of Athenian politics. For earlier examples see 120 above, for a later one, cf. App. *BC* 3.20, and note also the use of verbs such as *surreô* ('flow together': X. *HG* 2.3.18) and *katakluzô* ('swamp': Pl. *R.* 492c5) of popular activity. The image is reified in the anecdote that Demosthenes practised speaking against the din of a stormy sea to give him the confidence necessary to address the assembly (Lib. *Arg.D.* 11).

127 *Plt.* 266e; *Lg.* 905e, 906e; *R.* 566d; *Grg.* 516e (picking up the animal-taming imagery of 516ab [above 150]); for Plato's use of *euênios* ('responsive to the rein') in *Lg.* see above 138n.120, and note also the passing reference (in a medical image) to the authority of the ephors at Sparta as a curb-chain (*psalion*: *Lg.* 692a4–5).

128 D. 3.31, though he can use the yoke positively as an image of partnership (*Pro.* 55.2). There is a hint of social legislation as yoking in Aristotle's description of Lycurgus' attempt *tas ... gunaikas ... agein ... hupo tous nomous* (lit. 'to lead women beneath the laws': *Pol.* 1270a6–7) and their resistance (*antekrouon* lit. 'they knocked against'): see Newman (1887–1902) on a8; for the expression cf. D. 24.131.

129 Though conversely, Aristotle as biologist frequently describes bees and other social species in political terms: at *HA* 488a10–13 he notes that some social species, such as cranes and bees, have a 'leader' (*hêgemôn*), while ants and many others do not, and at 628a33–4 the wasp leaders are described as 'managing (*dioikousai*)'. He uses the neutral term *hêgemôn* much more frequently than the popular *basileus* ('king') with reference to bees and other insects (34 times as against 12: see the index to Balme 2002) and also applies it to bellwethers among sheep (573b24–5, cf. 574a10, 575b1, 577a15), cranes (614b21–5), partridges (614a11, 15) and migratory fishes (598a29–30 – but at 597b15 the reference is to species that 'pilot' quails: Arnott 2007 s.v. Glôttis); otherwise *basileus* is applied only to the Goldcrest or Firecrest (592b27, 615a19–20; also *tyrannos* at 592b23; Arnott 2007 s.vv.). For a later positive paradigm from the beehive, see Plut. *Lyc.* 25.5 on the identification of Spartiates with their community.

130 *HG* 3.2.28; since the context is military, Xenophon may have modelled the image on the simile of swarming bees in *Il.* 2.87–90.

131 A. *Pers.* 126–9 with Broadhead (1960) on 128; he also notes the intrusion of ground terminology in the substitution of the Homeric *orchamos* for *hêgemôn*, the word normally used of the queen.

132 *Plt.* 301de with Rowe (1995); however, he applies the image positively to the Rulers at *R.* 520ab.

133 Goodenough (1928) 84, though without any Persian parallels for the image as such (for the belief in the inherent natural superiority of Persian monarchs see above 12); Roscalla (1998) 97–101 sees the Persians' self-identification reflected in distorted form in the assertion that in ancient times the Greeks called them Kephenes (i.e. Drones: Hdt. 7.61.2) and notes an apparent allusion to the king of Assyria as a bee in *Isaiah* 7.18. Cf. also Pomeroy (1994) 240–2, 276–7 on the complex of queen bee imagery in *Oec.* 7.17, 32–4, 38–9, arguing for a link to the Persian content of ch. 4, though here Xenophon must also be trading on ideas of orderly and productive management in the hive, overseen by the queen, which go back at least to the Bee-Woman of Semonides (7.83–93, esp. 85). Callimachus (*Jov.* 66, *Aet.* fr.178.23Pf.) uses in the sense 'king' the

word *essên*, which on some accounts referred specifically to the king bee, and was applied to the *basileus* at Ephesus (*EM* 383.27; the priestesses of Artemis were called *melissai* 'bees'); at least in the former passage, the appearance of other bee motifs suggests that he has this sense in mind (so McLennan 1977 *ad loc.*). This cult-practice would seem to be ancient and perhaps of Hittite origin: Barnett (1948) 20–1; for other cultic and mythic associations with bees, see Cook (1895).

134 *R.* 552e, 555d, 556a, 559cd, 564b, 564d–5c; note the subordinate image of the need for a lawgiver-doctor to excise the drones (564bc), whose stings are toxic or infectious (*entiktei* 565c; Pelletier 1948, 140–1) and, among much interaction between tenor and vehicle, the buzzing of subordinate drones in assembly 564de; *prostatês*: 565cd, though the parallel with a werewolf is more prominent here, and the drones now represent the tyrant's bodyguard (567de). In the individual, the desires of the oligarchic character are also drones (554b-d), and the process culminates in the establishment in the tyrannical man of a master-passion as supreme drone with drone attendants (572e–3b, 573e, 574d). This imagery goes back to Hesiod *Op.* 304–6, to which Plato alludes in *Lg.* 901a, and there are strong parallels in fifth-century drama (and later: Adam 1902 on 552c cites Shakespeare *Pericles* 2.1.50): for stings and stinging to describe exploitation see E. *Supp.* 242 (see the mention of base *prostatai* in 243), Ar. *Vesp.* 1113, though as Pelletier (1948) notes, aggressive drones with stings are an invention of Plato's with no parallel in nature; for *blittein* (564e10) NB Ar. *Eq.* 794, *Lys.* 475); Liebert (2010) argues that Plato's ultimate target is the honeyed sweetness of poetry. Plato also describes colonization in terms of swarming: *Plt.* 293d, *Lg.* 708bc (and the inverse image occurs at X. *Oec.* 7.34).

135 The delay is even more striking if one accepts the arguments of Fisher (2008) 208–12 against Pritchard (2003), (2004) for substantially increased levels of participation socially as well as numerically in festival activity from the time of Cleisthenes' reforms on, although the musical imagery of the chorus seems to operate from the standpoint of the critic or observer rather than the practitioner.

136 Systematic theoretical approaches to art go back to the second half of the fifth century with the Canon of Polycleitus (Borbein 1996, 84–6), which laid down rules for the ideal ratios between measurements of parts of the body, and musical theory likewise gained pace through the fifth century, particularly under the influence of the 'New Music' (West 1992, 218–53, 356–72; Csapo 2004), while the principle of proportional equality emerges in the early fourth century: Harvey (1965). The influence of theoretical developments in music is evident in the *Republic* in Socrates' concern to identify the correct music for the ideal city (398c–402a), and the citation of Damon (also mentioned at 400bc) for the proposition that there can be no musical change without major constitutional change (424c): Wallace (2004) discusses public aspects of Damon's activity, and Csapo (2004) 235–45 considers the links between musical and political controversies.

137 *Pol.* 1309b21–31, 1302b33–1303a2; at 1287a14–16, in the discussion of proportional equality, he makes the related point that bodies (and their needs) vary, the implication being that the appropriate arrangements must be decided on a case-by-case basis by expert judgment – and indeed there were probably competing artistic canons: Pollitt (1974) 21–3; see especially Plin. *HN* 34.58 on Myron and 34.65 on Lysippus. Despite his openness to models derived from art, Aristotle rejects the image of the law as 'a likeness' of justice: *Top.* 140a7–8, 141a20–1.

138 *Paradeigma*: *R.* 500d–1c; the image is introduced to denote the basis of philosophic understanding at 484cd; at 592b the ideal city is itself a 'paradigm laid up in heaven'.

139 500d6; there is an instructive parallel at *Lg.* 671bc, where wine is said to heat men and make them pliable, like iron, in the hands of the lawgiver. However, at *Plt.* 261cd the objection is raised that kingly knowledge is nobler than that of the master-builder because it works with animate materials.

140 The word suits well the moulding of the matrix for a bronze sculpture in clay or wax (*Lg.* 746a specifies the latter). Although we tend to think in terms of sculptors working in marble, there is no Greek parallel to Michelangelo's concept of the artist liberating the sculpture from the stone, and it seems a reasonable assumption that, particularly for large sculptural programmes like the Parthenon frieze, the design will have been first produced as a clay maquette.

141 The painter is most prominent when Plato focuses on fidelity to a model (*R.* 484c8–9, 501c6), so that the creative process here is described largely in those terms: NB *pinax* ('canvas' [lit. 'wooden board'] 501a2), *hypographesthai* ('sketch' 501a9; also used of the legislator as artist providing judicial 'sketches' at *Lg.* 934c1–2), *exaleiphô* ('rub out' 501b9); the image also represents the exercise of practical expertise: Nightingale (2004) 127–31, Schofield (2006) 162–3. The cleaning of the canvas ('blank canvas', '*tabula rasa*') is also the best artistic analogue for the preparatory cleaning or purging which he usually anticipates (*katharan* 'clean' in 501a3 is cognate with *kathairô* 'clean', 'purge'): for other such images NB above nn.28, 38.

142 *dêmiourgoi*: *Pol.* 1273b32–3, 1274b18; *glaphuros*: *Pol.* 1271b21–2, 1274b8 (contrast the biological image 'more developed' in 1271b24); hence tyrants banish nobles as rival practitioners (*antitechnous*: 1311a17 with Newman 1887–1902).

143 Harmony in the cosmos: *R.* 617bc, *Ti.* 37a, 47d, 90d, *Cra.* 405cd; in the soul: *Phd.* 93cf.; hence it is also the objective of the education of the Guardians, to be achieved by harmony between its intellectual and physical aspects (*R.* 410e, 441e–2a; cf. *Lg.* 659e) and harmony is characteristic of the wise man (*R.* 591cd, *La.* 188d, *Prt.* 326b): so Socrates warns Gorgias of the danger of internal dissonance (*Grg.* 482bc). Compare also the discussion of pleasure or contentment as harmony at *Phlb.* 31cd, and NB Csapo (2004) 235–6.

144 *Lg.* 689cd with England (1921) on d2, 691a with England on a7; his note on 689d6 identifies this knowledge with *sophrosunê*. Plato also puns on the musical and legislative senses of *nomos* (cf. n. 29 above), often combined with the idea of the prelude (*prooimion*), particularly in the *Laws*, where it is associated with the persuasive model of law-giving: *R.* 531d–2a, 532d; *Lg.* 722d–3b, 734e, 772e, 774a, 799e, 854ac, 870de, 880ab, 887a, 907d, 916d, 923c, 925e, 932a; Csapo (2004) 239–40. This wordplay does not seem to have explicit argumentative force, though it may hint both at the harmony implicit in good law and at the idea of law as a tune to be followed; it also suggests the creativity of the lawgiver.

145 For the model of the best constitution as a harmonious balance see Arist. *Pol.* 1290a19–29, *Rh.* 1360a23–7, *EE* 1241b27–30 (and for the broader principle *EN* 1138b21–3) and cf. *Pol.* 1301b16–17 for tautening or slackening; particular changes at Athens: 1304a20–1 (tautening), [Arist.] *Ath.Pol.* 26.1 with helpful discussion in Rhodes (1981) *ad loc.* (slackening); NB also *rhuthmizein* of the creation of order in *Pol.* 1308b17.

146 *Pol.* 1273b11–12; 1277b29–30: Plato makes a similar point about the superior understanding of the piper as user at *R.* 601de. The *aulos* was a double-reed instrument, so 'pipe' is preferable as an approximate translation to the traditional 'flute'.

147 [Arist.] *Oec.* 1353b17–18; X. *Oec.* 8.3 (cf. 8.20), *Mem.* 3.5.18 with Dillery (2004) 261

and, for his fundamental concern with order, Dillery (1995) 27–35; Wilson (2000) 37–40, 46–7 highlights the similarities with military training. Perhaps the division of direction of a chorus between *chorodidaskalos* (trainer) and *choregos* (funder and manager) was another factor which made it unsuitable as a model of leadership: Wilson (2000) 81–6, but see also 130–6 for possible cases of the *choregos* personally leading the chorus in performance; in any case, there were substantial ideological tensions around the figure of the *choregos* as patron and representative of the wealthy elite (109–97). The relatively small size of the chorus (only 50 for dithyramb, fewer still for drama) may also have limited its appeal as a model for democratic arrangements.

There is an incidental theatrical image in Demosthenes' comparison of the danger that the demos will not give an equal hearing to both sides to the susceptibility of an audience to the actors who appear on stage first (*tôn prokatalambanontôn*: *Pro.* 34.2; cf. Arist. *Pol.* 1336b28f with Newman 1887–1902).

148 *Plt.* 305e–6a, 308c–11c; see the illuminating discussions of Lane (1998) 163–82 and Blondell (2005) 49–71.

149 The subordinate activities are distinguished by division (280a–1d, cf. 289cd; Lane 1998, 49–56) following the purportedly random choice of weaving at 279ab.

In the *Laws*, the combination of dissimilar elements in marriage is represented as the mixing of wine and water (*Lg.* 773cd, cf. 771e). Proper blending is an important element in Plato's thought, particularly in the *Philebus* (Gould 1955, 220–1), but he tends to refer to it in rather general terms and language (though NB *sugkrasis* in *Plt.* 308e in the context of weaving), so that it is frequently unclear whether the underlying thought is symposiastic or medical (or indeed from some other field such as weaving or music). The description of early Sparta as 'inflamed' and 'swollen' (above n.95 and 77n.8) suggests that the mixture of elements in the constitution described there is conceived in medical terms, particularly since more than two elements are involved (691e–2a, 693b), and indeed Jouanna (1978) 84–91 argues that a concern with balance and regimen is a new feature of Plato's model of the statesman as doctor in this work. The language of mixture is widespread elsewhere in the dialogue (Wibier 2010, 49–53 lists 36 instances), but not always clearly in a medical sense, as already noted: that might be in play in the passages concerned with legislation (722bc, 921e) but is less obviously the case when the Nocturnal Council is presented as a mixture (951d, 961d, 969b; Wibier 2010, 38–46).

Aristotle alludes to the idea of Sparta as a 'mixed' constitution (*Pol.* 1265b33–5, cf. 1266a4 for the advantage of blending from more elements) and to accounts of Solon as having created a similar arrangement at Athens by 'mixing' (1273b35–41) in a way that suggests that the concept was current in wider circles. His own enthusiasm for a form of mixed constitution which he labels *politeia* is well-known (Lintott 2000), though the idea of mixture is usually expressed more or less literally; however, in 1281b35–8 he compares the admixture of the demos to the superiority of a mixed diet over an unmixed one (and cf. 1286a29–30 on the advantages of a feast to which many people contribute).

150 Even if one accepts the tempting suggestion that Plato had in mind Lysistrata's wool-working image (above 122; Lane 1998, 164; Scheid and Svenbro 1996, 21–2 are somewhat guarded on the point), the same is true in that case – and of course there are important differences, too (below). For comic influence on Plato cf. nn. 79, 89–90 above.

151 Both points emphasized by Lane (1998) 167–71, 173; Blondell (2005) 67–71 goes

further on the former, arguing that women are actually excluded by the 'neutering' of weaving. It is a little surprising, given the frequent imagery of cleansing and purging elsewhere, that Plato barely alludes to this in terms of the image here (308c is general and anodyne) but describes it explicitly at 308e–9a; the significant implication is that culling is not part of statecraft as such: Lane (1998) 173. Aristotle uses the parallel of weaving to make the point about preparing the raw material entirely neutrally at *Pol.* 1325b40–6a5.

152 Complexity: Lane (1998) 171–82; diversity: Blondell (2005) 60–2, who also emphasizes collaboration: 'the central point of the paradigm of weaving is that the finished product requires the co-operation of many skilled agents besides the actual weaver' (67); NB also Lane (1998) 177–8 for the continuing role of the citizens. Clothing as a form of protection: *Plt.* 279cd, 280c-e, 288b; perhaps also evoked in the closing picture of the fabric 'covering all the other inhabitants in the cities' (311c3–4).

153 *Lg.* 734e–5a with England (1921), noted by Aristotle (*Pol.* 1265b19–21). In *R.* 557c the point of the comparison of democracy to a robe is its variegated nature (*pepoikilmenê*; LSJ s.v. *poikillô* I): for discussion see Rosenstock (1994) 377–8, Monoson (2000), 170–1, 223–6; Villacèque (2010) brings out well the critique underlying an implicit opposition between *poikilia* and *haplotês* (simplicity) that democracy is deceptive and lacks genuine coherence and consistency. There is also the suggestion that a concern with show and appearance reflects a self-indulgence and superficiality at odds with the proper function of weaving.

154 *Prostatês* and its cognates continue to be applied figuratively to leadership, most commonly with reference to political leadership, both singular (Ar. *Pl.* 920, [Andoc.] 4.12, X. *HG* 2.3.51, *Mem.* 3.6.2: the appearance in Xenophon of the verb *prostateuein* implies that the usage is becoming a commonplace; Theopompus *FGrH* 115 F121) and plural (Ar. *Ec.* 176, L. 13.7, 25.9, the last of factional leaders; X. *HG* 7.4.33, *Mem.* 2.8.4, Theopompus *FGrH* 115 F194): Isocrates (8.53) plays on the alternative technical use of the word for a metic's patron to make a point about the implications of the character of *prostatai* for the reputations of those they represent. The singular only appears once in the fifth-century formula *prostates tou demou* in a historical context (X. *HG* 1.7.2: Archedemos precipitating the Arginusae trial), though Plato applies this language in the *Republic* to the popular leader who turns into a tyrant (565c–e, 566cd and for the single leader cf. *Grg.* 519bc, *Lach.* 197e, *Phdr.* 241a; more generally, with an implication of plurality, *R.* 562d, 564d, 565a). In the fourth century the image is extended beyond the polis to denote the leading state in Greece, first Athens (L. 2.57), then Sparta (X. *HG* 3.1.3, 5.10, 14, *An.* 6.6.12, 7.1.30; cf. the aspirations of Mytilene within Lesbos: *HG* 4.8.28), hence the Spartans' position of patronage as *prostatai* of the Peace of Antalcidas (*HG* 5.1.36).

The only instance of the figurative use of the general is when Plato mentions him as one possible comparison for the gods in the *Laws* (905e); it may be that the military function of many authority figures, especially monarchs, made it otherwise ineffective as an image.

155 Socrates is made to say that one must adhere to the post in which one has been stationed by the god, be it philosophy (*Ap.* 28d–9a, an extended *a fortiori* argument) or life (*Phd.* 62b, where the word used is *phroura* ['guard-post']); the image need not be anachronistic: NB nn.157–8 below. On philosophical warfare, see Loraux (1989) 27–30, who sees an echo of ephebic service in *phroura*. *Taxis* is commonly used by Aristotle, too, often in a fairly neutral manner to denote the 'disposition' of a constitution (Rhodes 1981 on *Ath.Pol.* 3.1) but the implications are made clear

by his description of law as 'a *taxis*' (i.e. a form of order: *Pol.* 1287a18, 1326a29–30) and when he says that it is a sign of a good constitution when the demos 'maintains position in its *taxis*' (*Pol.* 1272b30–31) For an echo of the idea of the constitution as *taxis* (e.g. D.15.32–3; below) NB *Mx.* 246b (*taxis* must have the slightly more general sense of 'policy' or 'standards'): hence in *Lg.* 917c failure by a citizen to uphold the laws can be regarded as *prodosia* ('betrayal'). When Aristotle (*Pol.* 1270b34–5) echoes Plato's description (*R.* 548b; Aelian *VH* 13.38 attributes a similar expression to Alcibiades) of the Spartans 'running away from the laws', one naturally thinks of soldiers deserting, though the verb *apodidraskô* can also refer to slaves escaping their masters, which would suit the characterization of Law as *despotês* of the Spartans (Hdt. 7.104.4; below, n.190). The image of deserting one's post can be applied to standards or principles more generally: L. fr. 427 (Carey) concerns female morality.

156 D. 3.36: there is much play with *tax-* language in the peroration of this speech (3.34–6); the expression, which hints at the Athenian station at the battle of Plataea (Hdt. 9.26–8) is imitated at [D.] 13.34, and NB also the appeal to the same rhetoric in the ephebic oath and the oath of Plataea (R&O no.88 6–8, 23–31).

157 L. 31.28, cf. the *a fortiori* argument based on *prodosia* (treason) in 26; for the probable date (*c.* 398 BC) and the problems in pinning down the legal basis of the argumentation here see Carey (1989) 179, 197–200.

158 Evidence: Lycurg. 1.20; like Lysias and Aeschines (3.159, below), Lycurgus is playing on his opponent's literal desertion: contrariwise, at D. 21.120 Demosthenes turns back Meidias' literal accusation into a metaphorical denial of desertion (NB MacDowell (1990) *ad loc.*); juror: Aeschin. 3.7; cf. [D.] 25.4 for jurors 'occupying the position' of a prosecutor. We may compare the epigraphic expression for doing one's duty, *einai en tôi tetagmenôi* ('to be in the appointed [place]') which goes back to at least 426/5 BC: *IG* I³ 61.47 cf. *IG* II² 116.45–8, 212.63–5; *eutaxia* ('orderliness'), on the other hand, does not emerge as a 'cardinal virtue' in honorific inscriptions until after our period, being first attested in 304 BC, though its roots go back further into the fourth century: Whitehead (1993) 65 and n.101, 70. In the same way, Aristotle speaks of defence of the constitution as a kind of 'night watch' which needs the stimulus of fear (*Pol.* 1308a24–30); in the *Ath.Pol.*, it is the Areopagus which is said to have had the *taxis* of watching over (*diatêrein*) or guarding the laws (3.6, cf. 4.4, 25.2).

159 Courage and resolution: D. 8.71, 18.62 (Yunis 2001 has a good note *ad loc.*), 192, 221, 304; dangerous loyalty: 18.138 (note the contrasting juxtaposition of wrestling imagery: and cf. 15.31–2); consistency in crisis: 18.173 and cf. Plut. *Dem.* 13.1; on Aeschines: 19.9, 302. In a similar image, Solon is said to have imposed sanctions on the citizen who did not 'take up station (*thêtai ta opla*)' with one side or other in civil strife ([Arist.] *Ath.Pol.* 8.5. with Rhodes 1981). One wonders whether all Demosthenes' military imagery (he is by far the most frequent practitioner, even allowing for the volume of his corpus; around half of all his images in speeches before 346 come from this field: Ronnet 1951, 166) was intended consciously or otherwise to offset his rather inglorious military career in reality: compare the claim that in the matter of bribery, Athens avoided defeat where he was concerned (18.247). It is however noteworthy that military imagery is more frequent in *de Corona* than *F.L.*, while for commercial imagery the pattern is reversed (above, n.73). Cf. Christ (1998) 148–9 on the use of military imagery by volunteer prosecutors: he notes a further term, *boêthein* ('come/run to the aid of').

160 Aeschines' riposte: 3.75, 159; policies of others: D. 14.35, *Ep.* 3.2, 15, 29, 32; [D.] 58.45; siding with the enemy: D. 18.138, 292.

161 See MacDowell (1978) 160 for the legal sanctions; the gravity of the offence is also shown by the fact that to allege it falsely was covered by the law of slander (ibid. 127–9).
162 Note especially the contrast between drawing pay (*mistharnein*) and duty at 18.138, and for *misthophorein*, the normal word for mercenary service see D. 9.14, [D.] 17.11; bodyguards ([D.] 17.12, 25) were normally mercenaries. Isocrates plays on the same idea but with the opposite effect in his *Helen* when he describes Theseus as 'bodyguarded by the goodwill of the citizens' (10.37); 2.21 makes a similar point more neutrally in his instruction of Nicocles (NB Usher 1990 *ad loc.* for Roman parallels) and cf. X. *Cyr.* 8.7.13 for loyal friends as a king's truest and most reliable sceptre.
163 *polemô*: X. *HG* 2.3.48 (~ Critias' charge: §29). The closest parallel in earlier literature seems to be E. *Ion* 1385–6, where *polemô* means 'disagree with'; as with the language of *erôs* (above 134n.83) the change in grammatical format from *polemios eimi* ('I am an enemy of/hostile to') makes a significant difference. For the spread of military imagery into other fields compare Antisthenes' use of military imagery for philosophy (frr.71, 88, 90; Rankin 1986, 116–7); the comparison of disease to warfare alluded to in Pl. *Ti.* 88e, *Lg.* 905e is already present in Hippocratic writing by the late fifth century: Padel (1992) 56, Jouanna (1999) 330–1.
164 Demosthenes and pro-Macedonians: 18.31, 19.115; Meidias: 21.29; other politicians: 22.61, 63 and also found in [D.] 25.38, 58.44, Isoc. 15.136, Aeschin. 1.64, 135 (*katadromên*); for non-political quarrels cf. L. 32.22, Is. 1.15. At 3.35 Aeschines seems to imply that Ctesiphon is going to engage in siege warfare (*epoisei technas tois nomois*); note also Demosthenes' claim that it has never been his policy to whet (*akonôn*) the city against its own breast (*Ep.* 2.11).
165 Contrast the direct invective of Aeschines' denunciation of Demosthenes as a 'cutpurse' (3.207) and 'pirate' (3.253). The recurrent theme in Xenophon's *Hiero* that the tyrant is at war with his subjects (e.g. 2.8–18, 4.11, 6.7–8) is a metaphor that verges on the literal, and the same is true of his account of the conspiracy of Cinadon (*HG* 3.3.4–5): the seer's warning that the Spartans are, as it were, in the midst of their enemies, and Cinadon's description of the minority Spartiates as 'enemies' suggest an impending *stasis* in which the polis fragments into two mutually hostile communities.
166 Din. 1.64, referring to D. 18.299 (the word does not appear there, but does so at Aeschin. 3.236). Wankel (1976) 1269–74 has a detailed and illuminating discussion of the image; Demosthenes had already used it in a less developed form in *F.L.* (19.84); Aeschin. 3.84; Demad. fr.25 De Falco.
167 Lycurg. 1.47, speaking of the Athenians who died at Chaironeia; for the earlier tradition see above 89, 123.
168 Pl. *Lg.* 793c, *Plt.* 301e–2a (cf. *Lg.* 736e); D. 2.10. The latter two combine architectural and maritime imagery, while at *Lg.* 945c Plato juxtaposes the undergirding of a ship and sinews in a body which create a unity that amounts to *dikê*. Elsewhere, the terminology of bonding could refer either to physiology or architecture: *sundesmon* (*R.* 520a, *Lg.* 921c; NB *LSJ* s.v.v. σύνδεσμος, σύνδεσις, συνδέω). At *Lg.* 737a7 he applies the Homeric phrase *herma poleôs* (above 85) to a constitutional principle, while making the Nocturnal Council the anchor of the city (961c) comes close to integrating them into its fabric.
169 *Thêria*: of rivals in general: D. 18.322, 24.143, [D.] 25.8); of individuals: [D.] 25.31, 95 (referring to Aristogeiton 'the Dog'), 58.49; Aeschin. 2.20 (attributed to

Demosthenes), 34, 3.182 cf. 2.146; Din. 1.10, 2.10 (Aristogeiton again); Aristogeiton called Lycurgus and Demosthenes *knôdala*: fr.5 B-S. *Thêria* is also found in non-political contexts: D.34.52, [D.] 35.8, 43.83. Sycophants: Harvey (1990) 109, who specifies monkey, wolf, ox, dog, snake, scorpion and poisonous spider. Politicians are an assortment of animals in Pl. *Plt.* 291ab (with Rowe 1995 on b2).

170 Idrieus: Androtion *FGrH* 324 F72 = Arist. *Rh.* 1406b27–9; for the figure of the dangerous dog cf. X. *An.* 5.8.24. Thirty: X. *HG* 2.4.41, alluding to a practice established by a law of Solon (Plut. *Sol.* 24.3). Pernée (1979) sees a further image from hunting dogs in *perielêluthen* (the MS reading): the oligarchs have first been out-manoeuvred by their prey, and then handed over to them by their former masters. Dogs are not only dangerous when biting: Hippias of Erythrai (*FGrH* 421 F1) has a tale of flatterers called *prokunes* ('fawning dogs'), who overthrew an unsuspecting king.

171 Hyp. fr. 80 Jensen; Aesop 269a Perry = Arist. *Rh.* 1393b22–4a1; Plut. *Mor.* 790cd applies the fable slightly differently, to 'young men thirsty for fame and power'. Isocrates' comparison of rhetors to *korakes* ('crows': fr.15 = Apophth. δ1 Blass) is perhaps not more than a pun on the name of the early Sicilian rhetorician Korax, but also exemplifies the negative use of animal imagery.

172 Arist. *Pol.* 1284a15–17 = Antisthenes fr.100. Cf. D.S. 19.25.5–7 for another fable (related by Eumenes of Cardia) which underlines the positive value of possessing teeth.

173 D. 18.296 (translation from Yunis 2001; NB his notes on the chapter for the bravura sequence of images), 3.31; Aeschin. 3.166: notoriously, none of the phrases cited there appears in the published version of *de Corona*. Compare the demand for the excision or burning out of Aristogeiton like a cancer or ulcer ([D.] 25.95) and Aeschines' denunciation of Demosthenes for opening new wounds (*helkopoieis*: 3.208; above 73).

174 The phrase *anatetmêkasi tines ta klêmata tou dêmou* appears in the MSS of Aeschines but not in the citation in D.H. *Dem.* 57, and so is omitted by the Budé editors: however, it is not likely to be a marginal glossing of the preceding viticultural image, which is a simple accusation of peculation, and the fact that Herodian *de fig.* (Walz *Rhet. Gr.* VIII 590) preserves the word *klêmata* is in its favour; for the resonance of the destruction of growing vines, compare Arist. *Ach.* e.g. 183 (with Olson 2002), 233, 512, 984–5. *Phormorraphoumetha*: 'stitched up' = hampered (so *LSJ* s.v.), and the following phrase seems to come from the same field; NB Aeschin. 3.207 for D. as cutter-up of the constitution.

175 The farmer is one of the traditional figures to which the gods might be compared at Pl. *Lg.* 906a and attributed to Protagoras as a model for wise men and good speakers at *Tht.* 167bc; cf. Athena's description of herself as a gardener: A. *Eum.* 911–2. Meletus weeding like a good gardener: Pl. *Euthph.* 2d–3a; ears of corn are a familiar lesson for tyrants at Arist. *Pol.* 1284a, 1311a20–2, 1313a40–1, but applicable also to oligarchies and democracies (with particular reference to ostracism) and even imperial powers at *Pol.* 1284a26-b3; Aristotle also reverses the roles of Thrasybulus and Periander, perhaps because the latter as one of the Seven Sages seemed better fitted to the didactic persona: Felton (1998) 46 n.16; on Aristotle's handling of the anecdote see further Forsdyke (1999) 368–70. Tyranny a plant: Pl. *R.* 565cd (cf. Hdt. 1.60.1, 64.1, imitated in [Arist.] *Ath.Pol.* 14.3, for the 'rooting' of Peisistratus' tyranny); *sperma* and/or *rhiza* of trouble: D. 24.154, [D.] 25.48, Hyp. fr.204.

176 Jurors as *phulakes* of the laws: [D.] 25.6, Aeschin. 1.7; of the democracy: Aeschin.

3.7; of both: Din. 3.16; so also judges' power is *nomôn phulaka* at Pl. *Plt.* 305c. Magistrates: L. 27.3, though here the gamekeepers have turned to poaching; Isoc. 7.47 develops the notion of legal system as deterrence and likewise mentions punishment, though he is dismissive of communities which simply establish laws as barriers (*emphragmata*) to wrongdoing (7.40). At L. 25.28 it is claimed that abiding by oaths and contracts protects democracy (cf. below, n.182). Compare the language of guardianship and deposit on trust: above 27–8.

Law can itself be characterized as a contract ([D.] 25.16, Hyp. 3.30, perhaps also *Com. Adesp.* fr.1094.17 = *PHeid.* 182 [Gigante 1957]); Aristotle offers this as a possible argument in *Rh.* 1376b7–11, but dismisses the conception of the laws of a polis as merely a 'treaty' at *Pol.* 1280b6–12, and such a view is likely to have been superseded by the increasing characterization in this period of Law as a personality and agent (below).

177 Guardians against illegality: [D.] 58.34, 46; of the constitution: Isoc. 8.53; of the democracy: Aeschin. 3.250; watching the watchdogs: [D.] 26.22. In the *Hiero* (6.10), Xenophon, exploiting an ambiguity in *phulattô*, contrasts free cities, <u>protected</u> by sentries who are themselves <u>overseen</u> by the laws, with the lack of security of a tyrant, the implication being that the tyrant's arrogation of law to himself (a stock charge) actually serves to undermine his own security.

178 Likewise in the *Republic*, although the Guardians (*Phulakes*) are initially introduced as having a military function (374b-e), that role is hived off to the Auxiliaries (*Epikouroi* 414b, described at 414d3 as 'soldiers'), while the character of the Guardians as 'best' and 'most protective of the city' (412c) is characterized in more general terms (412c–3c; for the distinction cf. 434ab): hence it is natural to regard subsequent references to the Guardians as *phulakes* as substantially figurative (e.g. 421a, 463ab, 464c, 503b, 504c, 506a), though the same word is also applied to the Auxiliaries as watchdogs (e.g. 451d; note the jingle *phulakes ... skulakes*); for the figurative usage cf. *Ti.* 17d, *Lg.* 632c, 754d, 920a, 964b-d, 965b, 966b, 969c: in *Lg.* in particular the reference is frequently to law(s) and in Book XII the effect is to spell out the implications of the title *Nomophulakes* (which is also attested as an office at Athens by the 320s: Din. frr.6.11, 14.2).

179 Liturgy: Is. fr.30 Thalheim, cf. L. 21.19; *chorêgos*: D. 9.60, 19.216 (both of Philip); of politicians exploiting war for personal gain at Aeschin. 2.79; cf. the verb at [D.] 11.6. Symmories: D. 2.29, repeated with minor variations at [D.] 13.20; for their organization see de Ste Croix (1953) 56–62 (esp. 60), whose account implies a pun on the technical and non-technical senses of *hêgemôn*.

180 D. 1.28, 8.69, 18.189 (with Wankel 1976, 899–90), 245, cf. 18.196; 18.235 (Philip); other instances are vaguer, and in *Pro.* 53.1 *tas euthunas didonai* amounts to 'pay the price'. Alexis fr. 264 alludes to the system in constructing a comic paradox: the speaker argues that one is better off disenfranchised than married, since while those in the former condition cannot rule others, married men are not even their own masters and have to submit to daily *euthunai*. Logistai: 18.229 with Yunis (2001).

181 *Synêgoroi*: Aeschin. 3.37. Compare also n.154 above for Isoc. 8.53 on *prostatai* (and NB his use of *metoikein* at 4.105 to mean 'have no political rights' in an oligarchy) and 26–7 for Hyperides' ironic use of *tamias* and *epistatês*.

182 D. 18.170, Demad. fr.36 De Falco 9 (cf. Lycurg. 1.79 for oath 'holding together [*sunechon*]' the democracy), Aeschin. 3.199–200; for law as *kanôn* cf. Lycurg. 1.9 and above 135n.93; Aristotle objects to the image of the law as a measure (*metron*) of justice at *Top.* 140a7–8.

183 Timocrates: D. 24.212-4: there is anachronism in his reference to proceedings for *nomon mê epitêdeion theinai* as well as the association of Solon with coinage. Assembly as assayer: *Pro.* 32.4 (*dokimasai*: *LSJ* s.v. δοκιμάζω I.1); *Pro.* 55.3 (*zugon*: *LSJ* s.v. IVa cf. L. 10.18); juror as assayer: Arist. *Rh.* 1375b3-6; Leptines: 20.167. See the discussion in Kurke (1999) 317-20, who notes that it was around this time that Athens introduced small-denomination bronze coinage. For the quality of Athenian coinage see X. *Vect.* 3.2: Athenian concern to maintain its reputation is made plain by the law on approvers of silver coinage passed in 375/4 BC: R&O no. 25; the language of scrutiny and approval (*dokimazein*: ll.6, 14) could also be applied to citizenship: Kurke (1999) 310-13 (and note also *kibdêlos* 'counterfeit, fraudulent' [11] and *kôdônizô* 'test [metal]': Ar. *Ran.* 723, D. 19.167 with MacDowell 2000).

184 For examples in the later fifth century see above 145n.156. The increasingly entrenched position of law in the fourth century (above n.2) is reflected in the frequency of prosecutions for unconstitutional proposal (*graphê paranomôn*), a process first attested in 415 BC: Hansen 1991, 205-12. That procedure is itself invoked figuratively by Aristotle when he says that many jurists 'bring a charge of illegality (*hôsper rhêtora graphontai paranomôn*') against the doctrine of legal slavery (*Pol.* 1255a7-9). Cp. his use of *proedria* ('front-row seats', i.e. precedence: *Pol.* 1309a28, cf. 1292a9) for figurative allusion to the language of Athenian institutions; the comparison of 'the middle' to an arbitrator (*diaitêtês*: *Pol.* 1297a5-6) might be another case, since the Athenians had a system of public arbitrators: [Arist.] *Ath. Pol.* 53.2-6.

185 Guardians (of morals): Aeschin. 1.14 and cf. Din. 1.86, where the personified Meter is guardian (*phulax*) of Athens' public records in her temple, the Metroön; *sôizein*: D. 24.156, 216, [D.] 25.21, Aeschin. 1.5; democratic cities are administered (*dioikountai*) by the laws: Aeschin. 1.4, and cf. the same verb at [D.] 59.115; laws rule like magistrates (*tois tês poleôs archousi nomois*): [D.] 26.5); drive the democracy: [D.] 25.20. Laws as prosecutors: [D.] 59.115, reducing the case to The Laws v. Neaira; as executioners: L. 1.26 with Carey (1989); collaborate with prosecutor and democracy: Aeschin. 3.197-8 cf. 202, where they are linked with the democracy and the jurors; even legislate: [D.] 25.16; this somewhat far-fetched conceit is matched slightly earlier in the speech (11) by an emotive appeal to support Eunomia 'who preserves all cities and lands' and Dike (seen in Hesiodic terms, though the account is attributed to Orpheus). NB also the law as educator in Arist. *Pol.* 1287b25-6, and Rhodes (1981) 34 and n.177 for frequent instances of the law(s) issuing orders in [Arist.] *Ath.Pol*; likewise law(s) speak, give orders and forbid actions in *EN* 1129b14-24.

186 Reading *tôi tois nomois ischuein* ('that your power is derived from the laws'): see MacDowell (1990) *ad loc.*; perhaps the elite status of the litigants made the laws a more sympathetic victim?

187 Agathon: Pl. *Smp.* 196c; Alcidamas: Arist. *Rh.* 1406a17-23: it is a moot point whether the former depends on the latter (Dover 1980 prints it as a quotation) or whether the phrase is a sophistic commonplace; Pl. *Ep.* 8 354bc; Demad. fr.35 De Falco; Pl. *Prot.* 337d; cf. also L. 2.19 (above 21n.77) and NB already Anon. Iambl. 6.1 (above 145n.158). Plato's characterization of law in *Plt.* 294bc as a stubborn and ignorant man who permits no contravention of his rule reflects the depreciation of codified law in that dialogue.

188 For voluntary servitude to the laws as masters see esp. *Lg.* 698bc, 699c, 700a with the discussion of Schofield (2006) 78-82, noting the Herodotean echo in *despotis* ... *Aidôs* (698b5-6) and 715cd; refusal to accept it (701bc) and subjection of the laws to men (856b) threaten corresponding danger. The same policy is urged on the

Sicilians in Plato's letters (*Ep. 7* 334c, 337a, *Ep. 8* 355e), where the suggestion that the victors should make themselves more subject to the laws than the vanquished (337cd) perhaps hints at the idea of self-mastery as rule. Aristotle in commending the rule of law recommends that individual rulers should be appointed as guardians and servants (*hypêretas*) of the laws (*Pol.* 1287a20–2; for the milder terminology cf. Pl. *Lg.* 715c) and argues that subjection to the constitution is not *douleia* but *eleutheria* (*Pol.* 1310a35); compare his paradoxical description of the Orthagorid tyrants as 'enslaved to the law in many respects' (1315b15–16); X. *Ages.* 7.2 with Brock (2007) 209–10 for the resonances of *latreuein*; *endoxos douleia*: Ael. *VH* 2.20, attributed to Antigonos Gonatas; and above 30. The concept of the law as master presumably also underlies the image of the citizen who attempts to evade his liturgic responsibilities as a runaway slave (*drapeteuein* [D.] 42. 25, 32); for the image of running away from the law as parent see above n.155.

189 X. *Cyr.* 8.1.22 (tr. Miller [Loeb]); Farber (1979) 502–7 takes a pragmatic view of the concept as necessitated by the practicalities of expansive imperial rule. Cf. also *Lac.* 8.4 for the ephors' capacity for close supervision, like judges at the games (above n.47); fuller discussion above 14. Aristotle describes the man of outstanding virtue who should be made king as 'law in himself' (*Pol.* 1284a13–14, 1288a3); the principle is anticipated when he says that the man of judgement is *nomos heautôi*, i.e. can legislate for himself, regarding appropriate social behaviour (specifically, ridicule: *EN* 1128a32).

190 Pi. fr.169a.1–2 with discussion above 19n.52; Hdt. 7.104.4. Stier (1927–8) 250–2 saw a reaction to sophistic exegesis of the Pindar passage in the fourth-century figuring of law as legitimate king; for a more detailed exegesis of the influence of the passage, see Gigante (1956), especially in this context 253–67 on Plato, and NB also Svenbro (1993) 123–44 (stimulating if a shade fanciful).

191 *Plt.* 303b: ideal constitution is to be distinguished 'like a god from men'; *Lg.* 965c and perhaps 630e1 (so the scholiast *ad loc.* and Stephanus); submission to laws as to gods: *Lg.* 762e cf. 715c4 with England (1921); in *Ep. 8* he observes that the only moderate servitude is to the gods 'and law is a god for self-controlled men' (354e). Aristotle likewise reports the anti-monarchic argument that the rule of law is the rule of God and reason (*nous*) alone (*Pol.* 1287a28–30).

192 Lycurgus: *Phdr.*258c, *Lg.* 691e (and cf. X. *Resp.Lac.*15.9 on his funeral honours for Spartan kings); Nocturnal Council: *Lg.* 966d, 969b cf.945c; divine honours for Guardians: *R.* 540bc; *sôtêras te kai epikourous*: 463b with Adam 1902; for the title *Sôtêr*, see above 22n.88. On heroization see further above 13–14.

193 *FGrH* 124 F31, alluding to Hom. *Il.* 13.27–30 (the scholia in fact cite Callisthenes on 13.29); however, while obeisance would be appropriate to a god, it does not feature in the epic and more likely refers to Alexander's increasing claim to be lord of Persia (so Bosworth 1980 on Arr. *An.* 1.26.2). See also the careful discussion of Pearson (1960) 36–8, suggesting that Callisthenes was preparing his ancient readers for more explicit evidence of divinity at Siwah. The episode in Pamphylia gave rise to the later conceit that rulers had a quasi-divine power to control the weather: Hardie (1986) 206–7; it may be significant that this idea also featured in Achaemenid royal ideology: Briant (1996) 251–2.

Epilogue

The transition to the Hellenistic world marks a fundamental transformation in the political landscape, a shift to an environment dominated by monarchy which was to persist into the early modern period. As a result, political theory loses the plurality and dialectic between constitutional options which have characterized it hitherto and becomes almost exclusively concerned with the ideology of kingship. Both the radical change in the historical context and the fact that the ensuing period has been well studied make this a natural point at which to conclude this study.[1] Yet because political thought from this point onward concentrated so much on the person of the king, and because image and imagery therefore came to play a more prominent role, much of the groundwork for the kingship theory of the Hellenistic and later periods had already been done and the foundations, including its characteristic imagery, were already in place.[2]

The characteristic representations of the leader, now specifically concentrated on the figure of the monarch, were to remain in use for two millennia and more, and across a remarkable diversity of geographical, historical and cultural situations. If it is not surprising that Louis XIV, whose propaganda deliberately drew on classical models, should have been depicted in paintings as a helmsman,[3] it is remarkable that Joseph Mobutu, President of almost land-locked Zaire, should have chosen to borrow from Mao the title of The Helmsman. It would seem that by now the helmsman has become an abstracted ideal to which a ruler will aspire, whatever their situation in reality. The other models in the Greek toolkit, too, have retained their currency and lent themselves to adaptation to changing circumstances: thus the father-figure has in recent American politics bifurcated, according to the speaker's ideological slant, into the 'strict father' and the 'nurturant parent'.[4] More subtly, Yulia Tymoshenko, then prime minister of Ukraine, reflected the changing role of women in politics when she laid claim to the role of parent as leader for the mother, while simultaneously evoking the more traditional analogy between domestic and political administration which goes back to Lysistrata: 'You know how, when a family breaks up, in most instances the child stays with the mother? She is the more reliable caretaker. It is the same with a country. I simply think that we are more reliable…'.[5] More conventional – in a characteristic way – was the evocation of military and maritime imagery directed at Eduard Shevardnadze in the crisis of the Soviet Union: 'Mr Shevardnadze should stay at his post and not be a "deserter". [Another speaker claimed that he] was someone "who recognized Gorbachev's ship is sinking"'.[6] Whether traditional or adapted, such examples exemplify the deep-seated and perennial appeal of the images of community and leadership first formulated for us by the Greeks: whatever changes we may see in the conduct of politics in the modern world, the father and the watchdog, the helmsman and the doctor are likely to be with us for generations to come.

Notes

1 Scholarship in the field goes back at least to Goodenough (1928); more recently, see Walbank (1984) and Hahm (2000), both with extensive further bibliography.
2 Walbank (1984) 75–84 traces the antecedents of monarchic ideology.
3 Burke (1992) 62–3.
4 Lakoff (2002) chs 5–6. For Mobutu as (disputed) father see above 40n.36. It is striking that that the standing as father-figure of even a leader as widely admired as Nelson Mandela could be contested on the basis of their personal familial circumstances: 'One of the demonstrators was brandishing a poster with the words scrawled across it: "What happened to your family? You can never be the father to a nation!"' (*Guardian*, 5 November 1991).
5 Quoted in an interview in the *Financial Times*, 16/17 August 2008.
6 *Guardian*, 22 December 1990. Meichsner (1983) cites examples of the ship of state in the politics of 1960s West Germany; see also above 62n.5.

Bibliography

Adam, J. (1902). *The Republic of Plato*. Cambridge: Cambridge University Press.
Adcock, F. E. (1953). 'Greek and Macedonian kingship', *PBA* 39, 163–80.
Adkins, A. W. H. (1985). *Poetic craft in the early Greek elegists*. Chicago: Chicago University Press.
Adrados, F. R. (1999–2003). *History of the Graeco-Latin fable*, trans. by L. A. Ray, 3 Vols. Leiden: Brill.
Alföldi, A. (1952–4). 'Die Geburt der kaiserlichen Bildsymbolik. 3. Parens patriae', *MH* 9, 204–43; 10, 103–24; 11, 133–69.
Allen, D. S. (2000). *The world of Prometheus: the politics of punishing in democratic Athens*. Princeton: Princeton University Press.
Allen, T. W., Halliday, W. R. and Sikes, E. E. (1936). *The Homeric Hymns*, 2nd edn. Oxford: Clarendon Press.
Anderson, W. S. (1966). 'Horace *Carm*. 1.14: What kind of ship?' *CPh* 61, 84–98.
Anhalt, E. K. (1993). *Solon the singer: politics and poetics*. Lanham: Rowman & Littlefield.
Annas, J. (1981). *An introduction to Plato's Republic*. Oxford: Clarendon Press.
Arnott, W. G. (1991). 'A lesson from the *Frogs*', *G&R* 38, 18–23.
—(2007). *Birds in the ancient world from A to Z*. London: Routledge.
Ashmole, B. (1972). *Architect and sculptor in classical Greece*. New York: New York University Press.
Atran, S. (2002). *In gods we trust: the evolutionary landscape of religion*. Oxford: Oxford University Press.
Austin, M. M. (1990). 'Greek tyrants and the Persians 546–479 B.C.' *CQ* 40, 289–306.
Bakewell, G. (2008). 'Aeschylus' *Supplices* 11–12: Danaus as ΠΕΣΣΟΝΟΜΩΝ', *CQ* 58, 303–7.
Bakola, E. (2010). *Cratinus and the art of comedy*. Oxford: Oxford University Press.
Balme, D. M. (2002). *Aristotle Historia Animalium*. Cambridge: Cambridge University Press.
Bambrough, R. (1956). 'Plato's political analogies' in P. Laslett (ed.), *Philosophy, politics and society*. Oxford: Blackwell, 98–115.
Barlow, S. A. (1971). *The imagery of Euripides: a study in the dramatic use of pictorial language*. London: Methuen.
Barnett, R. D. (1948). 'Early Greek and oriental ivories', *JHS* 68, 1–25.
Barrett, W. S. (1973). 'Pindar's Twelfth *Olympian* and the fall of the Deinomenidai', *JHS* 93, 23–35.
Beck, F. A. G. (1964). *Greek education: 450–350 B.C.* London: Methuen.
Bernhardt, R. (1987). 'Die Entstehung der Legende von der tyrannenfeindlichen Aussenpolitik Spartas im sechsten und fünften Jahrhundert v. Chr.', *Historia* 36, 257–89.
Blondell, R. (2005). 'From fleece to fabric: weaving culture in Plato's *Statesman*' in *Oxford studies in ancient philosophy* XXVIII. Oxford: Oxford University Press, 23–75.
Blundell, M. W. (1989). *Helping friends and harming enemies: a study in Sophocles and Greek ethics*. Cambridge: Cambridge University Press.

Boardman, J. (1982). 'Herakles, Theseus and Amazons' in D. Kurtz and B. Sparkes (eds) *The Eye of Greece: Studies in the art of Athens*. Cambridge: Cambridge University Press, 1–28.
—(1998). *Early Greek vase painting*. London: Thames & Hudson.
Boedeker, D. and Raaflaub, K. (1998). *Democracy, empire, and the arts in fifth-century Athens*. Cambridge, MA: Harvard University Press.
Bond, G. W. (1981). *Euripides Heracles*. Oxford: Oxford University Press.
Borbein, A. H. (1996). 'Polykleitos' in O. Palagia and J. J. Pollitt (eds) *Personal styles in Greek sculpture*. Cambridge: Cambridge University Press, 66–90.
Bordes, J. (1982) *Politeia dans la pensée grecque jusqu'à Aristote*. Paris: Les Belles Lettres.
Bosworth, A. B. (1980). *A historical commentary on Arrian's History of Alexander I*. Oxford: Clarendon Press.
—(1988). *Conquest and empire: the reign of Alexander the Great*. Cambridge: Cambridge University Press.
—(1995). *A historical commentary on Arrian's History of Alexander II*. Oxford: Clarendon Press.
—(1996). *Alexander and the East. The tragedy of triumph*. Oxford: Clarendon Press.
Bourriot, F. (1995). *Kalos kagathos – kalokagathia: d'un terme de propagande de sophistes à une notion sociale et philosophique: étude d'histoire athénienne*. Hildesheim: Olms.
Bowie, A. M. (1993). *Aristophanes: myth, ritual and comedy*. Cambridge: Cambridge University Press.
Bowie, E. L. (1986). 'Early Greek elegy, symposium and public festival', JHS 106, 13–35.
Boyer, P. (2001). *Religion explained: the human instincts that fashion gods, spirits and ancestors*. London: Heinemann.
Braswell, B. K. (1988). *A commentary on the fourth Pythian ode of Pindar*. Berlin: de Gruyter.
Braund, D. (2000). 'Friends and foes: monarchs and monarchy in fifth-century Athenian democracy' in R. Brock and S. Hodkinson (eds) *Alternatives to Athens*. Oxford: Oxford University Press, 103–18.
Briant, P. (1996). *Histoire de l'Empire perse: de Cyrus à Alexandre*. Paris: Fayard.
Brickhouse, T. C. and Smith, N. D. (1994). *Plato's Socrates*. Oxford: Oxford University Press.
Broadhead, H. D. (1960). *The Persae of Aeschylus*. Cambridge: Cambridge University Press.
Brock, R. (1991). 'The emergence of democratic ideology', Historia 40, 160–9.
—(1994). 'The labour of women in classical Athens', CQ 44, 336–46.
—(2000). 'Sickness in the body politic' in E. Marshall and V. Hope (eds) *Death and disease in the Ancient City*. London: Routledge, 24–34.
—(2003). 'Authorial voice and narrative management in Herodotus' in P. Derow and R. Parker (eds) *Herodotus and his world*. Oxford: Clarendon Press, 3–16.
—(2004a). 'Political imagery in Herodotus' in V. Karageorghis and I. Taifacos (eds) *The world of Herodotus*. Nicosia: Foundation Anastasios G. Leventis, 169–77.
—(2004b). 'Xenophon's political imagery' in C. J. Tuplin (ed.) *Xenophon and his world*. Stuttgart: Steiner, 2004, 247–57.
—(2006). 'The body as a political organism in Greek thought' in F. Prost and J. Wilgaux (eds), *Penser et représenter le corps dans l'Antiquité*. Rennes: Presses Universitaires de Rennes, 351–9.
—(2007). 'Figurative slavery in Greek thought' in A. Serghidou (ed.) *Peur de l'esclave – Peur de l'esclavage en Méditerranée ancienne / Fear of Slaves – Fear of enslavement*

in the ancient Mediterranean (XXIXe colloque du GIREA, Rethymnon, 4–7 novembre 2004). Besançon: Presses universitaires de Franche-Comté, 217–24.
Brosius, M. (2000). *The Persian empire from Cyrus II to Artaxerxes I. LACTOR* 16, London: London Association of Classical Teachers.
Brown, E. L. (1974). 'Cleon caricatured on a Corinthian cup', *JHS* 94, 166–70.
Budelmann, F. (2000). *The language of Sophocles: communality, communication and involvement*. Cambridge: Cambridge University Press.
Bultrighini, U. (1999). *'Maladetta democrazia': studi su Crizia*. Alessandria: Edizioni dell'Orso.
Burke, P. (1992). *The fabrication of Louis XIV*. New Haven: Yale University Press.
Buxton, R. G. A. (1982). *Persuasion in Greek tragedy: a study of Peitho*. Cambridge: Cambridge University Press.
Cairns, D. L. (2001). 'Introduction' in *id*. (ed.) *Oxford readings in Homer's Iliad*. Oxford: Clarendon Press, 1–56.
—(2012). 'Introduction' in *id*. (ed.) *Tragedy and Archaic Greek Thought*. Swansea: Classical Press of Wales, ix–liv.
Cairns, F. (1982). 'Cleon and Pericles: a suggestion', *JHS* 102, 203–4.
Calhoun, G. M. (1935). 'Zeus the father in Homer', *TAPA* 66, 1–17.
Cambiano, G. (1982). 'Patologia e metafora politica. Alcmeone, Platone, Corpus Hippocraticum', *Elenchos* 3, 219–36.
Camp, J. McK II (2000). 'Walls and the *polis*' in P. Flensted-Jensen, T. H. Nielsen and L. Rubinstein (eds) *Polis and politics: Studies in ancient Greek history*. Copenhagen: Museum Tusculanum Press, 41–57.
Campbell, D. A. (1967). *Greek lyric poetry: a selection of early Greek lyric, elegaic and iambic poetry*. London: Macmillan.
—(1982–93). *Greek Lyric*. Loeb Classical Library, 5 Vols. Cambridge, MA: Harvard University Press.
—(1986). 'Ship imagery in the *Oedipus Tyrannos*' in M. J. Cropp, E. Fantham and S. E. Scully (eds) *Greek tragedy and its legacy: essays presented to D. J. Conacher*. Calgary: University of Calgary Press, 115–20.
Carey, C. (1980). 'The epilogue of Pindar's Fourth Pythian', *Maia* 32, 143–52.
—(1981). *A commentary on five odes of Pindar: Pythian 2, Pythian 9, Nemean 1, Nemean 7, Isthmian 8*. New York: Arno Press.
—(1989). *Lysias: selected speeches*. Cambridge: Cambridge University Press.
Carey, C. and Reid, R. A. (1985). *Demosthenes: Selected private speeches*. Cambridge: Cambridge University Press.
Carlier, P. (1984). *La royauté en Grèce avant Alexandre*. Strasbourg: AECR.
Cartledge, P. (1990). 'Fowl play: a curious lawsuit in classical Athens (Antiphon XVI, frr. 57–9 Thalheim)' in P. Cartledge, P. Millett and S. Todd (eds) *Nomos: essays in Athenian law, politics and society*. Cambridge: Cambridge University Press, 41–61.
—(1993). *The Greeks: a portrait of Self and Others*. Oxford: Oxford University Press.
—(1998). 'Writing the history of archaic Greek political thought' in N. Fisher and H. van Wees (eds) *Archaic Greece: new approaches and new evidence*. London: Duckworth/Classical Press of Wales, 379–99.
Carver, T. and Pikalo, J. (eds) (2008). *Political language and metaphor: interpreting **and** changing the world*. London: Routledge.
Caserta, C. (2007). 'Normale e patologico nel corpo e nella polis. *Isonomia* e armonia fra VI e V secolo' in G. Daverio Rocchi (ed.) *Tra concordia e pace*. Milan: Cisalpino, 65–87.

Cassio, A. C. (1985). 'Old Persian *Marîka-*, Eupolis *Marikas* and Aristophanes *Knights*', *CQ* 35, 38–42.
Casson, L. (1971). *Ships and seamanship in the ancient world*. Princeton: Princeton University Press.
Castriota, D. (1992). *Myth, ethos and actuality: official art in fifth-century B.C. Athens*. Madison, WI: University of Wisconsin Press.
Catenacci, C. (1991). 'Il τύραννος e i suoi strummenti: alcune metafore "tiranniche" nella *Pitica* II (vv. 72–96) di Pindaro', *QUCC* 39, 85–95.
Cawkwell, G. L. (1981). 'The King's Peace', *CQ* 31, 69–83.
Ceccarelli, P. (1993). 'Sans thalassocratie, pas de démocratie? La rapport entre thalassocratie et démocratie à Athènes dans la discussion du Ve et IVe siècle', *Historia* 42, 444–70.
Chantraine, P. (1968). *Dictionnaire étymologique de la langue grecque*. Paris: Klincksieck.
Charteris-Black, J. (2005). *Politicians and rhetoric: the persuasive power of metaphor*. Basingstoke: Palgrave Macmillan.
Chiasson, C. (1986). 'The Herodotean Solon', *GRBS* 27, 249–62.
Christ, M. R. (1998). *The litigious Athenian*. Baltimore: Johns Hopkins University Press.
Clarke Kosak, J. (2000). '*Polis nosousa*: Greek ideas about the city and disease in the fifth century BC' in E. Marshall and V. Hope (eds) *Death and disease in the ancient city*. London: Routledge, 35–54.
Clay, J. S. (1989). *The politics of Olympus. Form and meaning in the major Homeric hymns*. Princeton: Princeton University Press.
Coffee, N. (2006). 'The ΦΟΡΤΗΓΟΙ of Theognis 667–82', *CQ* 56, 304–5.
Cohen, E. E. (2002). 'An unprofitable masculinity' in P. Cartledge, E. E. Cohen and L. Foxhall (eds) *Money, labour and land: approaches to the economies of ancient Greece*. London: Routledge, 100–12.
Collard, C. (1975). *Euripides Supplices*. Groningen: Bouma's Boekhuis.
Collard, C., Cropp, M. J. and Lee, K. H. (1995). *Euripides Selected fragmentary plays*. Warminster: Aris & Phillips.
Collins, C. (1996). *Authority figures: metaphors of mastery from the Iliad to the Apocalypse*. Lanham: Rowman & Littlefield.
Conacher, D. J. (1980). *Aeschylus' Prometheus Bound. A literary commentary*. Toronto: University of Toronto Press.
Connor, W. R. (1971). *The new politicians of fifth-century Athens*. Princeton: Princeton University Press.
—(1977). 'Tyrannis polis' in J. H. d'Arms and J.W. Eadie (eds) *Ancient and modern*. Ann Arbor, Centre for Coordination of Ancient and Modern Studies, 95–109.
—(1984). *Thucydides*. Princeton, Princeton University Press.
—(1985). 'The razing of the house in Greek society', *TAPA* 115, 79–102.
Constantakopoulou, C. (2007). *The dance of the islands: insularity, networks, the Athenian empire, and the Aegean world*. Oxford: Oxford University Press.
Cook, A.B. (1895). 'The bee in Greek mythology', *JHS* 15, 1–24.
Cook, J. M. (1983). *The Persian empire*. London: Dent.
—(1985). 'The rise of the Achaemenids and establishment of their empire' in I. Gershevitch (ed.) *The Cambridge history of Iran*. Cambridge: Cambridge University Press, 200–91.
Cordes, P. (1994). *Iatros: das Bild des Artztes in der griechischen Literatur von Homer bis Aristoteles*. Stuttgart: Steiner.
Corner, S. (2010). 'Transcendent drinking: the symposium at sea reconsidered', *CQ* 60, 352–80.

Craik, E. (1988). *Euripides Phoenician Women.* Warminster: Aris & Phillips.
Csapo, E. (2004). 'The politics of the New Music' in P. Murray and P. Wilson (eds) *Music and the Muses: the culture of mousike in the classical Athenian city.* Oxford: Oxford University Press, 207–48.
Cucchiarelli, A. (2004). 'La nave e lo spettatore. Forme dell'allegoria da Alceo ad Orazio, I', *SFIC* 97, 189–206.
Currie, B. (2002). 'Euthymos of Locri: a case study of heroization in the Classical period', *JHS* 122, 24–44.
Dale, A. M. (1954). *Euripides Alcestis.* Oxford: Clarendon Press.
Dalfen, J. (1994/95). 'Die ὕβρις der Nachtigall', *WS* 107/108, 157–77.
Dalley, S. (1989). *Myths from Mesopotamia: Creation, the Flood, Gilgamesh and others.* Oxford: Oxford University Press.
Daube, D. (1972). *Civil disobedience in antiquity.* Edinburgh: Edinburgh University Press.
Davidson, J. (1990). 'Isocrates against imperialism: an analysis of the *De Pace*', *Historia* 39, 20–36.
—(1997). *Courtesans and fishcakes.* London: Fontana.
Davies, J. K. (2000). 'A wholly non-Aristotelian universe: the Molossians as ethnos, state and monarchy' in R. Brock and S. Hodkinson (eds) *Alternatives to Athens.* Oxford, Oxford University Press, 234–58.
—(2008 [actually 2011]). 'State-formation in Early Iron Age Greece' in M. Lombardo (ed.), *Forme sovrapoleiche e interpoleiche di organizzazione nel mondo Greco antico.* Galatina: Congedo Editore, 15–25.
Dawe, R. D. (1982). *Sophocles Oedipus Rex.* Cambridge: Cambridge University Press.
Delcourt, M. (1939). 'Notes d'histoire Grecque', *AC* 8, 371–82.
Denniston, J. D. and Page, D. L. (1957). *Aeschylus Agamemnon.* Oxford: Clarendon Press.
Denyer, N. (2001). *Plato Alcibiades.* Cambridge: Cambridge University Press.
De Souza, P. (1999). *Piracy in the Greco-Roman world.* Cambridge: Cambridge University Press.
Dickey, E. (1996). *Greek forms of address: from Herodotus to Lucian.* Oxford: Clarendon Press.
Diggle, J. (2004). *Theophrastus Characters.* Cambridge: Cambridge University Press.
Dillery, J. (1995). *Xenophon and the History of his Times.* London: Routledge.
—(2004). 'Xenophon, the military review and Hellenistic *pompai*' in C. J. Tuplin (ed.) *Xenophon and his world.* Stuttgart: Steiner, 259–76.
Dodds, E. R. (1929). 'Euripides the Irrationalist', *CR* 43, 97–104.
—(1959). *Plato Gorgias.* Oxford: Clarendon Press.
—(1960). *Euripides Bacchae,* 2nd edn. Oxford: Clarendon Press.
Donlan, W. (1999). *The aristocratic ideal and Selected Papers.* Wauconda: Bolchazy-Carducci. [*Aristocratic ideal* originally published Lawrence, Coronado 1980 with same pagination except Introduction].
Dorati, M. (1998). 'Lisistrata e la tessitura', *QUCC* 58, 41–56.
Dornseiff, F. (1927). 'Σωτήρ', *RE Zweite Reihe* III A1, 1211–21.
Dover, K. J. (1968). *Aristophanes Clouds.* Oxford: Clarendon Press.
—(1972). *Aristophanic comedy.* Berkeley: University of California Press.
—(1980). *Plato Symposium.* Cambridge: Cambridge University Press.
—(1993). *Aristophanes Frogs.* Oxford: Clarendon Press.
Drews, R. (1983). *Basileus: the evidence for kingship in Geometric Greece.* New Haven: Yale University Press.
Ducrey, P. (1995). 'La muraille est-elle un élément constitutif d'une cité?' in M. H. Hansen

(ed.) *Sources for the ancient Greek city-state*. Copenhagen: Royal Danish Academy of Sciences and Letters, 245–56.
Due, B. (1989). *The Cyropaedia: Xenophon's aims and methods*. Aarhus: Aarhus University Press.
Duff, T. E. (1999). *Plutarch's Lives: exploring virtue and vice*. Oxford: Oxford University Press.
Dunbabin, T. J. (1948). *The Western Greeks*. Oxford: Clarendon Press.
Dunbar, N. (1995). *Aristophanes Birds*. Oxford: Clarendon Press.
Duplouy, A. and Brock, R. (eds) (forthcoming). *Defining archaic citizenship*.
Dvornik, F. (1966). *Early Christian and Byzantine political philosophy*. Washington, DC: Dumbarton Oaks Center for Byzantine Studies.
Dyson, G. W. (1929). 'ΛΕΟΝΤΑ ΤΕΚΕΙΝ', *CQ* 23, 186–95.
Easterling, P. E. (1997). 'Constructing the heroic' in C. Pelling (ed.), *Greek Tragedy and the Historian*. Oxford: Clarendon Press, 21–37.
Eder, W. (1998). 'Aristocrats and the coming of Athenian democracy' in I. Morris and K. Raaflaub (eds) *Democracy 2500? Questions and challenges*. Dubuque: Archaeological Institute of America.
Edmunds, L. (1987). *Cleon, Knights, and Aristophanes' politics*. Lanham: University Press of America.
Edwards, M. (1995). *Greek orators IV: Andocides*. Warminster: Aris & Phillips.
Eide, T. (1988). 'δημοβόρος', *Glotta* 66, 142–4.
England, E. B. (1921). *The Laws of Plato*. Manchester: Manchester University Press.
Fantham, E. (1972). *Comparative studies in Republican Latin imagery*. Toronto: University of Toronto Press.
Farber, J. J. (1979). 'The *Cyropaedia* and Hellenistic kingship', *AJP* 100, 497–514.
Farquharson, A. S. L. (1912). *De motu animalium, De incessu animalium* in J. A. Smith and W. D. Ross (eds) *The Works of Aristotle volume V*. Oxford: Clarendon Press.
Fatouros, G. (2002). 'ΚΙΩΝ-ΣΤΥΛΟΣ. Zur Geschichte einer Metapher', *Glotta* 76, 168–76.
Felton, D. (1998). 'Advice to tyrants: the motif of "enigmatic counsel" in Greek and Roman texts', *Phoenix* 52, 42–52.
Finley, M. I. (1978). *The world of Odysseus*, 2nd rev. edn. London: Chatto & Windus.
—(1981). *Economy and society in ancient Greece*, B. D. Shaw and R. Saller (eds). London: Chatto & Windus.
Fisher, N. (2001). *Aeschines Against Timarchos*. Oxford: Clarendon Press.
—(2008). 'The bad boyfriend, the flatterer and the sycophant: related forms of the "*Kakos*" in democratic Athens' in I. Sluiter and R. Rosen (eds) *KAKOS: Badness and Anti-Value in Classical Antiquity, Mnemosyne* suppl. 307. Leiden: Brill, 185–232.
Flower, M. A. and Marincola, J. (2002). *Herodotus Histories Book IX*. Cambridge: Cambridge University Press.
Fontenrose, J. (1978). *The Delphic oracle, its responses and operations, with a catalogue of responses*. Berkeley: University of California Press.
Fornara, C. W. (1966). 'The hoplite achievement at Psyttaleia', *JHS* 86, 51–4.
Forrest, W. G. (1966). *The emergence of Greek democracy*. London: Weidenfeld & Nicolson.
—(1975). 'An Athenian generation gap' *YCS* 24, 37–52.
Forsdyke, S. (1999). 'From aristocratic to democratic ideology and back again: the Thrasybulus anecdote in Herodotus' *Histories* and Aristotle's *Politics*', *CPh* 94, 361–72.
Foucault, M. (2002). '"*Omnes et singulatim*": towards a critique of political reason' in J. D. Faubion (ed.), *Power: essential works of Foucault 1954–1984 volume III*. London: Penguin, 298–325. [originally delivered 1979].

Fowler, B. H. (1967). 'Aeschylus' imagery', C&M 28, 1–74.
Fowler, R. L. (2000). *Early Greek mythography volume 1: Text and introduction.* Oxford: Clarendon Press.
Fraenkel, E. (1950). *Aeschylus Agamemnon.* Oxford: Clarendon Press.
Fränkel, H. (1975). *Early Greek poetry and philosophy*, trans. by M. Hadas and J. Willis. Oxford: Blackwell.
Frankfort, H. (1948). *Kingship and the gods: a study of ancient Near Eastern religion as the integration of society and nature.* Chicago: University of Chicago Press.
Frankfort, H., Frankfort, H. A., Wilson, J. A., Jacobsen, T. and Irwin, W. A. (1946). *The intellectual adventure of ancient man: an essay on speculative thought in the ancient Near East.* Chicago: Chicago University Press.
Früchtel, L. (1952). 'Was bedeutet die ἔνδοξος δουλεία des Antigonos Gonatas?', *Gymnasium* 59, 350–1.
Garvie, A. F. (1986). *Aeschylus Choephoroi.* Oxford: Clarendon Press.
—(1998). *Sophocles Ajax.* Warminster: Aris & Phillips.
—(2009). *Aeschylus Persae.* Oxford: Oxford University Press.
Gentili, B. (1975). 'La giustizia del mare: Solone, fr.11 D., 12 West', *QUCC* 20, 159–62.
—(1988). *Poetry and its public in ancient Greece*, trans. by A. T. Cole. Baltimore: Johns Hopkins University Press.
Gera, D. L. (1993). *Xenophon's Cyropaedia: style, genre and literary technique.* Oxford: Clarendon Press.
Gernet, L. (1981). *The anthropology of ancient Greece*, trans. by J. Hamilton and B. Nagy. Baltimore: Johns Hopkins University Press.
Gigante, M. (1956). *NOMOS BASILEUS.* Napoli: Edizioni Glaux.
—(1957). 'Un nuovo frammento politico (P. Heid 182)', *Maia* 9, 68–74.
Gildersleeve, B. L. (1907). *Pindar, the Olympian and Pythian Odes*, rev. edn. London: Macmillan.
Gilula, D. (1989). 'A Career in the Navy (Arist. *Knights* 541–4)', *CQ* 39, 259–61.
Glotz, G. (1929). *The Greek city and its institutions*, trans. by N. Mallinson. London: Kegan Paul, Trench and Trubner.
Glowacki, K. (2003). 'A personification of Demos on a new Attic document relief', *Hesperia* 72, 447–66.
Goheen, R. F. (1951). *The imagery of Sophocles' Antigone: a study of poetic language and structure.* Princeton: Princeton University Press.
Golden, M. (1998). *Sport and society in ancient Greece.* Cambridge: Cambridge University Press.
—(2003). *Sport in the ancient world from A to Z.* London: Routledge.
Goldhill, S. (1988). 'Battle narrative and politics in Aeschylus' *Persae*', *JHS* 108, 189–93.
Gomme, A. W. (1933). 'A forgotten factor of Greek naval strategy', *JHS* 53, 16–24.
Gomme, A. W., Andrewes, A. and Dover, K. J. (1945–81). *A historical commentary on Thucydides.* 5 Vols. Oxford: Clarendon Press.
Goodenough, E. R. (1928). 'The political philosophy of Hellenistic kingship', *YCS* 1, 55–102.
Gould, J. (1955). *The development of Plato's ethics.* Cambridge: Cambridge University Press.
Graf, F. (2009). *Apollo.* Abingdon: Routledge.
Graham, A. J. (1992). 'Thucydides 7.13.2 and the crews of Athenian triremes', *TAPA* 122, 257–70.
—(1998). 'Thucydides 7.13.2 and the crews of Athenian triremes: an addendum', *TAPA* 128, 89–114.

Gray, V. J. (1989). *The character of Xenophon's Hellenica*. London: Duckworth.
—(2007). *Xenophon on government*. Cambridge: Cambridge University Press.
—(2011). *Xenophon's mirror of princes: reading the reflections*. Oxford: Oxford University Press.
Graziosi, B. and Haubold, J. (2010). *Homer Iliad Book VI*. Cambridge: Cambridge University Press.
Griffin, J. (1980). *Homer on Life and Death*. Oxford, Clarendon Press.
Griffith, M. (1983). *Aeschylus Prometheus Bound*. Cambridge: Cambridge University Press.
—(1998). 'The king and eye: the rule of the father in Greek tragedy', *PCPS* 44, 20–84.
Griffiths, A. (1995). 'Non-aristocratic elements in archaic poetry' in A. Powell (ed.) *The Greek world*. London: Routledge, 85–103.
van Groningen, B. A. (1966). *Theognis: le premier livre*. Amsterdam: Noord-Hollandsche Uitgevers Maatschappij.
Grossmann, G. (1950). *Politische Schlagwörter aus der Zeit des Peloponnesischen Krieges*. Zurich: Leeman.
Guthrie, W. K. C. (1962-81). *A history of Greek philosophy*. Cambridge: Cambridge University Press.
Gutzwiller, K. J. (1991). *Theocritus' pastoral analogies: the formation of a genre*. Madison: University of Wisconsin Press.
Hahm, D. E. (2000). 'Kings and constitutions: Hellenistic theories' in C. Rowe and M. Schofield (eds) *The Cambridge history of Greek and Roman political thought*. Cambridge: Cambridge University Press, 457–76.
Hainsworth, B. (1993). *The Iliad: a commentary. Vol. 3, Books 9–12*. Cambridge: Cambridge University Press.
Hall, E. (1989). *Inventing the barbarian*. Oxford: Clarendon Press.
—(1996). *Aeschylus Persians*. Warminster: Aris & Phillips.
Halliwell, S. (1993). *Plato Republic 5*. Warminster: Aris & Phillips.
Hamilton, J. R. (1969). *Plutarch Alexander*. Oxford: Clarendon Press.
Hansen, M. H. (1989). 'Athenian democracy' [review of Sinclair (1988)], *CR* 39, 69–76.
—(1991). *The Athenian democracy in the age of Demosthenes*. Oxford: Blackwell.
—(1998). *Polis and city-state: an ancient concept and its modern equivalent*. Copenhagen: Munksgaard.
—(2002). 'The Game called *Polis*' in T. H. Nielsen (ed.) *Even more studies in the ancient Greek polis*. Stuttgart: Steiner, 9–15.
—(2008). 'Thucydides' description of democracy (2.37.1) and the EU-Convention of 2003' *GRBS* 48, 15–26.
Hardie, P. (1986). *Virgil's Aeneid: cosmos and imperium*. Oxford: Clarendon Press.
Harrison, A. R. W. (1968–71). *The law of Athens*. Oxford: Clarendon Press.
Harrison, T. (2000). *The emptiness of Asia*. London: Duckworth.
Hartog, F. (1988). *The mirror of Herodotus*, trans. by J. Lloyd, Berkeley: University of California Press.
Harvey, F. D. (1965). 'Two kinds of equality', *C&M* 26, 101–46. [with 27 (1966), 99–100].
—(1985). 'Dona ferentes: some aspects of bribery in Greek politics' in P. A. Cartledge and F. D. Harvey (eds) *CRUX: Essays in Greek history presented to G.E.M. de Ste. Croix*. London: Duckworth, 76–117.
—(1990). 'The sykophant and sykophancy: vexatious redefinition?' in P. Cartledge, P. Millett and S. Todd (eds) *Nomos: essays in Athenian law, politics and society*. Cambridge: Cambridge University Press, 103–21.

Haubold, J. (2000). *Homer's people*. Cambridge: Cambridge University Press.
Henderson, J. (1987). *Aristophanes Lysistrata*. Oxford: Clarendon Press.
—(1991). *The maculate muse: obscene language in Attic comedy*, 2nd edn. Oxford: Oxford University Press.
—(2003). 'Demos, demagogue, tyrant in Attic old comedy' in K. A. Morgan (ed.) *Popular tyranny: sovereignty and its discontents in ancient Greece*. Austin: University of Texas Press, 155–79.
Hesk, J. (2000a). 'Intratext and irony in Aristophanic comedy' in A. Sharrock and H. Morales (eds) *Intratextuality and classical literature*. Oxford: Clarendon Press, 227–61.
—(2000b). *Deception and democracy in classical Athens*. Cambridge: Cambridge University Press.
Heubeck, A., West, S. and Hainsworth, J. B. (1990). *A commentary on Homer's Odyssey. Vol. 1, Introduction and books i–viii*. Oxford: Clarendon Press.
Hirsch, S. W. (1985). *The friendship of the barbarians*. Hanover, NH: University Press of New England.
Hölscher, T. (1998). 'Images and political identity' in D. Boedeker and K. Raaflaub (eds) *Democracy, empire, and the arts in fifth-century Athens*. Cambridge, MA: Harvard University Press, 153–83.
Honohan, I. (2008). 'Metaphors of solidarity' in T. Carver and J. Pikalo (eds) *Political language and metaphor*. London: Routledge, 69–82.
Hordern, J. H. (2002). *The fragments of Timotheus of Miletus*. Oxford: Clarendon Press.
Hornblower, S. (1987). *Thucydides*. London: Duckworth.
—(1991–2008). *A commentary on Thucydides*, 3 Vols. Oxford: Clarendon Press.
—(2000). 'The *Old Oligarch* (Pseudo-Xenophon's *Athenaion Politeia*) and Thucydides. A fourth-century date for the *Old Oligarch*?' in P. Flensted-Jensen, T. H. Nielsen and L. Rubinstein (eds) *Polis and politics: Studies in ancient Greek history*. Copenhagen, 363–84.
—(2002). *The Greek world 479–323 BC*, 3rd edn. London: Routledge.
—(2004). *Thucydides and Pindar*. Oxford: Oxford University Press.
—(2006). 'Pindar and kingship theory' in S. Lewis (ed.) *Ancient tyranny*. Edinburgh: Edinburgh University Press, 151–63.
How, W. W. and Wells, J. (1928). *A Commentary on Herodotus*, corrected 1st edn. Oxford: Clarendon Press.
Hubbard, T. K. (1995). 'Hesiod's fable of the Hawk and the Nightingale reconsidered', *GRBS* 36, 161–71.
—(1998). 'Popular perceptions of elite homosexuality in classical Athens', *Arion* (ser.3) 6, 48–78.
Humphreys, S. C. (1978). *Anthropology and the Greeks*. London: Routledge.
—(1983). *The family, women and death: comparative studies*. London: Routledge.
Hunter, R. L. (2012). *Plato and the traditions of ancient literature: the silent stream*. Cambridge: Cambridge University Press.
Hunter, V. (1994). *Policing Athens*. Princeton: Princeton University Press.
Hutchinson, G. O. (1985). *Aeschylus Septem contra Thebas*. Oxford: Clarendon Press.
—(2012). 'Image and world in epinician poetry' in P. Agócs, C. Carey and R. Rawles (eds) *Reading the victory ode*. Cambridge: Cambridge University Press, 277–302.
Inwood, B. (2001). *The poem of Empedocles: a text and translation*, rev. edn. Toronto: University of Toronto Press.
Irwin, E. (2005). *Solon and early Greek poetry*. Cambridge: Cambridge University Press.
Jackson, M. W. (1988). 'Plato's political analogies', *International studies in philosophy* 20, 27–42.

Jameson, M. H. (1990). 'Domestic space in the Greek city-state' in S. Kent (ed.) *Domestic architecture and the use of space: an interdisciplinary cross-cultural study*. Cambridge: Cambridge University Press, 92–113.
—(1994). 'The ritual of the Athena Nike parapet' in R. Osborne and S. Hornblower (eds) *Ritual, finance, politics: Athenian democratic accounts presented to David Lewis*. Oxford: Clarendon Press, 307–24.
Janko, R. (1992). *The Iliad: a commentary. Vol. 4, Books 13–16*. Cambridge: Cambridge University Press.
Jebb, R. C. (1887). *Sophocles Oedipus tyrannus*, 2nd edn. Cambridge: Cambridge University Press.
—(1891). *Sophocles Antigone*, 2nd edn. Cambridge: Cambridge University Press.
Jesch, J. (2001). *Ships and men in the late Viking age: the vocabulary of runic inscriptions and skaldic verse*. Woodbridge: Boydell & Brewer.
Jones, A. H. M. (1957). 'The Athenian democracy and its critics' in *id.*, *Athenian democracy*. Oxford: Blackwell, 41–72.
Jouanna, J. (1978). 'Le médecin modèle du législateur dans les *Lois* de Platon', *Ktema* 3, 77–91.
—(1980a). 'Politique et médecine. La problématique du changement dans le *Régime des maladies aiguës* et chez Thucydide (livre VI)' in M. D. Grmek (ed.) *Hippocratica*. Paris: Éditions du CNRS, 299–318.
—(1980b). 'Médecine et politique dans la *Politique* d'Aristote (II 1268 b 25–1269 a 28)', *Ktema* 5, 257–66.
—(1999). *Hippocrates*, trans. by M. B. DeBevoise. Baltimore: Johns Hopkins University Press.
Kallet, L. (1999). 'The diseased body politic, Athenian public finance, and the massacre at Mykalessos (Thucydides 7.27–29)', *AJP* 120: 223–44.
—(2003). '*Dêmos tyrannos*: wealth, power and economic patronage' in K. A. Morgan (ed.) *Popular tyranny: sovereignty and its discontents in ancient Greece*. Austin: University of Texas Press, 117–53.
Kallet-Marx, L. (1993). 'Thucydides 2.45.2 and the status of war widows in Periclean Athens' in R. M. Rosen and J. Farrell (eds) *Nomodeiktes: Greek studies in honor of Martin Ostwald*. Ann Arbor: University of Michigan Press, 133–43.
Kamerbeek, J. C. (1967). *The plays of Sophocles: commentaries. Pt. 4: the Oedipus tyrannus*. Leiden: Brill.
Kannicht, R. (1969). *Euripides Helena*. Heidelberg: Winter.
Kantorowitz, E. H. (1957). *The King's two bodies*. Princeton: Princeton University Press.
Kearns, E. (1990). 'Saving the city' in O. Murray and S. Price (eds) *The Greek city from Homer to Alexander*. Oxford: Clarendon Press, 323–44.
Killy, W. (ed.) (1988–93). *Literatur-Lexicon: Autoren und Werke deutsche Sprache*. Gütersloh: Bertelsmann.
Kirk, G. S. (1990). *The Iliad: a commentary. Vol. 2, Books 5–8*. Cambridge: Cambridge University Press.
Kirk, G. S., Raven, J. E. and Schofield, M. (1983). *The Presocratic philosophers*, 2nd edn. Cambridge: Cambridge University Press.
Kirkwood, G. M. (1969). 'Eteocles Oiakostrophos', *Phoenix* 23, 9–25.
Knipping, J. B. (1974). *Iconography of the Counter-reformation in the Netherlands*. Nieuwkoop: B de Graaf/Leiden: A. W. Sijthoff.
Knox, B. M. W. (1957). *Oedipus at Thebes*. New Haven: Yale University Press.
—(1961). 'The *Ajax* of Sophocles', *HSCP* 65, 1–37.

Kraut, R. (1984). *Socrates and the State*. Princeton: Princeton University Press.
Krentz, P. (1989). *Xenophon Hellenika I-II.3.10*. Warminster: Aris & Phillips.
Kurke, L. (1999a). *Coins, bodies, games and gold: the politics of meaning in archaic Greece*. Princeton: Princeton University Press.
Kurke, L. (1999b). 'Ancient Greek board games and how to play them', *CPh*. 94, 247–67.
Kyle, D. G. (1987). *Athletics in ancient Athens*. Leiden: Brill.
Labarbe, J. (1972). 'Les premières démocraties de la Grèce antique', *BAB* 58, 223–54.
Lakoff, G. (2002). *Moral politics: how liberals and conservatives think*. Chicago: University of Chicago Press.
Lakoff, G. and Johnson, M. (1980). *Metaphors we live by*. Chicago: University of Chicago Press.
Lakoff, G. and Turner, M. (1989). *More than cool reason: a field guide to poetic metaphor*. Chicago: University of Chicago Press.
Landfester, M. (1967). *Die Ritter des Aristophanes*. Amsterdam: Grüner.
Lane, M. S. (1998). *Method and politics in Plato's Statesman*. Cambridge: Cambridge University Press.
Lane Fox, R. (2000). 'Theognis: an alternative to democracy' in R. Brock and S. Hodkinson (eds) *Alternatives to Athens*. Oxford: Oxford University Press, 35–51.
Last, D. M. and Ogilvie, R. M. (1958). 'Claudius and Livy', *Latomus* 17, 476–87.
Lavelle, B. M. (1991). 'The compleat angler: observations on the rise of Peisistratos in Herodotus (1.59–64)', *CQ* 41, 317–24.
Lebeck, A. (1971). *The Oresteia: a study in language and structure*. Washington: Center for Hellenic Studies.
Leclerc, M.-C. (1992). 'L'épervier et le rossignol d'Hésiode: une fable à double sens', *REG* 105, 37–44.
Lee, K. H. (1976). *Euripides Troades*. Basingstoke: Macmillan.
Lefkowitz, M. (1984). 'Pindar's *Pythian* V' in A. Hurst (ed.) *Pindare* (*Entretiens du Fondation Hardt*, Vol. 31). Geneva: Fondation Hardt, 33–63.
Legrand, Ph.-E. (1946). *Hérodote Histoires V*. Paris: Les Belles Lettres.
Leidl, C. G. (2003). 'The harlot's art: metaphor and literary criticism' in G. Boys-Stones (ed.) *Metaphor, allegory and the classical tradition*. Oxford: Clarendon Press, 31–54
Lelli, E. (2006). *Volpe e leone: il proverbio nella poesia greca: Alceo, Cratino, Callimaco*. Rome: Edizioni dell'Ateneo.
Lentini, G. (2001). 'La nave e gli ἑταῖροι: in margine ad Alceo frr. 6, 73, 208a V', *MD* 46, 159–70.
Levine, D. B. (1985). 'Symposium and the polis' in T. J. Figueira and G. Nagy (eds) *Theognis of Megara: poetry and the polis*. Baltimore: Johns Hopkins University Press, 176–96.
Lewis, D. M. (1977). *Sparta and Persia*. Leiden: Brill.
—(1990). 'The political background of Democritus' in E. Craik (ed.) *Owls to Athens: essays on classical subjects for Sir Kenneth Dover*. Oxford: Clarendon Press, 151–4.
Lewis, S. (2004). 'καὶ σαφῶς τύραννος ἦν: Xenophon's account of Euphron of Sicyon', *JHS* 124, 65–74.
Liddel, P. (2007). *Civic obligation and individual liberty in ancient Athens*. Oxford: Oxford University Press.
Liebert, R. S. (2010). 'Apian imagery and the critique of poetic sweetness in Plato's Republic', *TAPA* 140, 97–115.
Lintott, A. (2000). 'Aristotle and the mixed constitution' in R. Brock and S. Hodkinson (eds) *Alternatives to Athens*. Oxford: Oxford University Press, 152–66.

Lloyd, A. B. (1975-89). *Herodotus Book II. A Commentary*, 3 Vols. Leiden: Brill.
Lloyd, G. E. R. (1966). *Polarity and analogy*. Cambridge: Cambridge University Press.
—(1987). *The revolutions of wisdom*. Berkeley: University of California Press.
—(1996). *Adversaries and authorities: investigations into ancient Greek and Chinese science*. Cambridge: Cambridge University Press.
—(2003). *In the grip of disease: studies in the Greek imagination*. Oxford: Oxford University Press.
Lloyd-Jones, H. (1968). 'The Cologne fragment of Alcaeus', *GRBS* 9, 125-39.
—(1972). 'Pindar fr.169', *HSCP* 76, 45-56.
Lloyd-Jones, H. and Wilson, N. G. (1990). *Sophoclea: studies on the text of Sophocles*. Oxford: Clarendon Press.
Long, A. A. (1978). 'Sophocles, *O.T.* 879-81', *LCM* 3, 49-53.
Longo, O. (1974). 'Ad Alceo 112,10 L.-P.: per la storia di un topos', *BIFG* 1, 211-28
Longrigg, J. (1993). *Greek rational medicine*. London: Routledge.
Lonsdale, S. H. (1990). *Creatures of speech: lion, herding and hunting similes in the Iliad*. Stuttgart: Teubner.
Loraux, N. (1984). 'Solon au milieu de la lice' in *Aux origines de l'Hellénisme: La Crète et la Grèce. Hommage à Henri van Effenterre*. Paris: Sorbonne, 199-214.
—(1986). *The invention of Athens*, trans. by A. Sheridan. Cambridge, MA: Harvard University Press.
—(1989). 'Therefore, Socrates is immortal' in M. Feher with R. Naddaf and N. Tazi (eds) *Fragments for a history of the human body, Vol. 2*. New York: Zone Books, 12-45.
—(1993). *The children of Athena*, trans. by C. Levine. Princeton: Princeton University Press.
Louis, P. (1945). *Les metaphors de Platon*. Paris: Les Belles Lettres.
Low, P. (2007). *Interstate relations in classical Greece: morality and power*. Cambridge: Cambridge University Press.
Luccioni, J. (1959). 'Platon et la mer', *REA* 61, 15-47.
Ludwig, P. W. (2002). *Eros and Polis: desire and community in Greek political theory*. Cambridge: Cambridge University Press.
MacDowell, D. M. (1971). *Aristophanes Wasps*. Oxford: Clarendon Press.
—(1978). *The law in classical Athens*. London: Thames & Hudson.
—(1982). *Gorgias Encomium of Helen*. Bristol: Bristol Classical Press.
—(1990). *Demosthenes Against Meidias*. Oxford: Clarendon Press.
—(2000). *Demosthenes On the false embassy (Oration 19)*. Oxford: Oxford University Press.
MacGregor, N. (2010). *A history of the world in 100 objects*. London: Allen Lane.
Macleod, C. (1983). *Collected essays*. Oxford: Clarendon Press.
Mainoldi, C. (1984). *L'image du loup et du chien dans la Grèce ancienne d'Homère à Platon*. Paris: Éd. Ophrys.
Manger, K. (1983). *Das Narrenschiff: Entstehung, Wirkung und Deutung*. Darmstadt: Wissenschaftliche Buchgesellschaft.
Marcovitch, M. (1967). *Heraclitus*. Merida: Los Andes University Press.
Marincola, J. (1997). *Authority and tradition in ancient historiography*. Cambridge: Cambridge University Press.
Marshall, E. (2000). 'Death and disease in Cyrene: a case study' in E. Marshall and V. Hope (eds) *Death and disease in the Ancient City*. London: Routledge, 8-23.
Martin, R. P. (2006). 'Solon in no man's land' in J. Blok and A. P. M. H. Lardinois (eds) *Solon of Athens: new historical and philological approaches*. Leiden: Brill, 157-72.

Mastronarde, D. J. (1994). *Euripides Phoenissae*. Cambridge: Cambridge University Press.
Mathieu, G. (1960). *Isocrate Discours III*. Paris: Les Belles Lettres.
McDermott, W. C. (1935). 'The ape in Greek literature', *TAPA* 66, 165–76.
McDonnell, M. (1991). 'The introduction of athletic nudity: Thucydides, Plato and the vases', *JHS* 111, 182–93.
McGlew, J. F. (1993). *Tyranny and popular culture in ancient Greece*. Ithaca: Cornell University Press.
—(2002). *Citizens on stage*. Ann Arbor: University of Michigan Press.
McLennan, G. R. (1977). *Callimachus, Hymn to Zeus: introduction and commentary*. Rome: Edizioni dell'Ateneo & Bizzarri.
McNellen, B. (1997). 'Herodotean symbolism: Pericles as lion cub', *ICS* 22, 11–23.
McQueen, E. I. (1986). *Demosthenes: Olynthiacs*. Bristol: Bristol Classical Press.
Meichsner, I. (1983). *Die Logik von Gemeinplätzen vorgeführt an Steuermannstopos und Schiffsmetapher*. Bonn: H. Grundmann.
Meiggs, R. 1972). *The Athenian empire*. Oxford: Clarendon Press.
Merkelback, R. (1949). 'Politischer Dialog in einem Florentiner Papyrus', *Aegyptus* 29, 56–8.
Michelini, A. (1978). 'Ὕβρις and plants', *HSCP* 82, 35–44.
Miller, M. H. Jr. (1980). *The philosopher in Plato's Statesman*. The Hague: Martinus Nijhoff.
Miller, S. G. (2004). *Ancient Greek athletics*. New Haven: Yale University Press.
Millett, P. (1990). 'Patronage and its avoidance in classical Athens' in A. Wallace-Hadrill (ed.) *Patronage in ancient society*. London: Routledge, 15–47.
—(1991). *Lending and borrowing in ancient Athens*. Cambridge: Cambridge University Press.
Missiou, A. (1993). 'ΔΟΥΛΟΣ ΤΟΥ ΒΑΣΙΛΕΩΣ: the politics of translation', *CQ* 43, 377–91.
Mitchell, L. G. (2007). *Panhellenism and the barbarian in archaic and classical Greece*. Swansea: Classical Press of Wales.
Mondi, R. (1980). 'Σκηπτοῦχοι Βασιλεῖς. Divine kingship in early Greece', *Arethusa* 13, 203–16.
Monoson, S. (1994). 'Citizen as *Erastes*: erotic imagery and the idea of reciprocity in the Periclean funeral oration', *Political theory* 22, 253–76.
Monoson, S. S. (2000). *Plato's democratic entanglements: Athenian politics and the practice of philosophy*. Princeton: Princeton University Press.
Morawetz, T. (2000). *Der Demos als Tyrann und Banause*. Frankfurt am Main: Lang.
Morgan, C. (1990). *Athletes and oracles*. Cambridge: Cambridge University Press.
Morgan, K. A. (2003). 'The tyranny of the audience in Plato and Isocrates' in *id.* (ed.) *Popular tyranny: sovereignty and its discontents in ancient Greece*. Austin: University of Texas Press, [2003a], 181–213.
Morris, I. (1991). 'The early polis as city and state' in J. Rich and A. Wallace-Hadrill (eds) *City and country in the ancient world*. London: Routledge, 24–57.
—(1996). 'The strong principle of equality and the archaic origins of Greek democracy' in J. Ober and C. Hedrick (eds) *Dêmokratia: a conversation on democracies ancient and modern*. Princeton: Princeton University Press, 19–48.
—(2001). 'The use and abuse of Homer' in D. Cairns (ed.) *Oxford readings in Homer's Iliad*. Oxford: Clarendon Press, 57–91.
Morrison, J. S. (1984). '*Hyperesia* in naval contexts in the fifth and fourth centuries BC', *JHS* 104, 48–59.
Morrison, J. S. and Coates, J. F. (1986). *The Athenian trireme*. Cambridge: Cambridge University Press.

Moulton, C. (1977). *Similes in the Homeric poems.* Göttingen: Vandenhoeck & Ruprecht.
—(1981). *Aristophanic poetry.* Göttingen: Vandenhoeck & Ruprecht.
Mülke, C. (2002). *Solon's politische Elegien und Iamben (Fr. 1-13, 32-7 West) Einleitung, Text, Übersetzung, Kommentar.* München: Saur.
Murray, O. (1990). 'The idea of the shepherd king from Cyrus to Charlemagne' in P. Godman and O. Murray (eds) *Latin Poetry and the Classical Tradition.* Oxford: Clarendon Press, 1-14.
—(1993). *Early Greece,* 2nd edn. London: Fontana.
Nagy, G. (1985). 'Theognis of Megara: a poet's vision of his city' in T. J. Figueira and G. Nagy (eds) *Theognis of Megara: poetry and the polis.* Baltimore: Johns Hopkins University Press, 22-81.
Neer, R. T. (2002). *Style and politics in Athenian vase-painting : the craft of democracy, circa 530-470 B.C.E.* Cambridge: Cambridge University Press.
Neil, R. A. (1901). *The Knights of Aristophanes.* Cambridge: Cambridge University Press.
Nelson, S. (1997). 'The Justice of Zeus in Hesiod's Fable of the Hawk and the Nightingale', *CJ* 92, 235-47.
van Nes, D. (1963). *Die maritime Bildersprache des Aischylos.* Groningen: Wolters.
Nestle, W. (1927). 'Die Fabel des Menenius Agrippa', *Klio* 21: 350-60.
Newman, W. L. (1887-1902). *The Politics of Aristotle.* Oxford: Clarendon Press.
Nielsen, T. H. (2004). 'The concept of *patris* in archaic and classical sources' in T. H. Nielsen (ed.) *Once again: studies in the ancient Greek polis.* Stuttgart: Steiner, 49-76.
Nightingale, A. W. (1995). *Genres in dialogue: Plato and the construct of philosophy.* Cambridge: Cambridge University Press.
—(2004). *Spectacles of truth in classical Greek philosophy.* Cambridge: Cambridge University Press.
Nock, A. D. (1972). 'Soter and euergetes' in *Essays on religion and the ancient world* Z. Stewart (ed.). Oxford: Clarendon Press, 720-35.
Nouhaud, M. (1982) *L'Utilisation de l'histoire par les orateurs Attiques.* Paris: Les Belles Lettres.
Noussia, M. (2001). *Solone. Frammenti dell'opera poetica.* Milan: Rizzoli.
—(2006). 'Strategies of persuasion in Solon's Elegies' in J. Blok and A. P. M. H. Lardinois (eds) *Solon of Athens: new historical and philological approaches.* Leiden: Brill, 134-56.
Noussia-Fantuzzi, M. (2010). *Solon the Athenian: the poetic fragments.* Leiden: Brill.
Ober, J. (1989). *Mass and elite in democratic Athens.* Princeton: Princeton University Press.
—(1998). *Political dissent in democratic Athens: intellectual critics of popular rule.* Princeton: Princeton University Press.
Ogden, D. (1997). *The crooked kings of ancient Greece.* London: Duckworth.
OKell, E. (2004). 'Orestes the contender: chariot-racing and politics in fifth-century Athens and Sophocles' *Electra*' in S. Bell and G. Davies (eds) *Games and festivals in classical antiquity, BAR* Int. Ser. 1220. Oxford: Archaeopress, 33-43.
Olson, S.D. (1998). *Aristophanes Peace.* Oxford: Clarendon Press.
—(2002). *Aristophanes Acharnians.* Oxford: Oxford University Press.
—(2007). *Broken laughter: select fragments of Greek comedy.* Oxford: Oxford University Press.
O'Neil, J. L. (1995). *The origins and development of Ancient Greek democracy.* Lanham, MD: Rowman & Littlefield.
Ortony, A. (1975). 'Why metaphors are necessary and not just nice', *Educational theory* 25, 45-53.

Orwell, G. (1961). 'Politics and the English language' in *Collected essays*. London: Secker & Warburg, 337–51.
Osborne, R. (1997). 'Law, the democratic citizen and the representation of women in classical Athens', *P&P* 155, 3–33.
—(2000). 'An Other view: an essay in political history' in B. Cohen (ed.) *Not the classical ideal*. Leiden: Brill, 23–42.
—(2003). 'Changing the discourse' in K. A. Morgan (ed.) *Popular tyranny: sovereignty and its discontents in ancient Greece*. Austin: University of Texas Press, 251–72.
Ostwald, M. (1965). 'Pindar, ΝΟΜΟΣ, and Heracles', *HSCP* 69, 109–38.
—(1969). *Nomos and the beginnings of the Athenian democracy*. Oxford: Clarendon Press.
—(1982). *Autonomia: its genesis and early history*. Chico, CA: Scholars Press.
Padel, R. (1992). *In and out of the mind: Greek images of the tragic self*. Princeton: Princeton University Press.
Page, D. L. (1938). *Euripides Medea*. Oxford: Clarendon Press.
—(1955). *Sappho and Alcaeus*. Oxford: Clarendon Press.
—(1965). 'The song of Hybrias the Cretan', *PCPS* 11, 62–65.
Pakaluk, M. (1998). *Aristotle Nicomachean ethics Books 8 and 9*. Oxford: Clarendon Press.
Papazarkadas, N. (2009). 'Epigraphy and the Athenian Empire: Reshuffling the Chronological Cards' in J. Ma, N. Papazarkadas and R. Parker (eds) *Interpreting the Athenian empire*. London: Duckworth, 67–88.
Parke, H. W. and Wormell, D. E. W. (1949). 'Notes on Delphic oracles', *CQ* 43, 138–40.
—(1956). *The Delphic oracle*. Oxford: Blackwell.
Parker, R. (1983). *Miasma*. Oxford: Clarendon Press.
—(1996). *Athenian religion: a history*. Oxford: Clarendon Press.
Parry, A. (1969). 'The Language of Thucydides' Description of the Plague', *BICS* 16: 106–18.
Pearson, A. C. (1909). *Euripides, the Phoenissae*. Cambridge: Pitt Press.
—(1917). *The Fragments of Sophocles*. Cambridge: Cambridge University Press.
Pearson, L. (1960). *The lost histories of Alexander the Great*. Philadelphia: American Philological Association.
Pelletier, A. (1948). 'L'image du "frelon" dans la *République* de Platon', *RPh* 3.22, 131–46.
Pelliccia, H. (1995). *Mind, body and speech in Homer and Pindar*. Göttingen: Vandenhoeck & Ruprecht.
Pelling, C. (1997). 'Aeschylus' *Persians* and History' in *id*., (ed.) *Greek Tragedy and the Historian*. Oxford: Clarendon Press) 1–19.
—(2004a). 'Plutarch on the outbreak of the Roman civil war' in H. Heftner and K. Tomaschitz (eds) *Ad Fontes!* (Festschrift G. Dobesch) (Wien, im Eigenverlag der Herausgeber), 317–27.
—(2004b). 'Do Plutarch's politicians never learn?' in L. de Blois, J. Bons, T. Kessels and D. M. Schenkeveld (eds) *The statesman in Plutarch's works*. Leiden: Brill, 87–103.
Pender, E. E. (2000). *Images of persons unseen: Plato's metaphors for the gods and the soul*. Sankt Augustin: Academia Verlag.
—(2003). 'Plato on metaphors and models' in G. Boys-Stones (ed.) *Metaphor, allegory and the classical tradition*. Oxford: Clarendon Press, 55–81.
Pernée, L. (1979). 'Quand l'intelligence est en défaut (Xénophon, Helléniques, II, 4, 41)', *REG* 92, 552–4.
Péron, J. (1974). *Les images maritimes de Pindare*. Paris: Klincksieck.
Petit, T. (2004). 'Xénophon et la vassalité achéménide' in C. J. Tuplin (ed.) *Xenophon and his world*. Stuttgart: Steiner, 175–99.

Piepenbrink, K. (2003). 'Medizinische Paradigmata im politischen Diskurs der athenischen Demokratie des 4. Jahrhunderts v. Chr.', *AncSoc* 33, 209–22.

Podlecki, A. J. (1966). *The political background of Aeschylean tragedy*. Ann Arbor: University of Michigan Press.

Pohlenz, M. (1913). *Aus Platos Werdezeit: philologische Untersuchungen*. Berlin: Weidmann.

Poliakoff, M. B. (1987). *Combat sports in the ancient world: competition, violence and culture*. New Haven: Yale University Press.

Pollitt, J. J. (1974). *The ancient view of Greek art*. New Haven: Yale University Press.

Pomeroy, S. B. (1994). *Xenophon Oeconomicus: a social and historical commentary*. Oxford: Clarendon Press.

Porro, A. (1995). 'Alceo e le metafore dei giochi simposiali' in L. Belloni, G. Milanese and A. Porro (eds) *Studia Classica Iohanni Tarditi oblata*. Milan: Vita e Pensiero, I.357–68.

Powell, A. (1995). 'Athens' pretty face: anti-feminine rhetoric and fifth-century controversy over the Parthenon' in *id.*, (ed.) *The Greek world*. London: Routledge, 245–70.

Powell, J. E. (1938). *A lexicon to Herodotus*. Cambridge: Cambridge University Press.

Pritchard, D. (2003). 'Athletics, education and participation in classical Athens' in D. Philips and D. Pritchard (eds) *Sport and festival in the ancient Greek world*. Swansea: Classical Press of Wales, 293–350.

—(2004). 'Kleisthenes, participation and the dithyrambic contests of late archaic and classical Athens', *Phoenix* 58, 208–28.

Pritchard, J. B. (ed.), (1969). *Ancient Near Eastern Texts relating to the Old Testament*, 3rd edn. with supplement, Princeton: Princeton University Press.

Pucci, P. (1998). *The song of the sirens: essays on Homer*. Lanham, MD: Rowman & Littlefield.

Pulleyn, S. (2000). *Homer Iliad 1*. Oxford: Clarendon Press.

Purcell, N. (1990). 'Mobility and the *Polis*' in O. Murray and S. Price (eds) *The Greek City from Homer to Alexander*. Oxford: Clarendon Press, 29–58.

—(1995). 'Eating fish: the paradoxes of seafood' in J. Wilkins, D. Harvey and M. Dobson (eds) *Food in antiquity*. Exeter: University of Exeter Press, 132–49.

Qviller, B. (1981). 'The dynamics of the Homeric society', *SO* 56, 109–55.

Raaflaub, K. (1989) 'Contemporary perceptions of democracy in fifth-century Athens', *C&M* 40, 33–70.

—(1994). 'Democracy, power and imperialism in fifth-century Athens' in J. P. Euben, J. R. Wallach and J. Ober (eds), *Athenian political thought and the reconstruction of American democracy*. Ithaca, NY: Cornell University Press, 103–46.

—(1996). 'Equalities and inequalities in Athenian democracy' in J. Ober and C. Hedrick (eds) *Dêmokratia: a conversation on democracies, ancient and modern*. Princeton: Princeton University Press, 139–74.

—(2003). 'Stick and glue: the function of tyranny in fifth-century Athenian democracy' in K. A. Morgan (ed.) *Popular tyranny: sovereignty and its discontents in ancient Greece*. Austin: University of Texas Press, 59–93.

—(2004). *The Discovery of Freedom in ancient Greece*, trans. by R. Franciscono. Chicago: University of Chicago Press.

—(2009). 'Learning from the enemy: Athenian and Persian 'instruments of empire' in J. Ma, N. Papazarkadas and R. Parker (eds) *Interpreting the Athenian empire*. London: Duckworth, 89–124.

Radt, S. (1970). 'Sapphica', *Mnem.* Ser.4, 23, 337–47.

Rahner, H. (1963). *Greek myths and Christian mystery*, trans. by B. Battershaw. London: Burns & Oates.
Rankin, H. D. (1986). *Antisthenes Sokratikos*. Amsterdam: Hakkert.
Rechenauer, G. (1991). *Thukydides und die hippokratische Medizin*. Hildesheim: Georg Olms.
Rhodes, P. J. (1980). 'Athenian democracy after 403 B.C.', *CJ* 75, 305–23.
—(1981). *A Commentary on the Aristotelian Athenaion Politeia*. Oxford: Clarendon Press.
—(2008). 'After the three-bar *sigma* controversy: the history of Athenian imperialism reassessed', *CQ* 58, 501–6.
Rhodes, P. J. with Lewis, D. M. (1997). *The decrees of the Greek states*. Oxford: Clarendon Press.
Rhodes, P. J. and Osborne, R. (2003). *Greek historical inscriptions 404–323 BC*. Oxford: Oxford University Press.
Richardson, N. J. (1974). *The Homeric Hymn to Demeter*. Oxford: Clarendon Press.
—(2010). *Three Homeric hymns: To Apollo, Hermes, and Aphrodite*. Cambridge: Cambridge University Press.
Ringmar, E. (2008). 'Metaphors of social order' in T. Carver and J. Pikalo (eds) *Political language and metaphor*. London: Routledge, 57–68.
Roberts, J. T. (1982). *Accountability in Athenian government*. Madison, WI: University of Wisconsin Press.
—(1994). *Athens on trial: the antidemocratic tradition in western thought*. Princeton: Princeton University Press.
Robinson, E. W. (1997). *The first democracies: early popular government outside Athens*. Stuttgart: Steiner.
Robinson, G. M. (1987). *Heraclitus Fragments*. Toronto: University of Toronto Press.
Robinson, R. (1995). *Aristotle Politics Books III and IV*. 2nd edn. Rev. D. Keyt. Oxford: Oxford University Press.
Robinson, T. M. (1979). *Contrasting arguments: an edition of the Dissoi logoi*. New York: Arno.
de Romilly, J. (1974). 'Fairness and kindness in Thucydides', *Phoenix* 28, 95–100.
—(1976). 'Alcibiade et le mélange entre jeunes et vieux: politique et médecine.' *WS* n.s.10, 93–105.
—(1998). *The great Sophists in Periclean Athens*, trans. by J. Lloyd, Oxford: Clarendon Press.
Ronnet, G. (1951). *Etude sur le style de Démosthène dans les discours politiques*. Paris: de Boccard.
Rood, T. (1998). *Thucydides: narrative and explanation*. Oxford: Clarendon Press.
Roscalla, F. (1998). *Presenze simboliche dell' ape nella Grecia antica*. Pavia: La Nuova Italia.
Rose, P. (1997). 'Ideology in the *Iliad*', *Arethusa* 30, 151–99.
Rosen, R. M. (1997). 'The gendered polis in Eupolis' *Cities*' in G. W. Dobrov (ed.) *The City as comedy*. Chapel Hill, NC: University of North Carolina Press, 149–76.
Rosenstock, B. (1994). 'Athena's Cloak: Plato's critique of the democratic city in the *Republic*', *Political Theory* 22, 363–90.
Rosivach, V. J. (1987). 'Autochthony and the Athenians', *CQ* 37, 294–306.
Rösler, W. (1980). *Dichter und Gruppe: eine Untersuchung zu den Bedingungen und zur historischen Funktion früher griechischer Lyrik am Beispiel Alkaios*. München: Fink.
Rowe, C. J. (1995). *Plato: Statesman*. Warminster: Aris & Phillips.
Roy, J. (1999). '*Polis* and *oikos* in classical Athens', *G&R* 46, 1–18.

Rutherford, R. B. (1995). *The art of Plato*. London: Duckworth.
—(1996). *Homer* (*Greece & Rome* New Surveys 26). Oxford: Clarendon Press.
—(2012). *Greek tragic style*. Cambridge: Cambridge University Press.
Salmon, J. (1984). *Wealthy Corinth*. Oxford: Clarendon Press.
—(1997). 'Lopping off the heads? Tyrants, politics and the polis' in L. Mitchell and P. J. Rhodes (eds) *The development of the polis in archaic Greece*. London: Routledge, 60–73.
Sancho Rocher, L. (1994). 'Tucídides y el tema de la polis-tyrannos', *QS* 20, 59–83.
Sancisi-Weerdenburg, H. (1993). 'Exit Atossa: images of women in Greek historiography on Persia' in A. Cameron and A. Kuhrt (eds) *Images of women in antiquity*, rev. edn. London: Routledge, 20–33.
Schaefer, H. (1962). 'προστάτης', *RE Supp.* IX, 1287–304.
Scheid, J. and Svenbro, J. (1996). *The craft of Zeus: myths of weaving and fabric*. Cambridge, MA: Harvard University Press.
Schibli, H. S. (1990). *Pherekydes of Syros*. Oxford: Clarendon Press.
Schofield, M. (2006). *Plato: political philosophy*. Oxford: Oxford University Press.
Scholtz, A. (1996). 'Perfume from Peron's: the politics of pedicure in Anaxandrides fr.41KA' *ICS* 21, 69–86.
—(2007). *Concordia discors: eros and dialogue in classical Athenian literature*. Cambridge, MA: Center for Hellenic Studies.
Schubert, S. (1997). 'Menschenbild und Normwandel in der klassischen Zeit' in H. Flashar and J. Jouanna (eds) *Médicine et morale dans l'antiquité* (*Entretiens du Fondation Hardt*, Vol. 43). Geneva: Fondation Hardt, 121–43.
Schwarze, J. (1971). *Die Beurteilung des Perikles durch die attische Komödie und ihre historische und historiographische Bedeutung* (*Zetemata* 51). Munich: C.H. Beck.
Scott, L. (2005). *Historical commentary on Herodotus Book 6*. Leiden: Brill.
Scully, S. (1990). *Homer and the Sacred City*. Ithaca: Cornell University Press.
Seaford, R. (1994). *Reciprocity and ritual*. Oxford: Clarendon Press.
—(1996). *Euripides Bacchae*. Warminster: Aris & Phillips.
—(2012). *Cosmology and the polis*. Cambridge: Cambridge University Press.
Sennett, R. (1980). *Authority*. London: Secker & Warburg.
Silk, M. S. (1974). *Interaction in poetic imagery*. Cambridge: Cambridge University Press.
Sinclair, R. K. (1988). *Democracy and participation in Athens*. Cambridge: Cambridge University Press.
Skemp, J. B. (1952). *Plato's Statesman*. London: Routledge & Kegan Paul.
Skutsch, O. (1985). *The Annals of Quintus Ennius*. Oxford: Clarendon Press.
Slatkin, L. M. (2001). 'The Wrath of Thetis' in D. L. Cairns (ed.) *Oxford Readings in Homer's Iliad*. Oxford: Clarendon Press, 409–34. [revised from *TAPA* 1986 1–24].
Smith, A. C. (1999). 'Eurymedon and the evolution of political personifications in the early classical period', *JHS* 119, 128–41.
Smith, C. F. (1918). 'Personification in Thucydides', *CPh* 13, 241–50.
Smith, C. J. (1907). 'What constitutes a state?', *CJ* 2, 299–302.
Snodgrass, A. (1983). 'Heavy Freight in Archaic Greece' in P. Garnsey, K. Hopkins and C. R. Whittaker (eds) *Trade in the Ancient Economy*. Berkeley: University of California Press, 16–26, 182–3.
Sommerstein, A. (1980). *Aristophanes Acharnians*. Warminster: Aris & Phillips.
—(1983). *Aristophanes Wasps*. Warminster: Aris & Phillips.
—(1989). *Aeschylus Eumenides*. Cambridge: Cambridge University Press.
—(1993). 'Kleophon and the restaging of *Frogs*' in A. H. Sommerstein, S. Halliwell,

J. Henderson and B. Zimmerman (eds) *Tragedy, comedy and the polis*. Bari: Levante, 461–76.
Sontag, S. (1991). *Illness as metaphor* and *AIDS and its metaphors*. Harmondsworth: Penguin. [*Illness as Metaphor*, first published 1978. New York: Farrar, Straus & Giroux].
Spivey, N. (1994). 'Psephological heroes' in R. Osborne and S. Hornblower (eds) *Ritual, finance, politics: Athenian democratic accounts presented to David Lewis*. Oxford: Clarendon Press, 39–51.
Stadter, P. A. (1989). *A commentary on Plutarch's Pericles*. Chapel Hill, NC: University of North Carolina Press.
Stafford, E. (2000). *Worshipping virtues: personification and the divine in ancient Greece*. London: Duckworth/Classical Press of Wales.
—(2003). 'Brother, son, friend and healer: Sleep the god' in K. Dowden and T. Wiedemann (eds) *Sleep*. Bari: Levante, 71–106.
—(2012). *Herakles*. Abingdon: Routledge.
Stagakis, G. (1966). 'Therapontes and hetairoi in the *Iliad*, as symbols of the political structure of the Homeric state', *Historia* 15, 408–19.
Stanford, W. B. (1958). *Aristophanes The Frogs*. London: Macmillan.
—(1959). *The Odyssey of Homer*, 2nd edn. London: Macmillan.
—(1963). *Sophocles Ajax*. London: Macmillan.
de Ste. Croix, G. E. M. (1953). 'Demosthenes' *timema* and the Athenian *eisphora* in the fourth century BC', *C&M* 14, 30–70.
—(1972). *The origins of the Peloponnesian war*. London: Duckworth.
—(1981). *The class struggle in the ancient Greek world*. London: Duckworth.
Stehle, E. (2006). 'Solon's self-reflexive political persona and its audience' in J. Blok and A. P. M. H. Lardinois (eds) *Solon of Athens: new historical and philological approaches*. Leiden: Brill, 79–113.
Steiner, D. (1986). *The crown of song: metaphor in Pindar*. London: Duckworth.
—(1994). *The tyrant's writ: myths and images of writing in ancient Greece*. Princeton: Princeton University Press.
—(2010). *Homer Odyssey Books XVII and XVIII*. Cambridge: Cambridge University Press.
Stevens, P. T. (1971). *Euripides Andromache*. Oxford: Clarendon Press.
Stevenson, T. R. (1992). 'The ideal benefactor and the father analogy in Greek and Roman thought', *CQ* 42, 421–36.
Stewart, A. (1996). *Art, desire and the body in ancient Greece*. Cambridge: Cambridge University Press.
Stier, H. E. (1927–8). 'ΝΟΜΟΣ ΒΑΣΙΛΕΥΣ', *Philologus* 83, 225–58.
Storey, I. C. (2003). *Eupolis, poet of Old Comedy*. Oxford: Oxford University Press.
Strauss, B. (1986). *Athens after the Peloponnesian war*. London: Croom Helm.
—(1993). *Fathers and sons in Athens*. Princeton: Princeton University Press.
—(1996). 'The Athenian trireme, school of democracy' in J. Ober and C. Hedrick (eds) *Dêmokratia: a conversation on democracies, ancient and modern*. Princeton: Princeton University Press, 313–25.
Stylianou, P. J. (1998). *A historical commentary on Diodorus Siculus Book 15*. Oxford: Clarendon Press.
Svenbro, J. (1993). *Phrasikleia: an anthropology of reading in ancient Greece*, trans. by J. Lloyd. Ithaca: Cornell University Press.
Swain, S. (1994). 'Man and medicine in Thucydides', *Arethusa* 27: 303–27.

Taillardat, J. (1962). *Les images d'Aristophane: études de langue et de style*. Paris: Les Belles Lettres.
Taplin, O. (1977). *The stagecraft of Aeschylus*. Oxford: Clarendon Press.
Tarrant, D. (1946). 'Imagery in Plato's *Republic*', *CQ* 40, 27–34.
—(1960). 'Greek metaphors of light', *CQ* 10, 181–7.
Tatum, J. (1989). *Xenophon's imperial fiction*. Princeton: Princeton University Press.
Taylor A. E. (1928) *A commentary on Plato's Timaeus*. Oxford: Clarendon Press.
Taylor, C. C. W. (1999). *The Atomists: Leucippus and Democritus*. Toronto: University of Toronto Press.
Tedeschi, G. (1991). 'Il canto di Hybrias Cretese: un esempio di poesia conviviale' and 'Il canto di Hybrias: edizione critica e commento' in K. Fabian, E. Pellizer and G. Tedeschi (eds) 'Οινηρὰ τεύχη. *Studi triestini di poesia conviviale*. Alessandria: Edizioni dell'Orso, 119–26, 173–85.
Thomas, E. (2007). *Monumentality and the Roman empire*. Oxford: Oxford University Press.
Thomas, R. (1989). *Oral tradition and written record in classical Athens*. Cambridge: Cambridge University Press.
Trevett, J. (1992). *Apollodorus the son of Pasion*. Oxford: Clarendon Press.
Triebel-Schubert, C. (1984). 'Der Begriff der Isonomie bei Alkmaion', *Klio* 66, 40–50.
Tucker, T. G. (1889). *The 'Supplices' of Aeschylus*. London: Macmillan.
Tuplin, C. J. (1985). 'Imperial tyranny: some reflections on a classical Greek political metaphor' in P. A. Cartledge and F. D. Harvey (eds) *CRUX: Essays in Greek history presented to G.E.M. de Ste. Croix*. London: Duckworth, 348–75.
—(2007a). 'Fear of slavery and the failure of the *polis*' in A. Serghidou (ed.) *Peur de l'esclave – Peur de l'esclavage en Méditerranée ancienne / Fear of slaves – Fear of enslavement in the ancient Mediterranean (XXIXe colloque du GIREA, Rethymnon, 4–7 novembre 2004)*. Besançon: Presses universitaires de Franche-Comté) 57–74.
—(2007b). 'Treacherous hearts and upright tiaras: on the head-gear of Persian kings' in id., (ed.) *Persian responses: political and cultural interaction with(in) the Achaemenid Empire*. Swansea: Classical Press of Wales, 67–98.
—(2009). 'The Gadatas letter' in L. G. Mitchell and L. Rubinstein (eds) *Greek history and epigraphy: essays in honour of Peter Rhodes*. Swansea: Classical Press of Wales, 155–84.
Usher, S. (1968). 'Xenophon, Critias and Theramenes', *JHS* 88, 128–35.
—(1990). *Greek orators III: Isocrates*. Warminster: Aris & Phillips.
Ussher, R. G. (1973). *Aristophanes Ecclesiazusae*. Oxford: Clarendon Press.
Vannicelli, P. (2002). '*Moritur et ridet*: indizi di *logos epitaphios* nella *Lisistrata* di Aristofane', *QUCC* n.s. 72, 63–72.
Vermeule, E. (1979). *Aspects of death in early Greek art and poetry*. Berkeley: University of California Press.
Vernant, J. P. (1982). *The origins of Greek thought*. London: Methuen.
Villacèque, N. (2010). 'De la bigarrure en politique (Platon *République* 8.577c4–61e7), *JHS* 130, 137–52.
Villard, P. (1988). 'Le mélange et ses problèmes', *REA* 90, 19–33.
Vlastos, G. (1946). 'Solonian justice', *CPh*. 41, 65–83.
—(1947). 'Equality and justice in early Greek cosmologies', *CPh*. 42, 156–78.
—(1953). 'Isonomia', *AJP* 74, 337–66.
—(1994). 'The historical Socrates and Athenian democracy in *id.*, *Socratic studies* (ed. M. Burnyeat). Cambridge: Cambridge University Press, 87–108.
Vox, O. (1984). *Solone autoritratto*. Padova: Antenore.

Wade-Gery, H. T. (1932). 'Thucydides son of Melesias', *JHS* 52, 205–27.
Walbank, F. W. (1984). 'Monarchies and monarchic ideas' in F. W. Walbank, A. E. Astin, M. W. Frederiksen and R. M. Ogilvie (eds) *The Cambridge Ancient History* VII². Cambridge: Cambridge University Press, 62–100
Wallace, R. W. (2004). 'Damon of Oa: a music theorist ostracized?' in P. Murray and P. Wilson (eds) *Music and the Muses: the culture of mousike in the classical Athenian city*. Oxford: Oxford University Press, 249–67.
Wallach, J. R. (2001). *The Platonic political art: a study of critical reason and democracy*. University Park, PA: Pennsylvania State University Press.
Wankel, H. (1976). *Demosthenes: Rede für Ktesiphon über den Kranz*. Heidelberg: Winter.
Watkins, C. (2001). *How to kill a dragon: aspects of Indo-European poetics*. Oxford: Oxford University Press.
Webster, T. B. L. (1954). 'Personification as a mode of Greek thought', *JWI* 17, 10–21.
—(1970). *Sophocles Philoctetes*. Cambridge: Cambridge University Press.
van Wees, H. (1992). *Status Warriors*. Amsterdam: Gieben.
—(1995). 'Politics and the battlefield: ideology in Greek warfare' in A. Powell (ed.) *The Greek world*. London: Routledge, 153–78.
—(1998). 'Greeks bearing arms: the state, the leisure class and the display of arms in archaic Greece' in N. Fisher and H. van Wees (eds), *Archaic Greece: new approaches and new evidence*. London: Duckworth/Classical Press of Wales, 338–78.
—(2007). 'Attic Vikings: society and state in Athens, c. 750–450 BC', Inaugural lecture, UCL, 18/10/2007.
—(2008). '"*Stasis*, destroyer of men": security in archaic Greece' in P. Ducrey and C. Brelaz (eds) *Sécurité collective et ordre public dans les societés anciennes* (*Entretiens du Fondation Hardt*, Vol. 54). Geneva: Fondation Hardt, 1–44.
—(2009). 'The economy' in K. A. Raaflaub and H. van Wees (eds) *A companion to archaic Greece*. Chichester: Wiley-Blackwell, 444–67.
Weinstock, S. (1971). *Divus Julius*. Oxford: Clarendon Press.
Welcker, F.G. (1850). 'Schneiden und Brennen' in *Kleine Schriften* III. Bonn: E. Weber, 209–17.
West, M.L. (1966). *Hesiod Theogony*. Oxford: Clarendon Press.
—(1971). *Iambi et elegi ante Alexandrum cantati*. Oxford: Clarendon Press.
—(1974). *Studies in Greek elegy and iambus*. Berlin: de Gruyter.
—(1978a). *Hesiod Works and Days*. Oxford: Clarendon Press.
—(1978b). 'An unrecognised fragment of Archilochus?', *ZPE* 32, 1–5.
—(1983). *The Orphic poems*. Oxford: Clarendon Press.
—(1992). *Ancient Greek music*. Oxford: Clarendon Press.
—(1997). *The East face of Helicon*. Oxford: Clarendon Press.
—(2002). '"Eumelos": a Corinthian epic cycle?', *JHS* 122, 109–33.
—(2007). *Indo-European poetry and myth*. Oxford: Oxford University Press.
Whitehead, D. (1993). 'Cardinal virtues: the language of public approbation in democratic Athens', *C&M* 44, 37–75.
—(2000). *Hypereides: the forensic speeches*. Oxford: Oxford University Press.
Wibier, M. (2010). *Medical metaphor and mixed constitution in Plato's Laws*. MA Diss: Leiden.
Wilamowitz-Möllendorf, U. von (1893). *Aristoteles und Athen*. Berlin: Weidmann.
Wilkins, J. (2000). *The boastful chef: the discourse of food in ancient Greek comedy*. Oxford: Oxford University Press.
Willcock, M. M. (2001). 'Mythological paradeigma in the *Iliad*' in D. L. Cairns (ed.)

Oxford Readings in Homer's Iliad. Oxford: Clarendon Press, 435–55. [revised from *CQ* 1964, 141–54].
Willets, R. F. (1962). *Cretan cults and festivals*, London: Routledge & Kegan Paul.
Wilson, P. (2000). *The Athenian institution of the khoregia: the chorus, the city, and the stage*. Cambridge: Cambridge University Press.
Willi, A. (2008). 'νόσος and ὁσίη: etymological and sociocultural observations on the concept of disease and divine (dis)favour in ancient Greece', *JHS* 128, 153–71.
Winnington-Ingram, R. P. (1980). *Sophocles: an interpretation*. Cambridge: Cambridge University Press.
Wiseman, T. P. (2012). 'Cicero and the Body Politic', forthcoming in *Politica antica* 2.
Wohl, V. (2002). *Love among the ruins: the erotics of democracy in classical Athens*. Princeton: Princeton University Press.
Wolff, C. (1979). 'A note on lions and Sophocles *Philoctetes* 1436' in G. W. Bowersock, W. Burkert and M. C. J. Putman (eds) *Arktouros: Hellenic studies presented to Bernard M.W. Knox on the occasion of his 65th birthday*. Berlin: de Gruyter, 144–50.
Woodman, A. J. (1988). *Rhetoric in classical historiography*. London: Croom Helm.
Wooten, C. W. (1978). 'La funzione delle metafore e delle similitudini nelle orazioni di Demostene', *QUCC* 29, 123–5.
—(1979). 'Unnoticed medical language in Demosthenes', *Hermes* 107, 157–60.
Wright, M. R. (1981). *Empedocles: the extant fragments*. New Haven: Yale University Press.
Yatromanolakis, Y. (2005). '*Poleos erastes*: The Greek city as the beloved' in E. Stafford and J. Herrin (eds) *Personification in the Greek world: from Antiquity to Byzantium*. Aldershot: Ashgate, 267–83.
Young, T. C. (1988). 'The early history of the Medes and the Persians and the Achaemenid empire to the death of Cambyses' and 'The consolidation of the empire and the limits of its growth under Darius and Xerxes' in J. Boardman, N. G. L. Hammond, D. M. Lewis and M. Ostwald (eds) *The Cambridge Ancient History* IV². Cambridge: Cambridge University Press, 1–52, 53–111.
Yunis, H. (1996). *Taming democracy: models of political rhetoric in classical Athens*. Ithaca, NY: Cornell University Press.
—(1997). 'Thrasymachus B1: discord, not diplomacy', *CPh* 92, 58–66.
—(2001). *Demosthenes On the crown*. Cambridge: Cambridge University Press.
Zuntz, G. (1971). *Persephone: three essays on religion and thought in Magna Graecia*. Oxford: Clarendon Press.

Index of Authors and Images

Authors only cited once or twice are omitted here unless a passage is discussed in the text, but can be located through the Index locorum; for convenience pseudo-Demosthenes is incorporated with Demosthenes, [Arist.] under Aristotle and P.V. under Aeschylus.

Aeschines
    animals, abusive comparisons 163
    commerce 154
    democracy, imagery from 164–5
    freedom and slavery 157
    household 28, 154
    law as agent 165
    maritime 57, 156
    medical 73, 156
    military xi, 162–3
    protection 164
    sport 157
    wage labour 29, 154
Aeschylus
    architecture 125
    bees 160
    birds of prey 118
    Demos as *polissouchos* (guardian) 16n. 23
    freedom and slavery 111
    gods as kings 5–8
    kings as gods 12
    lion 118
    maritime 55–6, 113
    medical 75, 112
    military 139n. 127
    shepherd 44, 107–8
    sport 119, 173n. 47
    taming of animals 111
    water, law as pure 125
Aesop
    animals 164
    medical 70–1
Alcaeus
    architecture 89, 123
    board games 93
    elements 88–9
    fox 90
    gods as kings 18n. 37
    maritime 53–4, 59, 85–6
    myth as example 93
    predator, tyrant as 90
    proverbs 104n. 91
Alcidamas
    gods as kings 10, 164
Alcmaeon of Croton
    medical 9, 75, 114, 152
Alexis
    Democracy, imagery from 194n. 180
Anacreon
    gods as kings 8, 16n. 23
    shepherd (divine) 44
Anaxagoras
    gods as kings 9–10, 20n. 36
Anaximander
    gods as kings 8
Andocides
    democracy, imagery from 125
    freedom and slavery 157–8
    protection 125
Anonymus Iamblichi
    gods as kings 10
    tyrant as trustee 27, 125
Antimachus
    gods as kings 18n. 39
Antiphanes
    god as helmsman 174n. 50
    gods as kings 8
    writing tablet 179n. 81
Antiphon
    taming of animals 121
    law as agent 145n. 156

Antisthenes
    maritime 180n. 89
    military 192n. 163
Archelaus
    gods as kings 10
Archilochus
    maritime 53–4, 59, 85
Aristophanes
    animals, abusive comparisons 119
    bees 137n. 106
    chariot of state 121
    coinage 122
    elements 61, 120
    eranos 154
    household 27–8, 115
    lion 118
    lover of the demos 116
    maritime 57, 117
    politicians as gods 13, 120
    shepherd 50n. 17
    sport 119–20
    stasis 125
    tyrant city 124
    watchdog 118–19
    wool-working 122
Aristophon
    gods as kings 7
Aristotle
    animals 164
    art 160
    coinage 165
    crop destruction 164
    elements 159
    father 31, 156, 179n. 86
    freedom and slavery 157
    gods as kings 9
    household 26, 28, 30, 32, 34, 149
    king as living law 14, 166
    law as agent 165
        as divine 166
        as master 166
    maritime 150
    medical 79n. 28, 81n. 49, 150, 173n. 44
    military 162
    mixture 189n. 149
    music 161
    protection 125
    rule of reason 152
    shepherd 48

sport 152
Attic skolia
    kings as gods 12

Bacchylides
    gods as kings 5, 7, 18n. 38

Comedy, anonymous
    animals, abusive comparisons 119
    gods as kings 7
    taming of animals 120–1
Cratinus
    fire 138n. 118
    politicians as gods 13, 120

Delphic oracle
    boulder 89
    helmsman 55, 86
    kings as gods 11–12
    lion 89
    medical 70
Demades
    architecture 163
    democracy, imagery from 165
    law as tyrant 166
    maritime 57, 156
    medical 72, 156
Democritus
    bodily microcosm 152
    freedom and slavery 183n. 112
    gods as kings 10
Demosthenes
    animals, abusive comparisons 163
    architecture 163
    carpet-making 164
    coinage 165
    commerce 154
    democracy, imagery from 164–5
    elements 61, 159
    eranos 154
    freedom and slavery 157–8
    gods as kings 18n. 39
    household 28–9, 32–3, 154, 156
    law as agent 165
    lover of the demos 155
    maritime 57, 156
    medical 70, 72–3, 156, 164
    military xi, 162–3
    protection 164

Index of Authors and Images 223

religion 24n. 101
rule of reason 153
sport 157
taming of animals 159
theatre 189n. 147
viticulture 164
wage labour 29, 154
watchdog 156
Dinarchus
  animals, abusive comparisons 163
  architecture 163
  commerce 154
  freedom and slavery 158
  household 37n. 14
  law as agent 165
  lover of the demos 155
  medical 70, 156
  protection 164
  sport 157
Diogenes
  gods as kings 9

Empedocles
  gods as kings 5–6, 8, 20n. 63, 114
Epimenides
  gods as kings 4–5, 114
Eupolis
  animals, abusive comparisons 180n. 91
  clothing 141n. 129
  politicians as gods 11, 13
  sport 119
Euripides
  crop destruction 124
  elements 61, 120
  freedom and slavery 110–11
  gods as kings 6–9, 19n. 49
  household 25
  kings as gods 12
  maritime 55–6
  master and slave 108, 128n.16
  medical 75
  military 139n. 127
  shepherd 44

Gorgias
  gods as kings 6–7
  kings as gods 12
  legislators as craftsmen 135n. 93
  protection 125

Heraclitus
  gods as kings 8–9
  law as city wall 93
Hermippus
  politicians as gods 13
Herodotus
  bull 89–90
  crop destruction 101n. 62, 124
  elements 61, 100n. 49, 120
  father 31
  gods as kings 4, 6
  household 25, 37n. 15, 110
  kings as gods 12–13
  lion 89–90, 118
  maritime 54, 117
  master and slave 108–9
  medical 71
  sport 119
Hesiod
  gods as kings 1–4
  hawk and nightingale 84
  kings as gods 11
  predator, king as 90
  shepherd 44
Hippocratic Corpus
  master and slave 128n. 16
  'powers' in body 7, 9, 114, 152
Hipponax
  gods as kings 5
Homer
  architecture 85
  gods as kings 1–4, 7
  king as father 30, 83–4
  kings as gods 11
  predator, king as 90
  shepherd 43–4, 83–4
Homeric hymns
  gods as kings 2–4
  kings as gods 11
Hypereides
  animals, abusive comparisons 163
  commerce 154
  freedom and slavery 158
  household 26, 154
  medical 70, 156

Iambic, anonymous
  elements 61
Ion of Chios

gods as kings 8
Isaeus
   imagery from democracy 164
Isocrates
   bad living as treason or stasis 42n. 61, 175n. 55
   elements 61, 159
   freedom and slavery 157
   gods as kings 6–7, 19n. 49, 152, 174n. 49
   household 26–7, 32–3, 154, 156
   kings as gods 14
   lover of the demos 155
   maritime (of soul) 174n. 50
   medical 70
   military 162–3
   protection 164
   rule of reason 152
   sport 152

Lycophron
   law as guarantor 37n. 14
Lycurgus
   architecture 163
   democracy, imagery from 165
   eranos 154
   freedom and slavery 158
   household 32–3
   military 162
Lyric, anonymous
   gods as kings 18n. 40
   Hybrias the Cretan as master 92, 98n. 37
Lysias
   democracy, imagery from 164
   freedom and slavery 158
   gods as kings 10
   household 33
   military 162

Orphic poems
   gods as kings 4, 6

Pherecydes
   gods as kings 4
Philemon
   freedom and slavery 185n. 119
Pindar
   architecture 85, 89, 112

   birds of prey 112
   elements 138n. 116
   father 30, 112
   gods as kings 3, 5–7, 16n. 23, 18, 166
   household 26, 112
   light 100n. 49, 112
   maritime 113
   medical 75, 112
   military 139n. 127
   shepherd 44, 112
   tree 112
Plato
   animals, abusive comparisons 159
   architecture 163
   art 160
   bees 160, 176n. 59
   chariot of state 159
   father 31
   freedom and slavery 157
   gods as kings 8–10
   horticulture 164
   household 25, 28, 32–4, 149, 155–6
   king as living law 14
   kings as gods 12
   law as master 166
      as god 166
      as king 166
   lover of the demos 155
   maritime 58, 150–1, 156
   medical 70–3, 75, 81n. 50, 150–2
   military 162
   music 161
   mythological 13
   rule of reason 152–3
   shepherd 45–6, 48, 148, 150
   trainer 72, 151–2
   tyranny of demos 159
   watchdog 46, 156
   wool-working 161
Plato Comicus
   animals, abusive comparisons 119
   medical 181n. 97
   politicians as gods 13, 120
   sport 119
Pratinas
   gods as kings 8
Pythagorean School
   gods as kings 9

Scylax
    kings as gods 12
Simonides
    gods as kings 5, 18n. 39
    light 89
    teacher 118
Solon
    animals 90-1
    boundary stone (*horos*) 91
    chariot of state 88
    cream 91
    elements 61, 88
    gods as kings 18n. 37
    hunting 90
    master and slave 92
    medical 69-70, 73, 92
    shield 91
Sophocles
    architecture 145n. 155
    chariot of state 113, 121
    elements 120
    father 30-1, 41n. 43, 111
    freedom and slavery 111
    gods as kings 6-9
    hunting 112
    kings as gods 12
    maritime 55-6, 113
    military 139n. 127
    sport 119
    taming of animals 111
    teacher 118
Stesichorus
    animal fable 87
    gods as kings 18n. 37
Stesimbrotus
    gods as kings 5, 114

Telecleides
    politicians as gods 13
Theognis
    architecture 89
    gods as kings 5, 18n. 37
    kings as gods 11
    maritime 54, 85-6
    medical 69-70, 73, 92
    predator, tyrant as 90
    taming of animals 87
Thucydides
    eranos 154
    freedom and slavery 123, 158
    lover of the demos 115-16
    medical 75, 117, 122
    men identified with city 123
    sport 119
    tyrant city 123-4
    see also prostatês
Tragedy, anonymous
    architecture 145n. 155
    gods as kings 8
Tyrtaios
    taming of animals 87

Xenophanes
    gods as kings 9-10
Xenophon
    animals, abusive comparisons 163
    bees 159-60
    father 31, 156
    freedom and slavery 157
    gods as citizens 19n. 50
    household 25-6, 30, 32, 149
    kings as gods 12
    law as master 166
    maritime 55, 150
    medical 70, 150
    rule of reason 152
    ruler as law 14, 166
    shepherd 43, 45-7, 150
    sport 151
    tyranny of demos 159

Index locorum

This index is selective and restricted to passages of political (or, occasionally, other) imagery and does not include passages cited to establish historical or literary context. Passages cited in or alluded to in the main text are cited by the text page(s) but will generally be found in the corresponding footnotes. Authors are 'amalgamated' for convenience as in the index of authors and images.

Aelian
VH 2.20 30, 166
13.38 191n. 155

Aeschines
1.4, 5 165
1.7 27–8, 164
1.14 165
1.51–2 29
1.64 163
1.72 29
1.135 163
1.153 25
1.154, 163–4 29
1.187 27–8
2.20, 34 163
2.79 165
2.146 163
2.176 140n. 127, 157
2.177 80n. 37, 181n. 95
2.253 130n. 36
3.3 28, 154
3.7 162, 164
3.13, 15–16 26, 36n. 8, 154
3.35 192n. 164
3.37 165
3.66 154
3.75 162
3.84 163
3.86 29, 154
3.91, 92–4 154
3.132 157
3.158 57, 156
3.159 162
3.166 164

3.179–80 157
3.182 163
3.197–8, 199–200 165
3.200 29
3.202 165
3.205–6 157
3.207 192n. 165, 193n. 174
3.208 72–3, 193n. 173
3.218 29
3.220 154
3.225 72–3
3.226 154
3.233–4 185n. 121
3.236 163
3.250 164
3.251 28, 154
3.253 192n. 165

Aeschylus
Ag. 6 7
49 118
50 108
113–15 118
171 119
181–96 108
182–3 56
200 139n. 127
256 145n. 155
410 139n. 127
483 141n. 127
509 6
587 127n. 7
594 108
650–1 8
666 127n. 7

717–36 118
795 45
848–50 75, 112
899 120
966–72 xxn. 30, 120
1617–18 56, 113
1639–42 111
Cho. 357–9, 405 6
630 141n. 127
809, 863, 1046 111
Eum. 16 64n. 23
127–8 7
399 139n. 127
456, 566, 569, 668, 683, 762 140n. 127
765 64n. 23
775, 883 16n. 23, 142n. 136
889 140n. 127
694–5, 701, 706 125
911–12 164
948 125
1010 16n. 23, 142n. 136
Pers. 74–5 44
80 12
126–9 160
157 12
215 31, 111
241–2 44, 107–8, 140n. 127
634, 642–3, 651, 655 12
656 55, 113
664, 671 31, 111
711, 856 12
859–60 145n. 155
P.V. 50 5, 129n. 29
122 5
149–50 55, 113
171, 186f., 198f. 5
208 111
221 5
224–5 5, 74
228–31, 310, 324, 389 5
405 141n. 127
515 56
671–2 111
756–7, 761, 767, 908–10, 912 5
918–21 119
927, 930 111
Sept. 2–3, 62–4, 208–10, 652 55, 113
Supp. 248 140n. 127
345 64n. 29, 113

373 12
524, 595f. 6
905 139–40n. 127
Fr. 47a.2 140n. 127
132c.8 44
281a.24 140n. 127
451q.8 44

Aesop
130 Perry 70–1
269a Perry 164

Aglaosthenes (*FGrH* 499)
F2 18n. 39, 152

Alcaeus
Fr.6 54, 86
69.6, 70.6–7 90
73 xvii–xviiin. 7, 97n. 26
74 88–9
112.10 89
129.23–4 90
208 53–4, 86
296.3 18n. 37
306 (i) col. II a xvii–xviiin. 7, 97n. 26
308b.3–4, 387 18n. 37
344 104n. 91
351 93
426 89
S262 93–4

Alcidamas
Fr.17B–S 10, 166

Alcmaeon
B4 9, 75, 114, 152

Alexis
Fr.264 194n. 180

Anacreon
fr. 346 (2) xviin. 7
348 16n. 23, 44
360 99n. 41
396, 398, 403 xviin. 7
417 99n. 41
449 102n. 77
505d 8

Index locorum

Anaxagoras
A48 9
A55 20n. 63
B12 9–10

Anaxandrides
Fr.4 64n. 31

Anaximander
A15 64n. 31
B1 8

Andocides
1.9 145n. 156
2.27 158
3.29 182n. 102
4.7 125
4.12 190n. 154
4.16 125

Androtion (*FGrH* 324)
F72 163

Anonymus Iamblichi
6.1 10, 195n. 187
7.13–14 27, 125

Antimachus
Fr.3 18n. 39, 152

Antiphanes
Fr.19.4 8
42 174n. 50
194 179n. 81

Antiphon
1.13 56, 174n. 50
3.1.1 125
B70DK 121

Antisthenes
Fr.15.8 168n. 14
71, 88, 90 192n. 163
100 164
185–6 168n. 14

Archilochus
Fr.23.20 102n. 77
105–6 53, 85

Aristodicus (*FGrH* 36)
F1 18n. 39, 152

Aristogeiton
Fr.5B–S 163

Aristophanes
Ach. 143–4 116
385 xixn. 17
530–1 13
565 xixn. 17
598 119
704 xixn. 17, 119
710 119
Av. 977–9 136n. 99
1753 19n. 49
Eccl. 176 140n. 127, 190n. 154
210–12, 455–6 27, 115
466 121
600 27, 115
Eq. passim 26, 28, 115
41 145n. 160
47–8 137n. 103
60 28
75 134n. 82
212 27, 115
213–6 132n. 68
256 50n. 17
264 119
326 50n. 23
388 119
426 27, 115
461–3 134n. 82
491–2 119
511 13, 120
589–90 125
716–8 28
732–4 116
841–2 119
974 137n. 106
859 132n. 68
862–3 134n. 82
887 119
908 28
947–8, 949 27, 115
956 136n. 97
1011–12 136n. 99
1017–19, 1023–4 118–19
1025–6, 1031–4 119

1037–43 118
1038 28
1051–3 118
1086–7 136n. 99
1098 27, 115
1099 134n. 82
1109 121
1111–14 124
1128 140n. 127
1151–1226 28, 115
1163 116
1259 27, 115
1330, 1333 124
1340–4 116
1353 119–20
Lys. 170 61, 120
493–5 27, 115
567–86 27, 115, 122
648–55 177n. 71
1155 128n. 24
Nub. 591 136n. 97
1203 119
Pax 313–5, 641 119
684 140n. 127
686 27, 136n. 102
752, 754–9 13, 119–20
Pl. 920 140n. 127, 190n. 154
Ran. 359–60 120
361 57, 117
689–90 119
704 57, 117
708 119
718–37 122
1085 119
1431 118
Vesp. 29 57, 117
32, 34 119
35 136n. 97
419 140n. 127
596–7 28
650–1 77n. 7, 117
704–5 119
712 28, 132n. 68
891–930, 971–2 118–19
1030–6 13, 120
Fr.241 136n. 99
305 27
409 119
699 28, 132n. 68

Aristophon
Fr.11 7

Aristotle
APo. 76a16–18 152
Ath.Pol. 3.6, 4.4 191n. 158
6.4 69, 156
8.5 191n. 159
13.3 69, 156
14.3 164
24.2 158
25.2 191n. 158
26.1 161
28.5 32
41.2 158
De An. 410b12–14, 429a18–20 152
EE 1219b26–20a2 152
1241b27–30 161
1242a1–13 34
1242a32–5 179n. 86
1242b27–31 34
1246b8–12, 1249b7–13 152
EN 1113a6–7 152
1128a32 196n. 189
1129b14–24 194n. 185
1132a21–2 14
1138b21–3 161
1143b33–5, 1145a6–9 152
1145a28–9 11
1151b15–16, 1152a20–4 175n. 55
1160b22–61b10 34, 170n. 24
1161a12–15 48, 170n. 27
1166b19 175n. 55
1180b4–7 179n. 86
HA 488a10–13, 628a33–4 186n. 129
MA 701b25, 29, 702a37 175n. 56
703a37–b1 152
MM 1177a13–16, 1198b9–20 152
1203b8–9 175n. 55
Metaph. 1076a3–4 9, 174n. 51
Oec. 1353b17–18 161
Part.An. 670a26 77n. 11, 175n. 56
Pol. 1252a7–16 26, 149
1252b19–27 170n. 24
1253b18–20 149
1254b5–7 152
1255a7–9 195n. 184
1255b16–20 149
1258b31–3 34

1259a37–b17 17n. 26, 34, 149
1265b33–5, 1266a4 189n. 149
1270a6–7 186n. 128
1270b24–5 173n. 47
1270b34–5 41n. 48, 191n. 155
1271b21–2, 24 160
1273b11–12 161
1273b18–24 77n. 7, 79n. 28, 156
1273b32–3 160
1273b35–41 189n. 149
1274a17–18 158
1274a25–7 152
1274b8, 18 160
1277a23–5 184n. 117
1277b29–30 161
1278b30–79a2 149
1278b40–79a21 171n. 34
1280b6–12 194n. 176
1280b10–11 37n. 14
1281b35–8 189n. 149
1284a 164
1284a3–15 14, 196n. 189
1284a15–17, a26–b3 164
1284b17–22 77n. 7, 79n. 28, 156
1284b25–34 14
1285b29–33 170n. 24
1286a9–14 173n. 44
1286a29–30 189n. 149
1286a31–3 159
1287a10–16 81n. 49, 187n. 137
1287a18 191n. 155
1287a20–2 30, 166
1287a28–30 153, 196n. 191
1287a32–b3 173n. 44
1287b25–6 194n. 185
1287b29–31 22n. 89, 77n. 10
1288a3 196n. 189
1290a19–29 161
1292a9 195n. 184
1295a40–1 176n. 57
1295b19–22, 1297a2 158
1297a5–6 195n. 184
1301b16–17 161
1302b20 79n. 28
1302b33–1303a2 160
1304a20–1 161
1305a32 79n. 28
1308a24–30 191n. 158
1308b17 188n. 145

1308b26 79n. 28
1309a28 195n. 184
1309b21–31 160
1310a35 166
1310b40–11a1 136n. 102
1311a17 160
1311a19–20 158
1311a20–2, 1313a40–1 164
1313b7–9, 1314a7–9, 19–21 158
1314b6–7, 14–18 28
1314b17 136n. 102
1314b37–8 28
1315a21 31, 149
1315a40–b2 28
1315b15–16 166
1317b10–13 158
1320b33–21a1 171n. 35
1321a16 79n. 28
1324a35–b3 158
1324b29–33 171n. 34
1326a29–30 191n. 155
1332b38–41 177n. 71
1336b28f. 189n. 147
Rh. 1360a23–7 161
1375b3–6 165
1375b20–5 173n. 44
1376b7–11 194n. 176
1376b19–20 173–4n. 47
1393b4–8 148
1393b8–22 87
1393b22–4a1 164
1396a17–19 158
1399b11–13 182n. 102
1406a17–23 10, 166
1406b27–9 163
1410a17–20 178n. 73
1410a34–6 158
Top. 129a10–16 152
140a7–8 187n. 137, 194n. 182
141a20–1 187n. 137
Fr.548R 45
658R 182n. 102

Arrian
An. 4.9.7 14

Bacchylides
5.19–20, 179 18n. 38
9.45 7

9.100 18n. 39
13.185 56
19.21 18n. 40

Callimachus
Jov. 66, *Aet.* Fr.178.23Pf. 186–7n. 133

Callisthenes (*FGrH* 124)
F31 167

Com. Adesp.
Fr.209 119
288 13
310 119
700 120–1
701, 704 13
881, 883,1062 7
1094.15–17 135n. 93, 194n. 176

Cratinus
Fr.61.3 119
73 13,120
95 138n. 118
118, 171 13,120
214 50n. 23
258–9 13, 120

Critias
A13DK 144n. 153
TrGF 43 F19.6–7 7

Ctesias (*FGrH* 688)
F9.8, 19 157–8

Demades
Fr.13, 17 De Falco 57, 156
24 180n. 93
25 163
26 180n. 93
35 166
36.9 165
42–3 57, 156
64 72, 156

Democrates
Fr.1 B–S 28, 154

Democritus
B34 152

B37, 125, 159, 187 174–5n. 53
B214 158
B223 174–5n. 53
B251 183n. 112
B288 174–5n. 53

Demosthenes
1.4 158
1.23 158, 183n. 109
1.28 165
2.8 158
2.10 163
2.14 28, 69, 154, 156
2.21 70, 156–7
2.29 164–5
2.30 37n. 18, 184n. 116
3.22 177n. 70
3.24 154–5
3.30–1 28, 154
3.31 73, 137n. 104, 159, 164, 181n. 96
3.33 73
3.36 162
5.12 178n. 73
6.25 158
7.7 29, 154
7.17 154
7.32 158
8.36 181n. 95
8.46, 59–60 158
8.61 29
8.62 158
8.69 165
8.71 162
8.74 158
9.9 154
9.12 69, 156
9.14 162
9.22, 26, 32 158
9.35 181n. 96
9.38–40 154
9.39 156
9.43 36n. 8, 157–8
9.50 69, 156
9.53 36n. 8
9.54 29, 154
9.56 36n. 8, 158
9.59 158
9.60 164
9.66 158

Index locorum 233

9.69 65n. 35, 156
9.70, 10.4 158
10.6 181n. 96
10.9 29
10.19 29, 154
10.25 158
10.40–1 33, 179n. 86
10.59 29
10.61–2 158
10.63 29
10.64, 11.4 158
11.6 164
11.14 70–1, 156–7
11.18 154
13.19 24n. 101
13.20 164–5
13.31 28, 154
13.34 162
14.31–2 157–8
14.35 162
15.3 158
15.15, 17–20 157–8
15.23, 27 157
15.30–1 181n. 101
15.32 29, 154
15.32–3 162
17.8 158
17.11–12 162
17.13 29
17.17 36n. 8
17.25 162
18.21 29, 154
18.23, 28 154
18.31 163
18.32 154
18.33 29, 154
18.38, 42 29
18.46–7 29, 154, 158
18.49, 51–2 29
18.62 162
18.65, 72, 100 158
18.131 29
18.138 29, 157, 162
18.149 29, 119, 154
18.159 181n. 96
18.170 165
18.173 162
18.177 154
18.189 165

18.192 162
18.194 57, 156
18.196 165
18.198 181n. 96
18.203 158
18.205 33, 158
18.206 26
18.208 158
18.221 162
18.229 165
18.235 158, 165
18.236 29
18.243 72
18.245 165
18.247 154, 191n. 159
18.281 65n. 35, 156
18.284 29
18.286 181n. 96
18.292 162
18.295–6 158
18.296 73, 164, 177n. 70
18.298 178n. 73
18.299 163
18.304 162
18.305 158, 183n. 109
18.307 29
18.311 26, 154
18.320 29
18.322 163
18.324 73, 156
19.9 162
19.13, 16 29
19.28 154
19.29 29, 153
19.30 29
19.68 29, 154
19.69 36n. 8, 158
19.81 158
19.84 163
19.85 36n. 8
19.90 154
19.99 37n. 14
19.102, 109, 110 29
19.112 158
19.115 163
19.116, 118 29
19.122, 133 154
19.136 159
19.141–2, 149 154

19.156, 167 29
19.178, 180, 207–8 154
19.216 164
19.224 71, 181n. 96
19.226 181n. 96
19.229 154
19.236 29
19.250 57, 156
19.253 154
19.259 80n. 37, 181n. 95
19.259–61 158
19.262 80n. 37
19.286 29
19.289 29, 181n. 95
19.299 36n. 8
19.300 154
19.302 162
19.314 159
19.316 29, 154
19.329 154
19.331 29
19.334, 343 154
20.15–16, 69, 70 158
20.107 173n. 47
20.107–8 158
20.167 165
21.29 163
21.101 177n. 71
21.120 162
21.177 27–8
21.184–5 177n. 71
21.223–5 165
22.54f. 28, 154
22.61, 63 163
23.201 154
23.209–10 28
24.14 154
24.14–5 29
24.67 29, 154
24.75 158
24.124 28, 154
24.143 28, 163
24.154 193n. 175
24.156 165
24.200 29
24.210 153
24.212–4 165
25.4 162

25.6 164
25.8 163
25.11 27–8, 194n. 185
25.16 165, 194n. 176
25.20, 21 165
25.21–2 177n. 71
25.31 163
25.37 29, 154
25.38 163
25.40 156
25.46 154
25.48 193n. 175
25.91 163
25.95 73, 156, 193n. 173
26.3 57, 180n. 88
26.5 165
26.22 156, 164
26.23 154–5
26.26 156
26.27 153
35.40 18n. 39, 152
42.25, 32 196n. 188
47.42, 48 36n. 8
50.2 26, 154
51.7 26
51.22 29, 154
58.30 154–5
58.34 164
58.44 163
58.45 162
58.46 164
58.49 163
58.61 37n. 18
59.115 165
60.4 32
61.37–8 153
61.48 157
Pro. 32.4 165
34.2 189n. 147
53.3 154–5
53.4 72
55.2 186n. 128
55.3 24n. 101, 165
Ep. 1.8 65n. 35, 156
2.11 26, 192n. 164
3.2, 15, 29, 32 162
3.45 41n. 45
6.1 36n. 8

Fr.11.2 29, 156
13. 16 65n. 35, 156
13.23 70, 175n. 57

Dinarchus
1.10 163
1.15 29, 154
1.19 158
1.20, 28 29, 154
1.38 158
1.44 158
1.64 163
1.81 37n. 14
1.86 194n. 185
1.88 154
1.110 70, 156
2.1 154
2.10 163
3.12 29, 154
3.16 164
3.22 154–5
fr.I.2 Conomis 29
9.3 157

Diodorus Siculus
8 fr.24 87
14.8 183n. 110
16.91.2–3 101n. 58
19.25.5–7 193n. 172
20.78 183n. 110

Diogenes
B5 9, 64n. 31

Dissoi Logoi
7 168n. 12

Empedocles
B17, 30, 35 8
B115 6
B128.2–3 6
D135 20n. 63

Epic fragments
Asius fr.1.3 49n. 5
Iliupersis fr.4.2D/6.2B 49n. 5
Panyassis fr.6cD/25B 16n. 19
Phoronis fr.4.1–2, 4 16n. 19

Epimenides
B23–4 4
Fr.10 (Fowler) 4–5

Eupolis
Fr.102.1–3 119
104 22n. 85, 141n. 129
220 137n. 103, 180n. 91
267, 294 13
316.1 134n. 82
384.6 11
438 23n. 98

Euripides
Alc. 30, 49, 53, 60, 70 7
743 19n. 49
Andr. 471–5, 479–82 131n. 53
Ba. 200, 800 xixn. 17
803 110
El. 22 140n. 127
386–7 25
Hcld. 206 140n. 127
670 139n. 127
964 140n. 127
Hec. 9 141n. 127
533, 606–8 138n. 117
816 8
Hel. 276 108
878–9 7
1428 108
HF 34 69
141–2, 251, 258, 270 110
272–3 69
274 110
542–3 69
1317–18, 1344 111
Hipp. 538 8
I.A. 28, 373 140n. 127
699 139n. 127
1400–1 109
Ion 416 140n. 127
595 56, 113
Med. 5 140n. 127
Or. 698–701 61, 120
772 140n. 127
Pho. 74–5 56, 113
430 xviiin. 13
486 xxn. 30, 36n. 4

506, 520 110–11
535–50 9
1226 140n. 127
1244 139n. 127
1245 xviiin. 13, 140n. 127
Rh. 29 140n. 127
410–11 108
479 140n. 127
Supp. 118 xviiin. 13
191–2 44
243 140n. 127
312–3 145n. 156
448–9 124
473–4, 507–9, 879–80 56, 113
Tro. 31 139n. 127
1169 12
fr.21 75, 122
136 8
194 140n. 127
200 25
295 140–1n. 127
703.1 xviiin. 13
719 109
744 44
774 65n. 32, 140n. 127
912 6

Gorgias
A19 135n. 93
B5a 12
B11.3, 6 6
B11.8 7
B11a.30 125

Heniochus
Fr.5 144n. 153

Heraclitus
B41 64n. 31
B44 93
B52 xixn. 27, 9
B53 8–9
B64 64n. 31
B94, 114 8

Hermippus
Fr.47 13

Herodorus (*FGrH* 31)
F30 174n. 49

Herodotus
1.6.3 109
1.8.3, 11.4 108
1.27.1 109
1.59.1–2 100n. 49
1.59.3 140n. 127
1.60.1 163
1.62.1 110
1.62.4 101n. 64
1.64.1 164
1.65.4 44
1.87.3 12, 110
1.90.2 109
1.91.1, 6 108
1.94.7, 95.2 109
1.99.2, 100.2 12
1.111.2, 112.3 108
1.120.5, 126.3, 126.5, 126.6 109
1.127.1 109, 140n. 127
1.129.3–4 109
1.130.1 108
1.141.1–2 101n. 64
1.155.1–2 31, 111
1.164.2, 169.1–2, 170.2, 174.1 109
1.204 12
1.210.2 109
2.80.2 13
2.115.6 12, 110
2.123.1 6
2.144.2 4
2.147.2 110
2.172 21n. 78
2.172.5 110
3.14.9, 19.1 109
3.20.2 12
3.21.2 109
3.32.3 124, 128n. 21
3.34.2, 35.4 108
3.36.2 140n. 127
3.62.3 108
3.65.7 109
3.76.2 70, 114
3.81.2 61, 120
3.82.3 xviiin. 13
3.82.4 140n. 127
3.82.5 109
3.83.2–3 110, 119
3.88.1 109
3.89.3 31, 109–11
3.127.1 70, 114

3.134.2 140n. 127
3.137.2, 140.5 109
3.142.3, 4, 143.2 110
4.20.1 109
4.79.5 140n. 127
4.91.2 12, 110
4.93, 118.4 109
4.118.5 108
4.126, 127.4, 128.1, 136.4, 137.1,
139.2, 142 109
4.149.1 137n. 105
4.163.3 90
5.2.2 108
5.18.3 109
5.23.2 140n. 127
5.28 69, 114, 117
5.29 25, 94
5.31.4, 46.2 110
5.49.2–3 109
5.55 110
5.56.1 89–90
5.62.1, 2, 63.1, 64.2, 65.5, 78, 91.1, 2 110
5.92β.2–3 89–90
5.92ζ2–η1 101n. 62, 124, 143n. 142
5.105.2 108
5.109.2–3, 116 109
6.5.1 110
6.9.3 110
6.11.2, 12.3 109
6.22.1 110
6.25.2 108
6.32, 43.1, 44.1, 45.1 109
6.71 139n. 121
6.74.1 140n. 127
6.100.2 117
6.106.2 109
6.109.3 108–10
6.109.5 54, 71, 80n. 37, 117
6.109.6 109–10
6.123.2 110
6.131.2 118
7.1.3, 5.1 109
7.5.2 12, 108, 110
7.8β.3 109
7.8γ 12, 108
7.9.1 108
7.9.2, 11.4 109
7.16α.1 99n. 46
7.35.2 109
7.38.1–2 108

7.39.1, 51.1 109
7.56.2 12
7.96.2, 102.1 109
7.104.4 125, 166
7.108.1, 111.1 109
7.136.1 13
7.139.5 109
7.140.2 70
7.147.3 108
7.148.3 70
7.154.2 110
7.157.2 80n. 37, 109, 117
7.168.1, 178.2 109
7.180 89
7.187.2 12, 110
7.194.2 110
7.203.2 12
7.204 44
7.220.4 89
7.235.2, 8.22.1 109
8.68α1, β1 108
8.68γ 12, 109
8.88.2, 100.2 108
8.100.3, 5, 101.3 109
8.102.2 108–10
8.102.3 109–10
8.116.1 109
8.118.3 108
8.132.1, 140α.1 109
8.140β.2 12, 110
8.142.3 109–10
8.144.4 109
9.27.2 110
9.41.3 140n. 127
9.45.2–3, 48.2, 60.1, 90.2 109
9.107.1 110
9.111.3, 5 108
9.116.3 12, 108, 110
9.122.4 109

Hesiod
Op. 39 90
111, 173a 15n. 12
202–12 84
263–4 90
668 15n. 7
Th. 71 15n. 7
81f. 11
403 15n. 7
462, 476, 486 15n. 12

491, 493, 506 15n. 7
837 2
850 16n. 20
883, 886, 897 15n. 7
1000 49n. 5
Sc. 41 49n. 5
56 15n. 7, 16n. 20
328 15n. 7
Fr.5 15n. 7, 16n. 20
10a47 49n. 5
10(d).9 16n. 19
40.1 49n. 5
308 15n. 7

Hippias of Erythrai (*FGrH*421)
F1 193n. 170

Hippocrates
Aër 12 9, 152
16.4–5, 7, 23.5–8 109
*Flat.*3, 15 7, 20n. 68, 131n. 60, 152
Nat.Hom. 4.2 114, 152
Vict. 10.3 65n. 31, 131n. 60, 174n. 50
VM 9.4 171n. 31
16.1, 8 114, 152
17.2, 19.4–5, 20.4, 6, 22.1, 24.1 152

Hipponax
Fr.3 18n. 40
38 18n. 38

Homer
Il. 1.231 90
1.396–406 2
1.502 15n. 7
1.518–23 84
2.204 9
2.474f. 43
2.669 15n. 7
3.196–8 43
3.230–1 11
3.276, 320 16n. 23
4.61 15n. 7
5.78 11
7.202 16n. 23
8.5–27 3
9.97, 155, 297, 302, 603, 10.33, 11.58 11
11.751 16n. 20
11.761 11

12.242 15n. 7
12.312 11
13.28 3
13.491–5 43
14.72–3, 205–6 11
14.233, 259 7
15.187–92, 196–9 3
16.234 16n. 23
16.440–3 84
16.549 85
16.605 11
18.366 15n. 7
20.61 16n. 20
22.178–81 84
22.394, 434–5, 24.258 11
24.308 16n. 23
24.770 30
Od. 1.64–79 84
2.47, 234 30
4.386 3
5.7–20 4
5.12 30
7.71–2, 74, 8.169f. 11
8.332, 347–56 4
8.467 11
9.106, 112–15, 273–80 4
9.552 15n. 7
11.484 11
11.556 85
13.25 15n. 7
15.181, 520 11
16.260–5 3
20.112 15n. 7
23.121 85
24.473 15n. 7

Homeric hymns
hAp. 29 3
151 11
hDem. 31, 84, 87, 347, 357 16n. 20
358 15n. 7
365 3
376 16n. 20
*hMerc.*2 16n. 23
259 3
264, 312, 324, 364 17n. 25
367 15n. 7, 16n. 20
370–3 17n. 25
hVen. 292 16n. 23

Hyperides
2 frr.1, 8 158
2 fr.10 71, 156–8
3.30 194n. 176
5.12 26–7
5.15 154
5.25 70, 156
5.30 26, 154
6.20, 24–5, 34, 39 158
Fr.27 158
80 163–4
204 193n. 175
Against Diondas 36n. 8, 109, 158

Iamb. Adesp.
29D 61, 120

Ibycus
Fr.287 99n. 41, 101n. 64

Ion of Chios
Fr.26.12W 8
Fr.27.1W 19n. 56, 22n. 88, 39n. 31
PMG 744.5 8

Isaeus
1.15 192n. 164
Fr.30 Thalheim 164

Isocrates
1.21 158
1.37 36n. 8
2.5–6 14
2.11, 13 152
2.14–15 14
2.15 169n. 22
2.15–16 36n. 8
2.19 25, 32, 149, 156
2.21 32, 149, 156, 192n. 162
2.23 14
2.29 158
2.32, 34 14
2.51 14, 152
3.9 7, 174n. 49
3.22 36n. 8, 178n. 73
3.26 6, 24n. 103, 152
4.25–31 32
4.76 27, 30, 154
4.80 158

4.90 157
4.104 158
4.105 184n. 115, 194n. 181
4.127 157–8
4.150, 5.139 157
6.44–5 183n. 110
6.93 162
6.108 33
7.14 70, 153
7.25–6 26, 36n. 8, 158, 177n. 68
7.40, 47 194n. 176
7.65, 69 158
8.53 164, 190n. 154, 194n. 181
8.89–115, 125 158
8.127 36n. 8
8.142–4 158
9.15 19n. 49, 174n. 49
9.44 14
9.45 158
9.46 36n. 8
9.56, 68 158
10.34 74
10.35 183n. 111
10.37 192n. 162
12.56 36n. 8
12.99 69
12.124–5 32–3
12.138 70, 153
12.141 154–5
12.146 36n. 9, 177n. 68
12.147 158
12.165 69
15.64 158
15.72 14
15.103, 116, 131, 133 36n. 8
15.136 163
15.172 61, 159
15.180 152
15.257 7, 174n. 49
15.305 42n. 61
16.25, 37, 20.10 158
Ep. 3.5 14
Fr. 31 175n. 55
37 = Apophth. δ3 174n. 50
40 158

Lycurgus
1.20 162
1.47 163

1.47-8 32-3
1.50 158
1.53 32-3
1.60, 61 158
1.79 194n. 182
1.104, 125 158
1.143 177n. 71
1.149 158
Fr.12.1 158

Lyric adespota
PMG Adesp. 867 13
869 104n. 91
894 12
909.8-10 92, 98n. 37
925 (e).11, 960, S415.4 18n. 40

Lysias
1.26 145n. 156, 165
1.34-5 145n. 156
2.17 40n. 42
2.18 183n. 111
2.19 10, 166
2.56 158
2.57 190n. 154
2.58-60 158
2.59 184n. 115
2.61-2, 64, 12.35, 39, 67, 73, 78, 94, 97 158
13.7 140n. 127, 190n. 154
13.17 158
13.91 33
14.34, 18.5, 24, 27 158
21.19 164
25.9 190n. 154
25.28, 27.3 164
28.13 158
31.26 158, 162
31.28 162
31.31-2 158
32.22 192n. 164
33.6 158
34.2 183n. 111

Menander
Fr.247 40n. 42
372 64n. 31, 174n. 50
Mon. 145, 511 40n. 42
Fr.1100K 174n. 50

Orphic tablets
A1-2 (Zuntz) 6

Parmenides
B12 64n. 31

Pherecydes
F78 Schibli 4

Philemon
Fr.31 185n. 119

Philistus (*FGrH* 556)
F59/T4 183n. 110

Phrynichus Com.
Fr.21.1-2 119

Pindar
O. 1.113-14 xviiin. 13
2.6 89, 112
2.9-10 103n. 84
2.58-9 18n. 39
2.76 7
2.81-2 85
5.31 140n. 127
6.60 44, 112
7.34 18n. 37
7.64f 3
8.30 26
9.57 18n. 38
10.13 16n. 23
11.17 140n. 127
12.3 56
13.24 18n. 38
P. 1.3 19n. 57
1.6 18n. 39
1.39 3
1.86 55, 113, 140n. 127
1.88 26, 112
1.91-2 113
2.46 140n. 127
2.87 138n. 116, 140n. 127
3.27 3
3.71 112
3.94 6
4.181 7
4.263-9 112
4.270 130n. 43

Index locorum 241

4.271–2 70, 75, 112
4.274 56, 113
5.55–7 103n. 84
5.62 26, 112
5.111–12 112
5.122–3 56
9.7, 54, 56–7, 69–70 3
9.107, 10.8 140n. 127
10.72 55, 113
11.50 140n. 127
N. 1.39 18n. 40
1.51 140n. 127
3.10 18n. 38
4.67, 5.35 18n. 37
7.1 7
7.82 18n. 37
8.11 140n. 127
10.16 18n. 37
10.25 140n. 127
11.2 18n. 40
11.4 5
I. 2.17 100n. 49, 112
5.53 18n. 38
8.20 18n. 37
8.21–2 3, 7
8.29f., 49–50, 65 6
Fr.33 7
36 18n. 38
40 56
52k.44 140n. 127
52v.3,11,19 18n. 40
70b.7 18n. 39
76.2 85
105 30, 112
169a1–2 7, 166
214 56

Plato
Alc I 119b 151
120ab 155
122b 158
130a–c 152
131a 151
132a 178n. 76
132b 151, 173n. 45
134e–5a 171n. 33
Apol. 28d–9a 162
30a 33, 155
30e 159

Chrm. 173a, 174de 175n. 54
Clit. 407e 152
408ab 172n. 38
Cra. 396a 152
405cd 161
412d, 413b 152
Cri. 47b 151
50d–1c, 51e 33, 155
54b 152
Criti. 109c 56, 152
121b 152
Ep. 7 325e 186n. 126
326a 172n. 37
330c–31a 71, 172n. 37
331cd 41n. 46
334c, 337a, cd 166
Ep 8 354b 180–1n. 95
354bc 166
354cd 184n. 117
354de 158
354e 166
355e 166
Epin. 980de, 983d 152
Euthd. 277d xixn. 17
291cd 172n. 36
Euthphr. 2c 33, 155
2d–3a 164
Grg. 456b 151
456c–7b 181n. 99
463b–6a 29, 151, 155
464bc 72, 151
466bc 158
477e–9e 73
481d–2a 155
484a 185n. 122
491de 158
492ab 185n. 122
494e 155
500b, e–501a 151
502e 28
503a 29
504a 151
510d 185n. 122
511b–12b 172n. 36
513a 185n. 122
513a–c 155
513d 29
516ab 150
516e 159

517ab 155
517b–8a 29
517c–9a 151
517e 151
518e–19b 71, 155
519bc 190n. 154
520e 25
521a–2a 151
521ab 29, 155
521e–2a 29, 72
Lg. 626e 184n. 118
627b 185n. 122
627b–8a 179n. 85
628cd 69, 156
630a 80n. 37
630b 181n. 95
630e 166
632c 194n. 178
671bc 188n. 139
680e 31
684c 72, 151
689ab 177n. 67
689cd 161
690a 31, 149
691a 161, 180–1n. 95
691e 12, 70, 166, 180–1n. 95, 189n. 149
692a 70, 180–1n. 95, 186n. 127, 189n. 149
693b 189n. 149
694a–5b 48, 150
697c, 698a 182n. 103
698bc, 699c 166
699e 182n. 103
700a 166
701bc 158, 166
701e 182n. 103
709b 56, 152
712e–3a 158
713d 51n. 27
714a 25, 171n. 29
715cd 166
719e–20e 72, 151
720c 158
722d–3b 188n. 144
722e 158
722e–3a 151
726 158
726–7a 152
728c 172n. 38
734e 188n. 144

734e–5a 161
735b–6c 48, 72, 144–5n. 154, 170–1n. 29, 172n. 38
736e 163
737a 192n. 168
744d 69, 156
754d 194n. 178
757a 182n. 103
758ab 171–2n. 35
758cd 180n. 95
762e 166, 185n. 119
769a–c 160
772e 188n. 144
773cd 189n. 149
774a 188n. 144
790b 25
793c 163
799e, 854ac 188n. 144
854e 172n. 38
856b 166
857c–e 173n. 43
859a 33, 173n. 43
862bc 172n. 38
863d 184n. 118
863e 184n. 117
863e–4a 177n. 67
870de 188n. 144
875cd 152
880ab, 887a 188n. 144
890a 185n. 119
896b, de, 897c 152
904a 174n. 51
905e 58, 159, 190n. 154, 192n. 163
905e–6a 148, 164, 171–2n. 35
906e 58, 159
907d 188n. 144
916a 151
916d 188n. 144
917c 191n. 155
920a 194n. 178
921c 192n. 168
923c, 925e, 932a 188n. 144
934c 160
942e 70, 153
945c 12, 56, 166, 192n. 168
961c 56, 192n. 168
961d 153
964b–d 194n. 178
964d–5b 70, 153

965b 194n. 178
965c 166
966b 194n. 178
966d 12, 166
967d 152
969b 12, 166
969c 194n. 178
Lach. 197e 190n. 154
Men. 73a, 91a 25
99d 11
Min. 321bc 171n. 29
Mx. 237e 40n. 42
238c 175–6n. 57
238e 158
238e–9a 32, 155
239d–40a 157
242a–c 158
243e 69, 156
246b 191n. 155
Phd. 62b 162
79e–80a 152
80a 158
93cf. 161
94b 152
94de 158
Phdr. 238b, e 184n. 117
241a 190n. 154
246e 152
256b 184n. 118
258c 166
258e 12
266c 158
Phlb. 28d, 35d, 64b 152
Plt. 258e–9c 25, 149
261b–e 46
261cd 188n. 139
263e–4a, 265b–6c, 266d–8c 46
266e 159
272e, 273cd 152
274e–6e 46
279cd, 280c–e, 288b 161
291ab 193n. 169
291e–2a 185n. 122
293d 72, 151
294bc 195n. 187
295b–e 151
295d–300a 151
295e 171n. 29
296e–7a 58, 151

297e 167–8n. 6
297e–9d 58–9
298a–9d 151, 171n. 33
300c 14
301de 160
301e–2a 163
303b 166
304c–5e 152
305c 164
305e–6a 161
307d 69, 156
308a 158
308c–11c 161
Prot. 313d 151
318e–9a 25
322d, 325a 180n. 95
326cd 135n. 93
337d 166
R. 329cd 158
340de 151
341c–2e 150
343ab 45, 150
344b 158
345cd 45, 150
352a 176n. 62
368c–9a 153
372e 70, 180–1n. 95
374b–e 194n. 178
375a–6c 45–6
389b–d 72, 151
389de 158
412c–3c 414b, d 194n. 178
414e 179n. 85
415e–6e 45–6, 150
416b, 417b 158
421a 194n. 178
422d 45–6
425e–6c 71, 172n. 37
426c 28, 172n. 37, 178n. 78
426e 13
430e 161
430e–1b 184n. 118
431e–2a 161
434ab 194n. 178
434d–444e 153
440b 176n. 62
440cd 45–6, 150
440e 176n. 62
441e 152

442cd 161, 176n. 62
443c–e 161
443d 184n. 118
444b 176n. 62
451cd 45–6, 150
451d 194n. 178
463ab 158, 194n. 178
463b 12, 166
464c 194n. 178
466a 170n. 29
470d 179n. 85
484cd 160
488a–9a 58, 156
489bc 72, 150–1, 172n. 37
493a–c 159
496c 180–1n. 95
496d 159
500d–1c 160
501a–c 160
503b, 504c, 506a 194n. 178
509d 152
520a 192n. 168
521b 184n. 117
531d–2a, 532d 188n. 144
537a, 539b 170n. 29
540bc 12, 166
544c 74, 180n. 95
544cd, 545bc 153
547c 158
548b 33, 179n. 82, 191n. 155
550ab 153
551c 171n. 33
551d 176n. 62
552c 176n. 59, 180n. 95
552e 160
553cd 8, 153, 158
554b–d 187n. 133
555d, 556a 160
556e 156, 176n. 62, 180n. 95
557c 190n. 153
559cd 160
559d 176n. 61
559d–60d 153
560b 176n. 59
561ab 153
562cd 28
562d 190n. 154
563d 158
563e 158, 180n. 95

564b 158, 160, 180n. 95
564bc 70, 172n. 38, 187n. 134
564d 190n. 154
564d–5c 160
565a 190n. 154
565c–e 164, 176n. 63, 190n. 154
565e 33, 155
566d 159
566cd 190n. 154
567de 187n. 133
568e–9c 33, 179n. 82
569a 158
572e–3b 154, 158, 174n. 49, 187n. 133
573bc 184n. 117
573d 56, 152
573e, 574d 154, 187n. 133
575a 158
575a–d 154
575d, 576a, 577c, 577d, 578d–9e 158
579c 176n. 65
579e 180n. 95
580c 184n. 118
586e 176n. 62
590cd 158
590d 152, 174n. 50
590e–1a 176n. 65
591d 161
591e 174n. 50
592b 160
600d 25
601de 188n. 146
603d 176n. 62
605b, 606d, 608b 176n. 65
617bc 161
Smp. 183b, 184c 178n. 78
187a 56, 152
196c 166
197b, e 56, 152
Soph. 228a 69, 180n. 95
Tht. 153a 152
167bc 193n. 175
174de 45, 170n. 25
Ti. 17d 194n. 178
34bc 152
34c 158
37a 161
42de 56, 152
44d 153, 158
45a 153

47d 161
48a 152
69c–70b 70, 154
82a 180n. 95
85e–6a 79n. 23, 180n. 95
88e 192n. 163
90a 175n. 56
90d 161

Plato Comicus
Fr.65.3, 132 119
201 71
202 13, 120
207 13
236 137n. 103

Plutarch
Alex. 52.2–4 14, 167
Dem. 13.1 162
23.5 180n. 91
Dion 46.1, *Pelop.* 12.4 22n. 88
Per. 8.5 137n. 109
12.2 124, 133n. 75
Sol. 14 55, 98n. 29
14.8 124
29.5 74

Polyaenus
3.9.22 70

Pratinas
Fr.708.9 8

Pseudepicharmeia
Fr.240.3KA 56

Pythagorean school
DK58 B37, D2 9

Pytheas
Fr.3B–S 154

Scylax (*FGrH* 709)
F5 12

Simonides
76D = ep.1 Page 89
Fr.90W 118
614 5

Solon
fr.4.17 69, 92
5 91
6.1–2 88
9 88, 92
11.5–6 90
12 61, 88
31.1 18n. 37
33a 92, 103n. 82
36.7–8 91
36.20–2 88
36.26–7 90–1
37 91

Sophocles
Aj. 35 56
669f. 8–9
675–6 7
1253–4 111
Ant. 189–90 55
290–2, 477–8 111
608 6
738 23n. 91
994 55, 113
El. 749 140n. 127
1462 111
O.C. 884 139n. 127
1267, 1382 7
O.T. 1, 6 31, 111–12
14 12
22–4 55
31–3, 48 12
58 31, 111–12
103–4 55
142 31, 111–12
216f. 12
380 135n. 93
535, 540–2 112
695 120
879–81 119
903–5 6, 12
922–3 64n. 26, 113
1200–1, 1418 145n. 155
Phil. 138 135n. 93
385–8 118
989 6
Tr. 127–8 6
217 8
795 140n. 127

Fr.85 111
133.6 129n. 33
524 56, 113
683 113, 121
873 111
941.15 19n. 58

Stesichorus
S14.1–2 18n. 37

Stesimbrotus (*FGrH* 107)
F17 5

Telecleides
Fr.18 13

Theognis
39–40 69, 92
233–4 89
257–60 99n. 41
285 18n. 37
338–40 11
373–6 18nn. 37–9
457–60 xviin. 7
667–82 54, 86
743 18n. 37
803 18n. 38
847–50 87
855–6 54
949–50 101n. 64
952 99n. 41
1023–4 87
1081–2 103n. 83
1133–4 69, 82
1181 90
1249–52, 1267–70 99n. 41
1273–4 xviin. 7
1357–8 99n. 41
1361–2, 1375–6 xviin. 7

Theophrastus
Char. 26.3 25
29.5 180n. 91

Theopompus (*FGrH* 115)
F121, 194 190n. 154

Thucydides
1.8.3, 98.4, 122.3, 124.3 123

2.43.1 115–16, 177n. 71
2.63.2 124
2.65.5, 11, 3.11.7 140n. 127
3.37.2 124
3.70.3, 75.2, 82.1, 8, 4.64.4, 66.3 140n. 127
6.14 75, 117
6.18.6–7 75, 117, 122
6.28.2, 35.2 140n. 127
6.38.3 119
6.77.1 123
6.85.1 124
6.89.4, 6 140n. 127
7.77.7 123
8.17.2 140n. 127
8.64.5 78n. 16, 135n. 88
8.65.2, 81.1, 89.4, 90.1 140n. 127
8.97.2 75, 122–3

Timotheus
Pers. 115–16, 152 108
206–7 139n. 121

TrGF Adespota
Fr.129 8
348g 56
506 7
570 8
646.12 145n. 155
655.19–20 19n. 49
656.7 185n. 122
668.5 139n. 127

Tyrtaios
6.1 87

Xenophanes
A32 98n. 37, 107
B23, 25 9–10

Xenophon
Ages. 1.38 31, 156
7.2 30, 166
7.3 31, 156
An. 1.7.3, 9.29, 2.3.17 157
2.5.23 182n. 104
2.5.38 157
2.6.12 173n. 46
3.1.12, 2.13, 4.1.35–6 157
5.8.18 31, 149, 156

5.8.18–20 168n. 6
5.8.20 171n. 35
5.8.24 193n. 170
6.6.12, 7.1.30 190n. 154
7.4.24, 7.29 158
7.6.38 31, 156
Cyr. 1.1.1–4 47, 150
1.1.5 171n. 31
1.3.18 157
1.6.21 171n. 31
5.1.24 160
5.3.6, 5.9 157
5.5.28–30 32, 149
7.1.12 177n. 71
8.1.1 31, 156
8.1.22 14, 166
8.1.43 157
8.1.44, 2.9 31, 156
8.2.14 47, 150
8.6.13 157
8.7.13 192n. 162
8.8.1 31, 156, 171n. 31
HG 1.7.2 190n. 154
2.2.23, 3.24 158
2.3.31 55, 180n. 89
2.3.48 38n. 22, 158, 162, 178n. 73
2.3.51 190n. 154
2.4.17, 20 158
2.4.41 163
3.1.3 158, 190n. 154
3.1.16, 21 158
3.2.28 159–60
3.3.3 70
3.5.10 190n. 154
3.5.12–13 158
3.5.14 190n. 154
4.1.35–6 158
4.4.6 184n. 115, 185n. 122
4.8.2 158
4.8.28, 5.1.36 190n. 154
5.4.1–2, 9, 13 184n. 115
6.1.2 157
6.3.6 19n. 49
6.3.8 184n. 115

7.1.44 158
7.3.7 184n. 115
7.3.8, 7.5.1, 3 158
7.4.33 190n. 154
Hiero 6.10 194n. 177
6.15–6 32, 149
11.11 169–70n. 23
11.14 32, 149
Lac. 8.4 14, 173n. 47, 196n. 189
10.3 173n. 47
15.9 12
Mem. 1.1.7 25
1.2.9 148
1.2.24 151
1.2.32, 37 45
1.2.32–8 148
1.2.40–6 30, 159
1.2.56 158
2.1.9 30, 159
2.1.10–12 38n. 26, 159
2.3.16 183–4n. 115
2.3.18 70
2.3.49 184n. 115
2.6.13 178n. 78
2.8.4 38n. 26, 159, 190n. 154
3.2.1 47, 170n. 27
3.4.7–12 26
3.5.13 184n. 115
3.5.18 161
3.6.2 190n. 154
3.7 151–2
3.9.10–11 171n. 31
3.9.11 169n. 18
4.1.2 25
4.2.5 171n. 31
4.2.11 26, 149
4.5.2–5 184n. 118
Oec. 7.17, 32–4, 38–9 186n. 133
8.3, 20 161
9.14–15, 13.5, 21.2, 10 25, 149
Smp. 4.32 38n. 26, 159
4.45 30, 159
8.42 38n. 23

General Index

For individual authors *see* the Index of authors and images.

Agesilaus 31, 166
Alcibiades 75, 117–18, 122, 125, 141n. 129, 151, 178n. 76
Aleuadae of Thessaly 55, 113
Alexander III 14, 29, 156, 167, 182n. 102
allegory 26, 54
Archelaus, king of Macedon 147
Argos 70
Aspasia 13, 120
Athena 2–3, 5, 16, 125
autochthony 32, 34, 155–6

balance, harmony, mixture, ideas of 9–10, 75–6, 93, 114, 122, 152, 160–1
biblical imagery 10–11, 15, 43–4, 47–9, 87, 90
Blair, Tony xix n. 19, 67n. 56
bodily microcosm 9, 56, 93, 152, 154

Cambyses 109, 124
China, medical imagery 77n. 2
Cicero 40, 62, 65n. 38, 77n. 5, 79n. 26, 176n. 62
Cleon xiii, 13, 115–16, 118–20, 124, 132n. 68, 134n. 82, 137n. 106, 138n. 118, 155
Clinton, Bill xix n. 19, 67n. 56
community, definition 59, 85–6, 92, 94
Corinth 89–90, 124, 184n. 115, 185n. 122
corruption 28–9, 115, 119, 154, 164
cosmos, political order xv, 8–10, 93, 114
    living organism 93
Critias 55, 180n. 89
Croesus 31, 109, 111
Cypselus 89–90
Cyrus 31, 108–9, 111, 128n. 18

Darius 31, 55, 109–11, 128n. 18

democracy 107
    Athenian, ideology xiv, 29, 32, 59–60, 66n. 48, 112, 114–17, 120–1, 124–6, 142n. 141, 145n. 160, 147, 149, 156, 158, 164–5
    changes in fourth century 147, 154, 157, 163
    opposition to *see* élites
Dionysius I 147, 183n. 110
divine honours, conferred on men 13–14, 166–7

élites
    anti-democratic imagery of 30, 61, 87–8, 120–1, 148, 158–61, 190n. 153
    ideology 56, 60, 86–9, 91, 93–4, 141n. 131
    oligarchy 86, 89, 92, 114, 135n. 85, 141n. 131, 142n. 141, 158
epitropos 27, 115
equality 8–10, 20n. 74
    proportional 93, 160
Evagoras, king of Cypriot Salamis 126n. 4, 147

fable xv, 78n. 15, 84, 87, 90, 93, 103n. 84, 164

gods
    divine succession 2
    as household 4, 84
    political institutions 3–4, 114
    possible images for 148
    society 1–7, 15n. 4
    timai 3, 84
    see also paredros
grammatical variation 133n. 74, 134n. 83, 192n. 163

Greek political imagery
  absent images xiii–xiv, 60, 70, 118, 121, 124–5
  functioning xii–xv
  inverse images xv, 1, 93, 152 see also bodily microcosm; political analogy
  working definition xiii–xiv
  see also entries for individual fields of image

Hades 3, 5–7
Hera 2–3, 5, 84
Hieron, tyrant of Syracuse 26, 30, 55, 112–13
horses in Greek élite culture 87–8, 121

imagery, fields of
  animals, abusive comparisons 119, 163–4
  architecture 85, 89, 93, 112, 125, 163
    city identified with men 89, 123, 163
  art 160
  bees 137n. 106, 159–60
  birds of prey 84, 90, 112, 118
  board games 20n. 69, 93
  boulder 89
  boundary-stone (*horos*) 91
  bull 89–90
  chariot of state 56, 86–7, 113, 121, 159
  clothing 141n. 129 see also wool-working
  coinage 122, 165
  cream 91
  crop destruction 124
  democracy, imagery from 164–5
  elements 61, 88, 120, 125, 159
  eranos 154
  family, state as 30–5, 111–12, 114, 149, 155–6
    mother or nurse, land as 32–3, 116, 156
    ruler as father 30–1, 83–4, 111–12, 149, 156, 197
  food, feeding and starvation 28, 73, 91, 115, 119, 154
  gods as kings 1–10
  household, state as 25–30, 94, 114–5, 149, 154–5
    possession of ruler 32, 110, 124, 149
    servant, politician as 26, 114–5, 149, 154–5
    see also *epitropos, tamias*
  hunting 90, 112
  kings as gods 10–14, 166–7
  light xviii n. 13, 11, 89, 100n. 49, 112, 129n. 28
  lion 44, 89–90, 118
  lover of the demos 29, 115–16, 154–5
  maritime xii, xviii n. 13, 85–6, 113, 117, 151, 156
    helmsman 54–9, 86, 113, 147–8, 150, 156, 197
      divine 56, 152
    ship of state a merchantman 60
    spatial articulation 56
  master and slave 92, 107–10, 154, 158, 166
    freedom and slavery 110–11, 123–4, 157–8
  medical
    body politic 69–76, 92, 112, 117, 122
    doctor 71–3, 75–6, 112, 117, 147–8, 150, 156–7
    head 70, 93, 153
    health, loyalty to Greece, 74, 135n. 88, 156
    treatment 69, 71, 76, 92, 151, 156
    see also purging
  military 121, 125, 139–41n. 127, 161–3, 197
    see also *prostatês*
  music 161
  predator, monarch as 90
  prostitution 29, 38n. 23, 154
  protection (*phulax*) 27, 125, 164–5
  shepherd 43–8, 50n. 17, 83–4, 107–8, 112, 148–50
  shield 91
  soul of city, constitution as 153
  spatial xviii n. 13
  sport xiv, 119–20, 151, 157
  taming of animals 87–8, 108, 111, 115, 119–21, 150, 159

yoke 108, 111, 129n. 32, 186n. 128
teacher 31, 118, 168n. 6, 173n. 46
    law as outline letters/ruler 135n. 93
tree 112
watchdog 116, 118–19, 150, 155–6
wolf 90–1
wool-working 122, 161
isonomia 9–10, 75, 114

Jason, tyrant of Pherae 184n. 117

law
  agent or ruler 10, 33, 93, 125, 164–6
  contract 194n. 176
  service to 30
  nomos 10, 19n. 52, 171n. 29, 188n. 144
    nomos empsuchos 14, 166
Long, Gov. Huey 143n. 147
Lycurgus 12, 166, 172n. 37
Lysander 13

Mandela, Nelson 198n. 4
Mao Zedong 117, 197
Megara 92
metaphor
  conceptual xiii, xvii–xix
  dead xiii–xiv
  Greek ideas of xiv–xv
  literary xii–xiii
  revived 26–7
  and 'semantic stretch' xiv–xv, 76n. 1
Mitterand, François 23
Mobutu, Joseph 40n.36, 197
monarchy 1–10, 26, 30, 32, 34, 44–8, 56,
    83–4, 89–90, 110–14, 121, 125,
    135n. 85, 147, 149–52, 160,
    166–7, 197
  ideal monarch 14, 151, 166, 197
  magic of kingship 21n. 78, 22n. 90,
    196
  see also tyranny

Near East, political imagery xi, 1,
    10–12, 30–1, 43–4, 83, 87, 89,
    100n. 58, 102n. 75, 111–12, 125,
    138nn. 115, 119
Nicias 75, 117, 122–3

Oligarchy, *see* élites

Orwell, George xviii n. 10

pandering 28–9, 115, 151, 155
paredros, divinity as 7, 14, 174n. 49
paternalism, avoided 35
Pericles xviii n.14, 13, 23n. 93, 115–18,
    120–1, 124, 150, 155
Persia 11–12, 31, 47, 61, 87, 92, 107–10,
    113, 117–19, 123, 125,
    139n. 121, 147, 150, 157–8, 160,
    166
  ideology 12, 14, 77n. 10, 107, 109–10,
    124, 157, 160, 196n. 193
personification(s) 7–8, 26, 115, 125,
    133n. 75, 145n. 156, 165–6
Philip II 14, 29, 158, 162–3, 165
plague narratives 71, 74
political analogy in Plato 152–4, 161
Poseidon 2–3, 84
Presocratic philosophers 8–10, 55, 86, 93,
    152, 175n. 53
proskunêsis 12–14
prostatês 140, 190n. 154
Protagoras xix n. 17, 25, 135n. 93,
    168nn. 8–9
proverbs 36n. 4, 104n. 91
punishment 31, 149
purging 48, 72, 170n. 29, 188n. 141,
    190n. 151

reason, rule of 9–10, 152–3
Rome, imagery 39n. 31, 40n. 36, 41n. 45,
    51n. 34, 67n. 54, 71, 79n. 26,
    80n. 38, 96n. 19, 143n. 142,
    170n. 29 *see also* Cicero

'Saviour' (*Sôtêr*) 22, 166
Seleucids, anchor emblem 65n. 32
Shevardnadze, Eduard 197
Sicily 133n. 79, 138n. 111
Socrates, Socratic tradition xiii, 33–4, 45,
    148, 150–2, 162, 181n. 97
Sparta 11, 14, 33, 44, 70, 87, 89, 124,
    139n. 121, 158, 162, 172n. 37,
    173n. 47, 181n. 95, 189n. 149,
    190nn. 154–5, 192n. 165
stasis (civil strife) 54, 69, 73, 93, 114, 117,
    119–20, 125, 153, 156
sunkrasis see balance

tamias (steward), *tamieuein* 26–7, 112, 115
technê (craft), images from 45, 135n. 93, 148, 150–2, 161
Thatcher, Margaret xi–xii, xvii
Thebes 158
Themistocles 123
Theramenes 38n. 22, 55, 64n. 24, 162, 178n. 73, 180n. 89, 184n. 115
therapeia ('care') 29, 115, 155
Theron (tyrant of Acragas) 89, 100n. 49
Tymoshenko, Yulia 197
tyranny, tyrant 27, 31, 33, 55–6, 74, 87–92, 94, 107, 110–11, 114, 149, 157, 162, 166, 192n. 165, 193n. 175
  of the demos 30, 158–9
  of Four Hundred at Athens 158
  imperial 185n. 120
  of Thirty at Athens 45, 148, 150, 154, 158, 163
  tyrant city (Athens) 123–4

Vikings, lack of maritime imagery 62n. 1

wage labour 29, 115, 154
women, basis of imagery 27, 115, 122, 169n. 18, 197

Xenophon
  ironic interpretation of xvi, 169n. 23
Xerxes 12, 107–10

Zaleukos of Locri (lawgiver) 45
Zeus 1–9, 30, 84, 137n. 110, 174n. 49
  opposition to 2–5
  stable cosmic rule of 2–4
  as tyrant 5–6, 111

Printed in Great Britain
by Amazon.co.uk, Ltd.,
Marston Gate.